The Critical Response to Nathaniel Hawthorne's *The Scarlet Letter*

Recent Titles in
Critical Responses in Arts and Letters

The Critical Response to Mark Twain's *Huckleberry Finn*
Laurie Champion, editor

The Critical Response to Nathaniel Hawthorne's *The Scarlet Letter*

Edited by
Gary Scharnhorst

Critical Responses in Arts and Letters, Number 2
CAMERON NORTHOUSE, Series Adviser

GREENWOOD PRESS
New York • Westport, Connecticut • London

Library of Congress Cataloging-in-Publication Data

The critical response to Nathaniel Hawthorne's The Scarlet letter /
edited by Gary Scharnhorst.
p. cm.—(Critical responses in arts and letters, ISSN 1057-0993 ;
no. 2)
Includes bibliographical references and index.
ISBN 0-313-27599-8 (alk. paper)
1. Hawthorne, Nathaniel, 1804-1864. Scarlet letter.
I. Scharnhorst, Gary. II. Series.
PS1868.C76 1992
813'.3—dc20 91-35630

British Library Cataloguing in Publication Data is available.

Library of Congress Catalog Card Number: 91-35630
ISBN: 0-313-27599-8
ISSN: 1057-0993

First published in 1992

Greenwood Press, 88 Post Road West, Westport, CT 06881
An imprint of Greenwood Publishing Group, Inc.

Printed in the United States of America

The paper used in this book complies with the
Permanent Paper Standard issued by the National
Information Standards Organization (Z39.48-1984).

10 9 8 7 6 5 4 3 2

Copyright Acknowledgments

The author and publisher gratefully acknowledge permission for use of the following material:

Gary Scharnhorst, " 'Now You Can Write Your Book': Two Myths in Hawthorne Biography," *Nathaniel Hawthorne Review* 15 (Fall 1989): 6-9. Reprinted by permission of *The Nathaniel Hawthorne Review*.

Neal Frank Doubleday, "Hawthorne's Hester and Feminism," *PMLA* 54 (1939): 825-28. Reprinted by permission of the Modern Language Association of America.

Elizabeth Aycock Hoffman, "Political Power in *The Scarlet Letter*," *ATQ* 4 (March 1990): 13-29. Reprinted by permission of *ATQ*.

Carl Van Doren, "The Flower of Puritanism," *The Nation* magazine/The Nation Co., Inc., December 1920.

Introduction by Elizabeth Deering Hanscom to Nathaniel Hawthorne's *The Scarlet Letter*. Reprinted with permission of Macmillan Publishing Company. Copyright 1927, renewed © 1955 by Macmillan Publishing Company.

" 'Scarlet Letter' Badly Done/Direction, Writing, Ruin Classic Novel," *Hollywood Reporter*, 6 July 1934, p. 3. Courtesy of *The Hollywood Reporter*.

"Scarlet Letter," *Variety*, 25 September 1934, 14:1-2. © Variety Inc. Reproduced with permission.

Every reasonable effort has been made to trace the owners of copyright materials in this book, but in some instances this has proven impossible. The author and publisher will be glad to receive information leading to more complete acknowledgments in subsequent printings of the book and in the meantime extend their apologies for any omissions.

As ever, to my friend and mentor William T. Stafford

Contents

Foreword

Critical Responses in Arts and Letters is designed to present a documentary history of highlights in the critical reception to the body of work of writers and artists and to individual works that are generally considered to be of major importance. The focus of each volume in this series is basically historical. The introductions to each volume are themselves brief histories of the critical response an author, artist, or individual work has received. This response is then further illustrated by reprinting a strong representation of the major critical reviews and articles that collectively have produced the author's, artist's, or work's critical reputation.

The scope of *Critical Responses in Arts and Letters* knows no chronological or geographical boundaries. Volumes under preparation include studies of individuals from around the world and in both contemporary and historical periods.

Each volume is the work of an individual editor, who surveys the entire body of criticism on a single author, artist, or work. The editor then selects the best material to depict the critical response received by an author or artist over his/her entire career. Documents produced by the author or artist may also be included when the editor finds that they are necessary to a full understanding of the materials at hand. In circumstances where previous, isolated volumes of criticism on a particular individual or work exist, the editor carefully selects material that better reflects the nature and directions of the critical response over time.

In addition to the introduction and the documentary section, the editor of each volume is free to solicit new essays on areas that may not have been adequately dealt with in previous criticism. For volumes on living writers and artists, new interviews may be included, again at the discretion of the volume's editor. The volumes also provide supplementary bibliography and are fully indexed.

While each volume in *Critical Responses to Arts and Letters* is unique, it is also hoped that in combination they will form a useful, documentary history of the critical response to the arts, and one that can be easily and profitably employed by students and scholars.

Cameron Northouse

Introduction

Whatever else may be said of *The Scarlet Letter*, the romance is virtually unique among works of American fiction: it has not lapsed from print in over a hundred and forty years. The history of its reception is, in fact, nothing less than a case-study in canon formation. As Wendell V. Harris has observed, moreover, "canons are made up of readings, not of disembodied texts."[1] Hershel Parker adds in the *Norton Anthology of American Literature* that *The Scarlet Letter* has appealed "to tastes of changing generations in different ways."[2] The present volume is not so much a comprehensive sampling of critical approaches to the story, then, as a collection of documents—canon-fodder, as it were—which detail what Jane Tompkins has called, in a different context, "the politics of Hawthorne's literary reputation."[3]

The plan of the volume is simple enough. The various items in the first section silhouette the background and composition- history of the romance. Hawthorne began to write *The Scarlet Letter*, as these items indicate, after he lost his patronage job in the Salem Custom-House in June 1849. His dismissal was rationalized by much of the Whig press, though Epes Sargent in the *Boston Transcript* blasted the Polk administration for its failure to rise above petty partisan politics. Ironically, Hawthorne's firing would prove a blessing in disguise. Compelled by circumstances to earn his living by his pen, Hawthorne produced an eminently marketable book which the Boston firm of Ticknor, Reed and Fields shrewdly promoted well in advance of its publication with blurbs in such papers as the *Transcript*, the dowager of Boston polite society. James T. Fields, "one of the great geniuses of American literary merchandising,"[4] recounts in his memoir *Yesterdays with Authors* how he first encouraged Hawthorne to elaborate the "germ" of the story and cites several letters the author wrote him in late 1849 and 1850 as he worked on the romance. As Richard H. Brodhead explains, "It was

Fields, in 1850, who produced the book that clinched Hawthorne's fame: in his own lurid account, Fields, Chillingworth-fashion, forcibly dragged to light the half-completed manuscript that Hawthorne was keeping secret."[5] Though Fields obviously embellished the part he had played in the process of composition, Hawthorne freely admitted his debt to him in 1861: "My literary success, whatever it has been or may be, is the result of my connection with you. Somehow or other, you smote the rock of public sympathy on my behalf."[6] In my own piece on the composition-history, I trace the sources of the mistaken biographical tradition that Hawthorne began to write *The Scarlet Letter* literally on the day he was "decapitated" in Salem.

From all indications, Hawthorne was unsure of the merit of the story even while he was completing it. "It is either very good or very bad—I don't know which," he reportedly told Fields. He confessed to a friend the day after finishing the manuscript that it was "positively a h—l-fired story, into which I found it almost impossible to throw any cheering light."[7] Still, it was immediately hailed, at least by some native literary folk cited in section two, as a minor masterpiece. *The Scarlet Letter* "set the seal upon an already promising reputation," as Bertha Faust has concluded.[8] On March 15, 1850, the day before it went on sale, the *Transcript* pronounced it "a first rate romance" which would prove Hawthorne belonged among "the first writers of our time." American reviewers would often compare Hawthorne, even in the first blush of his greatest success, to Addison, Steele, Goldsmith, Lamb, Scott, Irving, and Shakespeare; and before the end of the year Hawthorne's college classmate Henry Wadsworth Longfellow would rank *The Scarlet Letter* above Boccaccio's tales in the course of a lecture at Harvard.

The book soon proved to be more popular than even the publishers had anticipated, with some six thousand copies sold within the first six months. Hawthorne attributed its initial celebrity to the controversy which raged over "The Custom-House" introduction much as, later, Mark Twain thought the decision to remove *Adventures of Huckleberry Finn* from the shelves of the Concord Free Library would "sell 25,000 copies for us sure."[9] Indeed, much of the critical commentary on *The Scarlet Letter* focused on Hawthorne's caricatures of his former co-workers in the introduction. He no doubt had planned to exact a little revenge on his political enemies in Salem in this part of the book. "I feel an infinite contempt for them," he admitted to his friend Horatio Bridge, "and probably have expressed more of it than I intended." This preliminary chapter soon provoked "the greatest uproar that ever happened here since witch-times."[10] In its review, the *Salem Register* excoriated Hawthorne for "vilifying some of his former associates," particularly William Lee and James Miller, in the "outrageous personalities which disfigure" the chapter. The "venomous, malignant, and unaccountable assault" on these venerable gentlemen, according to the *Register*, was akin to character-assassination and proved the prescient wisdom "of the Administration in relieving" Hawthorne of "dignified employment" within the government. These sentiments were widely expressed in many of the other Whig newspapers that had condoned or approved his removal some nine months earlier. Such Democratic papers as the New York *Evening Post*, however, protested that there had been no "malignant intention in the writer." Charles C. Hazewell, who subsequently claimed to have memorized every word of *The Scarlet Letter*, asserted in the *Boston Times* that Hawthorne "could hardly have said less at the expense of the miserable, wretched Vandals who dismissed him from office." In any event, Hawthorne was unrepentant: in his preface to the second edition of the romance, dated March 30, 1850, he insisted the opening sketch "could not have been done in a better or kindlier spirit" and he reprinted it without alteration. According to C. E. Frazer Clark, Jr., this preface to the second edition quelled the controversy, at least "as far as Hawthorne was concerned, although neither he nor the outraged Salemites ever forgot the matter."[11]

Another complaint about the romance—that it was demoralizing if not downright immoral—was leveled by most reviewers for religious periodicals. From this perspective, Hawthorne had designed the story to be a *succes de scandale*, a titillating tale about a fornicator, an adulteress, and their illegitimate child written in the best (that is, worst) French style. "We are painfully tempted to believe that it is a book made for the market," Arthur Cleveland Coxe opined in the *Church Review*. It is a "dirty story" with a "running undertide of filth" and "dissolute conversation" about "the nauscous amour of a Puritan pastor." Dimmesdale is, according to this logic, the central actor in the naughty novel, the most culpable sexual transgressor because he is the male aggressor. Hester is, by implication, but the "frail creature of his charge" whom he seduces. Such a view, with minor variations, was widely shared across the theological spectrum, from the Episcopalian poet Coxe and the Roman Catholic convert Orestes Brownson to the anonymous reviewers of the romance for the liberal Unitarian weeklies. Each of these critics predictably scorned Hawthorne's achievement: "it is utterly and entirely a failure" when read as a religious narrative, according to the *Christian Register*, because it "nowhere recognise[s]" the "peculiar office of Christianity in the conversion of sinners and their restoration to purity and peace." The *Christian*

Inquirer went so far as to claim that the characters in *The Scarlet Letter*, reprobates all, "suffer intensely, agonize acutely, but tenderly or truly they cannot feel. The mother and child do not love each other." This critic confidently predicted the tale "will not survive a temporary importance."

Closely related to the complaint about the moral effect of *The Scarlet Letter* were questions about its historical accuracy. That Hawthorne, in the introduction, professed to have discovered the very letter Hester had worn on her breast and "half a dozen sheets of foolscap" sketching her life seemed to suggest the basis of the story in fact. Henry T. Tuckerman asserted in the *Southern Literary Messenger*, for example, that the romance "is as reliable as the best of Scott's novels" in its "truth to costume, local manners and scenic features." Yet the religious reviewers were at pains to deny that any such scandal as Hawthorne depicted had rocked Puritan Boston. While Governor Bellingham and Reverend Wilson were historical figures, they argued, Arthur Dimmesdale and Hester Prynne were figments of Hawthorne's imagination and, indeed, were a slander to the faith of the colonial forebears. Andrew Preston Peabody, Plummer Professor of Christian Morals at Harvard, concluded that Hawthorne had "defamed the fathers of New England"—again, Dimmesdale seems by implication to be the protagonist in this reading—"by locating his pictures of gross impurity and sacrilegious vice where no shadow of reproach, and no breath but of immaculate fame, had ever rested before." Similarly, C. C. Smith charged in the *Christian Examiner* that *The Scarlet Letter* "contains the grossest and foulest falsification of truth in history and personal character, that we have ever encountered."[12] His reticence to defend "those stern old Popery- haters" the Puritans notwithstanding, Orestes Brownson dismissed Hawthorne's characterization of them as precisely the sort of thing he would expect from "a moderate transcendentalist and liberal of the modern school."

The Scarlet Letter was almost immediately pirated in England, and the British reviews, a selection of which appear in section three of this volume, were perhaps even more favorable than the contemporary American notices. Henry Chorley, in an oft- reprinted comment on the romance in the June 15, 1850, issue of the London *Athenaeum*, described it as "powerful and painful."[13] In October 1851, the *English Review* praised it as "quaint," "passionate," "powerful," and "original," and rated Hawthorne "above all the authors of America" except Irving and perhaps Longfellow and Cooper. Eight months later, Samuel Smiles thought it "pure, severe, and truthful." This brand of comment was uncomplicated by either the topical overtones of Hawthorne's introduction or the parochial worries of the religious reviewers. Indeed, the pseudononymous reviewer for the *New Monthly Review* in February 1852 defended Hawthorne from the didacticists on the very grounds from which they had complained: *The Scarlet Letter,* he declared, was fundamentally a story of sin and penance, if not repentance, set against the "vivid" and "graphic" backdrop of the "patriarchal era of New England life." This latter phrase also hints at a reading of the romance which emphasizes Hester's plight, her dual role as both sinner and victim of sexual subjugation. Her character, according to the *North British Review,* was "of a stronger mould" than Dimmesdale's: "Without being unwomanly, she is of far less effeminate texture than the man she loved so truly, and for whom she suffered so bravely." These British notices also acknowledge for the first time the ambiguity of the letter A, the mystic symbol the American had simply associated with the adulterous union of Hester and the minister. In all, the early British reviewers, including Margaret Oliphant, Richard Holt Hutton, and Leslie Stephen, underscored the psychological and even allegorical dimensions of the romance, especially of the chapter entitled "The Interior of a Heart," rather than (like the Americans) its satirical or theological implications. The romance was also translated into German and French within months of its original American publication and into dozens of other languages over the next hundred and forty years.

After his death in 1864, Hawthorne's reputation within the genteel tradition of American letters steadily improved. This rising tide also lifted *The Scarlet Letter* to the rank of a classic, as the various documents in section four may suggest. The romance was reprinted "with an impression or more almost every year" well into the 1880s by Fields, Osgood & Company and its corporate successors.[14] Herman Melville obtained the only copy he is known to have owned in 1870.[15] The low-priced "Little Classics" edition of 1875 was welcomed by the *Liberal Christian,* the renamed organ of New York Unitarianism, as "the most powerful, if not the most remarkable, of Hawthorne's works." According to the Unitarian clergyman Robert Collyer, *The Scarlet Letter* was an elaboration of Pauline holy writ. Unlike the sectarian reviewers of the first edition, E. P. Whipple claimed Hawthorne was but a type of Puritan after all: "If Jonathan Edwards, turned romancer, had dramatized his sermon on 'Sinners in the Hand of an Angry God,' he could not have written a more terrific story of guilt and retribution than *The Scarlet Letter.*" In an essay for the *Catholic Presbyterian,* A. C. Roe summarized the entire plot as though it were a gloss on Proverbs 28:13. And Thomas Selby, in *The Theology of*

Modern Fiction, insisted that the characters who figure in the romance "represent influences providentially appointed to stimulate the laggard conscience" and concluded that Hawthorne "dramatises with transcendent skill some of those great facts of human nature which are at the very roots of all theology." The terms of this particular debate had scarcely changed since the romance was first published in 1850: it was still weighed and measured by standards of religious doctrine.

In most ways, however, the response to *The Scarlet Letter* had matured over the years. Though critical opinion was divided during Hawthorne's lifetime whether it or *The Marble Faun* was his masterpiece, the tale of Hester, Dimmesdale, Chillingworth, and Pearl was by the 1870s generally conceded to have the better claim to the title. Gilderoy Griffin declared it "perhaps his greatest creation" in 1871, and W. D. Howells referred to it as "Hawthorne's supreme romance" six years later. The Boston *Women's Journal*, the leading suffragist journal in America, commended the so-called Red-Line edition of 1877 in tacit recognition of its feminist overtones, and Howells discussed at length Mary Hallock's illustrations for this edition in his review of it for the *Atlantic*. Hallock's portrayal of the scene at Governor Bellingham's mansion in chapter VII was, he wrote, "quite unapproached in power by anything in American illustrative art." By 1879, no less a luminary than Henry James hailed *The Scarlet Letter* as "the finest piece of imaginative writing yet put forth in the country" and Hawthorne's "most substantial title to fame." James's praise reverberated, like an echo in a closed chamber, through dozens of essays and critical introductions over the next fifty years. But James also subtly condescended to the "provincial" Hawthorne. He thought the romance was, if anything, filled with "too much" symbolism, such as the "mystic A" that appears in the sky after Dimmesdale's midnight vigil on the scaffold or the one the minister "finds imprinted upon his breast and eating into his flesh." Such contrivances, according to James, were foreign to "real psychology." He also disputed all claims for the historicity or realism of the romance: "The historical colouring is rather weak than otherwise," he noted; "there is little elaboration of detail, of the modern realism of research; and the author has made no great point of causing his figures to speak the English of their period." Still, James's critical biography—the first volume devoted to an American writer to appear in the English Men of Letters series—suggests the extent to which Hawthorne's fame was institutionalized during the Gilded Age. In 1883, he was accorded the paramount literary tribute: a definitive edition of his work in twelve volumes, edited by his son-in-law George Parsons Lathrop and issued by Houghton Mifflin.[16]

Hawthorne was, by the turn of the century, the brooding crown prince of the *ars republica*. In an 1893 poll conducted by *The Critic* to select the greatest American books, *The Scarlet Letter* came in second, barely outdistanced by Emerson's *Essays*.[17] The same year, the Wesleyan weekly *Zion's Herald* pronounced it "Hawthorne's masterpiece of fiction," even if it was "not suited to the fancy of the multitude."[18] In 1904, the centenary of Hawthorne's birth, Theodore Munger cracked in the *Atlantic* that "it would be as safe to wager" on the "permanent high estimate of the Scarlet Letter" as on the solvency of the Bank of England. In his chapter on Hester Prynne in *Heroines of Fiction*, Howells made the case for it as "the modernest and maturest" of Hawthorne's romances. Unlike his friend James, Howells assumed the centrality of Hester to the plot, commended the "strong reality" in the material Hawthorne used to construct the story, and even defended the "stateliness of the dialogue" spoken by the characters. Similarly, in his Hawthorne volume for the American Men of Letters series, George Woodberry applauded the intense "sense of reality" of the romance, its critique of the harsh and forbidding Puritanism which ostracizes the heroine. The biographical critics of the Woodberry school attributed the melancholy that ostensibly marked all of Hawthorne's fiction to his Puritan ancestry, as if he had inherited their gloomy view of life. While Hawthorne distorted history in *The Scarlet Letter*, Woodberry asserted, he "symbolized historical New England by an environment that he created round a tragedy that he read in the human heart." The romance is, from this perspective, unremittingly sad and depressing, "a chapter in the literature of moral despair," its tone and expression shaped inexorably by the author's own "blood and breeding." According to William C. Brownell, Hawthorne was a fatalist who nurtured vicious habits. As Harry Thurston Peck sniffed in 1909, Hawthorne "was burdened with a secret pessimism which was ever a dark blot on his secret soul." The author had become, according to this critical estimate, the very type of character he had depicted in such tales as "The Minister's Black Veil" and "Young Goodman Brown." To such writers as Woodberry, Munger, Peck, and others of their stripe, in short, *The Scarlet Letter* was something of a Greek tragedy in modern dress, Hester an admirable and perhaps saintly heroine, the author an unhappy recluse if not a misanthrope. Ironically, the romance was not recommended for classroom use for precisely this reason. Because children should not "associate with those who are constantly dejected or morbidly sensitive," E. W. Barrett averred in the journal *Education* in 1894, teachers should "reject" assigning *The Scarlet Letter* in favor of *Twice-told Tales* or *The Marble Faun*: "There is little in Hawthorne's character to place before our pupils."[19]

This fashionable brand of biographical criticism dominated Hawthorne scholarship over the next several decades. In the introductions to and comments upon a series of popular editions of the romance between 1919 and 1929, the author was routinely portrayed as the sombre heir of an austere and diseased Puritanism. "Old-fashioned Nathaniel, with his little-boy charm, he'll tell you what's what. But he'll cover it with smarm," as that Puritan-baiter D. H. Lawrence observed at the time.[20] "To whatever disadvantages New England birth and breeding exposes the artist, Hawthorne was exposed," Stuart P. Sherman opined.[21] He was "bone of the bone, blood of the blood of Puritan New England," according to Elizabeth Deering Hanscom. "An ancestral strain, no doubt," explains his obsession "with human nature under circumstances of sin," Ernest E. Leisy suggests.[22] The "old Puritan tradition" was "in his blood," wrote Carl Van Doren in 1920: "Some ancestral strain accounts for this conception of adultery as an affair not of the civil order but of the immortal soul." To be sure, Van Doren also outlines a psychoanalytical rather than narrrowly theological approach to the story reminiscent of its early British reception: "The newest schools of psychology cannot object to a reading of sin which shows Dimmesdale and Chillingworth as the victims of instincts and antipathies which fester because unnatural repressed while Hester Prynne is cleansed through the discovery of her offense and grows healthier by her confession." Sin in these terms is "a violation less of some supernatural law than of the natural integrity of the soul." Of course, such observations beg the question whether Hester, the ostensible "free spirit liberated in a moral wilderness,"[23] actually confesses her sin, and if so where in the narrative such an event is recorded. Surely not in chapter XVII, where she defiantly declares to Dimmesdale that "What we did had a consecration of its own." The vexing question of Hawthorne's affiliation with Transcendentalism also runs like a subtext through the scholarship of this period. Did the author intend to lampoon the movement in Hester, as Sherman implies, or was his writing "touched" with "transcendental doctrines," as Hanscom and Leisy claim? In 1927, in any case, William Lyon Phelps pronounced *The Scarlet Letter*, with pardonable hyperbole, "the greatest book ever written in the Western Hemisphere," one of "the fifteen best novels of the world." Translated into Chinese three times since 1934, the romance has served as a standard introduction to American literature in both pre- and post-revolutionary China.[24] For better or worse, it has been required reading in middle- and high-school English courses throughout the U. S. for much of the recent past, enshrined in the list of books three generations of adolescents have been taught to despise.

Over the past half-century, *The Scarlet Letter* has become an academic shibboleth, prompting dozens of New Critical, contextual, psychoanalytical, feminist, New Historical, post-structural, and other readings. In 1971, Roy R. Male outlined "the ways in which Hawthorne's work has responded to rapidly shifting expectations during the last two decades" in *American Literary Scholarship*:

> In the fifties it rewarded the explicatory and mythic analyses of the New Critics; in the mid-sixties it survived, at the cost of some diminution, the rigorous inquest of the new historicists and the neo-Freudians; and now his fiction seems more vital than ever for readers aware of new developments in psychology and related fields.[25]

These modern readings, represented in this volume by the selections in the fifth section, are all indebted, at least indirectly, to the work in the 1930s of Perry Miller, who reclaimed the Puritans as a topic for serious intellectual inquiry, and Randall Stewart, who demythologized the events in Hawthorne's life. In his histories of early New England, Miller corrected the caricature of the Massachusetts Bay colonists as thin-lipped philistines, even as they had been portrayed in *The Scarlet Letter*; and, in his biographical notes and sketches of the author, Stewart revised the mistaken estimates of Hawthorne's character. In his view, Hawthorne was a fairly normal and well-adjusted fellow, albeit a closet Christian. Stewart's work, coupled with the New Critics' emphasis upon the intrinsic qualities of the text, finally freed Hawthorne scholars from the biographical barrel in which they had been confined like frogs.

By the late 1930s, then, *The Scarlet Letter* had become something more than a great novel by a child of the Puritans. F. O. Matthiessen, for example, devoted over a dozen pages of *American Renaissance* (1941) to a detailed analysis of its structure and design. Indeed, as Tompkins fairly observes, the text of the romance has been continually reinvented over the years: "*The Scarlet Letter* is a great novel in 1850, in 1876, in 1904, in 1942, and in 1966, but each time it is great for different reasons."[26] Nevertheless, its place in the canon has never been seriously disputed. It remains one of the most frequently reprinted works of American fiction, and it appears in its entirety in the *Heath Anthology of American Literature*, the most decentered of the new recanonized collections. The Norton Critical Edition of the romance, the standard college classroom text, recently entered its third edition in the past thirty years. It also remains the standard against which all other stories of the period are measured. After reading "the many novels by American women authors about women, written between 1820 and 1870," for example, Nina Baym did not "hit upon even one novel that I would propose to set alongside *The Scarlet Letter*"[27]—a frank admission for which she has been roundly criticized.[28] Yet even Tompkins, a radical protestant in the present literary reformation, does not claim "that the novels of Stowe, Fanny Fern, and Elizabeth Stuart Phelps are good in the same way that *Moby-Dick* and *The Scarlet Letter* are."[29]

Over the past fifty years, in any event, the meaning and significance of Hawthorne's romance have been hotly debated. Given his celebrated remark about the "d——d mob of scribbling women" with whom he competed in the literary marketplace[30] and his patronizing private comments about Margaret Fuller, who may have figured as a model for Hester Prynne, Hawthorne answered the so-called "woman question" of his day with a resounding No! in thunder—or so it has been widely assumed. In "Hawthorne's Hester and Feminism" (1939), the first article on *The Scarlet Letter* to appear in *PMLA*, Neal Frank Doubleday carefully distinguished between Hester's and Hawthorne's views; that is, according to Doubleday, "in his treatment of Hester, Hawthorne embodies his criticism of a movement contemporary with him." In "Pearl and the Puritan Heritage" (1951), Chester E. Eisinger reexamined the Puritan influence on the romance, though hardly in the simple-minded manner of the biographical critics earlier in the century. Employing the contextual method of the new discipline of American Studies, Eisinger contended that the figure of Pearl, in particular, may be best understood "by reference to the Puritan theories of nature and liberty." The elf-child "is the hypostatization, in miniature, of the Puritan conception of nature and notion of the state." The story in which she appears in less a realistic treatment of Puritan life than an allegory which illustrates Puritan ideas. Darrel Abel, in "Hawthorne's Hester" (1952), shared and elaborated Doubleday's view that *The Scarlet Letter* exhibits the "inadequacy" of its heroine's philosophy of "romantic individualism." Hester's "breach of her marriage obligations" is tinged with Godwinism, Abel argued, and the Puritans' condemnation of her adultery is in their terms no more harsh than it is illogical.

Nina Baym, one of the most perceptive of Hawthorne's contemporary critics, has forcefully disputed this judgment of Hester. "Hawthorne's work presented me with a teacher's dilemma" in the mid-1960s, Baym has recalled.[31] "I found it impossible to teach *The Scarlet Letter* to undergraduate students according to interpretations of that work then current." Whereas Doubleday had read the romance as a covert satire of Hester's misguided individualism, Baym averred that "Almost nothing that she does in *The Scarlet Letter* can be labeled as an example of romantic individualism." Whereas Abel and many New Critics had argued that the romance centered on the minister, that its plot consists of a "struggle between God and the Devil for the soul of Arthur Dimmesdale," Baym has repeatedly insisted upon Hester's "place as protagonist" of *The Scarlet Letter*.[32] She has been particularly critical of the attempts by such critics as Male, Richard Harter Fogle, and Hyatt Waggoner to remake Hawthorne in the image of a neo-orthodox Calvinist. In "Passion and Authority in *The Scarlet Letter*" (1970), Baym contends that Hawthorne deliberately misrepresented Puritanism in the romance as "a self-satisfied secular autocracy," that "what Hawthorne does give us" in the way of religious dogma "bears little resemblance to Puritan theology." Thus he "must be held accountable as one of the first shapers of that myth of the Puritans which turned them into dour Victorians." The Boston of *The Scarlet Letter* is "an authoritarian state with a Victorian moral outlook," a patriarchal community "dedicated to preserving the values and purposes of aging men." Dimmesdale, the youngest of these patriarchs, refuses to own his paternity of Pearl lest he "be thrown out of what is, to him, Heaven—the society of elders." On her part, however, Hester becomes after seven years of ostracism "what she was at most only implicitly before, a rebel." Her embroidered letter is "a masked defiance of the authorities," as the townswomen remark. Just as Pearl represents Hester's transgression, Chillingworth is the literal incarnation of the minister's guilty conscience. Yet, on the whole, Hester is the more sympathetic figure. She "must reject the judgment of the letter, no matter how she tries to assent to it; and Dimmesdale must take that letter on himself, no matter how much a part of him struggles to resist." These "two versions of the struggle between self and society," Baym concludes, are similarly "gloomy," for Hawthorne "does not believe that true self-fulfillment is possible."

Robert E. Todd offers yet another perspective on Hester's character in "The Magna Mater Archetype in *The Scarlet Letter*" (1972). Though Joseph Levi published a psychoanalytic interpretation of the romance as early as 1953,[33] Charles Feidelson and Frederick Crews fully legitimated this approach in the mid-1960s. Still, Crews devoted most of his chapter on *The Scarlet Letter* in *The Sins of the Fathers: Hawthorne's Psychological Themes* (1966) to Dimmesdale's repression of his self-destructive libidinal impulses. In his Jungian reading of the story, Todd identifies Hester, whose dual or ambivalent nature has been much remarked by earlier critics, with the "anima" or bipolar Magna Mater. Even in the first chapter, when she emerges from the jail as if from a womb with Pearl at her breast, her "kinship with the Great Mother is strikingly evident," according to Todd. In her relations with Dimmesdale, she is "both a source of destruction and death" and "a source of love and rebirth." Their meeting in the forest, depicted in "a succession of images that are important symbols of the elemental womb-tomb character of the Magna Mater archetype," results in Dimmesdale's psychic rebirth or, in Jung's term, "individuation." Holding the dying minister in her arms after his revelation of the stigma on his breast, Todd concludes, "Hester is the latter-day equivalent of the Magna Mater as the Pieta, who receives the crucified Jesus, embracing him in death as in birth."

In the present moment of critical dissensus, the romance has continued to inspire a wide variety of disparate approaches and readings. As Ross C Murfin has recently noted, "A great work of literature such as *The Scarlet Letter* elicits a host of different interpretive responses, no one of which stands alone or is entirely adequate to unpack its significance."[34] The best of these recent studies, such as Elizabeth Aycock Hoffman's "Political Power in *The Scarlet Letter*" (1990), focus on issues of gender and sexuality. Following Michel Foucault's lead in *Discipline and Punish*, Hoffman contends that "Hawthorne's failure to give Hester's individualism complete expression evolves from the restrictive terms of the discourse that he employs." The introduction to the romance functions as "a personal 'allegory' of the author's experience with conformative pressures" in the Salem Custom House. After his public "decapitation," Hawthorne thought he was free of those pressures and free to criticize them: "The publicly punished Hester plays out this aspect of the author's life." The "punitive relation between Chillingworth and Dimmesdale" suggests the extent to which "Hawthorne's concept of the self-reliant, self-willed individual is inseparable from the political powers of discipline." In the parallel relation of Pearl and Hester, he attempted to describe a more natural or benign form of discipline and valorized it "by replacing the intervention of overtly political powers of discipline with that of a child whose 'uncanny' behavior reminds the parent of the 'wild' past." Lacking the "self-perception" Hester gains through the surveillance of Pearl, "Dimmesdale cannot obtain the higher truth regarding justice" that she realizes. Yet, in the end, Hawthorne's "literary model" of discipline "subverts his critical observations about the expediencies of political mechanisms of social control." His suggestion that Pearl is a visitation of God "suppresses the political nature of her mediating position between her mother's adultery and its punishment." In "Paradigm and Paramour: Role Reversal in *The Scarlet Letter*," an essay prepared expressly for this volume, Marilyn Mueller Wilton also contends that Hawthorne inverted the conventional functions of hero and heroine. As Wilton explains, Hester assumes the "dominant" and Dimmesdale the subordinate role in the story. Like the traditional romantic hero, "Hester repeatedly rescues the heroine, Dimmesdale." Particularly in the "Conclusion," with Hester's return to Boston, Hawthorne underscored her primacy in the romance.

The sixth and final section of this volume, which reprints reviews of theatrical and cinematic adaptations of the story produced between 1876 and 1934, silhouettes an alternative history of *The Scarlet Letter* as cultural icon. As the items in this section indicate, the story has been continually reinvented—despite its apparent dearth of overt theatrics—for the stage and screen. The earliest dramatization was produced at Barnum's American Museum in New York in February 1858.[35] When Hawthorne learned of this attempt to adapt his story to the boards, he remarked that "I should think it might possibly succeed as an opera, though it would certainly fail as a play."[36] In 1877, however, shortly after the romance was first issued in the "Little Classics" edition, two separate dramatic versions of it appeared. The first of them was staged at the Boston Theatre, opening on the evening of January 1, with W. D. Howells, James Russell Lowell, and Henry Wadsworth Longfellow in attendance.[37] This five-act version "was mostly a work of selection from the splendid materials of our greatest American romance," as the critic for the *Transcript* noted, though it deserved to "rank in its classification" with such other tragedies as "Goethe's 'Faust' and Shakspeare's 'Hamlet.' " At virtually the same moment, Gabriel Harrison published his script of the story, which has apparently never been produced on stage. Harrison severely abridged the text, as the notice in the *Brooklyn Eagle* indicates; unfortunately, he also introduced several Indian characters, *a la* the witches in *Macbeth*, and a silly incantation scene over which Mistress Hibbins presides. Two more theatrical versions of the romance staged in London in 1888 also revised the story. The playwrights Stephen Coleridge and Norman Forbes, in an adaptation at the Royalty Theatre, changed the ending: in their scenario, Chillingworth is charged with fathering Pearl and is killed by a mob before Dimmesdale can confess, thus permitting him to conceal his guilt. When this play was "coldly received" by critics, they substituted "Hawthorne's tragic ending."[38] In another version produced simultaneously at the Olympic, the playwright Charles Charrington added a prologue set in England "which shows the early love which grew up between Hester Prynne and Arthur Dimmesdale" before all three principal characters emigrated to the New World. The net effect of these changes was, of course, to legitimitize the love of Hester and Dimmesdale, to render it less sensational to Victorian audiences.

By far the most commercially successful of the nineteenth- century adaptations of *The Scarlet Letter* was written by Joseph Hatton and first produced in England in 1876 and at Daly's Theatre in New York in 1892. The latter production starred the Shakespearean actor Richard Mansfield and his miscast blonde wife Beatrice Cameron. In Hatton's version, once again, there are "whole pages literally transcribed from the romance," such as the early scene in the marketplace. However, Hatton also interpolated several scenes of low comedy and introduced a number of new characters, including "the sensible and lighthearted village girl, Mary Willis, who believes in Hester's goodness and virtue." As Harry Thurston Peck observed in his review of the play, moreover, Hatton was forced by "the exigencies of stage management" to set three of the four acts in the public square and on the pillory. As a result, "We see nothing of the priest's suffering in his own house under the hideous and implacable vengeance of Chillingworth."[39] The critic for the *New York Tribune* complained that this play was "as didactic as it is stationary," more concerned with metaphysics than with physics.[40] Still, it ran on Broadway for most of a month and was revived briefly in 1894 and again in 1906. Ironically, another version of *The Scarlet Letter* staged in New York in 1925 consisted of a series of eight tableaux, with backdrops modeled upon F. O. C. Darley's illustrations for an 1882 edition of the romance. Such a method of dramatization, of course, underscored the essentially static quality of the story.

Hawthorne's own belief that the story "might possibly succeed as an opera" was not entirely lost on theatrical producers. The romance inspired a three-act Wagnerian opera by Walter Damrosch, with libretto by George Parsons Lathrop, which was produced at Carnegie Hall in January 1895 and the Academy of Music in March 1896. The rhymed libretto entirely omitted the part of Pearl, however, because Lathrop believed "the character was obviously impossible in opera." Not surprisingly, the consensus among critics was that this work, too, was "artistically a failure."[41]

Over the past eighty-plus years *The Scarlet Letter* has also been adapted no less than ten times for movies and television. The earliest of these movie versions were little more than thin-as-gruel satires of pop-Puritanism. In one of them, Hester and Dimmesdale even marry![42] The most significant of these silent films, directed by Victor Sjostrom and released in 1926, starred Lillian Gish. Though Mordaunt Hall, in his review of the film for the *New York Times*, thought it "as faithful a transcription of the narrative as one could well imagine,"[43] in point of fact the screenplay virtually reinvented Hawthorne's romance. As Gish later recalled, "My idea was to present Hester as a victim of hard circumstance, swept off her feet by love. Of course, that was what she was, but her innate innocence must be apparent."[44] The first half of the movie is devoted to Hester and Dimmesdale's courtship—the birth of Pearl does not occur until the second half and Chillingworth, who is "transformed into the stock villain of nineteenth-century melodrama,"[45] does not appear until its closing minutes. As Julian Smith concludes, "the film clearly departs from the novel on every level in order to make Hester the center and focus. . . . the film follows an entirely different temporal pattern putting almost total emphasis on Hester rather than on the interplay between Hester and Dimmesdale."[46] In this movie as in the book, Dimmesdale dies in Hester's arms—but here Hester in the person of Gish leads the townspeople in prayer just before the closing credits roll. Capitalizing on Gish's "stock virginal sweetness,"[47] the movie became a smash success. The shooting script was published the year after its release.[48] But it was scarcely a faithful adaptation: "What happened to Hawthorne's novel at M.G.M. should surprise no-one familiar with the history of that studio's early relationship to literary 'properties.' "[49] An even looser adaptation of the romance starring Coleen Moore was released by Majestic Pictures in 1934 and re-released in 1965. Meanwhile, CBS's *Studio One* and NBC's *Kraft Theatre* televised hour-long productions of the story in 1950 and 1954, and a European film version featuring Senta Berger was produced as recently as 1972. A celebrated four-hour adaptation, produced under the auspices of the National Endowment for the Humanities, was twice telecast in April 1979 and became the highest-rated PBS program of the season; still, as Larry Baker has demonstrated, this screenplay deviated at crucial points from the original story, particularly by casting Hawthorne as a character who repeatedly interrupts the narrative.[50]

The romance has been, in the end, so durable a literary text precisely because it has permitted such a wide diversity of readings. It has seemed at various times both a naughty novel and a moral allegory of sin and suffering, both a burlesque and a covertly sympathetic treatment of nineteenth-century feminism and Transcendentalism, both a satire of Puritanism and a reliable history of it. Like the scarlet letter worn by Hester and ostensibly found by Hawthorne in the attic of the custom house, *The Scarlet Letter* is "of a splendor in accordance with the taste of the age" when it was embroidered, and it remains a "riddle" no less "worthy of interpretation" by every successive generation of readers.

I am particularly grateful to Bruce F. Jaffe and Teresa Abeyta for helping me prepare the manuscript of this volume; to Margaret Shinn and Margaret Gilmore for various types of logistical support; to Hershel Parker for sending me some of the items I cite here; to Darrel Abel, Chet Eisinger, Nina Baym, Elizabeth Aycock Hoffman, and Marilyn Mueller Wilton for granting me permission to print their essays; and to my colleague Patrick Gallacher for translating the passage from the Latin Vulgate which Orestes Brownson quotes in his review.

Notes

[1]Wendell V. Harris, "Canonicity," *PMLA*, 106 (January 1991), 110.

[2]*Norton Anthology of American Literature* (New York and London: Norton, 1979), I, 878.

[3]Jane Tompkins, *Sensational Designs: The Cultural Work of American Fiction 1790-1860* (New York: Oxford Univ. Press, 1985), 3-39.

[4]Richard H. Brodhead, *The School of Hawthorne* (New York and Oxford: Oxford Univ. Press, 1986), 55.

[5]Brodhead, 56.

[6]*Centenary Edition of the Works of Nathaniel Hawthorne* (Columbus: Ohio State Univ. Press, 1987), XVIII, 365.

[7]*Centenary Edition*, XVI, 312.

[8]Bertha Faust, *Hawthorne's Contemporaneous Reputation* (Philadelphia: Univ. of Pennsylvania Press, 1939), 74.

[9]*Selected Letters of Mark Twain*, ed. Charles Neider (New York: Harper & Row, 1982), 153.

[10]*Centenary Edition*, XVI, 329.

[11]C. E. Frazer Clark, Jr., "Posthumous Papers of a Decapitated Surveyor: *The Scarlet Letter* in the Salem Press," *Studies in the Novel*, 2 (Winter 1970), 403.

[12]Charles Card Smith, "Notices of Recent Publications," *Christian Examiner*, 50 (May 1851), 509.

[13]*Athenaeum*, 15 June 1850, 634.

[14]*Centenary Edition*, XVI, lviii.

[15]F. O. Matthiessen, *American Renaissance: Art and Expression in the Age of Emerson and Whitman* (London, Oxford, New York: Oxford Univ. Press, 1941), 209.

[16]Edwin H. Cady, " 'The Wizard Hand': Hawthorne, 1864-1900," in *Hawthorne Centenary Essays*, ed. Roy Harvey Pearce (Columbus: Ohio State Univ. Press, 1964), 320.

[17]"The Ten Best American Books," *Critic*, 27 May 1893, 341; and 3 June 1893, 357.

[18]"Our Book Table," *Zion's Herald*, 29 November 1893, 379.

[19]E. W. Barrett, "Lessons on American Authors, Nathaniel Hawthorne," *Education*, 14 (March 1894), 420.

[20]D. H. Lawrence, *Studies in Classic American Literature* (New York: Viking, 1964), 96.

[21]Stuart P. Sherman, "Introduction" to *The Scarlet Letter* (New York: Scribner's, 1919), p. vii.

[22]Ernest E. Leisy, "Introduction" to *The Scarlet Letter* (New York: Thomas Nelson and Sons, 1929), p. x.

[23]Stuart P. Sherman, *Americans* (New York: Scribner's, 1922), 148.

[24]Xiao-huang Yin, "The Scarlet Letter in China," *American Quarterly*, 39 (Winter 1987), 551-562.

[25]Roy R. Male, "Hawthorne," in *American Literary Scholarship 1969*, ed. J. Albert Robbins (Durham: Duke Univ. Press, 1971), 19- 20.

[26]Tompkins, 35.

[27]Nina Baym, *Women's Fiction: A Guide to Novels By and About Women in America, 1820-1870* (Ithaca: Cornell Univ. Press, 1978), 11-14.

[28]E.g., Lillian S. Robinson, "Treason Our Text: Feminist Challenges to the Literary Canon," *Tulsa Studies in Women's Literature*, 2 (1983); rpt. in *Contemporary Literary Criticism*, 2nd edition, ed. Robert Con Davis and Ronald Schleifer (New York and London: Longman, 1989), 620. See also Susan K. Harris, *19th–Century American Women's Novels* (Cambridge and New York: Cambridge Univ. Press, 1990), 10.

[29]Tompkins, 126.

[30]*Centenary Edition*, XVII, 304.

[31]Nina Baym, *The Shape of Hawthorne's Career* (Ithaca and London: Cornell Univ. Press, 1976), 9.

[32]Nina Baym, "Plot in Hawthorne's Romances," in *Ruined Eden of the Present*, ed. G. R. Thompson and Virgil L. Lokke (West Lafayette, Ind.: Purdue Univ. Press, 1981); rpt. in *The Scarlet Letter*, 3rd edition, ed. Seymour Gross et al. (New York: Norton, 1988), 404.

[33]Joseph Levi, "Hawthorne's *The Scarlet Letter*: A Psychoanalytical Interpretation," *American Imago*, 10 (1953), 291- 305.

[34]Ross C Murfin, "Introduction: The Critical Background" to *The Scarlet Letter* (Boston: Bedford, 1991), 221.

[35]William Torbert Leonard, *Theatre: Stage to Screen to Television* (Metuchen, N.J.: Scarecrow, 1981), 1375.

[36]Quoted in Constance Rourke, *American Humor: A Study of the National Character* (New York: Harcourt Brace Jovanovich, 1931), 188.

[37]Templeton [pseudo.], "Boston Correspondence," *Hartford Courant*, 8 January 1877, 1:8.

[38]"The Scarlet Letter," *Theatre*, 2 July 1888, 37.

[39]H[arry] T[hurston] P[eck], "The Scarlet Letter," *Boston Transcript*, September 1892, 8:1-2.

[40]"Mr. Mansfield in 'The Scarlet Letter,' " *New York Tribune*, 13 September 1892, 7:2.

[41]"The Scarlet Letter," *Critic*, 14 March 1896, 185.

[42]Edward Wagenknecht, *The Movies in the Age of Innocence* (Norman: Univ. of Oklahoma Press, 1962), 54.

[43] Mordaunt Hall, "A Nathaniel Hawthorne Classic," *New York Times*, 10 August 1926, 19:2.

[44]Albert Bigelow Paine, *Life and Lillian Gish* (New York: Macmillan, 1932), 224.

[45]Mark W. Estrin, " 'Triumphant Ignominy': *The Scarlet Letter* on Screen," *Literature/Film Quarterly*, 2 (Spring 1974), 114.

[46]Julian Smith, "Hester, Sweet Hester Prynne—*The Scarlet Letter* in the Movie Market Place," *Literature/Film Quarterly*, 2 (Spring 1974), 103.

[47]*Photoplay*, 30 (October 1926), 53.

[48]Frances Taylor Patterson, *Motion Picture Continuities* (New York: Columbia Univ. Press, 1927), 89-156.

[49]Smith, 106.

[50]Larry Barker, "The PBS *Scarlet Letter*: Showing Versus Telling," *Nathaniel Hawthorne Journal*, 8 (1978), 219-229.

The Critical Response to Nathaniel Hawthorne's *The Scarlet Letter*

Background and Composition History

Epes Sargent, "Nathaniel Hawthorne," ***Boston Transcript*****, 13 June 1849, 2:3.**

We don't care how much of an outcry our locofoco neighbors raise about the removal of Nathaniel Hawthorne from his humble post in the Custom House at Salem. It was very small business, to say the best of it. It was what Talleyrand would have called "something worse than a crime—a blunder." The high authorities at Washington should make amends for it at once by giving Hawthorne a better berth. He was no politician; although, so far as his vote went, a supporter of the late administration. But if he had been ever so active in his politics, he should have been spared. Do his decapitators know who he is? Perhaps not. But if they will revisit the "glimpses of the moon" a hundred years hence, and ask the casual lover of elegant literature concerning him, an answer will be ready beyond a doubt; and a little indignation will mingle with the reply, when the speaker shall add, that this writer of some of the most exquisite prose in the language, while contributing unrewarded except by the accompanying fame, to his country's honor and to the delight of all good men and women, by his pen, and at the same time fulfilling his official duties unexceptionally, was removed from a paltry Surveyorship, the income of which was just sufficient for his modest wants, because, forsooth, he was on the wrong side politically. "Fie upon it! Oh, fie!"

Boston Transcript, **14 June 1849, 2:2.**

The Salem Register thinks, that Mr Hawthorne may congratuate himself "that he can hereafter turn his undivided attention to the cultivation of his fine talents, by which he can confer a more lasting benefit on the public than by his services as Surveyor." Is not the history of letters crowded with instances, showing that the reward of the highest order of literary labor,— labor, that posterity has consecrated by its applause; labor that has given absolute employment to unborn thousands, in the manufacture of new editions of books—has been often utterly inadequate to the supply of the ordinary necessities of life to the original laborer himself? What if Mr Hawthorne's case were one of these? Would it not have been well to have made the inquiry, before turning him adrift?

James T. Fields, *Yesterdays with Authors* **(Boston: J. R. Osgood, 1872), pp. 48-52.**

I came to know Hawthorne very intimately after the Whigs displaced the Democratic romancer from office. In my ardent desire to have him retained in the public service, his salary at that time being his sole dependence,—not foreseeing that his withdrawal from that sort of employment would be the best thing for American letters that could possibly happen,—I called, in his behalf, on several influential politicians of the day, and well remember the rebuffs I received in my enthusiasm for the author of the "Twice-Told Tales." One pompous little gentleman in authority, after hearing my appeal, quite astounded me by his ignorance of the claims of a literary man on his country. "Yes, yes," he sarcastically croaked down his public turtle-fed throat, "I see through it all, I see through it; this Hawthorne is one of them 'ere visionists, and we don't want no such a man as him round." So the "visionist" was not allowed to remain in office, and the country was better served by him in another way. In the winter of 1849, after he had been ejected from the custom-house, I went down to Salem to see him and inquire after his health for we heard he had been suffering from illness. He was then living in a modest wooden house in Mall Street, if I remember rightly the location. I found him alone in a chamber over the sitting-room of the dwelling; and as the day was cold, he was hovering near a stove. We fell into talk about his future prospects, and he was, as I feared I should find him, in a very desponding mood. "Now," said I, "is the time for you to publish, for I know during these years in Salem you must have got something ready for the press." "Nonsense," said he; "what heart had I to write anything, when my publishers (M. and Company) have been so many years trying to sell a small edition of the 'Twice-Told Tales'?" I still pressed upon him the good chances he would have now with something new. "Who would risk publishing a book for *me*, the most unpopular writer in America?" "I would," said I, "and would start with an edition of two thousand copies of anything you write." "What madness!" he exclaimed; "your friendship for me gets the better of your judgment. No, no," he continued; "I have no money to indemnify a publisher's losses on my account." I looked at my watch and found that the train would soon be starting for Boston, and I knew there was not much time to lose in trying to discover what had been his literary work during these last few years in Salem. I remember that I pressed him to reveal to me what he had been writing. He shook his head and gave me to understand he had produced nothing. At that moment I caught sight of a bureau or set of drawers near where we were sitting; and immediately it occurred to me that hidden away somewhere in that article of furniture was a story or stories by the author of the "Twice-Told Tales," and I became so positive of it that I charged him vehemently with the fact. He seemed surprised, I thought, but shook his head again; and I rose to take my leave, begging him not to come into the cold entry, saying I would come back and see him again in a few days. I was hurrying down the stairs when he called after me from the chamber, asking me to stop a moment. Then quickly stepping into the entry with a roll of manuscript in his hands, he said: "How in Heaven's name did you know this thing was there? As you have found me out, take what I have written, and tell me, after you get home and have time to read it, if it is good for anything. It is either very good or very bad,—I don't know which." On my way up to Boston I read the germ of "The Scarlet Letter"; before I slept that night I wrote him a note all aglow with admiration of the marvelous story he had put into my hands, and told him that I would come again to Salem the next day and arrange for its publication. I went on in such an amazing state of excitement when we met again in the little house, that he would not believe I was really in earnest. He seemed to think I was beside myself and laughed sadly at my enthusiasm. However, we soon arranged for his appearance again before the public with a book.

This quarto volume before me contains numerous letters, written by him from 1850 down to the month of his death. The first one refers to "The Scarlet Letter," and is dated in January, 1850. At my suggestion he had altered the plan of that story. It was his intention to make "The

Scarlet Letter" one of several short stories, all to be included in one volume, and to be called

OLD-TIME LEGENDS
together with sketches,
EXPERIMENTAL AND IDEAL.

His first design was to make "The Scarlet Letter" occupy about two hundred pages in his new book; but I persuaded him, after reading the first chapters of the story, to elaborate it, and publish it as a separate work. After it was settled that "The Scarlet Letter" should be enlarged and printed by itself in a volume he wrote to me:—

"I am truly glad that you like the Introduction, for I was rather afraid that it might appear absurd and impertinent to be talking about myself, when nobody, that I know of, has requested any information on that subject.

"As regards the size of the book, I have been thinking a good deal about it. Considered merely as a matter of taste and beauty, the form of publication which you recommend seems to me much preferable to that of the 'Mosses.'

"In the present case, however, I have some doubts of the expediency, because, if the book is make up entirely of 'The Scarlet Letter,' it will be too sombre. I found it impossible to relieve the shadows of the story with so much light as I would gladly have thrown in. Keeping so close to its point as the tale does, and diversified no otherwise than by turning different sides of the same dark idea to the reader's eye, it will weary very many people and disgust some. Is it safe, then, to stake the fate of the book entirely on this one chance? A hunter loads his gun with a bullet and several buckshot; and, following his sagacious example, it was my purpose to conjoin the one long story with half a dozen shorter ones, so that, failing to kill the public outright with my biggest and heaviest lump of lead, I might have other chances with the smaller bits, individually and in the aggregate. However, I am willing to leave these considerations to your judgment, and should not be sorry to have you decide for the separate publication.

"In this latter event it appears to me that the only proper title for the book would be 'The Scarlet Letter,' for 'The Custom-House' is merely introductory,—an entrance-hall to the magnificent edifice which I throw open to my guests. It would be funny if, seeing the further passages so dark and dismal, they should all chose to stop there! If 'The Scarlet Letter' is to be the title, would it not be well to print it on the title-page in red ink? I am not quite sure about the good taste of so doing, but it would certainly be piquant and appropriate, and, I think, attractive to the great gull whom we are endeavoring to circumvent."

Gary Scharnhorst, " 'Now You Can Write Your Book': A Myth in Hawthorne Biography," *Nathaniel Hawthorne Review*, **15 (Fall 1989), 6-8.**

For better or worse, Julian Hawthorne's reputation as an editor and biographer is roughly equivalent to that of a paid police informant. Edward Davidson has painstakingly demonstrated that the younger Hawthorne "allowed himself every license an editor could arrogate to himself" in the preparation of the manuscript of *Doctor Grimshawe's Secret* (1883).[1] Darrel Abel avers that he "was notoriously careless of veracity and exactness" in his literary projects.[2] Though his biography of his parents was perhaps the high-water mark of an otherwise lackluster career, even this work has had its detractors. Upon its publication in 1884, James Freeman Clarke declared some of the data "false" and "unworthy of the writer,"[3] and Thomas Wentworth Higginson complained it was rife with omissions and distortions.[4] More recently, Maurice Bassan has proved that the texts of documents cited in the two volumes "are not completely reliable."[5] At the risk of seeming to depreciate all criticism of Julian Hawthorne and the biography, I wish to discuss here the provenance of a controversial text cited in *Nathaniel Hawthorne and His Wife*: the "family legend" concerning Hawthorne's decision to begin *The Scarlet Letter* on the very day he was dismissed from the Salem Custom House. In retrospect, Nathaniel Hawthorne's son seems a more conscientious biographer than his reputation would suggest.

For well over half a century after the publication of *Nathaniel Hawthorne and His Wife*, it was assumed that the author began *The Scarlet Letter* on June 8, 1849, as Julian Hawthorne had claimed. However contrived it may seem today, the younger Hawthorne's account was the standard composition history:

> On the day he received the news of his discharge [from the custom house], Hawthorne came home several hours earlier than usual; and when his wife expressed pleasure and surprise at his prompt reappearance, he called her attention to the fact that he had left his head behind him. "Oh, then," exclaimed Mrs. Hawthorne, buoyantly, "you can write your book!"

When the author asked "where their bread and rice were to come from" while he was confined to his study, Sophia Hawthorne revealed that she had secretly saved "a large pile of gold" from her household allowance. So Nathaniel Hawthorne "began 'The Scarlet Letter' that afternoon; and blessed his stars, no doubt, for sending him such a wife.[6] Brander Matthews echoed this anecdote in his *Introduction to the Study of American Literature* (1896),[7] and Julian Hawthorne reiterated it, with minor variations, as late as 1931.[8] However, Randall Stewart marshaled evidence in 1948 that Nathaniel Hawthorne started the romance in late August or early September 1849,[9] and the general editor of the Centenary Edition of Hawthorne's works reiterated in 1962 that no hard facts support the earlier theory "that composition began so early" as June.[10] "Julian's version of the circumstances under which the masterpiece was written" is now considered, in the words of Alfred S. Reid, "a pretty little legend written for its sensational effect."[11] According to Arlin Turner, this account offers "little for the factual record."[12] Yet the question remains: Did Julian Hawthorne simply invent it for the biography, or was it, as James Mellow diplomatically contends, a "family legend" he preserved?[13]

In fact, the story was first published in 1871, and it had appeared in print at least four times before Julian Hawthorne cited it in *Hawthorne and His Wife*. Moncure Conway, an American Unitarian minister resident in London, first recounted a version of the anecdote in *Harper's Weekly* shortly after the death of Sophia Hawthorne. According to Conway, who often wrote about the Hawthornes over a period of thirty years, Nathaniel Hawthorne one day received notice of his dismissal from the Salem Custom House. Conway then shifts to present tense for an entire paragraph, as if imagining the scene:

> With heaviness of heart he repairs to his humble home. His young wife recognizes the change, and stands waiting for the gloomy silence to be broken. At length he falters out, "I am removed from office." Then the wife leaves the room; returns soon with fuel, and kindles a bright fire with her own hands; next brings paper, pen, and ink, and deposits them beside Hawthorne on the table. Then she touches the sad man on the shoulder, and as he turns it is to meet the beaming face of a little woman, who says to him,"Now you can write your book!"
>
> From that moment the cloud cleared away, never to return.[14]

Conway cites no source here. When he repeated the "pleasant story" verbatim twelve years later in a biography of Emerson, however, he claimed to have heard it from someone "very intimate" with Nathaniel and Sophia Hawthorne.[15] Might he have been told the story by a fellow mourner at Sophia's funeral in March 1871?

To judge from a third publication of the legend, the answer is yes.

George William Curtis, Hawthorne's acquaintance from Brook Farm days, recounts the anecdote in his " 'Editor's Easy Chair" in *Harper's* for August 1871. According to Curtis, who attributes the story to an unnamed friend "who had known [Sophia Hawthorne] for many years," when Nathaniel Hawthorne returned to the house "with the news that his office was gone" his wife "met his anxious face and words by telling him that she had saved from his earnings enough to keep them in bread and rice for a few weeks, and was so glad that he could now write his romance, and would have a fire kindled immediately in the study." In Curtis' version, Sophia Hawthorne then wrote "the friend just mentioned," "her most affectionate counsellor through life," to ask "what she could do to keep up the household supplies when the bread and rice were gone." The friend suggested that she "make lamp-shades of lovely forms" to sell. Sophia Hawthorne ostensibly "employed herself constantly with this work" until *The Scarlet Letter* appeared in March 1850.[16] Curtis also quotes a published account of Sophia Hawthorne's funeral written by her confidant. This clue serves to identify the friend as William Henry Channing, another American Unitarian minister in England, whose private letter about the funeral had been printed in the *Boston Transcript* the previous March.[17] From all indications, Channing seems to have been the original, unacknowledged source of the story in the versions cited by both Conway and Curtis. Unfortunately, there is no documentary evidence to corroborate it. Neither Sophia Hawthorne's letter to Channing in June 1849 nor his reply to her is apparently extant, if either ever existed. Obviously, however, the anecdote was no family tradition, for it originated among a circle of Hawthorne's friends after the deaths of both principal characters and some twenty years after the events it presumes to chronicle.

In a sense, however, the story became a family tradition even before Julian Hawthorne cited it in 1884. George Parsons Lathrop, Hawthorne's son-in-law, embellished the anecdote in a biographical sketch of the author published in 1883. In effect, Lathrop fictionalizes a legend of dubious authenticity. In his version, Hawthorne returned home early one day from the custom house

> and entering sat down in the nearest chair, without uttering a word. Mrs. Hawthorne asked him if he was well.
>
> "Well enough," was the answer.
>
> "What is the matter, then?" said she. "Are you 'decapitated?' "
>
> He replied with gloom that he was, and that the occurrence was no joke.
>
> "Oh," said his wife, gayly, "now you can write your

Romance!" For he had told her several times that he had a romance "growling" in him.

" 'Write my Romance!' " he exclaimed. "But what are we to do for bread and rice, next week?"

"I will take care of that," she answered, "and I will tell Ann to put a fire in your study, now."

According to Lathrop, Sophia Hawthorne had saved "about a hundred and fifty dollars" from her budget and "began making little cambric lamp-shades" for sale in Boston. In this way "the devoted wife contrived to defray the expenses of the household until the book was finished."[18] Lathrop has apparently fleshed out Curtis' account with imaginary dialogue and a number of invented details.

Thus Julian Hawthorne was, in 1884, at least the fourth writer to publish a version of the anecdote. Ironically, none of the other men who earlier reported it (Conway, Curtis, Lathrop) nor Channing, the apparent source of the story, was ever accused of falsifying evidence. Did the incident occur? No, at least not exactly as recorded. It is possible, however, that Sophia Hawthorne earned money to support the family in late 1849 and early 1850—a detail Julian Hawthorne, a scourge of feminism, conveniently omits from his biography. That is, the younger Hawthorne may have published that part of the legend which had no basis in fact and ignored that part with a kernel of truth. But he did not, in any case, fabricate a source from whole cloth.

Notes

[1]Davidson, *Hawthorne's Doctor Grimshawe's Secret* (Cambridge: Harvard UP, 1954), p. vi.

[2]Abel, "Who Wrote Hawthorne's Autobiography?" *American Literature*, 28 (March 1956), 75. See also Vernon Loggins, *The Hawthornes* (New York: Columbia UP, 1951), pp. 316-329.

[3]Clarke, "Hawthorne and Margaret Fuller," *Independent*, 1 January 1885, pp. 1-2.

[4]"Nathaniel Hawthorne and His Wife," *Atlantic Monthly*, 55 (February 1885), 259-265.

[5]Bassan, *Hawthorne's Son* (Columbus: Ohio State UP, 1970), p. 163. See also Bassan, "Julian Hawthorne Edits Aunt Ebe," *Essex Institute Historical Collections*, 100 (1964), 274-278.

[6]Hawthorne, *Nathaniel Hawthorne and His Wife* (Boston: J. R. Osgood, 1884), I, 340.

[7]Matthews, *An Introduction to the Study of American Literature* (New York: American Book Co., 1896), p. 115. See also Matthews, "Nathaniel Hawthorne," *St. Nicholas*, 22 (March 1895), 387.

[8]Hawthorne, "The Making of *The Scarlet Letter*," *Bookman*, 74 (December 1931), 402.

[9]Stewart, *Nathaniel Hawthorne: A Biography* (New Haven: Yale UP, 1948), pp. 93-94.

[10]W[illiam] C[harvat], "Introduction," *The Centenary Edition of the Works of Nathaniel Hawthorne* (Columbus: Ohio State UP, 1962), I, xix.

[11]Reid, "A Note on the Date of *The Scarlet Letter*," *Furman University Bulletin*, NS 4 (Winter 1957), 35. See also Hubert H. Hoeltje, "The Writing of *The Scarlet Letter*," *New England Quarterly*, 27 (March 1954), 342.

[12]Turner, *Nathaniel Hawthorne: A Biography* (New York: Oxford UP, 1980), p. 190.

[13]Mellow, *Nathaniel Hawthorne in His Times* (Boston: Houghton Mifflin, 1980), p. 303.

[14]Conway, "A Fresh Grave in Kensal Green," *Harper's Weekly*, 22 April 1871, p. 369.

[15]Conway, *Emerson at Home and Abroad* (Boston: J. R. Osgood, 1882), p. 217.

[16]"Editor's Easy Chair," *Harper's Monthly*, 43 (August 1871), 453.

[17]"The Late Mrs. Hawthorne," *Boston Transcript*, 21 March 1871, 2:1.

[18]Lathrop, "Biographical Sketch," in *The Works of Nathaniel Hawthorne* (Boston: Houghton Mifflin, 1883), XII, 496-497.

"Nathaniel Hawthorne," ***Boston Transcript*****, 22 January 1850, 2:1.**

The announcement of a new work by this distinguished author will create great interest among the reading community, as well as among the more prescribed and limited circle of writers and critics. We are glad to learn that Mr Hawthorne is to give us a novel during the spring, from the press of Messrs Ticknor, Reed & Fields of this city. Its title is "The Scarlet Letter," and the story is introduced by some autobiographical reminiscences of the author during his late sojourn in the Salem Custom House. Of Nathaniel Hawthorne, as a man of original and striking genius, the public does not need to be advised. At this present time, no man living, either in Europe or America, is comparable to him as a writer in his peculiar walk. Mr Whipple, in his last volume of lectures, says finely of this admirable author—"though we cannot do him justice, let us remember the name of Nathaniel Hawthorne, deserving a place second to none in that band of humorists, whose beautiful depth of cheerful feeling is the very poetry of mirth. In ease, grace, delicate sharpness of satire,—in a felicity of touch, which often surpasses the felicity of Addison, in a subtlety of insight which often reaches further than the subtlety of Steele,—the humor of Hawthorne presents traits so fine as to be almost too excellent for popularity, as, to every one who has attempted their criticism, they are too refined for statement."[1]

Note

[1]E. P. Whipple, *Lectures on Subjects Connected with Literature and Life* (Boston: Ticknor, Reed and Fields, 1849), pp. 154-55.

Christian Inquirer, **9 February 1850, 3:2.**

NATHANIEL HAWTHORNE is busy with the proof sheets of his new novel. Its title is "The Scarlet Letter," and from what has oozed out concerning its merits, there is no doubt of the interest its publication will excite. It is said to be admirably written, and the story so managed as to enchain attention through every scene it portrays. The power and beauty of HAWTHORNE'S style are always marked, but in the present work he seems to have produced more *effect* than he has elsewhere attempted. Should "The Scarlet Letter" place its distinguished author among the most attractive novelists of the present day, we shall not be surprised. He has genius, beyond a doubt, superior to any American story writer, and his touch is so delicate and skillful, that whatever he designs to accomplish is always successfully performed. The Salem Custom House comes in for a pictorial sketch in his Introduction to the novel, and every one will be on the *qui vive* to see how he has shown up an establishment which has connected itself with his name in no very enviable light.

Contemporary American Reception

"The New Romance," ***Boston Transcript*****, 15 March 1850, 4:1.**

The coil of a splendid reputation has long been lying safe in the brain of Nathaniel Hawthorne. After the publication of The Scarlet Letter, to be issued on Saturday morning next by Ticknor & Co, his fame will have secured a safe place for itself beside the first writers of our time, his name belonging of right to their catalogue. Following immediately a careful perusal of The Scarlet Letter we have no hesitation in saying that in imagination, power, pathos, beauty, and all the other essential qualifications requisite to the completeness of a first rate romance, Mr Hawthorne has equalled if not surpassed any other writer who has appeared in our country during the last half century. Indeed, we are inclined to the conclusion that he has not been eclipsed by the higher class of European minds which have led the way in that department to which his genius belongs. The author of the "Thrice Told Tales," and the "Mosses from an old Manse" has long been recognized at home and abroad as an original writer of exquisite tales, but "The Scarlet Letter" carries him an infinite distance farther on in his brilliant career to fame.

We shall not attempt to picture in advance of its publication the plot of the Romance. The subject is one that needed to be most carefully handled, and no man but Hawthorne could have traced so delicately and with so much effect. The Scarlet Letter is the work of infamy branded on the bosom of one, who has violated the seventh commandment and side by side with the partner of her guilt the sad heroine walks through a life of retribution crowded with incidents which the novelist has depicted with so much truth and vigor that the interest at every page of his book grapples to the reader with a powerful hold upon his sympathy, and he will not lay down the story till he knows its result at its close. As a great moral lesson this novel will outweigh in its influence all the sermons that have ever been preached against the sin, the effects of which The Scarlet Letter is written to exhibit. Mr Hawthorne has prefaced his Romance with an autobiographical introduction giving some account of his life in the Salem Custom House. These pages are full of wit and humor of the richest description, and show that the writer is as much at home with a smile on his countenance, as he is with a tear in his eye. * * *

"New Publications," ***Boston Transcript*****, 18 March 1850, 2:4.**

It is an ill wind that blows nobody any good. A few months since we gave expression to a sentiment of indignation, which was very generally felt in this community, at the news of the removal of Nathaniel Hawthorne from an humble post in the Salem Custom House. But how short-sighted we mortals are! It is to that very removal, that we, the public and posterity are probably indebted for this beautiful romance, decidedly one of the most powerful, original and memorable that American literature can boast. Every body must buy the book, and read it. The introductory portion, in which the author treats of his Custom-House experiences, is in the best vein of Goldsmith.

*Salem Gazette***, 19 March 1850, 2:2.**

A volume from the pen of Nathaniel Hawthorne will be seized with eagerness; for the dainty morsels which come to us from time to time, in the shape of sketches long enough to be contained in the story department of a newspaper, are snatched up and devoured by those who come within the reach of the newspaper, and who does not? We have often had an impatient desire 'for more' excited by this provoking taste of his quality, and the pleasure of sitting down to a volume of his is one which we could hardly wait for willingly, when it is announced to us as near at hand. With these highly raised expectations, we have taken up the volume before us, and have found ourselves completely enchained by it.

According to Mr Hawthorne, while in the office of Surveyor of the port of Salem, he came across, amidst a heap of rubbish in a neglected room in the Custom House, a mysterious package, which probably had escaped the eye of all of his predecessors in office, and but for him might have continued in obscurity during the dynasty of his successor. From its contents he has wrought a tale of thrilling interest, which he calls "the Scarlet Letter." It is founded upon an incident in the early history of New England. We shall not attempt a sketch of it, preferring that the book should tell its own story. Mr Hawthorne has a peculiar power of calling up from the past, not only the personages and incidents which most strongly stamped themselves upon its history, but he reproduces their spirit—their very presence. We have realized this in several of his earlier sketches, particularly in the matchless story of the "Gentle Boy." Nothing in the whole range of modern literature seems to us more absolutely perfect in its way than this exquisite creation. In the 'Scarlet Letter' we have a tale of much more exciting and absorbing interest, and we are hurried through it with a distressing eagerness.

In all his earlier writings, the interest of the story has been completely subordinated to the charm of fancy, and the unequalled power of language which has made a Carrier's Address or a Peter Parley's Universal History, as bewitching as a romance. We have been in love with our mother tongue, and have yielded ourselves to this fascination. But in the deep tragedy of Hester Prynne's experiences we are borne through the pages, as by an irresistible impulse—hardly stopping to notice the exquisite touches which are to be found in the midst of the most harrowing and distressing scenes. It is indeed a wonderful book, and we venture to predict that no one will put it down before he reaches the last page of it, unless it is forcibly taken out of his hands.

We are glad to notice that the book is published by Ticknor, Reed & Fields, and therefore is done up in perfect style. It is a pleasure to look at the printed page.

Salem Register, **21 March 1850, 2:1-2.**

The long expected Romance from the pen of Hawthorne has at length appeared, in all the attractive externals of binding, paper and typography, with which the celebrated Boston publishing firm of Ticknor & Co. love to adorn the volumes bearing their stamp. So far as the Scarlet Letter is concerned, it will more than meet the public expectation, and increase the enviable reputation which the author long ago acquired. It is a narrative of singular interest and originality, sustained throughout with a continuous power and pathos, and an affluence of imagination and bold and striking thought, that hold the reader a willing captive. It is marked by all the exquisiteness of Hawthorne's genius, but with less of that dreamy indistinctness which has sometimes made not a few of his productions unintelligible to an ordinary mind. The machinery and the plot are very simple. An erring woman and her child; the guilty father, bearing the burden of his sin in secret, while he is the esteemed and idolized pastor of his flock; and the wronged husband, are the chief characters in which the interest centres; the early days of the puritans, with their stern habits, principles, and modes of punishment, is the time in which the scenes are laid; and the public shame of the suffering woman, the secret tortures of the sinning minister, and the calm, cold-blooded, unceasing gloating for revenge of the vindictive husband, form the ground-work upon which Hawthorne has constructed this thrilling and powerful romance. The subsidiary characters and incidents are very skillfully interwoven into the narrative, and there is no break in the interest excited from the commencement to the close. We have rarely read a work which enchains the attention by so potent a spell—a spell with which only a rare genius could invest such umpromising materials. The moral which the tale enforces is: "Be true! Be true! Be true! Show freely to the world, if not your worst, yet some trait whereby the worst may be inferred!"

And here we wish we could pause, with only a word of praise upon our lips; but justice compels us to notice some other things, which, as citizens of Salem and taking an interest in our native place and in our neighbors, we can not suffer to pass in silence. Mr. Hawthorne, it may be remembered, some three or four years ago, supplanted another gentleman in the Surveyor's office of the Salem Custom House, where he continued until, by the fortune of politics, he was himself superseded, a few months since, and relieved from the burdens of the public service.—He has, accordingly, prefaced his Scarlet Letter with some fifty pages or more of autobiographical reminiscences during his incarceration in the Custom House, in which he developes some new traits in his character, or, at least, some which the public could never before have suspected, from his writings, that he possessed. Whether from an undue sensitiveness on account of his removal, or from what other reason we know not, he seeks to vent his spite on something or somebody, by small sneers at Salem, and by vilifying some of his former associates, to a degree of which we should have supposed any gentleman, to say nothing of a man of ordinary feeling, refinement, and kindliness of heart, incapable.—Indeed, while reading this chapter on the Custom House, we almost began to think that Hawthorne had mistaken his vocation—that, instead of indulging in dreamy transcendentalism, and weaving exquisite fancies to please the imagination and improve the heart, he would have been more at home as a despicable lampooner, and in that capacity would have achieved a notoriety which none of his tribe, either of ancient or modern times, has reached. We were almost induced to throw down the book in disgust, without venturing on the Scarlet Letter, so atrocious, so heartless, so undisguised, so utterly inexcusable seemed his calumnious caricatures of inoffensive men, who could not possibly have given occasion for such wanton insults. We could have tolerated some pleasantry in regard to the place—we could smile at his conceit that "it would be quite as reasonable to form a sentimental attachment for a disarranged checkerboard" as for his flat, tame, wearisome, joyless native town, with its "old wooden houses," its "mud and dust," its "dead level of site and sentiment," its "chill east wind" and "chilliest of social atmospheres."—We could readily believe that our author was entirely out of place here—he who had fellowshipped "with the dreamy brethren of Brook Farm"—who had lived "for three years within the subtile influence of an intellect like Emerson's"—who had indulged "fantastic speculations" with Ellery Channing— talked with Thoreau in his hermitage—grown "fastidious by sympathy with the classic refinement of Hillard's culture"—and become "imbued with poetic sentiment at Longfellow's hearth- stone." We could have submitted with composure to the doom imposed upon us, that Hawthorne was henceforth to be "a citizen of somewhere else," and that his children, so far as he can control their fortunes, "shall strike their roots into unaccumstomed earth." We could have borne all this, only wondering how $900, more or less, per year, for the irksome toil of three and a half hours daily waste of time at the Custom House,—"pacing from corner to corner, or lounging on the long-legged stool, with his elbow on the desk, and his eyes wandering up and down the columns of the morning newspaper," "doing what was really of no advantage or delight to any human being,"—only wondering, we say, how filthy lucre could have made such a place at all endurable, after such an experience. But we wonder still more that such a mind, with such culture, and such previous exercise, could stoop to perpetrate the outrageous personalities which disfigure this chapter on the Custom House.—What can be more heartless and irreverent, after ridiculing the infirmities of aged man, two of whom he admits to have been discharged thro' his own influence, than the following passage?

"They were allowed, on my representation, to rest from their arduous labors, and soon afterwards—as if their sole principle of life had been zeal for their country's service, as I verily believe it was—withdrew to a better world. It is a pious consolation to me, that, through my interference, a sufficient space was allowed them for repentance of the evil and corrupt practices into which, as a matter of course, every Custom House officer must be supposed to fall. Neither the front nor the back entrance of the Custom House opens on the road to Paradise."

This strange antipathy to the aged manifests itself even in the Scarlet Letter. Witness the following unkind cut:—

"Hurrying along the street, the Reverend Mr. Dimmesdale encountered the eldest female member of his church; a most pious and exemplary old dame; poor, widowed, lonely, and with a heart as full of reminiscences about her dead husband and children, and her dead friends of long ago, as a burial-ground is full of storied grave-stones. Yet all this, which would else have been such heavy sorrow, was made almost a solemn joy to her devout old soul by religious consolations and the truths of Scripture, wherewith she had fed herself continually for more than thirty years."

What a cold and heartless sneer at one of the natural and commendable propensities of the aged mind!

But the most venomous, malignant and unaccountable assault is made upon a venerable gentleman, whose chief crime seems to be that he loves a good dinner, has preserved a youthful flow of cheerfulness, and can tell a graphic story. Why this officer of fourscore years—the son of a Revolutionary Colonel—a perfect gentleman of the old school in his manners, and a rare specimen of vivacious age—courteous and polite to every body—ready to join in genial mirth, but never obtruding himself or his opinions upon any one's notice, unless invited—intelligent, benevolent, and of business capacities infinitely above any the Ex-Surveyor ever displayed—having children in this community, heads of families, respectable and respected—why this gentleman should be dragged so rudely and abusively before the public, and his and his children's feelings lacerated and outraged so unjustifiably, is a mystery beyond our power to fathom. The only thing we can liken it to, in refinement of cruelty, is the fell purpose with which old Roger Chillingworth sets about wrecking his vengeance on Arthur Dimmesdale—but without the visible motive for so much malice, which is palpable in the *avowed* Romance. Indignation and surprise are uppermost in all men's minds who read and see the application of this chapter on the Custom House. Even where the writer seems to praise, the picture is so overdrawn as to appear intended for a caricature, and the language so extravagant as to wear a strong tinge of irony.

We could wish for Mr. Hawthorne's sake, that this chapter had never been written. It has obliterated whatever sympathy was felt for his removal, in this community; and, could it be read in the Senate, with proper comments, whenever his case comes up, would put any advocate to the blush who should undertake to sympathize with or defend him. It is only by a strong effort to reconcile the incongruities of poor human nature that we can possibly recognize in the malignant Hawthorne of the Salem Custom House, the reputed "*gentle* Hawthorne," of former days.—Whether he places himself in the category of those who "suffer moral detriment from this peculiar mode of life," as he says most Custom House officials do, or whether he has only developed features which previously existed, we fear that he has been but too painfully true to his own moral, and has shown freely to the world, if not his worst, yet a "trait whereby the worst may be inferred." If we had any doubt before, we have not a single scruple remaining in regard to the full justification of the Administration in relieving him from the dignified employment of "pacing to and fro across [his] room, or traversing with a hundred fold repetition, the long extent from the front-door of the Custom House to the side entrance, and back again." The "*Posthumous Papers of a Decapitated Surveyor*" amply vindicate the justice of this application of the political guillotine.

"Literary Notices," ***Boston Post*****, 21 March 1850, 1:6.**

Hundreds of our readers must already be conversant with this book; and as we were compelled by its attractiveness to read every word between the covers, it is probable that our praise or blame is a little behind the times, and therefore of small account. But without going far into details, we must pass a vote of thanks for gratification received at the hands of Mr Hawthorne. "The Scarlet Letter" is, in essence, almost identical with the previous works of the author. It is a wild, poetical and symbolic story of remorse—of remorse and repentance in rags, of remorse and half repentance in high places. The scene is laid in Boston, some twenty years subsequent to its foundation. "The Scarlet Letter" is the "Letter A," worn on the bosom of a discovered adulteress, according to the old Puritan enactment or legend. There is no incident to the tale—it opens with the exposure of Hester Prynne, and its argument relates to her sufferings and those of him who had sinned with her, to the life of the little Pearl, the child of the guilty ones, and to the revenge of the old and injured Chillingworth. The adulteress is known to the world, but her seducer is hidden from all but the husband. The merits of the book lie in its vigorous conception of scenes, its vivid master-strokes of character, and its thickly-scattered gems of thought and expression. It has very little dialogue. The whole is a prose poem, and must be regarded as such, and judged by poetical standards only. In this view, Hester Prynne, Dimmesdale and Chillingworth and that wild, beautiful and unfathomable little Pearl are as true as they are original—they are poetical embodiments of the highest, strongest, most tenacious and most inconsistent principles of our nature. As prose creations, they are unnatural—as poetic fancies, they are fixed as the pole to the truth which is in man. We think there are few if any passages in literature, which are better, in their way, than the two scenes at the pillory, the walk in the forest, the revelation, and all the chapters through which Pearl dances; to say nothing of those wherein the physician goads on the minister to madness and death. Moreover, the catastrophe is grandly wrought out. It was a fine idea to make the solitary and long repentant woman finally willing to break the bonds of society for the life's sake of her crushed idol, while the passion-ridden priest, an involuntary compound of seeming and reality, manfully overcomes, in his dying hour, the fascinating temptation by which he was entranced. Mr Hawthorne writes as a man as well as a poet, and while building his romance upon the usages of society, and thereby occupying artificial ground, his pen is above all cant and creed, and his characters are of the real stuff, either God-born or devil-born, and not the offspring of man's ceremonials. We think Mr Hawthorne has largely increased his reputation by the "Scarlet Letter." Though of the same family, it is worth a score of "Twice Told Tales," and it will be read by thousands, to whom the preceding tid-bits of quaint, mystic and eccentric literature are but *caviare*.

"Literary Notices," ***Albany Daily State Register*****, 25 March 1850, 2:6.**

There are some authors, the sight of whose name on the title page of a new work comes with a freshness to our minds, prophetic of the pleasure the perusal is to give us. Among these is Hawthorne. Year after year we have taken up his works, as they issued from the press, and always with unabated interest. His very style is a relief. It is an exception to the exaggerated inflated verbiage of the day. Hawthorne writes in the simple words of one who cares only to convey the ideas with which his mind is so richly teeming. There is, too, about his writings, an air of sympathy with mortal sorrow and weakness. It is "the still sad music of humanity," and as we read, we feel that we are following the lead of one, who has obeyed Sir Philip Sidney's rule,— "Look into thy heart and write."

We glean from the first chapter of this work a little piece of auto-biography,—we have a picture of the quiet old Custom- house at Salem, where, for three years, our author presided over a set of aged officials, who slumbered away their time, and lived on their salaries, as he describes them, "a row of venerable figures, sitting in old fashioned chairs, which were tipped on their hind legs back against the wall." The sketches of character, however, of the old Inspector, and of General Miller, the hero of Niagara, are admirable. It was in the garret of this quiet dozing place, that—a usual piece of luck with authors—he found the manuscript which contained the history of the Scarlet Letter.

It proves to be a story of New England life two hundred years ago, and it is in this field that Hawthorne particularly excels. A thorough New England man, he understands the old Puritan character in all its phases. He has too the power—and a great power it is, where it exists—to cast himself back into those ages, live with their people, and clothe the dead of centuries gone with all the warm lineaments of life, calling up again before us a stern social system which has long since passed away.

The scene opens at the gates of the old prison of Boston, and the crowds have gathered to see Hester Prynne come forth to punishment, and in the Scripture phraseology of the day discuss the sentence which the magistrates, "the God-fearing gentlemen," had bestowed upon her who was to be always "the people's victim and the life-long bond-slave." But her thoughts are far away from that wild New England scene. In imagination she lived again the days of her girlish beauty in the old home over the ocean. There rises before her the decayed house of gray stone—her father's venerable beard flowed over his Elizabethian ruff—the quaint architecture of the cathedral—until she suddenly awakes to find herself in the place of shame, the sport of a deriding mob. But this quiet scene of old England forms a beautiful contrast in the narrative.

Each of the characters is indeed a life-like portrait. Old Governor Bellingham in his official stateliness—Mr. [W]ilson, the popular preacher of the day—Arthur Dimmesdale, going on thro' life with a secret burning at his heart's core—Mrs. Hibbins, the old witch-mother—and Chillingworth, the crafty leach, worming himself into the young man's confidence to plot against his soul, and by discovering the dark problem of his life, to answer his own revenge—are all delineations beautifully elaborated. There are some scenes of more passion than we remember elsewhere in Hawthorne's writings. Such are the Minister's Vigil—the interview with Hester in the forest—the fear, the remorse, the agony, the ineffectual repentance, the backward rush of sinful thoughts, which affected the heart of him who had fallen, until he loathed his miserable self—and the solemn ending to this life of human frailty and sorrow.

But we must say nothing to forestall our readers as to the conclusion. For although Hawthorne's works do not depend for their interest upon the plot, and we are rather inclined to linger on each page for the quiet beauty of the writing, yet still it is better for the tale gradually to unfold before the reader, and that it should not be anticipated by us.

"Recent Publications," *Philadelphia Cummings' Evening Telegraphic Bulletin*, **25 March 1850, 1:5.**

After reading this charming romance, one can scarcely find fault with the political fiat which turned Nathaniel Hawthorne out of the Salem Custom House. To that act of inexcusable severity the world is indebted for this story, with its beautiful pictures and its impressive lessons; and in this light alone can we see reason for approving of this exercise of the stern doctrine that "to the victors belong the spoils." But this is neither here nor there. The book is what we have to deal with, and as it has probably been read by many of our readers, the more brief we are, the better. To those who have not read it, we will say that the first fifty odd pages describe Hawthorne's life in this Salem Custom House—a classic spot now, like the India House where Charles Lamb wrote for his daily bread. This part of the book is filled with the most exquisite pen-portraits, and with passages of rich humor, quiet wit, and genial sentiment, that will warm the heart of every reader. Turning the last page of this with regret, we come to the strange, wild story of the Scarlet Letter, the materials for which are found among the rubbish of an unoccupied room of the Custom House.

An old Puritan Law, rigidly enforced in the early days of Boston, required the adulteress to wear upon her breast the letter "A," worked in red. An erring, but strong minded woman, is sentenced to bear this brand. The partner of her guilt is a clergyman, high in the veneration of the colony; and rather than expose him and destroy his influence as a divine teacher, she goes heroically through her bitter expiation. The erring woman, the no less erring man, the elfin offspring of their guilty love and the injured husband, pass through a history of almost agonizing interest; and prominent over all is the Scarlet Letter—the strange sign, mysteriously affecting all, and itself seeming invested with a species of supernatural vitality. The two passions, Remorse and

Revenge were never more strongly wrought out than in this romance. Having given this inkling of the meaning of the Scarlet Letter, we shall say no more of the plot. The book abounds in fine passages descriptive of early colonial life, which no one but Hawthorne could write. The author of "Thrice-told Tales" and "Mosses from an Old Manse," has acquired a new and higher fame as the author of the "Scarlet Letter." We are glad to see in the introductory chapter a promise of other tales from materials found in the Old Custom House.

"Nathaniel Hawthorne," ***Literary World*****, 30 March 1850, pp. 323-325.**

MR. HAWTHORNE introduces his new story to the public, the longest of all that he has yet published, and most worthy in this way to be called a romance, with one of those pleasant personal descriptions which are the most charming of his compositions, and of which we had so happy an example in the preface to his last collection, the Mosses from an Old Manse. In these narratives everything seems to fall happily into its place. The style is simple and flowing, the observation accurate and acute; persons and things are represented in their minutest shades, and difficult traits of character presented with an instinct which art might be proud to imitate. They are, in fine, little cabinet pictures exquisitely painted. The readers of the Twice Told Tales will know the pictures to which we allude. They have not, we are sure, forgotten Little Annie's Ramble, or the Sights from a Steeple. This is the Hawthorne of the present day in the sunshine. There is another Hawthorne less companionable, of sterner Puritan aspect, with the shadow of the past over him, a reviver of witchcrafts and of those dark agencies of evil which lurk in the human soul, and which even now represent the old gloomy historic era in the microcosm and eternity of the individual; and this Hawthorne is called to mind by such tales as the Minister's Black Veil or the Old Maid in the Winding Sheet, and reappears in the Scarlet Letter, a romance. Romantic in sooth! Such romance as you may read in the intensest sermons of old Puritan divines, or in the mouldy pages of that Marrow of Divinity, the ascetic Jeremy Taylor.

The Scarlet Letter is a psychological romance. The hardiest Mrs. Malaprop would never venture to call it a novel. It is a tale of remorse, a study of character in which the human heart is anatomized, carefully, elaborately, and with striking poetic and dramatic power. Its incidents are simply these. A woman in the early days of Boston becomes the subject of the discipline of the court of those times, and is condemned to stand in the pillory and wear henceforth, in token of her shame, the scarlet letter A attached to her bosom. She carries her child with her to the pillory. Its other parent is unknown. At this opening scene her husband from whom she had been separated in Europe, preceding him by ship across the Atlantic, reappears from the forest, whither he had been thrown by shipwreck on his arrival. He was a man of a cold intellectual temperament, and devotes his life thereafter to search for his wife's guilty partner and a fiendish revenge. The young clergyman of the town, a man of a devout sensibility and warmth of heart, is the victim, as this Mephistophilean old physician fixes himself by his side to watch over him and protect his health, an object of great solicitude to his parishioners, and, in reality, to detect his suspected secret and gloat over his tortures. This slow, cool, devilish purpose, like the concoction of some sublimated hell broth, is perfected gradually and inevitably. The wayward, elfish child, a concentration of guilt and passion, binds the interests of the parties together, but throws little sunshine over the scene. These are all the characters, with some casual introductions of the grim personages and manners of the period, unless we add the scarlet letter, which, in Hawthorne's hands, skilled to these allegorical, typical semblances, becomes vitalized as the rest. It is the hero of the volume. The denouement is the death of the clergyman on a day of public festivity, after a public confession in the arms of the pilloried, branded woman. But few as are these main incidents thus briefly told, the action of the story, or its passion, is "long, obscure, and infinite." It is a drama in which thoughts are acts. The material has been thoroughly fused in the writer's mind, and springs forth an entire, perfect creation. We know of no American tales except some of the early ones of Mr. Dana, which approach it in conscientious completeness. Nothing is slurred over, superfluous, or defective. The story is grouped in scenes simply arranged, but with artistic power, yet without any of those painful impressions which the use of the words, as it is the fashion to use them, "grouping" and "artistic" excite, suggesting artifice and effort at the expense of nature and ease.

Mr. Hawthorne has, in fine, shown extraordinary power in this volume, great feeling and discrimination, a subtle knowledge of character in its secret springs and outer manifestations. He blends, too, a delicate fancy with this metaphysical insight. We would instance the chapter towards the close, entitled "The Minister in a Maze," where the effects of a diabolic temptation are curiously depicted, or "The Minister's Vigil," the night scene in the pillory. The atmosphere of the piece also is perfect. It has the mystic element, the weird forest influences of the old Puritan discipline and era. Yet there is no affrightment which belongs purely to history, which has not its echo even in the unlike and perversely commonplace custom-house of Salem. Then for the moral. Though severe, it is wholesome, and is a sounder bit of Puritan divinity than we have been of late accustomed to hear from the degenerate successors of Cotton Mather. We hardly know another writer who has lived so much among the new school who would have handled this delicate subject without an infusion of George Sand. The spirit of his old Puritan ancestors, to whom he refers in the preface, lives in Nathaniel Hawthorne. * * *

And a literary man long may he remain, an honor and a support to the craft, of genuine worth and fidelity, to whom no word is idle, no sentiment insincere. Our literature has given to the world no truer product of the American soil, though of a peculiar culture, than Nathaniel Hawthorne.

Nathaniel Hawthorne, "Preface to the Second Edition" of *The Scarlet Letter*

Much to the author's surprise, and (if he may say so without additional offence) considerably to his amusement, he finds that his sketch of official life, introductory to THE SCARLET LETTER, has created an unprecedented excitement in the respectable community immediately around him. It could hardly have been more violent, indeed, had he burned down the Custom House, and quenched its last smoking ember in the blood of a certain venerable personage, against whom he is supposed to cherish a peculiar malevolence. As the public disapprobation would weigh very heavily on him, were he conscious of deserving it, the author begs leave to say that he has carefully read over the introductory pages, with a purpose to alter or expunge whatever might be found amiss, and to make the best reparation in his power for the atrocities of which he has been adjudged guilty. But it appears to him, that the only remarkable features of the sketch are its frank and genuine good-humor, and the general accuracy with which he has conveyed his sincere impressions of the characters therein described. As to enmity, or ill-feeling of any kind, personal or political, he utterly disclaims such motives. The sketch might, perhaps, have been wholly omitted, without loss to the public, or detriment to the book; but, having undertaken to write it, he conceives that it could not have been done in a better or a kindlier spirit, nor, so far as his abilities availed, with a livelier effect of truth.

The author is constrained, therefore, to republish his introductory sketch without the change of a word.

SALEM, March 30, 1850.

"Book Notices," ***Portland Transcript*****, 30 March 1850, p. 3.**

We have read this work with admiration and delight. It is a romance of singular merit and originality—a life story, a story of the heart-saddening errors and woes of life, in all their stern reality, yet clad in a beautiful garb of poetry. The author's peculiar genius—his refined humor, his deep pathos, and his power of delineating character are displayed in their highest excellence. The introduction to the tale describes the author's three years experience in the Salem Custom House, from which he was ejected upon the coming into power of the present administration. In this sketch he describes his associates and their mode of life in a strain of exquisite humor, worthy of Goldsmith himself. We see, by the Salem Register, that the good people of Salem, or a portion of them, are somewhat excited and indignant, at the freedom of description in this introduction. Upon this subject we have nothing to say, further than that we admire the picture, whoever may have been the original. The story of the Scarlet Letter traces the consequences of a deadly sin committed by a godly minister, beloved, and reverenced, almost idolized by his people, as a model of human excellence. Hester Prynne, the erring but heroic woman, her strange child, Pearl, and her wronged but malicious and horribly revengeful husband, are the other principal characters of the drama. The plot is simple, and the characters boldly and truthfully drawn. The ever knawing remorse and anguish of the minister; his piety, his timidity and weakness, are vividly depicted. The fortitude of Hester; her uncomplaining, yet almost proud submission to the indignities inflicted upon her by the stern Puritans, and to the humiliation of the Scarlet Letter, which ever burns upon her breast as a mark for the finger of scorn, are brought before the reader with almost painful distinctness. The scene of the "minister's vigil," and his final public shame and death, are p[or]trayed with touching pathos and depth of power. The work will give its author a high place among our writers, and a world- wide fame.

"New Publications," ***Boston Advertiser*****, 3 April 1850, 2:3.**

This new work of Mr. Hawthorne's, recently published by Messrs. Ticknor & Co., is written with great power and is deeply interesting, although the interest is of the most painful character. One cannot but regret, in reading it, that the author had not chosen a more pleasing subject on which to exercise his great powers as a writer. Pictures of martyrdoms of the body, however well executed, must always give more pain than pleasure in the contemplation, and pictures of martyrdoms of the heart and soul, are not less agonizing. Still there are some readers, who, like Tony Lumpkin's mother, and sister, like a thing better the more it makes them cry, and they will doubtless find nothing to complain of in this work.

Beta [pseudo.], "Personal Gossip—Literary Matters," ***Springfield Republican*****, 5 April 1850, 2:3.**

* * * Of new books, few of any great interest have appeared since my last letter on this subject. Hawthorne's Scarlet Letter, you have probably already seen and noticed. The author gets hard hits on all hands for the bad feeling displayed in his wholly uncalled for introduction, in which he caricatures and abuses his former fellow officers in the Salem Custom-House. If I am not mistaken, he will yet regret that he ever wrote it. Apart from this, the book is well received, though there seems to me to be but little plot to found so long a story on.

"Literary Intelligence," ***Boston Transcript*****, 12 April 1850, 2:2.**

Hawthorne's Scarlet Letter has been one of the most successful romances ever published in America. It was issued three weeks ago by Ticknor & Co, and they are now printing the fifth thousand. Hawthorne will, no doubt, devote himself to literary pursuits, and no author, now before the public, is destined to greater prosperity. He has lately taken up his residence at Lenox and added another celebrity to that genial atmosphere of talent and genius.

"The Scarlet Letter," ***Christian Register*****, 13 April 1850, p. 58.**

We have here a handsomely printed duodecimo volume, of three hundred and twenty-two pages. Prefixed to the "romance" is an introduction of fifty-four pages, giving an account, half serious and half humorous, of the Salem Custom House, and its inmates, in a style that would do credit to the author of the Sketch Book. We have seen nothing of Mr. Hawthorne's which indicates so much literary skill as this introduction. There is a certain airy grace about it, an easy insight into character, a power of sketching likenesses by a few delicate strokes, a depth of feeling partially concealed under apparently sportive expressions, and withal an interfusion of living emotion, such as give to the whole composition an unusual charm. There are few things in English prose finer in their way than the author's account of his attachment to his native place, and, were it not for the little touch of bitterness which mars the effect and leads us to doubt the perfect good faith of the writer, the sketch would be perfect. The account of the Collector is in the finest style of portrait writing, and is only a fitting tribute to one known through the country only as a warrior, but known to his friends and neighbors as a man of strong intellect, of immoveable firmness of moral purpose, of quiet humor, of warm affections and the utmost kindliness of feeling towards every living thing. We must quote a few detached sentences from the picture of General Miller, "New England's most distinguished soldier." "The closer you penetrated to the substance of his mind, the sounder it appeared." "Weight, solidity, firmness; this was the expression of his repose." "What I saw in him, were features of stubborn and ponderous endurance; of integrity, that, like most of his other endowments, lay in a somewhat heavy mass, and of a benevolence, which, fiercely as he led the bayonets on at Chippewa or Fort Erie, I take to be of quite as genuine a stamp as what actuates any or all the polemical philanthropists of the age. There was never in his heart so much cruelty as would have brushed the down off a butterfly's wing. A trait of native elegance, seldom seen in the masculine character after childhood or early youth, was shown in the General's fondness for the sight and fragrance of flowers. An old soldier might be supposed to prize only the bloody laurel on his brow; but here was one, who seemed to have a young girl's appreciation of the floral tribe."

The whole Custom House and Salem picture, as a piece of English composition, is almost unsurpassed; but whether a writer is justified in drawing such portraits as some of these are, of his old associates while they are still living, is, to say the least, a questionable matter. There are also a few sentences relating to the author which constrain us to think less well of his kindliness of nature than we should, if they had been omitted. No little act of party despotism has ever made us feel more indignant than Mr. Hawthorne's removal from his small office in Salem; but he here indicates a state of feeling toward his associates such as to show that they who procured his removal were guilty of no great injustice to him, though they may have done an act unworthy of themselves.

But what of the Scarlet Letter? Like Mr. Dana's Paul Felton, it is a tale of marked ability, vigorous in its conceptions, and as a literary performance almost faultless. There is no redundance, but a condensed energy of language and emotion, the horror of the main features relieved by some smiling accompaniments. It is unquestionably a work of genius.

But, morally, we doubt whether the annals of literature furnish a single instance of success in any work, where the one act around which the whole interest of the narrative gathers and on which it all depends, is an act of moral pollution. As in The Heart of Mid-Lothian, such an act may incidentally add to the moral interest and instruction of the story, but not when it is the one thing on which the imagination is obliged to rest from beginning to end. The intensity of the interest only increases the painfulness of the emotion. Another moral objection to the Scarlet Letter is, that while falsehood is very justly made through the conscience the source of the most fearful torture and self-reproach, the crime which falsehood is employed to cover up is not presented in such a way as to awaken the same kind of self-condemnation and horror. But notwithstanding these qualifications, there are few writers of fiction, if any, who bring out in more terrible colors the retributions of guilt through the conscience of the offender, nor do we know of any book which in this respect is more fearfully true to man's moral nature than the Scarlet Letter. It may serve as a warning to deter others from pursuing the same evil course.

But as a Christian narrative, detailing the experience of a Christian man and woman, falling away from their purity, and struggling to get back again, it is utterly and entirely a failure. The peculiar office of Christianity in the conversion of sinners and their restoration to purity and peace is nowhere recognised throughout the volume. It is a powerfully wrought story of crime and suffering—of crime without redemption and of suffering without purification. The terrible retributions that follow the transgressor through all the mazes of his guilty course are placed before us, every step only leading down to a deeper anguish so long as the one great sin that weighs upon the conscience is concealed under what would otherwise be a blameless religious life. This is as it should be. But on the other hand, the partner of his crime is hardly less wretched than he. Her guilt is atoned for by public exposure and contempt, through years of uncomplaining humiliation and sorrow, in offices of charity and self-denial, and by an outward life of unsullied purity, yet in the furnace of protracted and intense sufferings, never so expelled, but that, under the guise of a specious fidelity, the wicked passion still lurks, and the soul in consequence never rises to a religious peace. Nor is there any intimation that such a result is possible. The author nowhere recognises the transforming and redeeming power of that Christian faith through which the spiritually dead may yet live and the lost be restored,—through which the most sinful may be converted and leave their sins behind, and, regenerated, purified and sanctified in their affections, may walk in newnesses of life, and amid the wreck of earthly hopes find a peaceful satisfaction in a life of religious fidelity, in offices of Christian charity, in a sense of God's pardoning mercy and his constant love.

The great office of Christ, as a Redeemer, is overlooked. The remedial character of his religion is not understood. The grace of God in the soul, purging away its iniquities and leading it through many sorrows up the mountain of purification, till the rays of divine love rest upon it, and it has gained the victory over all its enemies, is a power which finds no place in Mr. Hawthorne's religious tales. His skill, as a moral writer, and in this respect it is very great, is like that of a physician, who knows how to trace out through all its fatal passages the workings of a disease, but who can do little towards curing it.

In many respects, Mr. Hawthorne brings up most vividly the state of things here two centuries ago. But he who, in a volume of three hundred pages, attempts to give the inmost religious experiences of a Puritan minister and a woman under his charge through the most trying scenes, without any reference to the distinguishing doctrines of redemption through Christ and justification or salvation by faith, is wanting in that which, above all things else, is essential to a faithful delineation of those times. There may be, as there are, powerful descriptions of inward struggling and outward events, abounding in marks of genius, and full of moral and religious interest, but they are not true to the character of the persons whom they would represent.

If we thought less highly than we do of Mr. Hawthorne's power, we should have let his book pass by, as we do so many others, with no decided marks of commendation or reproach, instead of administering so large a portion of both.

Charles C. Hazewell, "The Scarlet Letter," ***Boston Times*****, 18 April 1850, 2:2.**

This is the most thoroughly original work of the day, so far as American publications are concerned, and will probably be the means of making its author familiarly known to the million; for we see that upwards of five thousand copies have already been sold, and the demand for it still continues. Heretofore, Mr. Hawthorne's writings, which have generally assumed the form of short tales or essays, have found their way to the people through the media of magazines and newspapers. Several of his works have been published, it is true, but they, we fear, never added much to his means, however pleasing they were in the eyes of his admirers. Very different has been the fate of "The Scarlet Letter," which has proved as successful as if it had been thoroughly worthless, instead of being one of the most worthy of American volumes. We attribute this success, to some extent, to the very clever introduction to the story itself, in which our author evinces more sympathy with the every day world than can be found in all the rest of his writings together. Generally, he deals with those things that lie in the deepest recesses of the human heart, and the presence of which there is unknown to most of us until some magician like Mr. Hawthorne discloses them to our startled sight. His knowledge of the darker mysteries of humanity—of those things which are known rarely save to those who have been thoroughly initiated into the Eleusinia of life—is altogether Shakspearian, as he is said to live a life almost as retired as, but we presume rather more comfortable than, that of the very pious but somewhat eccentric Simon Stylites. Let any one who does not understand our meaning, read "The Minister's Black Veil," "The Wedding Knell," "The Christmas Banquet," "Dr. Heidegger's Experiment," "David Swan," and a score of others that might be named, and which would have been in the hands of every one had they been written by some German with a name utterly unpronouncable except at the price of a dislocation of the jaw,— and he will at once comprehend us. "The Scarlet Letter,"in addition to this raising of the veil from the heart's secrets, is more genial than its predecessors, the tale itself partaking of the character of the introduction. The scene and time are Boston two hundred years ago, when those stern religionists, the Puritans, deemed they were doing God service by rendering themselves, and everybody within reach of their iron hands, as miserable as possible. The author has worked up a few materials into a story that has taken a permanent place in our literature.

Some fault has been found with the introduction by certain whig editors. It has a little quiet malice, we admit, but that man must be as skinless as St. Bartholomew after he was flayed, who can be deeply offended at it. Beside, Mr. Hawthorne could hardly have said less at the expense of the miserable, wretched Vandals who dismissed him from office.

"Review of New Books," ***Peterson's*****, 17 (May 1850), 231.**

Of all Hawthorne's works this is decidedly the best. And yet [it] is not so much a novel, as a psychological fiction: not so much a narrative of ordinary life, as a profound analysis of the two master-passions, Remorse and Revenge. The story is one of crime and sorrow, located in the early days of Massachusetts. Stern old Puritans, and meek, suffering women are the principal characters in the pages; and the tale is sombre to the last degree. Yet, in almost every line, the great genius of Hawthorne shines forth. An introductory chapter, written with much delicate humor, gives the author's experience as a Custom House Officer, and relieves the otherwise too profound melancholy of the book. We regard "The Scarlet Letter" as one of the most valuable contributions yet made to American literature.

"The Scarlet Letter," ***Christian Inquirer*****, 25 May 1850, 2:4-6.**

A certain crudity seems inevitable to American writers of any originality. Sometimes it is in the style, and sometimes in the thought. EMERSON, BROWNSON, POE, HAWTHORNE, among the most accomplished artists in style, are in different ways crude in thought. PARKER, JUDD, M. FULLER, among the most vigorous thinkers, are crude alike in thought and power of expression; while our lively and fresh reviews furnish a copious supply of clear, strong and sound thoughts, clothed in the most tattered garments of style. The inlaid scabbard carries an untempered blade, or the Damascus blade wears a wooden sheath, or both sword and scabbard are as rude as strong.

Mr. Hawthorne possesses a nearly perfect style, connected with a defective taste; but his artistical power is much more conspicuous in the manner than the substance of his book. In regard to the matter, it is difficult for the critic to deal with its contrasted power and puerility, wonderful subtilty, and equally wonderful clumsiness, exquisite art, and false taste. A perfect master of language, and a magician of original thoughts, he seems often compelled to enshrine in the pure amber of his style, every brilliant and poisonous fly that buzzes through his populous brain. Fertile and bold in invention, he is not apt and magisterial in selection, and appears the servant of his own thoughts, rather than the genius who commands them. Continuous, vigorous, unique in his conceptions, the conceptions themselves need to be exorcised. They are malignly potent over the author as well as the reader; and while their genius, originality, and general consistency cannot be questioned, any more than their power over the imagination and the attention, it pains and offends us that such needless creations should, under the spell of genius, force their melancholy presence upon our chambers of imagery. The famous picture of St. Lawrence's martyrdom, by Rubens, does not by its admirable skill atone for its painful subject. And the Scarlet Letter, alike in its cruel design and severe execution, wounds the heart in extorting its interest, and wrings the reader[']s sympathy and admiration out of an offended judgment and a protesting taste.

The theme of the Scarlet Letter is saved from being vulgar or indelicate, only as death hallows nakedness, and surgery puts ordinary notions of modesty aside. The solemnity, gravity, and coldness of the treatment, give a sort of judicial sanctity to the forbidden theme, which in part saves it from censure. And yet this apology points to the chief defect of the book—aside from its subject—which is the total absence of human affections. It is guarded from moral offensiveness by its cool tone; but this marble paleness of the passions, is purchased by the death of all tender feeling. So entirely is natural affection banished from the "Scarlet Letter," whether con[j]ugal or filial, that we are compelled to yield an immoral sympathy, when the guilty parties in the plot are about doubling their crime, nearly expiated by years of suffering, with an elopement!

The author treats passion with an anatomical nicety of dissection and absence of sympathy. Hesther [sic], Dimmesdale, Chillingworth, and Pearl, have hearts capable of every thing but love. As the black drop was squeezed by the angel from Mahomet's heart, the red drop seems to have been omitted by the genius who made theirs. They can suffer intensely, agonize acutely, but tenderly or truly they cannot feel. The mother and child do not love each other. The injured husband has no wounded affection in his revenge. The guilty minister no touch of tenderness for Esther [sic], in his remorse; the haughty, wilful, self-punishing woman, no feminine sensibility in her shame and sorrow.

And yet we do not deny a human character to these creations. The potency of the writer's genius can almost dispense with some of the unfailing attributes of humanity, and yet preserve reality in his characters. His imagination is mysteriously powerful. It conjures with us. By another method, he attains the result of dramatic power. Weak in Shakspear's and Scott's faculty, to bring his characters before us, speaking their own language and acting in their own way, he possesses the power of detailing their minute and characteristic thoughts and qualities, until elaborate description finally does the work of graphic outline— and a book exceedingly feeble in proper dramatic power, is wonderfully strong in dramatic effect. We hold Hesther [sic], Dimmesdale, Chillingworth, and Pearl, to be real creatures, whom the new census will have to include among the population. Chillingworth is first cousin to Caliban and Shylock; Dimmesdale knew Hamlet in Denmark; Esther [sic] is a sort of Puritan Meg- Merriles and Norna of the fitful head combined; and Pearl doubtless plays somewhere with Puck and Peas-blossom, Ariel and Fenella—nor is there any want of originality in these persons.

In vigor of imagination and subtilty of perception, and in a certain love of the terrible and weird, Hawthorne reminds us more of Browning than of any other writer. Indeed, "the Blot in the Scutcheon," and "the Scarlet Letter," without any formal resemblance or echo, are marvellously related in spirit. We can very well conceive of Browning as writing Hawthorne's prose, and of Hawthorne as writing Browning's poetry. They are kindred and lofty geniuses.

For admirableness of style and flashes of insight into the more recondite mysteries of the conscience and the will, we hardly know Hawthorne's superior. In the transparent meshes of the simplest language, he catches and confines the most complete and subtle thoughts. With an analysis, costly and searching as a chemist's, he sometimes presents us the secrets of our nature in such elementary purity of appearance, that we hardly know, except on reflection, that we are beholding anything extraordinary. Evanescent emotions, too fleeting to be more than felt by others, he quietly lays down before us for leisurely examination, as one might bring in a section of the rainbow, and put it on the table without remark. Without loss of breath, he comes up from the pearl-diver's exploraton of the deep, and while we are handling his prize, he is down again and up with another gem, until we are rather disposed to cheapen the exploit.

Yet it is usually in the morbid, or at any rate, the eccentric and exceptional regions of our nature, that his discoveries are made, and while we own their truth to the possible, and for the time being, to the probable and real, yet we rejoice to escape into the society of more common and feebler, but more natural and easy thoughts.

In regard to the moral tone of this book, it seems to us somewhat strained where it is good, and only natural where it is questionable. The retributive principle in it is theatrically exaggerated. Remorse is represented as having all its agony, without any of its uses. The guilty suffer, confess that they suffer justly, live lives of voluntary penance, do works of utmost usefulness and die deaths of poetical justice—but do not *repent*; are just as bad at the close as at the beginning of their guilty career—and what is worse, just as *good*, for aught we see, after their crime, as before it. For it is impossible not to respect both Hesther [sic] and Dimmesdale. Their suffering, while it is made severe enough, is not made to carry the reader's sense of justice with it; and their remorse, while it produces all the effects of penitence in every thing else, does not produce it where we see no reason for its not doing so—in respect to the crime itself. Esther [sic], somehow, with all her humiliation, is proud of her guilty relations to Dimmesdale—and Dimmesdale rather cherishes, even while he brands with burning iron, the memory of his error. We seem to see no hearty condemnation of the crime in the author's heart, and are not permitted to feel it in our own.

The conscience of the book is neither a natural nor a Christian conscience, but a sort of cross between the classic and the romantic conscience. We are not, with some of our contemporaries, offended with the falsification of the history of the time; for we do not imagine the Scarlet Letter will be regarded as documentary authority. We are more disturbed by the caustic, cynical, perhaps even bitter tone of parts of it, and with some flings wholly unjustifiable and in very bad taste, in the introduction.

A few small particulars may be specified as quite unworthy of Mr. Hawthorne's genius. The circumstances of Esther [sic] *embroidering* the letter, detracts much from the dignity and reality of her character; and her dressing the child in imitation of it, is really a device worthy only of the Bowery theatre. The description of the minister's voice reads like nonsense, and his "hand over his heart" grown inexpressibly flat, before the book closes. Such melodramattic blotches misbecome so great an artist as the author. We accord to Pearl extraordinary license. She is the tint with which the author has supernaturalized his romance. We pardon the weird and flitting aspect of the little goblin, as we do the kaleidoscopic effects of the stained windows in an old cathedral, where we go to indulge unusual and strange thoughts. But Mr. Hawthorne must not Germanize himself too much. He is likely to be an imitator in that direction only; yet it evidently has dangerous fascination for him.

The essentials of the Scarlet Letter will forever prevent its taking a high and permanent place in the public heart. Like WILSON'S "Passages in the Life of the Rev. Adam Blair," containing the utmost proofs of vigor and genius, on a most painful theme, it will not survive a temporary importance. We hope it is only the purging of the author's mind of some perilous stuff, a relief necessary to his literary health, and that he will now devote his splendid and purified powers to a work that shall rival the Vicar of Wakefield in its genial humanity and extensive popularity, as the Scarlet Letter does in purity of style, force of imagination, and copiousness of thought.

New York *Evening Post*, 8 June 1850, 2:2.

THE SCARLET LETTER of Hawthorne has reached a second edition, which may be had at Putnam's, in Broadway. It is written with extraordinary talent—we might mend the expression, and call it a work of genius. The characters are skilfully individualized, the scenes of passion wrought up with great strength, and the style beautiful to a degree with few American writers have attained. With all these merits, there is a defect in the plot of the work, which is made to turn a crime against the laws of society, a crime kept painfully and repulsively in sight. The introductory chapter, called the Custom House, is one of the cleverest portions of the book, and parts of it show infinite comic power, but the sketches of character are understood to have been drawn from real life, and to have given great offence to those for whom they were intended. There does not appear to have been any malignant intention in the writer; but the fact that they give pain to unoffending people, is enough to show that it was a great error to publish them.

Orestes Brownson, "Literary Notices and Criticisms," *Brownson's Quarterly*, NS 4 (October 1850), 528-532.

MR. HAWTHORNE is a writer endowed with a large share of genius, and in the species of literature he cultivates has no rival in this country, unless it be Washington Irving. His *Twice-told Tales*, his *Mosses from an Old Manse*, and other contributions to the periodical press, have made him familiarly known, and endeared him to a large circle of readers. The work before us is the largest and most elaborate of the romances he has as yet published, and no one can read half a dozen pages of it without feeling that none but a man of true genius and a highly cultivated mind could have written it. It is a work of rare, we may say of fearful power, and to the great body of our countrymen who have no well defined religious belief, and no fixed principles of virtue, it will be deeply interesting and highly pleasing.

We have neither the space nor the inclination to attempt an analysis of Mr. Hawthorne's genius, after the manner of the fashionable criticism of the day. Mere literature for its own sake we do not prize, and we are more disposed to analyze an author's work than the author himself. Men are not for us mere psychological phenomena, to be studied, classed, and labelled. They are moral and accountable beings, and we look only to the moral and religious effect of their works. Genius perverted, or employed in perverting others, has no charms for us, and we turn away from it with sorrow and disgust. We are not among those who join in the worship of passion, or even of intellect. God gave us our faculties to be employed in his service, and in that of our fellow-creatures for his sake, and our only legitimate office as critics is to inquire, when a book is sent us for review, if its author in producing it has so employed them.

Mr. Hawthorne, according to the popular standard of morals in this age and this community, can hardly be said to pervert God's gifts, or to exert an immoral influence. Yet his work is far from being unobjectionable. The story is told with great naturalness, ease, grace, and delicacy, but it is a story that should not have been told. It is a story of crime, of an adulteress and her accomplice, a meek and gifted and highly popular Puritan minister in our early colonial days,—a purely imaginary story, though not altogether improbable. Crimes like the one imagined were not unknown even in the golden days of Puritanism, and are perhaps more common among the descendants of the Puritans than it is at all pleasant to believe; but they are not fit subjects for popular literature, and moral health is not promoted by leading the imagination to dwell on them. There is an unsound state of public morals when the novelist is permitted, without a scorching rebuke, to select such crimes, and invest them with all the fascinations of genius, and all the charms of a highly polished style. In a moral community such crimes are spoken of as rarely as possible, and when spoken of at all, it is always in terms which render them loathsome, and repel the imagination.

Nor is the conduct of the story better than the story itself. The author makes the guilty parties suffer, and suffer intensely, but he nowhere manages so as to make their sufferings excite the horror of his readers for their crime. The adulteress suffers not from remorse, but from regret, and from the disgrace to which her crime has exposed her, in her being condemned to wear emblazoned on her dress the Scarlet Letter which proclaims to all the deed she has committed. The minister, her accomplice, suffers also, horribly, and feels all his life after the same terrible letter branded on his heart, but not from the fact of the crime itself, but from the consciousness of not being what he seems to the world, from his having permitted the partner in his guilt to be disgraced, to be punished, without his having the manliness to avow his share in the guilt, and to bear his share of the punishment. Neither ever really repents of the criminal deed; nay, neither ever regards it as really criminal, and both seem to hold it to have been laudable, because they *loved* one another,—as if the love itself were not illicit, and highly criminal. No man has the right to love another man's wife, and no married woman has the right to love any man but her husband. Mr. Hawthorne in the present case seeks to excuse Hester Prynne, a married woman, for loving the Puritan minister, on the ground that she had no love for her husband, and it is hard that a woman should not have some one to love; but this only aggravated her guilt, because she was not only forbidden to love the minister, but commanded to love her husband, whom she had vowed to love, honor, cherish, and obey. The modern doctrine that represents the affections as fatal, and wholly withdrawn from voluntary control, and then allows us to plead them in justification of neglect of duty and breach of the most positive precepts of both the natural and the revealed law, cannot be too severely reprobated.

Human nature is frail, and it is necessary for every one who standeth to take heed lest he fall. Compassion for the fallen is a duty which we all owe, in consideration of our own failings, and especially in consideration of the infinite mercy our God has manifested to her erring and sinful children. But however binding may be this duty, we are never to forget that sin is sin, and that it is pardonable only through the great mercy of God, on condition of the sincere repentance of the sinner. But in the present case neither of the guilty parties repents of the sin, neither exclaims with the royal prophet, who had himself fallen into the sin of adultery and murder, *Misere mei Deus, secundum magnam misericordiam; et secundum multitudinem miserationum tuarum, dele iniquitatem meam. Amplius lava me ab iniquitate mea; et a peccato munda me. Quoniam iniquitatem meam cognosco, et peccatum meum contra me est semper.*[1] They hug their illicit love; they cherish their sin; and after the lapse of seven years are ready, and actually agree, to depart into a foreign country, where they may indulge it without disguise and without restraint. Even to the last, even when the minister, driven by his agony, goes so far as to throw off the mask of hypocrisy, and openly confess his crime, he shows no sign of repentance, or that he regarded his deed as criminal.

The Christian who reads *The Scarlet Letter* cannot fail to perceive that the author is wholly ignorant of Christian ascetisicm, and that the highest principle of action he recognizes is pride. In both the criminals, the long and intense agony they are represented as suffering springs not from remorse, from the consciousness of having offended God, but mainly from the feeling, especially on the part of the minister, that they have failed to maintain the integrity of their character. They have lowered themselves in their own estimation, and cannot longer hold up their heads in society as honest people. It is not their conscience that is wounded, but their pride. *He* cannot bear to think that he wears a disguise, that he cannot be the open, frank, stainless character that he had from his youth aspired to be, and *she*, that she is driven from society, lives a solitary outcast, and has nothing to console her but her fidelity to her paramour. There is nothing Christian, nothing really moral, here. The very pride itself is a sin; and pride often a greater sin than that which it restrains us from committing. There are thousands of men and women too proud to commit carnal sins, and to the indomitable pride of our Puritan ancestors we may attribute no small share of their external morality and decorum. It may almost be said, that, if they had less of that external morality and decorum, their case would be less desperate; and often the violation of them, or failure to maintain them, by which their pride receives a shock, and their self-complacency is shaken, becomes the occasion, under the grace of God, of their conversion to truth and holiness. As long as they maintain their self-complacency, are satisfied with themselves, and feel that they have outraged none of the decencies of life, no argument can reach them, no admonition can startle them, no exhortation can move them. Proud of their supposed virtue, free from all self- reproach, they are as placid as a summer morning, pass through life without a cloud to mar their serenity, and die as gently and as sweetly as the infant falling asleep in its mother's arms. We have met with these people, and after laboring in vain to waken them to a sense of their actual condition, till completely discouraged, we have been tempted to say, Would that you might commit some overt act, that should startle you from your sleep, and make you feel how far pride is from being either a virtue, or the safeguard of virtue,—or convince you of your own insufficiency for yourselves, and your absolute need of Divine grace. Mr. Hawthorne seems never to have learned that pride is not only sin, but the root of all sin, and that humility is not only a virtue, but the root of all virtue. No genuine contrition or repentance ever springs from pride, and the sorrow for sin because it mortifies our pride, or lessens us in our own eyes, is nothing but the effect of pride. All true remorse, all genuine repentance, springs from humility, and is sorrow for having offended God, not sorrow for having offended ourselves.

Mr. Hawthorne also mistakes entirely the effect of Christian pardon upon the interior state of the sinner. He seems entirely ignorant of the religion that can restore peace to the sinner,— true, inward peace, we mean. He would persuade us, that Hester had found pardon, and yet he shows us that she had found no inward peace. Something like this is common among popular Protestant writers, who, in speaking of great sinners among Catholics that have made themselves monks or hermits to expiate their sins by devoting themselves to prayer, and mortification, and the duties of religion, represent them as always devoured by remorse, and suffering in their interior agony almost the pains of the damned. An instance of this is the Hermit of Engeddi in Sir Walter Scott's *Talisman*. These men know nothing either of true remorse, or of the effect of Divine pardon. They draw from their imagination, enlightened, or rather darkened, by their own experience. Their speculations are based on the supposition that the sinner's remorse is the effect of wounded pride, and that during life the wound can never be healed. All this is false. The remorse does not spring from wounded pride, and the greatest sinner who really repents, who really does penance, never fails to find interior peace. The mortifications he practices are not prompted by his interior agony, nor designed to bring peace to his soul; they are a discipline to guard against his relapse, and an expiation that his interior peace already found, and his overflowing love to God for his superabounding mercy, lead him to offer to God, in union with that made by his blessed Lord and Master on the cross.

Again, Mr. Hawthorne mistakes the character of confession. He does well to recognize and insist on its necessity; but he is wrong is supposing that its office is simply to disburden the mind by communicating its secret to another, to restore the sinner to his self-complacency, and to relieve him from the charge of cowardice and hypocrisy. Confession is a duty we owe to God, and a means, not of restoring us to our self-complacency, but of restoring us to the favor of God, and reëstablishing us in his friendship. The work before us is full of mistakes of this sort, in those portions where the author really means to speak like a Christian, and therefore we are obliged to condemn it, where we acquit him of all unchristian intention.

As a picture of the old Puritans, taken from the position of a moderate transcendentalist and liberal of the modern school, the work has its merits; but as little as we sympathize with those stern old Popery-haters, we do not regard the picture as at all just. We should commend where the author condemns, and condemn where he commends. Their treatment of the adulteress was far more Christian than his ridicule of it. But enough of fault- finding, and as we have no praise, except what we have given, to offer, we here close this brief notice.

[1]Psalm 50 (Vulgate numbering): "Have mercy on me God, according to [your] great mercy; and according to the multitude of your forgiving acts, blot out my iniquity. Generously wash me from my iniquity; and cleanse me from my sin. Because I acknowledge my iniquity, and my sin is always before me."

"New Publications," ***Boston Transcript*****, 4 November 1850, 2:2.**

Professor [Henry Wadsworth] Longfellow observed in one of his Lectures on the Italian Writers, at Harvard University last week, that Hawthorne's "Scarlet Letter" will always rank in point of genius, far above the famous stories of Boccaccio, and the praise thus awarded to our popular Romancer was received with much applause by the students.

Arthur Cleveland Coxe, "The Writings of Hawthorne," ***Church Review*****, 3 (January 1851), 506-510.**

* * * Why has our author selected such a theme? Why, amid all the suggestive incidents of life in a wilderness; of a retreat from civilization to which, in every individual case, a thousand circumstances must have concurred to reconcile human nature with estrangement from home and country; or amid the historical connections of our history with Jesuit adventure, savage invasion, regicide outlawry, and French aggression, should the taste of Mr. Hawthorne have preferred as the proper material for romance, the nauseous amour of a Puritan pastor, with a frail creature of his charge, whose mind is represented as far more debauched than her body? Is it, in short, because a running undertide of filth has become as requisite to a romance, as death in the fifth act to a tragedy? Is the French era actually begun in our literature? And is the flesh, as well as the world and the devil, to be henceforth dished up in fashionable novels, and discussed at parties, by spinsters and their beaux, with as unconcealed a relish as they give to the vanilla in their ice cream? We would be slow to believe it, and we hope our author would not willingly have it so, yet we honestly believe that "the Scarlet Letter" has already done not a little to degrade our literature, and to encourage social licentiousness: it has started

other pens on like enterprises, and has loosed the restraint of many tongues, that have made it an apology for "the evil communications which corrupt good manners." We are painfully tempted to believe that it is a book made for the market, and that the market has made it merchantable, as they do game, by letting everybody understand that the commodity is in high condition, and smells strongly of incipient putrefaction.

We shall entirely mislead our reader if we give him to suppose that "the Scarlet Letter" is coarse in its details, or indecent in its phraseology. This very article of our own, is far less suited to ears polite, than any page of the romance before us; and the reason is, we call things by their right names, while the romance never hints the shocking words that belong to its things, but, like Mephistophiles, insinuates that the arch-fiend himself is a very tolerable sort of person, if nobody would call him Mr. Devil. We have heard of persons who could not bear the reading of some Old Testament Lessons in the service of the Church: such persons would be delighted with our author's story; and damsels who shrink at the reading of the Decalogue, would probably luxuriate in bathing their imagination in the crystal of its delicate sensuality. The language of our author, like patent blacking, "would not soil the whitest linen," and yet the composition itself, would suffice, if well laid on, to Ethiopize the snowiest conscience that ever sat like a swan upon that mirror of heaven, a Christian maiden's imagination. We are not sure we speak quite strong enough, when we say, that we would much rather listen to the coarsest scene of Goldsmith's "Vicar," read aloud by a sister or daughter, than to hear from such lips, the perfectly chaste language of a scene in "the Scarlet Letter," in which a married wife and her reverend paramour, with their unfortunate offspring, are introduced as the actors, and in which the whole tendency of the conversation is to suggest a sympathy for their sin, and an anxiety that they may be able to accomplish a successful escape beyond the seas, to some country where their shameful commerce may be perpetuated. Now, in Goldsmith's story there are very coarse words, but we do not remember anything that saps the foundations of the moral sense, or that goes to create unavoidable sympathy with unrepenting sorrow, and deliberate, premeditated sin. The "Vicar of Wakefield" is sometimes coarsely virtuous, but "the Scarlet Letter" is delicately immoral.

There is no better proof of the bad tendency of a work, than some unintentional betrayal on the part of a young female reader, of an instinctive consciousness against it, to which she has done violence, by reading it through. In a beautiful region of New England, where stage-coaches are not yet among things that were, we found ourselves, last summer, one of a traveling party, to which we were entirely a stranger, consisting of young ladies fresh from boarding-school, with the proverbial bread-and-butter look of innocence in their faces, and a nursery thickness about their tongues. Their benevolent uncle sat outside upon the driver's box, and ours was a seat next to a worshipful old dowager, who seemed to bear some matronly relation to the whole coach-load, with the single exception of ourselves. In such a situation it was ours to keep silence, and we soon relapsed into nothingness and a semi-slumberous doze. Meanwhile our young friends were animated and talkative, and as we were approaching the seat of a College, their literature soon began to expose itself. They were evidently familiar with the Milliners' Magazines in general, and even with Graham's and Harper's. They had read [G. P. R.] James, and they had read Dickens; and at last their criticisms rose to Irving and Walter Scott, whose various merits they discussed with an artless anxiety to settle forever the question whether the one was not "a charming composer," and the other "a truly beautiful writer." Poor girls! had they imagined how much harmless amusement they were furnishing to their drowsy, dusty, and very unentertaining fellow traveler, they might, quite possibly, have escaped both his praise and his censure! They came at last to Longfellow and Bryant, and rhythmically regaled us with the "muffled drum" of the one, and the somewhat familiar opinion of the other, that

"Truth crushed to earth will rise again."

And so they came to Hawthorne, of whose "Scarlet Letter" we then knew very little, and that little was favorable, as we had seen several high encomiums of its style. We expected a quotation from the "Celestial Railroad," for we were traveling at a rate which naturally raised the era of railroads in one's estimation, by rule of contrary; but no—the girls went straight to "the Scarlet Letter." We soon discovered that one Hester Prynne was the heroine, and that she had been made to stand in the pillory, as, indeed, her surname might have led one to anticipate. We discovered that there was a mysterious little child in the question, that she was a sweet little darling, and that her "sweet, pretty little name," was "Pearl." We discovered that mother and child had a meeting, in a wood, with a very fascinating young preacher, and that there was a hateful creature named Chillingworth, who persecuted the said preacher, very perseveringly. Finally, it appeared that Hester Prynne was, in fact, Mrs. Hester Chillingworth, and that the hateful old creature aforesaid had a very natural dislike to the degradation of his spouse, and quite as natural a hatred of the wolf in sheep's clothing who had wrought her ruin. All this leaked out in conversation, little by little, on the hypothesis of our protracted somnolency. There was a very gradual approximation to the point, till one inquired—"did n't you think, from the first, that he was the one?" A modest looking creature, who evidently had not read the story, artlessly inquired—"what one?"—and then there was a titter at the child's simplicity, in the midst of which we ventured to be quite awake, and to discover by the scarlet blush that began to circulate, that the young ladies were not unconscious to themselves that reading "the Scarlet Letter" was a thing to be ashamed of. These school-girls had, in fact, done injury to their young sense of delicacy, by devouring such a dirty story; and after talking about it before folk, inadvertently, they had enough of mother Eve in them, to know that they were ridiculous, and that shame was their best retreat.

Now it would not have been so if they had merely exhibited a familiarity with "the Heart of Mid-Lothian," and yet there is more mention of the foul sin in its pages, than there is in "the Scarlet Letter." Where then is the difference? It consists in this—that the holy innocence of Jeanie Deans, and not the shame of Effie, is the burthen of that story, and that neither Effie's fall is made to look like virtue, nor the truly honorable agony of her stern old father, in bewailing his daughter's ruin, made a joke, by the insinuation that it was quite gratuitous. But in Hawthorne's tale, the lady's frailty is philosophized into a natural and necessary result of the Scriptural law of marriage, which, by holding her irrevocably to her vows, as plighted to a dried up old book-worm, in her silly girlhood, is viewed as making her heart an easy victim to the adulterer. The sin of her seducer too, seems to be considered as lying not so much in the deed itself, as in his long concealment of it, and, in fact, the whole moral of the tale is given in the words—"Be true—be true," as if sincerity in sin were virtue, and as if "Be clean—be clean," were not the more fitting conclusion. "The untrue man" is, in short, the hang-dog of the narrative, and the unclean one is made a very interesting sort of a person, and as the two qualities are united in the hero, their composition creates the interest of his character. Shelley himself never imagined a more dissolute conversation than that in which the polluted minister comforts himself with the thought, that the revenge of the injured husband is worse than his own sin in instigating it. "You and I never did so, Hester"—he suggests: and she responds— "never, never! What we did had a *consecration of its own*, we felt it so—we said so to each other!" This is a little too much—it carries the Bay-theory a little too far for our stomach! "Hush, Hester!" is the sickish rejoinder; and fie, Mr. Hawthorne! is the weakest token of our disgust that we can utter. The poor bemired hero and heroine of the story should not have been seen wallowing in their filth, at such a rate as this.

Henry T. Tuckerman, "Nathaniel Hawthorne," *Southern Literary Messenger*, **17 (June 1851), 347-348.**

* * * In our view the most remarkable trait in [Hawthorne's] writings is this harmonious blending of the common and familiar in the outward work, with the mellow and vivid tints of his own imagination. It is with difficulty that his maturity of conception and his finish and geniality of style links itself, in our minds, with the streets of Boston and Salem, the Province House and even the White Mountains; and we congratulate every New Englander with a particle of romance, that in his native literature, "a local habitation and a name" has thus been given to historical incidents and localities;—that art has enshrined what of tradition hangs over her brief career—as characteristic and as desirable thus to consecrate, as any legend or spot, German or Scottish genius has redeemed from oblivion. The "Wedding Knell," the "Gentle Boy," the "White Old Maid," the "Ambitious Guest," the "Shaker Bridal," and other New England subjects, as embodied and glorified by the truthful, yet imaginative and graceful art of Hawthorne, adequately represent in literature, native traits, and this will ensure their ultimate appreciation. But the most elaborate effort of this kind, and the only one, in fact, which seems to have introduced Hawthorne to the whole range of American readers, is "the Scarlet Letter." With all the care in point of style and authenticity which mark his lighter sketches, this genuine and unique romance, may be considered as an artistic exposition of Puritanism as modified by New England colonial life. In truth to costume, local manners and scenic features, the Scarlet Letter is as reliable as the best of Scott's novels; in the anatomy of human passion and consciousness it resembles the most effective of Balzac's illustrations of Parisian or provincial life, while in developing bravely and justly the sentiment of the life it depicts, it is as true to humanity as Dickens. Beneath its picturesque details and intense characterization, there lurks a profound satire. The want of soul, the absence of sweet humanity, the predominance of judgment over mercy, the tyranny of public opinion, the look of genuine charity, the asceticism of the Puritan theology,—the absence of all recognition of natural laws, and the fanatic substitution of the letter for the spirit—which darken and harden the spirit of the pilgrims to the soul of a poet—are shadowed forth with a keen, stern and eloquent, yet indirect emphasis, that haunts us like "the cry of the human." Herein is evident and palpable the latent power which we have described as the most remarkable trait of Hawthorne's genius;—the impression grows more

significant as we dwell upon the story; the states of mind of the poor clergyman, Hester, Chillingworth and Penil [sic], being as it were transferred to our bosoms through the intense sympathy their vivid delineation excites;—they seem to conflict, and glow and deepen and blend in our hearts, and finally work out a great moral problem. It is as if we were baptized into the consciousness of Puritan life, of New England character in its elemental state; and knew, by experience, all its frigidity, its gloom, its intellectual enthusiasm and its religious aspiration.

Amory Dwight Mayo, "The Works of Nathaniel Hawthorne," ***Universalist Quarterly*****, 8 (July 1851), 285-290.**

Perhaps four years were never spent to better purpose, than those in Mr. Hawthorne's life, between the publication of "Mosses from an old Manse," and "The Scarlet Letter." The only account we have of them, is in the sketch of the "Custom House," which introduces the latter work. Like most men of genius, our author is not disposed to do full justice to those influences which have powerfully contributed to the growth of his mind. Often, when such men are receiving and appropriating most rapidly, they are tormented with a nervous suspicion of the decay of their power. But never was such want of faith more signally rebuked, than in the writer we are reviewing, for we suspect that "spacious edifice of brick" has seldom been turned to so good use, as by this man who looked through its machinery and its occupants to the facts which they unconsciously represent. The portrait of this place is wonderfully vivid, and from the author's point of observation, doubtless true.

The story so gracefully introduced, is the most remarkable of Mr. Hawthorne's works, whether we consider felicity of plot, sustained interest of development, analysis of character, or the witchery of a style which invests the whole with a strange, ethereal beauty. These qualities of the book are so evident, that we now desire to go beneath them to those which make it, in many respects, the most powerful imaginative work of the present era of English literature. No reader possessing the slightest portion of spiritual insight, can fail to perceive that the chief value of this romance is religious. It is an attempt to delineate the involved action of spiritual laws, and their effects upon individual character, with an occasional glimpse into the organization of society. Of course it has been a puzzle to the critics, and a pebble between the teeth of the divines, transcending the artificial rules of the former, and making sad work with the creeds and buckram moralities of the latter.

Standing as "The Scarlet Letter" does, at the junction of several moral highways, it is not easy to grasp the central idea around which it instinctively arranged itself in the author's mind. The most obvious fact upon its pages is, that the only safety for a human soul consists in appearing to be exactly what it is. If holy, it must not wrench itself out of its sphere to become a part in any satanic spectacle; if corrupt, it must heroically stand upon the low ground of its own sinfulness, and rise through penitence and righteousness.

This law of life is exhibited in the contrasted characters of Dimmesdale and Hester. Whatever errors of head or heart, or infelicity of circumstances, prevent Hester from fully realizing the Christian ideal of repentance, she sternly respects her moral relations to society. She embroiders the badge of her own infamy, and without complaint submits to isolation, the pity, scorn and indifference of the world, and the withering of her own nature under the blaze of a noonday exposure to the hot sun of social displeasure; she turns her face toward humanity, and begins the life-long task of beating up to virtue against the pitiless storm which overthrows so many an offender. If the impeding fate of the minister forces her to catch at the sole hope of escaping from her penance, and the closing scenes of the drama are necessary to make her an angel of mercy to the very community she had outraged by the sin of her youth, we may in mercy impute her falterings to that infirmity of our nature, which its greatest interpreter has represented by the concession of Isabella to the artifice of Mariana, and the untruth of Desdemona. As far as human fidelity to a spiritual law can go, did Hester live out the fact of the correspondence of seeming and being. Not so with the less heroic partner of her guilt. We cannot deny that all the arguments which may be used to palliate insincerity apply to Dimmesdale. The voluntary step he must take by confession, was from a more than mortal elevation to a more than human abasement. His constitutional weakness, too, is an excusing circumstance, and especially the genuineness of his repentance up to a certain point. Yet the radical vice of his soul was not submission to his passions, but cowardice; and the reflex action of this cowardice disarranged his whole life, placing him in false relation to the community and the woman he had wronged, and laying open his naked heart to the eye of the demon that was the appointed agent of his final ruin. Of the value of these two persons, considered as accurate delineations of character, nothing very flattering can be said. We see them in the midst of conflict, and in the strife of soul and law many wonderful revelations of human nature appear. Yet a strict fidelity to the engrossing object of the book, renders the author unfaithful to individual humanity. Dimmesdale and Hester are the incarnate action and reaction of the law of sincerity.

Another fact which appears in this book, is the downward tendency of sin; once let a soul be untrue, even though half in ignorance of its duty, and its world is disorganized, so that every step in its new path involves it in greater difficulties. The cardinal error, in this maze of guilt and wretchedness, is Hester's marriage with Chillingworth. She committed that sin which women are every day repeating, though never without retribution, as certain, if not as visible as hers, of giving her hand to a man she did not entirely love. There are souls great and good enough to stand firmly against the recoil of such an act, but Hester was not one of these. Her true husband at last came, and she could only give him a guilty love. By her fatal error she had cut herself off from the power to bless him by her affection as long as God should keep her in the bonds of a false marriage. The proclivity of her former error drove her on to sin again with more obvious consequences, if not with deeper guilt. And then came, in rapid succession, the ruin of Dimmesdale, the transformation of Chillingworth, the transmission of a diseased nature to her child, and the wide spread scandal of a whole community.

And growing out of this act, and its retribution, is the whole question of the relation of the sexes, and the organization of society. The author does not grapple with these intricate problems, though he knows as much of the falsity of what is called marriage, and the unnatural position of woman, as those who are more ready to undertake the cure of the world. And the hypocrisy of Dimmesdale, and the searing of heart in Hester, point to a social state in which purity will exist in connection with a mercy which shall throw no artificial obstacles in the way of a sinner's repentance.

Another fact more perplexing to a Christian moralist is here illustrated,—that a certain experience in sin enlarges the spiritual energies and the power to move the souls of men to noble results. The effects of Dimmesdale's preaching are perfectly credible, and moral, although he stood in false relations to those he addressed. True, the limitation at last came in his public exposure, yet we had almost said he could not have left his mark so deep upon the conscience of that community, had he lived and died otherwise. And Hester's error was the downward step in the winding stair leading to a higher elevation. This feature of the work, so far from being a blemish, is only a proof of the writer's insight, and healthy moral philosophy. He has portrayed sin with all its terrible consequences, yet given the other side of a problem which must excite our wonder, rebuke our shallow theories, and direct us to an all-embracing, infinite love for its solution.

In the character of Chillingworth appears another law,—the danger of cherishing a merely intellectual interest in the human soul. The Leech, is a man of diseased mental acuteness, changed to a demon by yielding to an unholy curiosity. Seduced by the opportunity to know the nature of Dimmesdale, he is drawn to the discovery of the fatal secret,—a discovery which he is not strong enough to bear. His character and fate are an awful rebuke to that insatiable desire for soul-gazing, which is the besetting devil of many men. Our human nature is too sacred to be applied to such uses, and he who enters its guarded enclosure from the mere impulse for intellectual analysis, risks his own soul as surely as he outrages that of another.

Passing from these points of the book to its general moral tone, we find the author's delineation of spiritual laws equalled by his healthy and profound religious sentiment. In justice to human nature, he shows all the palliative circumstances to guilt, while he is sternly true to eternal facts of morality. It is not improper for a novelist to do the former, if he leave the latter uppermost in the mind of the reader. Throughout the work we have not once detected the writer in a concession to that sophistical philanthropy, which, from the vantage-ground of mercy, would pry up the foundation of all religious obligation. His book is a fine contrast to the volumes of a class of modern novelists, who with a large developement of the humane sentiment, and an alarming briskness at catching the palliations of transgression, seem to have lost the sense of immutable moral distinctions. One side of Mr. Hawthorne's mind would furnish the heads of several first class French romancers. It may be that some of his statements on the side of destiny are too strong, and that human will appears to have a play too limited in his world, yet we look upon such passages rather as exaggerations of his idea of the omnipotence of God's law, than as indications of an irreligious fatalism.

We have already noticed the tendency to a symbolical view of nature and life, in this author's genius. In "The Scarlet Letter," it supplies the complete frame-work of the story—the age and social state in which the drama is cast being merely subsidiary to it. The gleam of the symbolical letter invests every object with a typical aspect. The lonely shores along which the minister walked, the wood in which he met Hester, the pillory and the street lit up by Mr. Wilson's lantern, are seen in this mysterious relation to the characters and plot of the story. But all the symbolism of the tale concentrates in the witch-child, Pearl. She seems to absorb and render back, by each developement of her versatile being, the secret nature of every thing with which she comes in contact. She is the microcosm of the whole history with its surroundings. As a poetical creation, we know not where to look for her equal in modern literature. She is the companion of Mignon and Little Nell, more original in conception than either, if not as strong in her hold upon our affections.

As a work of art, this book has great merits, shaded by a few conspicuous faults. We cannot too much admire the skill with which the tangled skein of counteracting law and character is unravelled, the compact arrangement and suggestive disposition of the parts. The analysis of character is also inimitable, and the style is a fit dress for the strange and terrible history it rehearses. Yet we shall be disappointed if we look for any remarkable delineation of character, or portraiture of historical manners. There is a certain ghastliness about the people and life of the book, which comes from its exclusively subjective character and absence of humor. The world it describes is untrue to actual existence; for, although such a tragedy may be acting itself in many a spot upon earth, yet it is hidden more deeply beneath the surface of existence than this, modified by a thousand trivialities, and joys, and humorous interludes of humanity. No puritan city ever held such a throng as stalks though the "Scarlet Letter;" even in a well conducted mad-house, life is not so lurid and intense. The author's love for symbolism occasionally amounts to a ridiculous melo-dramatic perversity, as when it fathers such things as the minister's hand over his heart, and the hideous disfigurement of his bosom, Dame Hibbins from Gov. Bellingham's window screeching after Hester to go into the forest and sign the black man's book, and the mete[ori]c "A" seen upon the sky during the midnight vigil.

Charles Hale, "Nathaniel Hawthorne," ***To-Day: A Boston Literary Journal*****, 18 September 1852, pp. 179-180.**

* * * When the "Scarlet Letter" was announced, we expected, judging from the character of his former works, some quaint delineation of Puritan life and character. But the story is an awful probing into the most forbidden regions of human consciousness. It is gloomy from beginning to end. Even his occasional sprightly remarks have a ghastly tinge. The plot serves only to develop the deep and unnatural revenge of Chillingworth, so refined and subtle as to make this part of the book a metaphysical curiosity. Connected with this is the adulterous union of his two victims, Hester and Dimmesdale. The desperate, almost insane, condition is also observable, of the minister who could with

difficulty refrain from blaspheming before his deacon, and dropping into the tender bosom of his maiden parishioner "a germ of evil that would be sure to blossom darkly soon, and bear black fruit betimes." And the book is demoralizing; for with his diabolic art he represents Hester and Dimmesdale, after seven years of separation, speaking of their sin as having "a consecration of its own," which they felt and had not forgotten. And yet it has its moral too; for when Hester, meditating flight and a renewal of her crime, together with oblivion of her former remorse and degradation, would throw the scarlet letter from her breast, Pearl, the offspring of her guilt, will not know her mother without the symbol of her shame upon her.

Andrew Preston Peabody, "Nathaniel Hawthorne," ***North American Review*****, 76 (January 1853), 232-233.**

* * * The early history of New England, more largely than any other source, has supplied Hawthorne with names, events, and incidents, for his creations. The manners, customs, beliefs, superstitions of the Puritans, and their immediate descendants, seem to have taken the strongest hold upon his fancy. Their times are his heroic age, and he has made it mythological. As illustrative of history, his stories are eminently untrustworthy; for, where he runs parallel with recorded fact in his narrative of events, the spirit that animates and pervades them is of his own creation. Thus, in the "Scarlet Letter," he has at once depicted the exterior of early New England life with a fidelity that might shame the most accurate chronicler, and defaced it by passions too fierce and wild to have been stimulated to their desolating energy under colder skies than of Spain or Italy. At the same time, he has unwittingly defamed the fathers of New England, by locating his pictures of gross impurity and sacrilegious vice where no shadow of reproach, and no breath but of immaculate fame, had ever rested before. He thus has violated one of the most sacred canons of literary creation. A writer, who borrows nothing from history, may allow himself an unlimited range in the painting of character; but he who selects a well- known place and epoch for his fiction, is bound to adjust his fiction to the analogy of fact, and especially to refrain from outraging the memory of the dead for the entertainment of the living.

Early British Reception

"Notices of Recent Publications," ***English Review*****, 16 (October 1851), 179-180.**

Quaint and passionate at once is this very powerful tale; spite of its strange horrors, an air of reality pervades it: it is an original creation, of which America may be proud, for which England may be grateful. This is a tale of sin, but also one of fearful punishment, and the human heart, with all its strength and weakness is therein most graphically delineated. We cannot wonder at the excitement which the appearance of this book has caused in literary as well as in fashionable circles: to both it brings something new and strange, a novel experience of humanity. So strongly are we impressed with a sense of the literary merits of "The Scarlet Letter," that we are inclined to rate its author above all the authors of America, excepting only Washington Irving, and perhaps Longfellow and Fenimore Cooper. * * *

Sir Nathaniel [pseudo.], "Nathaniel Hawthorne," ***New Monthly Magazine*****, 94 (February 1852), 203-205.**

There can be little question that the most powerful—if also the least pleasing—of Mr. Hawthorne's fictions, is "The Scarlet Letter," a work remarkable for pathos in the tale, and art in the telling. Even those who are most inclined (and with reason) to demur to the plot, are constrained to own themselves enthralled, and their profoundest sensibilities excited by

> The book along whose burning leaves
> His scarlet web our wild romancer weaves.

The invention of the story is painful. Like the "Adam Blair" of Mr. Lockhart, it is a tale of "trouble, and rebuke, and blasphemy:" the trouble of a guilty soul, the rebuke of public stigma, and the occasion thereby given to the enemy to blaspheme. For, of the two fallen and suffering creatures whose anguish is here traced out, little by little, and line upon line, with such harrowing fidelity, one, and the guiltiest of the twain, is, like Adam Blair, a venerated presbyter, a pillar of the faith; the very burden of remorse which crushes his soul increases the effect of his ministrations, giving him sympathies so intimate with the sinful brotherhood of mankind—keeping him down on a level with the lowest,—him, the man of etherial attributes, whose voice the angels might have listened to and answered: and thus his heart vibrates in unison with that of the fallen, and receives their pain unto itself, and sends its own throb of pain through a thousand other breasts, in gushes of sad, persuasive eloquence.

It has been objected to works of this class that they attract more persons than they warn by their excitement. Others have replied—"What is the real moral of any tale? is it not its permanent expression—the last burning trace it leaves upon the soul? and who ever read 'Adam Blair' "—we are citing the words of a critic of that book—"without rising from the perusal saddened, solemnised, smit with a profound horror at the sin which wrought such hasty havoc in a character so pure and a nature so noble? This effect produced, surely the tale has not been told in vain." However this may be, we find reviewers who moot the above objection to such fictions in general, avowing, with reference to the "Scarlet Letter" in particular, that if sin and sorrow in their most fearful forms are to be presented in any work of art, they have rarely been treated with a loftier severity, purity, and sympathy than here. What so many romancists would have turned into a fruitful hotbed of prurient description and adulterated sentiment, is treated with consummate delicacy and moral restraint by Mr. Hawthorne. As Miss Mitford observes, "With all the passionate truth that he has thrown into the long agony of the seducer, we never, in our pity for the sufferer, lose our abhorrence of the sin."[1] How powerfully is depicted the mental strife, so tumultuous and incessant in its agitation, of the young clergyman, Arthur Dimmesdale—whom his congregation deem a miracle of holiness—the mouthpiece of Heaven's messages of wisdom, and rebuke, and love—the very ground he treads being sanctified in their eyes—the maidens growing pale before him— the aged members of his flock, beholding his frame so feeble (for he is dying daily of that within which passeth show), while they themselves are rugged in their decay, believe that he will go heavenward before them, and command their children to lay their old bones close to their young pastor's holy grave; and all this time, perchance, when *he* is thinking of his grave, he questions with himself whether the grass will ever grow on it, because an accursed thing must there be buried. Irresistibly affecting is the climax, when he stands in the pulpit preaching the election sermon (so envied a privilege!), exalted to the very proudest eminence of superiority to which the gifts of intellect, rich lore, prevailing eloquence, and whitest sanctity could exalt a New England priest in those early days,—and meanwhile his much-enduring partner-in-guilt, Hester Prynne, is standing beside the scaffold of the pillory, with the scarlet letter still burning on her breast—still burning into it! There remains but for *him* to mount that scaffold—in haste, as one *in articulo mortis*, to take his shame upon him—and to lay open the awful secret, "though it be read like scarlet," before venerable elders, and holy fellow-pastors, and the people at large, whose great heart is appalled, yet overflowing with tearful sympathy. The injured husband, again, is presented with memorable intensity of colouring. He quietly pitches his tent beside the dissembler, who knows him not; and then proceeds—*festinat lentè*—with the finesse of a Machiavel, and the fiendish glee of a Mephistophiles, to unwind the *nexus* of the tragedy only to involve his victim inextricably in its toils. One feels how fitting it is that, when he has gained his purpose, old Roger Chillingworth should droop and his whole nature collapse—that all his strength and energy, all his vital and intellectual force, should seem at once to desert him, so that he withers up, shrivels away, and almost vanishes from mortal sight, like an uprooted weed that lies welting in the sun—such being the self-generated retribution of one who has made the very principle of his life to consist in the pursuit and systematic exercise of revenge. His it is to drain the dregs of the bitter truth, that

> To be wroth with one we love
> Doth work like madness in the brain.

And what shall we say of Hester Prynne, his ill-mated, ill-fated bride? Gazing at so mournful a wreck, we are reminded of the pathos and significance in the words of One of old time, of One who spake as never man spake: "Seest thou this woman?" The distinguishing characteristic of Christian ethics has been said to lie in the recognition of the fact, that the poor benighted pariah of social life will often, in the simple utterance of a cheerful hope in his behalf, see a window opening in heaven, and faces radiant with promise looking out upon him.[2] Mr. Hawthorne's "searching of dark bosoms" has taught him a humane p[sy]chology. He will not judge by the mere hearing of the ear or seeing of the eye; he can quite appreciate and illustrate by history—if history be philosophy teaching by example—the pregnant paradox of poor discrowned Lear, ending with "And then, handy-dandy, which is the justice, and which is the thief?" Not that he palliates the sin, or acts as counsel for the defendant; on the contrary, few have so explicitly surrounded the sin with ineffaceable deformities, or the criminal with agonising woes. But our casuistry is pervaded by ignorance of a thousand cumulative conditions, and this precludes him from judging peremptorily by the outward appearance. Masterly is his delineation of Hester in her life of penance—the general symbol at which preacher and moralist may point, and in which they may embody their images of frailty—and over whose grave the infamy she must carry thither will be her only monument. A mystic shadow of suspicion attaches itself to her little lonesome dwelling. Children, too young to comprehend why she should be shut out from the sphere of human charities, creep nigh enough to behold her plying her needle at the cottage-door, or labouring in her little garden, or coming forth along the pathway that leads townward; and then, discerning the scarlet letter on her breast, scamper off with a strange, contagious fear. She stands apart from moral interests, yet close beside them, like a ghost that revisits the familiar fireside, and can no longer make itself seen or felt; no more smile with the household joy, nor mourn with the kindred sorrow; or, should it succeed in manifesting its forbidden sympathy, awakening only terror and horrible repugnance. Of a tale so told it may be well said that

—In proud Hester's fiery pang we *share*.[3]

It is highly characteristic of our author to make little Pearl a source of wild foreboding to her remorseful mother. The elf-child is so freakish, tetchy, and wayward,—she has such strange, defiant, desperate moods,—she plays such fantastic sports, flitting to and fro with a mocking smile, which invests her with a certain remoteness and intangibility, as if she were hovering in the air, and might vanish like a glimmering light, whose whence and whither we know not,—that Hester cannot help questioning, many a time and oft, whether Pearl is a human child. Similarly it is devised that Hester should believe, with shuddering unwillingness, that the scarlet letter she wears has endowed her with a new sense, and given her a sympathetic knowledge of the hidden sin in other hearts. She is terror-stricken by the revelations thus made. Must she receive as truth these intimations, so obscure, yet so distinct? Surely, in all her miserable experience, there is nothing else so awful and so loathsome as this sense. What marvel if the vulgar, in those dreary old times, aver that the symbol is not merely scarlet cloth, tinged in an earthly dye-pot, but is red-hot with infernal fire, and can be seen glowing all alight whenever Hester Prynne walks abroad after dusk. "And, we must needs say, it seared Hester's bosom so deeply, that perhaps there was more truth in the rumour than our modern incredulity may be inclined to admit." The picture is one that leaves an indelible impression on the mind. Nor may we forget to notice how skilfully the background is filled in, and in what excellent keeping with the foremost figures are the puritan,. sombre shades behind. The patriarchal era of New England life has found no such vivid and graphic a painter as Nathaniel Hawthorne, and it is evidently one which he knows to be his *forte*—witness the constancy of his attachment to its grim and rugged aspect.

[1]Mary Russell Mitford, *Recollections of a Literary Life*
[2]Thomas De Quincy
[3]Oliver Wendell Holmes, *Astraea, or the Balance of Illusions*

Samuel Smiles, "Nathaniel Hawthorne," *Eliza Cook's Journal*, **19 June 1852, p. 123.**

* * * In The Scarlet Letter . . . Hawthorne for the first time fully brings out his great and peculiar powers. He lays decisive hand upon the apparition,—brings it near to us, so that we can see it face to face,—and unravels, skillfully and painfully, the dark mysteries of being. There is something extraordinarily fascinating in this book: we read on even while we shrink from it. The misery of the poor woman, Hesther [sic] Prynne,—she who wears the badge of disgrace,—stands prominent in every page; in strange contrast with her elfin child, little Pearl. We hang over that remarkable scene between the faithless priest and the guilty woman, in the deep shadow of the primeval forest,—while the mysterious child plays near at hand by the brookside, with a deeply-riveted interest. Then, that picture of the wronged husband, silently pursuing his revenge,—how terrible it is! Yet, harrowing though the subject be, there is nothing prurient or feverish about it. The whole story is told with simple power. The work is pure, severe, and truthful; and it holds every reader in thrall until the end of the dark story is reached.

Margaret Oliphant, "Modern Novelists Great and Small," ***Blackwood's*, 77 (May 1855), 563.**

* * * *The Scarlet Letter* glows with the fire of a suppressed, secret, feverish excitement; it is not the glow of natural life, but the hectic of disease which burns upon the cheeks of its actors. The proud woman, the fantastic and elfish child, the weak and criminal genius, and the injured friend, the husband of Hester, are exhibited to us rather as a surgeon might exhibit his pet "cases," than as a poet shows his men and women, brothers and sisters to the universal heart. In this book the imagination of the writer has been taxed to supply a world and a society in accordance with the principal actors in his feverish drama. The whole sky and air are tropical; and instead of the gentle monotony of ordinary existence, its long, wearing, languid sorrows, its vulgar weariness and sleep, we have a perpetual strain of excitement—a fire that neither wanes nor lessens, but keeps at its original scorching heat for years. The landscape is parched and scathed; the breeze is a furnace-blast; the volcano is muttering and growling in the depths of the earth; there is an ominous stillness, like the pause before a great peal of thunder. Nor is the air once clear, nor the fever dissipated, till, with a sigh of relief, we escape from the unwholesome fascination of this romance, and find ourselves in a world which is not always tending towards some catastrophe—a world where tears and showers fall to refresh the soil, and where calamities do not come from the blind and mocking hands of fate, but mixed with blessings and charities from the very gates of heaven.

Richard Holt Hutton, "Nathaniel Hawthorne," ***National Review*, 11 (October 1860), 458, 466-467, 469.**

* * * The stories of the *Scarlet Letter*, of the *House of the Seven Gables*, and of *Transformation*, might all have been included, in their full ideal integrity, and with all the *incident* they contain, in the *Twice-told Tales* without adding more than a few pages to the book. We do not mean that thus compressed they would produce the same, or any thing like the same, imaginative impression, but only that, as far as either the *aspect* of his characters or the circumstanial interest of the stories is concerned, there need be no compression in thus shortening them. The omissions would be most important, indeed, to the effect, but they would be the omission of minute contemplative touches, imaginative self-repetitions, and so forth, which seldom in-

deed give us a single glimpse of any other than the one side of his characters, or add a second thread to the one interest of the tale.

In the *Scarlet Letter*, for instance, there is but one conception, which is developed in three—perhaps we should say four—scenes of great power, and that is the analysis of the deranging effect of the sin of adultery on the intrinsically fine characters of those principally affected by it, with a special view to its different influence on the woman, who is openly branded with the shame, and on the man, whose guilt is not punished and who has a double remorse to suffer, for the sin, and for the growing burden of insincerity. The effect of the sin on the child who is the offspring of it is made a special study, as are the false relations it introduces between the mother and child. Throughout the tale every one of the group of characters studied is seen in the lurid light of this sin and in no other. The only failure is in the case of the injured and vindictive husband, whose character is subordinated entirely to the artistic development of the other three. * * *

In the *Scarlet Letter* [Hawthorne] has a subject naturally so painful as exactly to suit his genius. He treats it with perfect delicacy, for his attention is turned to the morbid anatomy of the relations which have originated in the sin of adultery, rather than to the sin itself. There are two points on which Mr. Hawthorne concentrates his power in this remarkable book. The first is the false position of the minister, who gains fresh reverence and popularity as the very fruit of the passionate anguish with which his heart is consumed. Frantic with the stings of unacknowledged guilt, he is yet taught by those very stings to understand the hearts and stir the consciences of others. His character is a pre-Raphaelite picture of the tainted motives which fill a weak but fine and sensitive nature when placed in such a position; of self-hatred quite too passionate to conquer self-love; of a quailing conscience smothered into insane cravings for blasphemy; of the exquisite pain of gratified ambition conscious of its shameful falsehood. The second point on which Mr. Hawthorne concentrates his power is the delineation of anomalous characteristics in the child who is the offspring of this sinful passion. He gives her an inheritance of a lawless, mischievous, and elvish nature, not devoid of strong affections, but delighting to probe the very sorest points of her mother's heart, induced in part by some mysterious fascination to the subject, in part by wanton mischief. The scarlet A, which is the brand of her mother's shame, is the child's delight. She will not approach her mother unless it be on her bosom; and the unnatural complication of emotions thus excited in Hester Prynne's heart present one of the most characteristic features of the book, and are painfully engraved on the reader's mind.

The scene of most marvellous power which the book contains contrives to draw to a focus all the many clashing affections portrayed. Mr. Dimmesdale, the unhappy minister, eager to invent vain penances in expiation of the guilt which he dares not avow, creeps out at midnight in his canonical robe to stand for an hour on the scaffold on which Hester and her child had been pilloried years before. * * * This strange vigil, the grim hysteric humour of the minister, the proud and silent fortitude of Hester, the mocking laughter of the child as she detects her unknown father's cowardice, together make as weird-like a tangle of human elements as ever bubbled together in a witches' caldron. Yet his scene, though probably the most powerful which Mr. Hawthorne has ever painted, scarcely exemplifies his uncanny fashion of awakening the most mutually- repellent feelings at the same moment towards the same person so characteristically as many of his other tales.

"Nathaniel Hawthorne," ***North British Review*****, 49 (September 1868), 195-198.**

The Scarlet Letter was the first of [Hawthorne's] larger works, and is perhaps unsurpassed in the concentrated power of one or two of its scenes by anything he afterwards wrote. The interest is centred in two chief and two subordinate characters,—the two natures, originally so fine, marred by their joint sin, the minister and Hester, and the two against whom they sinned, the husband and the child. There is nothing we know of in literature at once so tender and so unflinching, so harrowingly painful, and yet so irresistibly fascinating, as the dissection of the morbid heart of Dimmesdale,—or rather the history; for it is not its condition at any one moment, so much as its progress, step by step, from refined purity and almost saintly devotion, once wounded by momentary indulgence of unholy passion, through depths of beguiling self-knowledge and self-deception, of moral weakness and self-abasement, of passionate penance and miserable evasion, till, enfeebled to the point of collapse both physically and spiritually, his fall is perfected in yielding for an instant, under the stimulating sympathy and love of the stronger nature and more resolute will of his fellow-sinner, to a dream of unhallowed earthly life and passion, from which he is soon roused by the grim, chill, but to him not unwelcome, hand of death, to cleanse his conscience by confession. The constitution of the man is one of singular fineness and weakness. Every hour of his life he abhors himself in dust and ashes; he struggles, in almost mortal agony, to unburden himself of the concealed sin that rankles and festers in his conscience, till it eats out the whole pith of his being. In helpless cowardice and vanity he faints in the attempt, rendered doubly difficult by the devotedness and worship of his flock, and drifts into wild self-accusations of merely general sinfulness and depravity, which serve only to heighten their conception of his character and of his standard of moral purity. The misery of his life is augmented unspeakably by the fiendish process of refined torture to which he is subjected by the husband, who, living under the same roof with him, in the character of physician, seeks revenge, not in exposure, but in constantly fretting with poisonous touch the ever open wound. One cannot but regret that a nature endowed with so many noble qualities should not live, more visibly to retrieve its fall. Yet we cannot doubt the reality of his late repentance, and that in his dying confession, there was not only achieved the beginning of a higher life for himself, but a redeeming influence exerted for both mother and child.

Hester's character is of a stronger mould. Without being unwomanly, she is of far less effeminate texture than the man she loved so truly, and for whom she suffered so bravely. Under the hard Puritan treatment she somewhat hardens. The blazing brand upon her breast does not melt, but indurates her heart. It is true that for seven long years she had never been false to the symbol, and "it may be that it was the talisman of a stern and severe, but yet a guardian spirit." But an outcast from social intercourse and joy, her thoughts break loose from conventional limitations, and stray in bold and perilous speculation. Pitiless condemnation and scorn drive her to justify what she had better unfeignedly repented. "What we did had a consecration of it own. We felt it so. We said so to each other." Thrown out of her true relations to society, she sees its whole fabric in false perspective, awry. "For years past she had looked from an estranged point of view at human institutions, and whatever priests or legislators had established; criticising all with hardly more reverence than the Indian would feel for the clerical band, the judicial robe, the pillory, the gallows, the fireside, or the church. The tendency of her fate and fortunes had been to set her free. The scarlet letter was her passport into regions where other women dared not tread. Shame, Despair, Solitude! These had been her teachers—stern and wild ones—and they had made her strong, but taught her much amiss." Divine law broken becomes to her human prejudice. She not only seeks to justify the past; she would vainly aim at a higher and truer life in renewal and perpetuation of the sin; and in her wild daring she carries the poor bewildered soul of the minister with her. For deliberate power and skilful handling it might be difficult to find many passages equal to that in which she fans the dying embers of hope and passion into a short-lived glow before they expire for ever.

Arrived, however, at the very summit of his fame and influence, Dimmesdale is moved by a power and virtue beyond himself to count these and all else as loss that he may win truth; and in conquering himself he is "strangely triumphant" over more than himself. Stronger as Hester has all along shown herself, she "is impelled as if by inevitable fate against her stronger will" by the power of truth and right in his last moments. The child too is subdued: "the spell is broken" that seemed all her life to have inspired her with an elf-like nature that could not be bound by enduring human sympathies. Even Roger Chillingworth, become almost the incarnation of hate and revenge, though unsoftened, is withered up into impotence for evil by this "death of triumphant ignominy." This character, indeed, though at first apt to be thrown into shadow by the more intense interest that attaches to his wife and the minister, is truly the most painful in the narrative. The laborious student, the benevolent recluse of other days, has his whole nature poisoned, his learning and sage experience of human nature turned into a curse, by the sin that had been sinned against him. All human kindness is dried up within him, and he lives only to keep his enemy on the rack,—to prolong the wretched man's wasting life by care and healing art, only that he may the longer enjoy his devilish work. He miserably sinks out of the circle of human activity and life when his patient's death leaves him without a purpose more.

The early significance of Pearl's nature and disposition are deeply significant, full of reflex lights thrown on the modifying influences, not only of parental character and constitution, but of the deeds and circumstances and relations—of serious import to their own character, though perhaps foreign to its general tone—of our progenitors; and that less by their natural and generally recognised operation in habitual life and intercourse, than by a sort of natal affection of blood, and nerve, and spirit;—intimating to us in infinitely varied speech the truth, that what is sown must be reaped—the persistent cogency of moral law, the indestructible cohesion of moral order, either in recognition and observance, or in vindication and retribution. "The child's nature had something wrong in it, which continually betokened that she had been born amiss—the effluence of her mother's lawless passion." She was wayward, fitful, impulsive, never to be reckoned on, full of wild energy, gushing affection, and imperious self-will. "There was fire in her, and throughout her; she seemed the unpremeditated off-shoot of a passionate moment." She was at once the sting and the solace of her mother's heart, and that not only by virtue of the natural relationship of child and parent, as the constant memorial of the crime in which she had been begotten, and at the same time the blessing into which God in his mercy converts for us even the fruits of our sins; but far more in the peculiarity of her disposition, as a very "messenger of anguish," and a purger of her parent's conscience. Her first baby smile is not in her mother's face, but at the scarlet letter on her breast; its gold embroidery is the first plaything which her tiny fingers grasp at; it is the chief object of her later childish curiosity. She loves in imp-like prank to associate it in her remarks with the habit the minister has of keeping his hand over his heart. With malicious pertinacity she seeks ever and again to force his acknowledgment of herself and her mother on the most public occasions. It appeared to be the very end of her life to probe and keep ever open the hidden sores of both.

Leslie Stephen, "Nathaniel Hawthorne," ***Cornhill*****, 26 (December 1872), 727-728.**

* * * His idealism does not consist in conferring grandeur upon vulgar objects by tinging them with the reflection of deep emotion. He rather shrinks than otherwise from describing the strongest passions, or shows their working by indirect touches and under a side-light. An excellent example of his peculiar method occurs in what is in some respects the most perfect of his works, the *Scarlet Letter*. There, again, we have the spectacle of a man tortured by a life-long repentance. The Puritan clergyman, reverenced as a saint by all his flock, conscious of a sin which, once revealed, will crush him to the earth, watched with a malignant purpose by the husband whom he has injured, unable to summon up the moral courage to tear off the veil, and make the only atonement in his power, is undoubtedly a striking figure, powerfully conceived and most delicately described. He yields under terrible pressure to the temptation of escaping from the scene of his prolonged torture with the partner of his guilt. And then, as he is returning homewards after yielding a reluctant consent to the flight, we are invited to contemplate the agony of his soul. The form which it takes is curiously characteristic. No vehement pangs of remorse, or desperate hopes of escape, overpower his faculties in any simple and straightforward fashion. The poor minister is seized with a strange hallucination. He meets a venerable deacon, and can scarcely restrain himself from uttering blasphemies about the communion- supper. Next appears an aged widow, and he longs to assail her with what appears to him to be an unanswerable argument against the immortality of the soul. Then follows an impulse to whisper impure suggestions to a fair

young maiden, whom he has recently converted. And, finally, he longs to greet a rough sailor with a "volley of good round, solid, satisfactory, and heaven-defying oaths." The minister, in short, is in that state of mind which gives birth in its victim to a belief in diabolical possession; and the meaning is pointed by an encounter with an old lady, who, in the popular belief, was one of Satan's miserable slaves and dupes, the witches, and is said—for Hawthorne never introduces the supernatural without toning it down by a supposed legendary transmission—to have invited him to meet her at the blasphemous sabbath in the forest. The sin of endeavouring to escape from the punishment of his sins had brought him into sympathy with wicked mortals and perverted spirits.

This mode of setting forth the agony of a pure mind, tainted by one irremovable blot, is undoubtedly impressive to the imagination in a high degree; far more impressive, we may safely say, than any quantity of such rant as very inferior writers could have poured out with the utmost facility on such an occasion. Yet I am inclined to think that a poet of the highest order would have produced the effect by more direct means. Remorse overpowering and absorbing does not embody itself in these recondite and, one may almost say, over-ingenious fancies. Hawthorne does not give us so much the pure passion as some of its collateral effects. He is still more interested in the curious psychological problem than moved by sympathy with the torture of the soul. We pity poor Mr. Dimmesdale profoundly, but we are also interested in him as the subject of an experiment in analytical psychology. We do not care so much for his emotions as for the strange phantoms which are raised in his intellect by the disturbance of his natural functions. The man is placed upon the rack, but our compassion is aroused, not by feeling our own nerves and sinews twitching in sympathy, but by remarking the strange confusion of ideas produced in his mind, the singularly distorted aspect of things in general introduced by such an experience, and hence, if we please, inferring the keenness of the pangs which have produced them.

The Growth of Hawthorne's Posthumous Reputation

Robert Collyer, "Hawthorne," ***Western Monthly*****, 1 (January 1869), 32.**

Each one of HAWTHORNE'S great works is devoted to the gradual development of a great idea. The "Scarlet Letter" is a revelation of the truth of Paul's words, that "some men's sins are open beforehand going before them to judgment, and some men's sins follow after them." In opening this truth through the sin on which the story turns, it is wonderful to notice how the man manages to keep on the exact line between a Puritan reserve and a wild imagination. Esther's [sic] slow and painful purification is crowned by no perfect happiness. Dimmesdale's confessions is only the last relief of the soul on earth from what must have barred its entrance into heaven, and he has to bear the dreadful burden of his secret sin into the holiest places a man can enter, until the weight and corrosion of it kills him. While the tall woman in gray, whose dust in laid in the old King's Chapel graveyard at last, is not buried so near another grave that their dust can ever mingle.

Gilderoy W. Griffin, ***Studies in Literature*** **(Philadelphia: Claxton, Remsen & Haffelfinger, 1871), pp. 219-222, 224.**

HAWTHORNE is, we think, the ablest writer of pure fiction in the language. There is nothing commonplace about him. Unlike most novelists, he deals less with accidental manifestations than with universal principles. His characters are not mere shadowy abstractions, but "veritable human souls, though dwelling in a far-off world of cloud-land." He is a purist in style, and is at all times as scrupulously exact in his choice of words as if he were writing a complete and perfect poem. All his works, from his earliest productions, the "Twice Told Tales," to his later efforts, the "Marble Faun" and "Our Old Home," bear upon them the ineffaceable stamp of genius, and ever awaken ideas of beauty, of solemnity, and of grandeur. The SCARLET LETTER is perhaps his greatest creation.

There is a suggestiveness and an originality about it for which we may search in vain for a parallel outside of the writings of Shakspeare. In it he penetrates into the recesses of the heart, and touches the secret springs of our inmost passions and desires. It is a deep, a strange, a profound and an awful tragedy, in which the severest and most appalling sufferings known to man are not only depicted with wonderful naturalness and intensity, but laid bare as it were to the gaze even of persons of the dullest and most unimaginative sensibilities. Hawthorne is said to have derived his first conception of this story from reading a sentence written upon an old yellow parchment, accidentally found among some rubbish at the custom-house in Boston, decreeing that a woman convicted of adultery should stand upon the platform of a pillory in front of the market-place, with the letter "A" written on her breast. A friend who saw him read it remarked to a gentleman standing near: "We shall hear, I am sure, of the letter 'A' again." HAWTHORNE, in the introductory chapter to the romance, not only relates the story of reading the sentence, but says that he actually found a piece of fine red cloth, much worn and faded by time and wear, in the shape of the letter "A," and that he involuntarily put it upon his breast, and seemed to experience a sensation of burning heat, as if the letter were not of scarlet cloth but of red-hot iron, and that he shuddered and let it fall upon the floor. He added that it was the subject of meditation for many an hour while pacing to and fro across his room, or traversing with a hundred-fold repetition the long extent from the front door of the custom-house to the side entrance and back again. He felt that there was a mystic and a terrible meaning in it most worthy of interpretation.

The interpretation he gave will endure forever. He has portrayed, as no one else could portray, the religious faith of the Puritans. In depicting it in all its hideous deformity, he does not exaggerate anything or conceal anything. Its victim, Hester Prynne, whether or not a true type of her class, must forever be associated with the intolerance, narrow prejudices, and vindictive feelings of the bigoted sect who thought themselves especially chosen by Heaven to punish the guilty with the most damnable instruments of torture. The author, in discoursing upon the hard and unyielding severity of their laws, never allows his indignation to overmaster his judgment. In the very whirlwind of passion he begets a temperance which gives it smoothness. It has been urged as an objectionable feature in his writings, that he does not solve moral and psychological problems, "but exhibits their bearings and workings in concrete and living forms, for experiment and illustration." Now this is exactly what we most admire in him. It is a part of the peculiarity of genius not to be decisive, to raise questions rather than to settle them. HAWTHORNE seems to care more for giving his readers an opportunity of discovering truth for themselves than to point it out to them. But sometimes, we admit, he abuses this power; for instance, when he refuses to tell us in the "Marble Faun" whether Donatello has pointed and furry ears or not, or where he excites our curiosity by concealing the cause of the influence of the ill-omened Capuchin over the courageous and noble-hearted Miriam; or in the following comparison of hatred and love in the SCARLET LETTER: "It is a curious subject of observation and inquiry whether hatred or love be not the same thing at bottom. Each in its utmost development supposes a high degree of intimacy and heart-knowledge; each renders one individual dependent for the food of his affections and spiritual life upon another; each leaves the passionate lover, or the no less passionate hater, forlorn and desolate by the withdrawal of his subject. Philosophically considered, therefore, the two passions seem essentially the same, except that one happens to be seen in a celestial radiance, and the other in a dusky and lurid glow."

There is something about HAWTHORNE'S children that affects us with singular love and admiration. They are not prodigies, like Paul Dombey and Elinor Trench, but have all the natural bloom, freshness, and simplicity of childhood. They are imbued with a spell of infinite variety. They breathe an atmosphere of love and beauty, of enchanting hopes and dreams. We feel that theirs is the only flowery path, the golden period of existence, the unclouded dawn of life. We do not find anything inconsistent even in the conduct of little Pearl, one of the most shadowy, ethereal, and mystical of all the author's creations, when we recollect that "she seemed the unpremeditated offshoot of a passionate moment," and that "the child's nature had something wrong in it, which continually betokened that she had been born amiss, the effluence of her mother's lawless passion;" unless, indeed, we except the terrible scene at the brook side, where she refused to come to her mother, though called in accents of honeyed sweetness, until she placed the scarlet letter upon her breast, but stood motionless, pointing with her finger where she was accustomed to see it. The author, however, endeavors to reconcile her conduct in the following reflections of the mother: "Children will not abide any, the slightest change in the accustomed aspect of things that are daily before their eyes. Pearl misses something which she has always seen me wear."

We know of nothing in the whole range of literature that equals the sufferings of the mother when she again fastens the letter on her breast, feeling that she must bear the torture a while longer. "Hopefully but a moment ago as Hester had spoken of drowning it in the deep sea, there was a sense of inevitable doom upon her as she thus received back this deadly symbol from the hand of fate. She had flung it into infinite space! She had drawn an hour's free breath! and here again was the scarlet misery glittering on the old spot! So it ever is, whether thus typified or not, that an evil deed invests itself with the character of doom."

We have a hint at the conclusion of this mystical romance that little Pearl grew to womanhood, and that her wild, rich nature had been softened and subdued, and made capable of the gentlest happiness. The description of Hester's repentance is so full of divine philosophy that no one can rise from its perusal without a purer and deeper sympathy for the weaknesses of humanity. * * *

The entire book is filled with similar passages, illustrative of the author's delicate sentiment and mystical imagination, as well as of his suggestiveness and originality. He has the purest and loftiest ideas of love and virtue. Unlike Thackeray, he never indulges in petty and contemptible sneers at women, nor dwells with exquisite delight upon their "timorous debasements and self-humiliation." He does not stop to prove that "they are born timid and tyrants," and are terrified into humility, and bullied and frightened into devotion.

"Our Literary Record," ***Liberal Christian*****, 23 October 1875, p. 6.**

We are glad to see that Mr. Osgood is about to publish a new edition of Hawthorne's works in style nearly uniform with the "Little Classics," which have found their way so readily to the popular heart. The price of each volume will be $1.25, thus placing the works of the great novelist within the reach of many who could not afford to purchase more expensive editions.

This is certainly a step in the right direction. Hawthorne can never be what is commonly reckoned "popular." His genius was too fine and subtle to tickle the taste of the uncultivated reader. But very many so-called educated people have yet to learn that the author of the Scarlet Letter, the Marble Faun, and those wonderful Twice-Told Tales—which bear the mark of his genius as clearly as his larger works—was, perhaps, the finest flower of the intellectual life which our country has produced. We have had no touch more delicate, no imagination more far-reaching, no more subtle insight into character. His English is well-nigh faultless in its alertness and simple strength. His books will, doubtless, live when countless volumes that the world now holds famous have sunk into obscurity.

The Scarlet Letter is, perhaps, the most powerful, if not the most remarkable, of Hawthorne's works. Once to have read it is to remember it forever. It stands out from the mass of ordinary novels like some wonderful picture by a great artist, who has breathed into the canvas his own passionate soul.

Hester Prynne and Arthur Dimmesdale live and move before us as human beings into whose inmost nature, by some magician's power, we may look unquestioned—though we stand back awe-struck and afraid at what we find there. They seem scarcely of our own flesh and blood—so bare and naked do their hearts lie before us. We can recall few scenes in English fiction equal in strength and grandeur to the chapter in which Arthur Dimmesdale, before all the assembled multitude, makes the revelation of the Scarlet Letter. The whole description of Pearl—the wild, elfin creature—is full of Hawthorne's most subtle power. Such chapters as "Hester and Pearl," "A Forest Walk," and "The Child at the Brookside," make us wonder and grow still in thought of the man who wrote them.

E. P. Whipple, "The First Century of the Republic," ***Harper's Monthly*****, 52 (March 1876), 527-528.**

******The Scarlet Letter*, the romance by which Hawthorne first forced himself on the popular mind as a genius of the first class, was but the expansion of an idea expressed in three sentences, written twenty years before its appearance, in the little sketch of "Endicott and the [Red] Cross" which is included in the collection of *Twice-told Tales*. But *The Scarlet Letter* exhibited in startling distinctness all the resources of his peculiar mind, and even more than Scott's *Bride of Lammermoor* it touches the lowest depths of tragic woe and passion—so deep, indeed, that the representation becomes at times almost ghastly. If Jonathan Edwards, turned romancer, had dramatized his sermon on "Sinners in the Hand of an Angry God," he could not have written a more terrific story of guilt and retribution than *The Scarlet Letter*. The pitiless intellectual analysis of the emotions of guilty souls is pushed so far that the reader, after being compelled to sympathize with the Puritanic notion of Law, sighs for some appearance of the consoling Puritanic doctrine of Grace. Hawthorne, in fact, was a patient observer of the operation of spiritual laws, and relentless in recording the results of his observations. Most readers of romances are ravenous for external events; they demand that the heroes and heroines shall be swift in thought, confident in decision, rapid in act. In Hawthorne's novels the events occur in the hearts and minds of his characters, and our attention is fastened on the ecstasies or agonies of individual souls rather than on outward acts and incidents; at least, the latter appear trivial in comparison with the inward mental states they imperfectly express. * * * Hawthorne did not succeed in making his psychological pictures of sin and woe "enjoyable." The intensity of impassioned imagination which flames through every page of *The Scarlet Letter* was unrelieved by those milder accompaniments which should have been brought in to soften the effect of a tragedy so awful in itself. Little Pearl, one of the most exquisite creations of imaginative genius, is introduced not to console her parents, but, in her wild, innocent willfulness, to symbolize their sin and add new torments to the slow-consuming agonies of remorse.

"Literary Notices," ***Woman's Journal*****, 10 November 1877, p. 357.**

THE SCARLET LETTER is brought out by James R. Osgood & Co., on tinted paper, gilt edged, profusely illustrated, and beautifully bound, thus adding new attractions to that wonderful book, which, a quarter of a century ago, won a host of admiring readers, and made itself immortal. In its present form it is a handsome gift book.

W. D. Howells, "Recent Literature," ***Atlantic Monthly*****, 40 (December 1877), 753.**

The publishers have rather paid honor to the best and highest literature than consulted the ordinary holiday mood in choosing for illustration Hawthorne's supreme romance,—the great wonder-book in which the deep life of our Puritanic date suffers forever,—The Scarlet Letter, insurpassably tragic, as Evangeline is insurpassably pathetic, among works of imagination, and destined by the perfection of its form to endure with our language. They have given it due state in printing and paper; they have invited to illustrate the story the artist who perhaps unites more fine qualities than any other, and they have called to her aid the brilliant, sympathetic, and characteristic touch of our best engraver. If the result is not perfectly satisfactory, it must be because it is not within the scope of any one artist to interpret all the phases of the always deepening, always darkening tragedy. We all know in what Miss [Mary] Hallock has hitherto excelled: the innocent tenderness and grace of young girlhood; the entreating pathos of some unhappy woman's face; the sadness of an aged visage; the brightness, the light of some festival scene; the joyous gayety of love-making; the sweetness and serenity of family groups and all the aspects of domestic peace. Her successes in a different direction rather than her failures will surprise those already acquainted with her work; and we think that the more these illustrations are studied the more they will be found successful.

At first, as in the case of Hester Prynne on the scaffold, one does not accept them as expressions of the predominant feeling, yet a little reflection convinces that the air of joyless absence among other scenes, the look of dull oblivion, with its subconsciousness of present agony, in Hester's face,— half-averted and forgetful of the babe that hangs so heavy in her hold,—is the feeling which art could best and most movingly picture there. It is a triumph which contrasts with the failure of the second scene on the scaffold, when Dimmesdale, Hester, and Pearl stand there together, by night: Hester with rather a St. Cecilia-ish, Madonna-ish, upturned face, and Dimmesdale in a dishabille which does not at all correspond with the scrupulosity of costume attributed to him by the author on that occasion. The scenes of Hester, Dimmesdale, and Pearl in the forest are not so good, either, nor is the final scene on the scaffold after the election sermon; but that in Governor Bellingham's house, in which Hester appeals to Dimmesdale to keep the grim authorities from taking her Pearl away, is most finely and dramatically presented, and has a deep thrill in it. All the figures, in their various poses and expressions, are excellent. The mother and child, passing through the hall, are also admirable; in these two scenes chiefly does Miss Hallock seem to have caught the real Pearl, though we must except the pretty half-page in which the elfish child sits on a rock dabbling her foot in the pool. Hester Prynne's return to prison, after her hour on the pillory, is one of the good things; it is very good indeed; the figure is grand, and the heavy fatigue in the beautiful face most touchingly expressed; and the three studies of faces—the Puritan matron faces among the spectators, the young maiden faces in Mr.

Each of the following illustrations was drawn by May Hallock for the 1877 Osgood edition of *The Scarlet Letter* and reviewed by W. D. Howells.

Dimmesdale's congregation, and the faces of the magisterial group in the election-day procession—are all well imagined and extraordinarily well realized. Several landscape bits, too, are thoroughly and characteristically fine, especially that sad perspective of forest, with the white birch fallen across the pool in the foreground, and that winding woodland road with Hester and her babe in her arms in the foreground, and the Puritan figures in the background, following her with their eyes as she walks rapt and drearily brooding away. Chillingworth is often too theatrically fancied; Dimmesdale is most successfully portrayed in the scene at Governor Bellingham's, which is, on the whole, the most satisfactory, the most perfect scene in the book,—entirely and nobly beautiful, and as yet quite unapproached in power by anything in American illustrative art.

Anthony Trollope, "The Genius of Nathaniel Hawthorne," ***North American Review*****, 129 (September 1879), 208-213.**

"The Scarlet Letter" is, on the English side of the water, perhaps the best known [of Hawthorne's stories]. It is so terrible in its pictures of diseased human nature as to produce most questionable delight. The reader's interest never flags for a moment. There is nothing of episode or digression. The author is always telling his one story with a concentration of energy which, as we can understand, must have made it impossible for him to deviate. The reader will certainly go on with it to the end very quickly, entranced, excited, shuddering, and at times almost wretched. His consolation will be that he too has been able to see into these black deeps of the human heart. The story is one of jealousy,—of love and jealousy,—in which love is allowed but little scope, but full play is given to the hatred which can spring from injured love. A woman has been taken in adultery,— among the Puritans of Boston some two centuries since,—and is brought upon the stage that she may be punished by a public stigma. She was beautiful and young, and had been married to an old husband who had wandered away from her for a time. Then she has sinned, and the partner of her sin, though not of her punishment, is the young minister of the church to which she is attached. It is her doom to wear the Scarlet Letter, the letter A, always worked on her dress,—always there on her bosom, to be seen by all men. The first hour of her punishment has to be endured, in the middle of the town, on the public scaffold, under the gaze of all men. As she stands there, her husband comes by chance into the town and sees her, and she sees him, and they know each other. But no one else in Boston knows that they are man and wife. Then they meet, and she refuses to tell him who has been her fellow sinner. She makes no excuse for herself. She will bear her doom and acknowledge its justice, but to no one will she tell the name of him who is the father of her baby. For her disgrace has borne its fruit, and she has a child. The injured husband is at once aware that he need deal no further with the woman who has been false to him. Her punishment is sure. But it is necessary for his revenge that the man too shall be punished,—and to punish him he must know him. He goes to work to find him out, and he finds him out. Then he does punish him with a vengeance and brings him to death,—does it by the very stress of mental misery. After a while the woman turns and rebels against the atrocity of fate,—not on her own account, but for the sake of that man the sight of whose sufferings she can not bear. They meet once again, the two sinful lovers, and a hope of escape comes upon them,—and another gleam of love. But fate in the shape of the old man is too strong for them. He finds them out, and, not stopping to hinder their flight, merely declares his purpose of accompanying them! Then the lover succumbs and dies, and the woman is left to her solitude. That is the story.

The personages in it with whom the reader will interest himself are four,—the husband, the minister who has been the sinful lover, the woman, and the child. The reader is expected to sympathize only with the woman,—and will sympathize only with her. The husband, an old man who has knowingly married a young woman who did not love him, is a personfication of that feeling of injury which is supposed to fall upon a man when his honor has been stained by the falseness of a wife. He has left her and has wandered away, not even telling her of his whereabout. He comes back to her without a sign. The author tells us that he had looked to find his happiness in her solicitude and care for him. The reader, however, gives him credit for no love. But the woman was his wife, and he comes back and finds that she had gone astray. Her he despises, and is content to leave to the ascetic cruelty of the town magistrates; but to find the man out and bring the man to his grave by slow torture is enough of employment for what is left to him of life and energy.

With the man, the minister, the lover, the reader finds that he can have nothing in common, though he is compelled to pity his sufferings. The woman has held her peace when she was discovered and reviled and exposed. She will never whisper his name, never call on him for any comfort or support in her misery; but he, though the very shame is eating into his soul, lives through the seven years of the story, a witness of her misery and solitude, while he himself is surrounded by the very glory of sanctity. Of the two, indeed, he is the greater sufferer. While shame only deals with her, conscience is at work with him. But there can be no sympathy, because he looks on and holds his peace. Her child says to him,—her child, not knowing that he is her father, not knowing what she says, but in answer to him when he would fain take her little hand in his during the darkness of night,—"Wilt thou stand here with mother and me to-morrow noontide"? He can not bring himself to do that, though he struggles hard to do it, and therefore we despise him. He can not do it till the hand of death is upon him, and then the time is too late for reparation in the reader's judgment. Could we have sympathized with a pair of lovers, the human element would have prevailed too strongly for the author's purpose.

He seems hardly to have wished that we should sympathize even with her; or, at any rate, he has not bid us in so many words to do so, as is common with authors. Of course, he has wished it. He has intended that the reader's heart should run over with ruth for the undeserved fate of that wretched woman. And it does. She is pure as undriven snow. We know that at some time far back she loved and sinned, but it was done when we did not know her. We are not told so, but come to understand, by the wonderful power of the writer in conveying that which he never tells, that there has been no taint of foulness in her love, though there has been deep sin. He never even tells us why that letter A has been used, though the abominable word is burning in our ears from first to last. We merely see her with her child, bearing her lot with patience, seeking for no comfort, doing what good she can in her humble solitude by the work of her hands, pointed at from all by the finger of scorn, but the purest, the cleanest, the fairest also among women. She never dreams of supposing that she ought not to be regarded as vile, while the reader's heart glows with a longing to take her soft hand and lead her into some pleasant place where the world shall be pleasant and honest and kind to her. I can fancy a reader so loving the image of Hester Prynne as to find himself on the verge of treachery to the real Hester of flesh and blood who may have a claim upon him. Sympathy can not go beyond that; and yet the author deals with her in a spirit of assumed hardness, almost as though he assented to the judgment and the manner in which it was carried out. In this, however, there is a streak of that satire with which Hawthorne always speaks of the peculiar institutions of his own country. The worthy magistrates of Massachusetts are under his lash throughout the story, and so is the virtue of her citizens and the chastity of her matrons, which can take delight in the open shame of a woman whose sin has been discovered. Indeed, there is never a page written by Hawthorne not tinged by satire.

The fourth character is that of the child, Pearl. Here the author has, I think, given way to a temptation, and in doing so has not increased the power of his story. The temptation was, that Pearl should add a picturesque element by being an elf and also a charming child. Elf she is, but, being so, is incongruous with all else in the story, in which, unhuman as it is, there is nothing of the ghost-like, nothing of the unnatural. The old man becomes a fiend, so to say, during the process of the tale; but he is a man-fiend. And Hester becomes sublimated almost to divine purity; but she is still simply a woman. The minister is tortured beyond the power of human endurance; but neither do his sufferings nor his failure of strength adequate to support them come to him from any miraculous agency. But Pearl is miraculous,—speaking, acting, and thinking like an elf,—and is therefore, I think, a drawback rather than an aid. The desolation of the woman, too, would have been more perfect without the child. It seems as though the author's heart had not been hard enough to make her live alone;—as sometime when you punish a child you can not drive from your face that gleam of love which shoots across your frown and mars its salutary effect.

Hatred, fear, and shame are the passions which revel through the book. To show how a man may so hate as to be content to sacrifice everything to his hatred; how another may fear so that, even though it be for the rescue of his soul, he can not bring himself to face the reproaches of the world; how a woman may bear her load of infamy openly before the eyes of all men,—this has been Hawthorne's object. And surely no author was ever more successful. The relentless purpose of the man, in which is exhibited no passion, in which there is hardly a touch of anger, is as fixed as the hand of Fate. No one in the town knew that the woman was his wife. She had never loved him. He had left her alone in the world. But she was his wife; and, as the injury had been done to him, the punishment should follow from his hands! When he finds out who the sinner was, he does not proclaim him and hold him up to disgrace; he does not crush the almost adored minister of the gospel by declaring the sinner's trespass. He simply lives with his enemy in the same house, attacking not the man's body,—to which, indeed, he acts as a wise physician,—but his conscience, till we see the wretch writhing beneath the treatment.

Hester sees it too, and her strength, which suffices for the bearing of her own misery, fails her almost to fainting as she understands the condition of the man she has loved. Then there is a scene, the one graceful and pretty scene in the book, in which the two meet,—the two who were lovers,—and dare for a moment to think that they can escape. They come together in a wood, and she flings away, but for a moment, the badge of her shame, and lets down the long hair which has been hidden under her cap, and shines out before the reader for once,—just for that once,—as a lovely woman. She counsels him to fly, to go back across the waters to the old home whence he had come, and seek for rest away from the cruelty of his tyrant. When he pleads that he has no strength left to him for such action, then she declares that she will go with him and protect him and minister to him and watch over him with her strength. Yes; this woman proposes that she will then elope with the partner of her former sin. But no idea comes across the reader's mind of sinful love. The poor wretch can not live without service, and she will serve him. Were it herself that was concerned, she would remain there in her solitude, with the brand of her shame still open upon her bosom. But he can not go alone, and she too will therefore go.

As I have said before, the old man discovers the plot, and crushes their hopes simply by declaring that he will also be their companion. Whether there should have been this gleam of sunshine in the story the critic will doubt. The parent who would be altogether like Solomon should not soften the sternness of his frown by any glimmer of parental softness. The extreme pain of the chronicle is mitigated for a moment. The reader almost fears that he is again about to enjoy the satisfaction of a happy ending. When the blackness and the rumbling thunder-claps and the beating hailstones of a mountain storm have burst with all their fearful glories on the wanderer among the Alps, though he trembles and is awestruck and crouches with the cold, he is disappointed rather than gratified when a little space of blue sky shows itself for a moment through the clouds. But soon a blacker mantle covers the gap, louder and nearer comes the crash, heavier fall the big drops till they seem to strike him to the bone. The storm is awful, majestic, beautiful;—but is it not too pitiless? So it is with the storm which bursts over that minister's head when the little space of blue has vanished from the sky.

But through all this intensity of suffering, through this blackness of narrative, there is ever running a vein of drollery. As Hawthorne himself says, "a lively sense of the humorous again stole in among the solemn phantoms of her thought." He is always laughing at something with his weird, mocking spirit. The very children when they see Hester in the streets are supposed to speak of her in this wise: "Behold, verily, there is the woman of the scarlet letter. Come, therefore, and let us fling mud at her." Of some religious book he says, "It must have been a work of vast ability in the somniferous school of literature." "We must not always talk in the market-place of what happens to us in the forest," says even the sad mother to her child. Through it all there is a touch of burlesque,—not as to the suffering of the sufferers, but as to the great question whether it signifies much in what way we suffer, whether by crushing sorrows or little stings. Who would not sooner be Prometheus than a yesterday's tipsy man with this morning's sick-headache? In this way Hawthorne seems to ridicule the very woes which he expends himself in depicting.

Henry James, *Hawthorne* (New York: Harper & Bros., 1880), pp. 102-117.

The prospect of official station and emolument which Hawthorne mentions in one of those paragraphs from his Journal which I have just quoted, as having offered itself and then passed away, was at last, in the event, confirmed by his receiving from the administration of President Polk the gift of a place in the Custom-house of his native town. The office was a modest one, and "official station" may perhaps appear a magniloquent formula for the functions sketched in the admirable Introduction to *The Scarlet Letter*. Hawthorne's duties were those of Surveyor of the port of Salem, and they had a salary attached, which was the important part; as his biographer[1] tells us that he had received almost nothing for the contributions to the *Democratic Review*. He bade farewell to his ex-parsonage, and went back to Salem in 1846, and the immediate effect of his ameliorated fortune was to make him stop writing. None of his Journals of the period, from his going to Salem to 1850, have been published; from which I infer that he even ceased to journalise. *The Scarlet Letter* was not written till 1849. In the delightful prologue to that work, entitled *The Custom-house*, he embodies some of the impressions gathered during these years of comparative leisure (I say of leisure, because he does not intimate in this sketch of his occupations that his duties were onerous). He intimates, however, that they were not interesting, and that it was a very good thing for him, mentally and morally, when his term of service expired— or rather when he was removed from office by the operation of that wonderful "rotatory" system which his countrymen had invented for the administration of their affairs. This sketch of the Custom-house is, as simple writing, one of the most perfect of Hawthorne's compositions, and one of the most gracefully and humorously autobiographic. It would be interesting to examine it in detail, but I prefer to use my space for making some remarks upon the work which was the ultimate result of this period of Hawthorne's residence in his native town; and I shall, for convenience' sake, say directly afterwards what I have to say about the two companions of *The Scarlet Letter—The House of the Seven Gables* and *The Blithedale Romance*. I quoted some passages from the prologue to the first of these novels in the early pages of this essay. There is another passage, however, which bears particularly upon this phase of Hawthorne's career, and which is so happily expressed as to make it a pleasure to transcribe it— the passage in which he says that "for myself, during the whole of my Custom-house experience, moonlight and sunshine, and the glow of the firelight, were just alike in my regard, and neither of them was of one whit more avail than the twinkle of a tallow candle. An entire class of susceptibilities, and a gift connected with them—of no great richness or value, but the best I had—was gone from me." He goes on to say that he believes that he might have done something if he could have made up his mind to convert the very substance of the commonplace that surrounded him into matter of literature.

> "I might, for instance, have contented myself with writing out the narratives of a veteran shipmaster, one of the inspectors, whom I should be most ungrateful not to mention; since scarcely a day passed that he did not stir me to laughter and admiration by his marvelous gift as a story-teller. . . . Or I might readily have found a more serious task. It was a folly, with the materiality of this daily life pressing so intrusively upon me, to attempt to fling myself back into another age; or to insist on creating a semblance of a world out of airy matter. . . . The wiser effort would have been, to diffuse thought and imagination through the opaque substance of to-day, and thus make it a bright transparency . . . to seek resolutely the true and indestructible value that lay hidden in the petty and wearisome incidents and ordinary characters with which I was now conversant. The fault was mine. The page of life that was spread out before me was dull and commonplace, only because I had not fathomed its deeper import. A better book than I shall ever write was there. . . . These perceptions came too late. . . . I had ceased to be a writer of tolerably poor tales and essays, and had become a tolerably good Surveyor of the Customs. That was all. But, nevertheless, it is anything but agreeable to be haunted by a suspicion that one's intellect is dwindling away, or exhaling, without your consciousness, like ether out of phial; so that at every glance you find a smaller and less volatile residuum."

As, however, it was with what was left of his intellect after three years' evaporation, that Hawthorne wrote *The Scarlet Letter*, there is little reason to complain of the injury he suffered in his Surveyorship.

* * *

The work has the tone of the circumstances in which it was produced. If Hawthorne was in a sombre mood, and if his future was painfully vague, *The Scarlet Letter* contains little enough of gaiety or of hopefulness. It is densely dark, with a single spot of vivid colour in it; and it will probably long remain the most consistently gloomy of English novels of the first order. But I just now called it the author's masterpiece, and I imagine it will continue to be, for other generations than ours, his most substantial title to fame. The subject had probably lain a long time in his mind, as his subjects were apt to do; so that he appears completely to possess it, to know it and feel it. It is simpler and more complete than his other novels; it achieves more perfectly what it attempts, and it has about it that charm, very hard to express, which we find in an artist's work the first time he has touched his highest mark—a sort of straightness and naturalness of execution, an unconsciousness of his public, and freshness of interest in his theme. It was a great success, and he immediately found himself famous. The writer of these lines, who was a child at the time, remembers dimly the sensation the book produced, and the little shudder with which people alluded to it, as if a peculiar horror were mixed with its attractions. He was too young to read it himself; but its title, upon which he fixed his eyes as the book lay upon the table, had a mysterious charm. He had a vague belief, indeed, that the "letter" in question was one of the documents that come by the post, and it was a source of perpetual wonderment to him that it should be of such an unaccustomed hue. Of course it was difficult to explain to a child the significance of poor Hester Prynne's blood-coloured *A*. But the mystery was at last partly dispelled by his being taken to see a collection of pictures (the annual exhibition of the National Academy), where he encountered a representation of a pale, handsome woman, in a quaint black dress and a white coif, holding between her knees an elfish-looking little girl, fantastically dressed, and crowned with flowers. Embroidered on the woman's breast was a great crimson *A*, over which the child's fingers, as she glanced strangely out of the picture, were maliciously playing. I was told that this was Hester Prynne and little Pearl, and that when I grew older I might read their interesting history. But the picture remained vividly imprinted on my mind; I had been vaguely frightened and made uneasy by it; and when, years afterwards, I first read the novel, I seemed to myself to have read it before, and to be familiar with its two strange heroines. I mention this incident simply as an indication of the degree to which the success of *The Scarlet Letter* had made the book what is called an actuality. Hawthorne himself was very modest about it; he wrote to his publisher, when there was a question of his undertaking another novel, that what had given the history of Hester Prynne its "vogue" was simply the introductory chapter. In fact, the publication of *The Scarlet Letter* was in the United States a literary event of the first importance. The book was the finest piece of imaginative writing yet put forth in the country. There was a consciousness of this in the welcome that was given it—a satisfaction in the idea of America having produced a novel that belonged to literature, and to the forefront of it. Something might at last be sent to Europe as exquisite in quality as anything that had been received, and the best of it was that the thing was absolutely American; it belonged to the soil, to the air; it came out of the very heart of New England.

It is beautiful, admirable, extraordinary; it has in the highest degree that merit which I have spoken of as the mark of Hawthorne's best things—an indefinable purity and lightness of conception, a quality which in a work of art affects one in the same way as the absence of grossness does in a human being. His fancy, as I just now said, had evidently brooded over the subject for a long time; the situation to be represented had disclosed itself to him in all its phases. When I say in all its phases, the sentence demands modification; for it is to be remembered that if Hawthorne laid his hand upon the well-worn theme, upon the familiar combination of the wife, the lover, and the husband, it was, after all, but to one period of the history of these three persons that he attached himself. The situation is the situation after the woman's fault has been committed, and the current of expiation and repentance has set in. In spite of the relation between Hester Prynne and Arthur Dimmesdale, no story of love was surely ever less of a "love-story." To Hawthorne's imagination the fact that these two persons had loved each other too well was of an interest comparatively vulgar; what appealed to him was the idea of their moral situation in the long years that were to follow. The story, indeed, is in a secondary degree that of Hester Prynne; she becomes, really, after the first scene, an accessory figure; it is not upon her the *dénoûment* depends. It is upon her guilty lover that the author projects most frequently the cold, thin rays of his fitfully-moving lantern, which makes here and there a little luminous circle, on the edge of which hovers the livid and sinister figure of the injured and retributive husband. The story goes on, for the most part, between the lover and the husband—the tormented young Puritan minister, who carries the secret of his own lapse from pastoral purity locked up beneath an exterior that commends itself to the reverence of his flock, while he sees the softer partner of his guilt standing in the full glare of exposure and humbling herself to the misery of atonement—between this more wretched and pitiable culprit, to whom dishonour would come as a comfort and the pillory as a relief, and the older, keener, wiser man, who, to obtain satisfaction for the wrong he has suffered, devises the infernally ingenious plan of conjoining himself with his wronger, living with him, living upon him; and while he pretends to minister to his hidden ailment and to sympathize with his pain, revels in his unsuspected knowledge of these things, and stimulates them by malignant arts. The attitude of Roger Chillingworth, and the means he takes to compensate himself— these are the highly original elements in the situation that Hawthorne so ingeniously treats. None of his works are so impregnated with that after-sense of the old Puritan consciousness of life to which allusion has so often been made. If, as M. Montégut says,[2] the qualities of his ancestors *filtered* down through generations into his composition, *The Scarlet Letter* was, as it were, the vessel that gathered up the last of the precious drops. And I say this not because the story happens to be of so-called historical cast, to be told of the early days of Massachusetts and of people in steeple-crowned hats and sad-coloured garments. The historical colouring is rather weak than otherwise; there is little elaboration of detail, of the modern realism of research; and the author has made no great point of causing his figures to speak the English of their period. Nevertheless, the book is full of the moral presence of the race that invented Hester's penance—diluted and complicated with other things, but still perfectly recognizable. Puritanism, in a word, is there, not only objectively, as Hawthorne tried to place it there, but subjectively as well. Not, I mean, in his judgement of his characters in any harshness of prejudice, or in the obtrusion of a moral lesson; but in the very quality of his own vision, in the tone of the picture, in a certain coldness and exclusiveness of treatment.

The faults of the book are, to my sense, a want of reality and an abuse of the fanciful element—of a certain superficial symbolism. The people strike me not as characters, but as representatives, very picturesquely arranged, of a single state of mind; and the interest of the story lies, not in them, but in the situation, which is insistently kept before us, with little progression, though with a great deal, as I have said, of a certain stable variation; and to which they, out of their reality, contribute little that helps it to live and move. I was made to feel this want of reality, this over-ingenuity, of *The Scarlet Letter*, by chancing not long since upon a novel which was read fifty years ago much more than to-day, but which is still worth reading—the story of *Adam Blair*, by John Gibson Lockhart. This interesting and powerful little tale has a great deal of analogy with Hawthorne's novel—quite enough, at least, to suggest a comparison between them; and the comparison is a very interesting one to make, for it speedily leads us to larger considerations than simple resemblances and divergences of plot.

Adam Blair, like Arthur Dimmesdale, is a Calvinistic minister who becomes the lover of a married woman, is overwhelmed with remorse at his misdeed, and makes a public confession of it; then expiates it by resigning his pastoral office and becoming a humble tiller of the soil, as his father had been. The two stories are of about the same length, and each is the masterpiece (putting aside, of course, as far as Lockhart is concerned, the *Life of Scott*) of the author. They deal alike with the manners of a rigidly theological society, and even in certain details they correspond. In each of them, between the guilty pair, there is a charming little girl; though I hasten to say that Sarah Blair (who is not the daughter of the heroine, but the legitimate offspring of the hero, a widower) is far from being as brilliant and graceful an apparition as the admirable little Pearl of *The Scarlet Letter*. The main difference between the two tales is the fact that in the American story the husband plays an all- important part, and in the Scottish plays almost none at all. *Adam Blair* is the history of the passion, and *The Scarlet Letter* the history of its sequel; but nevertheless, if one has read the two books at a short interval, it is impossible to avoid confronting them. I confess that a large portion of the interest of *Adam Blair*, to my mind, when once I had perceived that it would repeat in a great measure the situation of *The Scarlet Letter*, lay in noting its difference of tone. It threw into relief the passionless quality of Hawthorne's novel, its element of cold and ingenious fantasy, its elaborate imaginative delicacy. These things do not precisely constitute a weakness in *The Scarlet Letter*; indeed, in a certain way they constitute a great strength; but the absence of a certain something warm and straight-forward, a trifle more grossly human and vulgarly natural, which one finds in *Adam Blair*, will always make Hawthorne's tale less touching to a large number of even very intelligent readers, than a love-story told with the robust, synthetic pathos which served Lockhart so well. His novel is not of the first rank (I should call it an excellent second-rate one), but it borrows a charm from the fact that his vigorous, but not strongly imaginative, mind was impregnated with the reality of his subject. He did not always succeed in rendering this reality; the expression is sometimes awkward and poor. But the reader feels that his vision was clear, and his feeling about the matter very strong and rich. Hawthorne's imagination, on the other hand, plays with his theme so incessantly, leads it such a dance through the moon-lighted air of his intellect, that the thing cools off, as it were, hardens and stiffens, and, producing effects much more exquisite, leaves the reader with a sense of having handled a splendid piece of silversmith's work. Lockhart, by means much more vulgar, produces at moments a greater illusion, and satisfies our inevitable desire for something, in the people in whom it is sought to interest us, that shall be of the same pitch and the same continuity with ourselves. Above all, it is interesting to see how the same subject appears to two men of a thoroughly different cast of mind and of a different race. Lockhart was struck with the warmth of the subject that offered itself to him, and Hawthorne with its coldness; the one with its glow, its sentimental interest—the other with its shadow, its moral interest. Lockhart's story is as decent, as severely draped, as *The Scarlet Letter*; but the author has a more vivid sense than appears to have imposed itself upon Hawthorne, of some of the incidents of the situation he describes; his tempted man and tempting woman are more actual and personal; his heroine in especial, though not in the least a delicate or a subtle conception, has a sort of credible, visible, palpable property, a vulgar roundness and relief, which are lacking to the dim and chastened image of Hester Prynne. But I am going too far; I am comparing simplicity with subtlety, the usual with the refined. Each man wrote as his turn of mind impelled him, but each expressed something more than himself. Lockhart was a dense, substantial Briton, with a taste for the concrete, and Hawthorne was a thin New Englander, with a miasmatic conscience.

In *The Scarlet Letter* there is a great deal of symbolism; there is, I think, too much. It is overdone at times, and becomes mechanical; it ceases to be impressive, and grazes triviality. The idea of the mystic *A* which the young minister finds imprinted upon his breast and eating into his flesh, in sympathy with the embroidered badge that Hester is condemned to wear, appears to me to be a case in point. This suggestion should, I think, have been just made and dropped; to insist upon it and return to it, is to exaggerate the weak side of the subject. Hawthorne returns to it constantly, plays with it, and seems charmed by it; until at last the reader feels tempted to declare that his enjoyment of it is puerile. In the admirable scene, so superbly conceived and beautifully executed, in which Mr. Dimmesdale, in the stillness of the night, in the middle of the sleeping town, feels impelled to go and stand upon the scaffold where his mistress had formerly enacted her dreadful penance, and then, seeing Hester pass along the street, from watching at a sick-bed, with little Pearl at her side, calls them both to come and stand there beside him—in this masterly episode the effect is almost spoiled by the introduction of one of these superficial conceits. What leads up to it is very fine—so fine that I cannot do better than quote it as a specimen of one of the striking pages of the book.

> "But before Mr. Dimmesdale had done speaking, a light gleamed far and wide over all the muffled sky. It was doubtless caused by one of those meteors which the nightwatcher may so often observe burning out to waste in the vacant regions of the atmosphere. So powerful was its radiance that it thoroughly illuminated the dense medium of clod betwixt the sky and earth. The great vault brightened, like the dome of an immense lamp. It showed the familiar scene of the street with the distinctness of mid-day, but also with the awfulness that is always imparted to familiar objects by an unaccustomed light. The wooden houses, with their jutting stories and quaint gable-peaks; the doorsteps and thresholds, with the early grass springing up about them; the garden-plots, black with the freshly-turned earth; the wheel-track, little worn, and, even in the market-place, margined with green on either side; —all were visible, but with a singularity of aspect that seemed to give another moral interpretation to the things of this world than they had ever borne before. And there stood the minister, with his hand over his heart; and Hester Prynne, with the embroidered letter glimmering on her bosom; and little Pearl, herself a symbol, and the connecting link between these two. They stood in the noon of that strange and solemn splendour, as if it were the light that is to reveal all secrets, and the daybreak that shall unite all that belong to one another."

That is imaginative, impressive, poetic; but when, almost immediately afterwards, the author goes on to say that "the minister looking upward to the zenith, beheld there the appearance of an immense letter—the letter A—marked out in lines of dull red light," we feel that he goes too far, and is in danger of crossing the line that separates the sublime from its intimate neighbour. We are tempted to say that this is not moral tragedy, but physical comedy. In the same way, too much is made of the intimation that Hester's badge had a scorching property, and that if one touched it one would immediately withdraw one's hand. Hawthorne is perpetually looking for images which shall place themselves in picturesque correspondence with the spiritual facts with which he is concerned, and of course the search is of the very essence of poetry. But in such a process discretion is everything, and when the image becomes importunate it is in danger of seeming to stand for nothing more serious than itself. When Hester meets the minister by appointment in the forest, and sits talking with him while little Pearl wanders away and plays by the edge of the brook, the child is represented as at last making her way over to the other side of the woodland stream, and disporting herself there in a manner which makes her mother feel herself, "in some indistinct and tantalizing manner, estranged from Pearl; as if the child, in her lonely ramble through the forest, had strayed out of the sphere in which she and her mother dwelt together, and was now vainly seeking to return to it." And Hawthorne devotes a chapter to this idea of the child's having, by putting the brook between Hester and herself, established a kind of spiritual gulf, on the verge of which her little fantastic person innocently mocks at her mother's sense of bereavement. This conception belongs, one would say, quite to the lighter order of a story-teller's devices, and the reader hardly goes with Hawthorne in the large development he gives to it. He hardly goes with him either, I think, in his extreme predilection for a small number of vague ideas which are represented by such terms as "sphere" and "sympathies." Hawthorne makes too liberal a use of these two substantives; it is the solitary defect of his style; and it counts as a defect partly because the words in question are a sort of specialty with certain writers immeasurably inferior to himself.

I had not meant, however, to expatiate upon his defects, which are of the slenderest and most venial kind. *The Scarlet Letter* has the beauty and harmony of all original and complete conceptions, and its weaker spots, whatever they are, are not of its essence; they are mere light flaws and inequalities of surface. One can often return to it; it supports familiarity, and has the inexhaustible charm and mystery of great works of art. It is admirably written. Hawthorne afterwards polished his style to a still higher degree; but in his later productions—it is almost always the case in a writer's later productions—there is a touch of mannerism. In *The Scarlet Letter* there is a high degree of polish, and at the same time a charming freshness; his phrase is less conscious of itself. * * *

[1]George Parsons Lathrop

[2]"Un Romancier Pessimiste en Amérique/Nathaniel Hawthorne," *Revue des Deux Mondes*, 1 August 1860.

A. C. Roe, "Hawthorne and His Teachings," ***Catholic Presbyterian*****, 6 (September 1881), 197-202.**

The "Scarlet Letter" was written in 1849, and published in the spring of 1850. Hawthorne had laid aside his pen for some time, when he was collector for the Custom House of Salem. The book is prefaced with a quaint description of that establishment and its ancient clerks, somnolently performing their office work, or creeping slowly about the wharves and ships. And in Hawthorne's peculiar way of mystifying his readers, and appropriately accounting for the light in which he chooses to set his picture, he would have us believe that an old chest in the loft furnished the materials for this inimitable story.

His plot is very simple, in fact, nothing more than a series of pictures carefully elaborated, kept before the mind till they have made their impression, and then dismissed. The style is perfect,—something less polished, perhaps, something stronger also, than the works that followed. The cast of characters, the wife, the lover, and the wronged husband, make the story very difficult to handle. The moral atmosphere of the book is saved, however, partly by Hawthorne's native purity, and yet more because passion is represented as past, and the hour of retribution has come. Indeed, James complains of it as cold and unreal, mistaking as usual Hawthorne's meaning, which was not an analysis of feeling, but sin working out its own punishment.

The book opens with Hester Prynne standing on the scaffold of the pillory with her babe on her arm, and a letter in fine scarlet cloth, artistically embroidered with gold thread, on the bosom of her gown—the fatal letter A, which she is condemned to wear thereafter for the remainder of her natural life. The scene is powerfully wrought, the cold glare of pitiless eyes, worse by far than cries and taunts; the open shame to a delicate shrinking nature; the wandering of the poor creature's imagination over the scenes of childhood, from mother love and father blessing down to the shameful hour. You are crushed yourself; and wonder at the strength that bore it all. And you get Hawthorne's first thought,—open sin, openly punished.

While she stands there, the Rev. Arthur Dimmesdale is called upon by the Governor to urge her to confess the companion of her guilt. He stands high for eloquence, learning, and saintly character; was, indeed, a noble man, but—fallen; and it is his *own* name he must urge her to speak. He does it nobly,—"Be not silent," says he, "from any mistaken pity or tenderness for him . . . . Heaven hath granted thee an open ignominy, that thou thereby mayest work out an open triumph over the evil within thee, and the sorrow without. Take heed how thou deniest to him—who, perchance, hath not the courage to grasp it for himself—the bitter, but wholesome, cup that is now presented to thy lips!"

"She will not speak," murmured Mr. Dimmesdale. He now drew back with a long respiration. "Wondrous strength and generosity of a woman's heart! She will not speak."

Dimmesdale had not the courage to avow himself, and went to face his conscience and struggle with remorse, while he perforce must meet his duties and accept the estimation of his flock as a saint. He is not a hypocrite. He loathes his position, hates his sin, but *dares* not face the consequences. This is the second aspect of Hawthorne's theme, darker than the first in crime and penalty—hidden sin and hidden suffering.

While Hester still stands there, a third character enters. Her husband is brought by the Indians to be ransomed. He is an old man, somewhat deformed, studious, intellectual, keen, but kind withal. He recognises her, and after she has returned to prison seeks an interview, and demands the name of the man who has wronged him. As between himself and Hester, he feels his own folly had betrayed her into circumstances that made the scales of wrong hang evenly between them. The world had been cheerless to him, and his large heart lonely and chill; and he had persuaded her into marriage, though he knew well she had nothing but friendship for him. He meditates her no evil more than to leave her to her fate and the scarlet letter which burns on her breast. She refuses the name.

Roger Chillingworth, as he is now called, scents his prey, and gives his life to refined revenge. Though he lost no time meanwhile, it was long, years in fact, before he attained actual certainty; for Dimmesdale guarded his secret well. This is the only part of the work where there is consecutive action. The play between two keen intellects, struggling to gain and keep possession of such a secret, is well given. The only safety for the minister would have been to cut away all ties between; but he believed him friendly, and was weighted by agony.

So Chillingworth becomes intimate with his victim, and, as his physician, shares his intellectual pursuits, and cares for his bodily ailments. But he keeps his thoughts on the symbol flaming on Hester's breast, stimulates conscience, harrows up remorse; and while he seems unaccountably to miss it, appears ever and anon on the very point of discovering his secret. The large-minded, genial-hearted student, deep in Nature's secrets, changes in the process. He appears to have his way; but has made evil his good, and goes visibly downward before our eyes towards a self-wrought doom. This gives us Hawthorne's third thought—devilish revenge developing into devilish character.

Under such circumstances Dimmesdale learned a peculiar message, which he gave with marvellous power. Multitudes crowded to hear; and swayed, as if he were inspired, to the burning words that smote sin and dragged to light the hidden evils of the heart—his own sin, his own heart. He realises to his stern age what a saint and prophet should be, and still the fame of his holiness grew, while conscience thundered in his ear, Thou hypocrite! He strove to believe that his work and evident usefulness required silence. He toiled, gave, denied himself, descended even to penance and the bloody scourge—did everything but confess. He *did* confess, and published his sin in words almost explicit, and declared himself most unfit to stand in his holy place. To his people he was but speaking of the general sin of the human heart; and the sainted Arthur Dimmesdale, in feeling so acutely his infinitesimal part therein, but rose the higher in their reverence and love.

More and more surely Chillingworth pursued the scent, till one day, the minister falling asleep over a vast black-letter volume, he thrust aside the vestment covering his breast, and saw something—Hawthorne does not say what—the counterpart of Hester's scarlet letter.

What use he made of his partial knowledge we have already seen. Now his torturing touch drove Dimmesdale almost frantic. Accusing visions peopled his dreams, came between him and his books, flitted about him by night and by day. He could see through them to realities by an effort of the mind. But, after all, *they* were the realities to him—his white-haired father frowning on him; his mother passing with averted face; Hester and little Pearl pointing first to his breast, and then at the letter on her mother's gown. He longed to confess, but dared not; while remorse and cowardice rent him by turns. So we get another solemn lesson: "Be true;" let the motives urging concealment and penalties of discovery be what they may.

Three pictures more will close our sketch. The first grows out of his morbid state of mind. It would be a relief, he thought, to stand on the pillory where Hester had borne her shame seven years before.

On a murky night in May he steals forth and takes his place. The hours pass in this mockery of penitence, till Dimmesdale is overcome with horror, and shrieks aloud. There is a little stir. Governor Bellingham looks forth. The witch-lady, Mrs. Hibbins, his sister, appears, listening as to the clamour of the night hags who were wont to meet her in the forest.

Presently the Reverend Mr. Wilson passes, going home from the chamber whence the noble Winthrop had gone to glory. In uncontrollable excitement he calls, or thinks he calls, to him to stand at his side, and shudders at the sound, as if the fiend had wrenched from him his doom. He had not spoken, and the holy man goes on.

Soon another light appears, Hester and Pearl coming from the same place where she had been to take the measure of the shroud. He calls to them. They mount the steps; and hand in hand, with the touch of truth and thrill of sympathy, a new, tumultuous life rushes through his heart. He is true now, and where he should be, and can pray.

Then little Pearl asks: "Wilt thou stand here with mother and me to-morrow noontide?" "Nay! not so, my little Pearl—one other day, the great judgment day, but not to-morrow." And all the old dread of public exposure returns. He was already trembling—with a strange joy, notwithstanding—at the circumstances in which he found himself.

Chillingworth, coming also from Governor Winthrop's, sees them, and gloats over the agony of his victim, but pretends to consider it the effect of overwork. "Aha! see now, how they trouble the brain—these books, these books! You should study less, good sir, and take a little pastime, or these night-whimseys will grow upon you."

"I will go home with you," said Mr. Dimmesdale.

Remorse had done her utmost; but cowardice won the day.

Touched by his condition, Hester will no longer be bound by her promise to keep Chillingworth's secret from the minister. She seeks Dimmesdale in the forest, as he returns from a visit to Eliot, the apostle to the Indians, to get relief, mayhap from pain, in society of the holy man, and tells him who was his bosom friend. The horror and shame overwhelm him, and he sinks on the forest leaves, and fain would die. Hester must think for him. He can live no longer where he is.

"I must die here," said he. "There is not strength or courage left me to venture into the wide, difficult world alone." He repeated the word, "Alone, Hester."

"Thou shalt not go alone." Then all was spoken.

It seemed the best good possible; and like another man, with an energy Dimmesdale had not felt for many a day, he made his way back to the town; but—it was surrender.

This, however, was not the only change the minister felt. Cowardly as he was, there had been a struggle, in its agony at least. Now he met his good old deacon, and the fiend, as if he were already his own, whispered some blasphemous suggestion touching the communion supper; and despite him, it seemed as if his tongue would wag. An aged sister came down the street, widowed, bereft, all her hopes beyond the grave. He can think of nothing but a brief and most specious argument against the immortality of the soul. A maiden, pure and fresh as a lily, the youngest of his flock, met him next. He hid his face with his cloak, and hurried past, lest he should blast her innocence with a word—a look, even, he felt would be enough. The old witch-lady, Mistress

Hibbins, from the other side of the street, smiled at him, and looked back, as one who would recognise a secret bond of sin.

"Have I sold myself, then?" thought the minister. He had done something very like it. And we get another lesson. Hidden warfare even, cowardly though it be, is better than surrender.[1]

One picture more.

How God had dealt with him, He only knows; but the minister had seen the abyss, recoiled, and was saved.

He was to preach the Election Sermon a few days after Hester, standing by the old pillory at the church door, saw him pass in the procession,—him whom she knew so well in the forest,—enveloped in the rich music, high in his position, and more distant in his abstracted thought. Hawthorne makes us see the pageant, the music, the civic guard, the strong New England magnates, and the Reverend Arthur Dimmesdale, the minister of the day, moving with a spiritual exaltation that scarce seemed to feel the earth, while the people looked on him as an angel soon to wing his flight.

The subject of the sermon was God's purpose in planting the New England colonies. We hear the discourse, full of eloquence, power, and withal a nameless thrill—the cry, even through its most triumphant tones, of a heart sorrow-laden, guilty, telling its secret in every aspect of his glorious theme. He ceased, and the audience drew their breath. Dimmesdale looked down on a sea of faces, strong, stern souls whom he had swayed at will. There was no higher position in the land. And thus side by side Hawthorne places their portraits—the sainted minister in his pulpit; Hester, with her scarlet letter, in the market-place—then brings them together in the revelation of the awful truth; and the story ends on the pillory, where it began.

Dimmesdale comes from the church, pale with exhaustion. The suffering of years, the strain of preparation, the shame and horror, the bliss and grandeur of his purpose have done their work. He is once more true; but he is a dying man. The procession passes Hester. He turns towards the scaffold, and reaches out his hands—

"Come, Hester, come, my little Pearl."

Chillingworth bursts through the crowd to keep him back. But with fainting strength and Hester's help, he struggles up; and, turning to the people, tells the truth, bares his breast, and shows the counterpart of Hester's scarlet letter, his own red stigma, type of what seared his inmost heart.

"Stand any here," he cries, "that question God's judgment on a sinner? Behold! behold a dreadful witness of it." Then he sank down.

Chillingworth with dull, blank countenance, knelt beside him.

"Thou hast escaped me," he repeated more than once. "Thou hast escaped me."

"God forgive thee," said the minister; "thou, too, hast deeply sinned."

He puts away the thought of meeting and of future bliss. "Shall we not meet again?" says she.

"Hush, Hester, hush. The law we broke—God knows . . . Had any of my agonies been wanting, I had been lost forever. Praised be His name. His will be done. Farewell."

A few pages more gather up the lessons of the wonderful book.

Chillingworth had transformed a noble nature by systematic pursuit of revenge, till it could live on no other food; and, having no more devil's work to do, wilted as a weed torn up by the roots, and died within the year, leaving a large property to little Pearl.

Hester soon after went to Europe, where the elf-child Pearl, sobered and changed by the awful scaffold scene, grew up capable of feeling a woman's gentle love. Years after, when Pearl had been honourably settled in life, Hester came back; and though she had long ago lived down her shame, took again the old badge upon her breast, and went to an fro a messenger of mercy. Women with wasted, wronged, and erring lives, came to one who had suffered more than they. The sick hailed her coming. The dying pillowed their heads upon the scarlet letter. It got a new meaning. The world said it stood for "able"—so strong, so helpful, was Hester Prynne for many years, till a new grave was dug near a green sunken hollow in King's Chapel Churchyard—near, but with a space between. And so this wonderful story ends.

Thus, gracefully, truthfully, and with infinite pathos, Hawthorne clothes in dress of modern story the solemn truth, the blessed word: "He that covereth his sins shall not prosper: but those confesseth and forsaketh them shall have mercy."

[1]We remark further, Hawthorne will not leave the thought of even temporary success of wrong. Chillingworth divines their purpose, and conveys to Hester his intention to take passage in the same vessel with them, though he keeps the knowledge from Dimmesdale, till at the proper moment he can feast on his horror and surprise.

George Parsons Lathrop, "Introductory Note" to *The Scarlet Letter* (Boston: Houghton Mifflin, 1883), pp. 9-14.

"The Scarlet Letter" was the first sustained work of fiction completed by Hawthorne after he had become known to the public through the "Twice-Told Tales;" and was the first among his books which attained popularity. He had meanwhile published "Grandfather's Chair," for children, and his "Mosses from an Old Manse." But it was not until he once more took up his residence in Salem, while occupying the post of surveyor at the Custom House of that port, that he began to hear—as he expressed it to a friend—"a romance growing in his mind." This romance was the now world-famous one, which is again offered to readers in the present volume. It was begun some time in the winter of 1849-50, after the author had been deprived of his official situation. He completed the book February 3, 1850, and on the following day wrote to Horatio Bridge:—

"I finished my book only yesterday, one end being in the press in Boston, while the other was in my head here in Salem; so that, as you see, the story is at least fourteen miles long. . . . Some portions of the book are powerfully written; but my writings do not, nor ever will, appeal to the broadest class of sympathies, and therefore will not attain a very wide popularity. Some like them very much; others care nothing for them and see nothing in them. There is an introduction to this book, giving a sketch of my Custom House life, with an imaginative touch here and there, which will perhaps be more attractive than the main narrative. The latter lacks sunshine."

So much, indeed, did the gravity and gloom of the situation in which he had placed Hester and Dimmesdale weigh upon him, that he described himself as having had "a knot of sorrow" in his forehead all winter. Like Balzac, he secluded himself while writing a romance, and, in fact, saw scarcely any one. It was noticed that he grew perceptibly thinner at such times; and how strongly the fortunes of his imaginary progeny affected him is well shown by a reminiscence in the "English Note-Books" (September 14, 1855):—

"Speaking of Thackeray, I cannot but wonder at his coolness in respect to his own pathos, and compare it with my emotions when I read the last scene of 'The Scarlet Letter' to my wife, just after writing it—tried to read it, rather, for my voice swelled and heaved, as if I were tossed up and down on an ocean as it subsides after a storm."

Nor was it only while in the act of composition with the pen that his fictions thus occupied all his faculties. During the time that he was engaged with "The Scarlet Letter," he would often become oblivious of his surroundings and absorbed in reverie. One day while in this mood he took from his wife's work-basket a piece of sewing and clipped it into minute fragments, without being aware of what he had done. This habit of unconscious destruction dated from his youth. The writer of these notes has in his possession a rocking chair used by Hawthorne, from which he whittled away the arms while occupied in study or in musing, at college. He is likewise said to have consumed an entire table in that manner during the same period.

Finished in February, "The Scarlet Letter" was issued the next month. Although the publisher, Mr. Fields, formed a high estimate of its merit as a work of art, his confidence in its immediate commercial value appears not to have been great, if we may judge from the following circumstance. The first edition printed numbered five thousand copies—in itself a sufficiently large instalment—but the type from which these impressions had been taken was immediately distributed; showing that no very extensive demand was looked for. But this edition was exhausted in ten days, and the entire work had then to be re-set and stereotyped, to meet the continued call for copies.

An illustration of Hawthorne's literary methods, and the extreme deliberation with which he matured his romances from the first slight germ of fancy or fact, is offered in the story of "Endicott and The Red Cross," written and published before 1845. Mention is there made of "a young woman with no mean share of beauty, whose doom it was to wear the letter *A* on the breast of her gown, in the eyes of all the world and her own children. And even her own children knew what that initial signified. Sporting with her infamy, the lost and desperate creature had embroidered the fatal token in scarlet cloth, with golden thread and the nicest art of needle-work; so that the capital A might have been thought to mean Admirable, or anything rather than Adulteress." When this story appeared, Miss E. P. Peabody remarked to a friend: "We shall hear of that letter by and by, for it evidently has made a profound impression on Hawthorne's mind." Years after the sentences quoted above had been printed in the second series of "Twice-Told Tales," the peculiar punishment referred to was elaborated and refined into the theme of "The Scarlet Letter."

The prescribing of such a punishment by the Puritan code is well authenticated. Hawthorne, it is understood, had seen it mentioned in some of the records of Boston, and it will be found among the laws of Plymouth Colony for 1658. A few years since, that close student of New England annals, the Rev. Dr. George E. Ellis, of Boston, stated incidentally in a lecture that there was not the slightest authenticity as to the person and character of the minister who plays the chief male part in the "Scarlet Letter" drama. Dr. Ellis held that, since Dimmesdale is represented as preaching the Election Sermon in the year of Governor Winthrop's death, he must be identified with the Rev. Thomas Cobbett, of Lynn, who actually delivered the Election Sermon in the year named; and he wished to defend the character of that clergyman against the suspicions of those who, like himself, conceived Dimmesdale to be simply a mask for the real Election preacher of that time. At the date under notice there was but one church in Boston, and its pastors were John Wilson and John Cotton. Wilson is mentioned under his own name in the romance; so that there can be no confusion of *his* identity with Dimmesdale's. Neither is there any reason for supposing that Hawthorne had the slightest intention of fixing the guilt of his imaginary minister on either John Cotton, or Thomas Cobbett of Lynn. The very fact that the name of Arthur Dimmesdale is a fictitious one, while the Rev. Mr. Wilson and Governor Bellingham are introduced under their true titles, ought to be proof enough that Dimmesdale's story cannot be applied to the actual Election preacher of 1649. The historic particularization must be understood as used simply to heighten the verisimilitude of the tale, while its general poetic truth and the possibility of the situation occurring in early New England remain unquestionable.

I believe it has not before been recorded that, when "The Scarlet Letter" had been written nearly through, the author read the story aloud, as far as it was then completed, to Mrs. Hawthorne; and, on her asking him what the ending was to be, he replied: "I don't know." To his wife's sister, Miss Peabody, he once said: "The difficulty is not *how* to say things, but *what* to say;" implying that, whenever he began to write, his subject was already so well developed as to make the question mainly one of selection. But it is easy to understand how, when he came to the final solution of a difficult problem, he might then, being carried away by the conflicting interests of the different characters, hesitate as to the conclusion.

When this romance was published it brought to Hawthorne letters from strangers, people who had sinned or were tempted and suffering, and who sought his counsel as they would that of a comprehensive friend or a confessor.

The introductory chapter on the Custom House, upon which Hawthorne relied to alleviate the sombreness of the story, successfully accomplished that result; but, at the time of its publication, its good-natured and harmless humor roused great ire in some of the Salem people, who recognized the sketches it contained of now forgotten officials. One individual, of considerable intelligence otherwise, was known to have firmly abstained from reading anything the author afterwards wrote; a curious revenge, which would seem to be designed expressly to injure the censor himself, without hurting or even being known to Hawthorne.

Henry S. Salt, *Literary Sketches* **(London: Swan Sonnenschein, Lowrey & Co., 1888), pp. 196-197.**

It can hardly be doubted that *The Scarlet Letter* is the best of all Hawthorne's productions. It is, indeed, one of the greatest of all works of fiction; for in the whole range of English literature there are few things more tragic and more sublime than this simple tale. The resemblance of its general structure to that of Lockhart's *Adam Blair* has more than once been commented on; it is also worth remark that *The Scarlet Letter* offers one or two very striking points of comparison with George Eliot's *Adam Bede*. The relation existing between the two guilty characters are almost identical in the two books; a forbidden love; a fatal secret; a disgrace borne at first by the woman alone, but finally shared by her lover—these form a strange coincidence in the plan of the novels, which is maintained even in the names of the characters, Hester Prynne and Hester Sorrel, Arthur Dimmesdale and Arthur Donnithorne. But with the names and situation of the characters the similarity ends; for Hawthorne's beautiful and pathetic story is happily free from the sensational incidents which so sadly mar the latter part of *Adam Bede*. In *The Scarlet Letter* the moral is not obtruded on the reader, yet the tone is altogether more lofty and spiritual, and aided by a power of poetical imagination of which George Eliot was wholly destitute. Nor can it be said that Hawthorne, on his side, was deficient in that keen insight and subtle analysis of character for which George Eliot is justly renowned. Indeed, this is one of the most striking features of *The Scarlet Letter*, after the publication of which Hawthorne is said to have been often consulted by various criminals and "spiritual invalids," who thus bore unconscious testimony to the keenness of his observation.

William Morton Payne, "The Scarlet Letter," *Dial*, 1 November 1892, p. 263.

Within this book is writ the tale of sin
And solemn expiation. From a soil
Virgin it sprang, the first-fruit of the toil
Whereof a nation new-create should win
Harvest of art immortal; herewithin
We read how memory, like a serpent's coil,
Clings round the guilty soul, which finds no foil
Against the fangs that strike still deeper in.

The glowing letter on the sable field
Burned to her heart, whose passion here revealed,
Strong both to err and to atone, deep burns
Into the mind, and holds in all men's sight
The law that sin committed ever earns
The bitter sorrow for the brief delight.

Thomas G. Selby, *The Theology of Modern Fiction* (London: C. H. Kelly, 1896), pp. 75-87.

The book by which Nathaniel Hawthorne is best known, *The Scarlet Letter*, gathers up and elaborates stray suggestions that are scattered through some of the shorter stories. That delineation of guilt, and all the mental purgatories through which it is swept, is a masterpiece no religious teacher can afford to overlook. A bit of New England history is brought before us with a dramatic impressiveness that has rarely, if ever, been rivalled; and the power, the mystery, the deathless judicial zeal which are inseparable attributes of the human conscience, imprint themselves upon our senses in lines that affright and agonise like fire. The chief characters of the romance are the Rev. Arthur Dimmesdale, a young preacher of mobile sensibility, with a vein of animalism running close under his finer qualities, and always ready to crop suddenly to the surface. He has fallen into sin with Hester Prynne, a young woman who, against her own choice, has been persuaded into marriage with a man much older than herself. The offspring of this guilty love is a child of strange and elfish disposition, known throughout the story by the name of Pearl. Hester has vowed that she will never reveal the name of her companion in sin. Whilst the faithless wife is enduring in the market-place of Salem the ordeal of public exposure and shame, as a punishment for her unchastity, the husband, who for some time past had been travelling amongst the Indians, returns to the settlement.

In the first scene Hester Prynne is being brought out of prison into the market-place to do penance in the pillory, which was one of the standing institutions of the Puritan townships. She holds in her arms the babe which is the proof of her shame, and on her breast, by the stern compulsion of those days, she wears the letter "A" embroidered upon a groundwork of scarlet cloth, announcing the fact that she is an adulteress. Whilst she is being made a spectacle for the gaze of indignant and unsympathising onlookers, it falls to the lot of Arthur Dimmesdale, as one of the ministers of the settlement, to exhort her to clear her soul by making known the paternity of her child, so that father and mother may share the humiliation belonging to both alike, and rise at last out of their abasement to a better life. At this juncture Roger Chillingworth appears upon the scene, and mixes with the bystanders. He has known nothing of his wife's fall, but she recognises him at once as he enters the crowd, through a disparity in the height of his two shoulders. At night he gains admission into the gaol, administers a sleeping draft to her restless and feverish child, fails to wrest from her the name of her fellow sinner, and extorts the vow that she shall never make known to the people of the settlement the fact that he is her husband. After the term of imprisonment has run out, Hester goes to live with her child in a cottage by the beach, where the two are almost entirely cut off from intercourse with the community. The very children scoff at her badge of shame, and mock her unoffending little one. The discipline of her forlornness, combined with a self-humiliation not inconsistent with dignity and independence, act as purifying forces in her life, and, little by little, she breaks down the harsh prejudice and hostility of her neighbours, and develops a strong, sympathetic, and magnanimous character, which compels silent esteem. The bitterness of death is past, for she has nothing to conceal, and has patiently borne the penalty of her misdoing.

In the meantime the minister goes about his work with this hideous secret eating away his very soul. Imagination . . . comes in to aid and abet the conscience in its work of punishing guilt and bringing to light the hidden things of darkness. The unresting pang which is ever throbbing in the breast of the minister, according to an organic law more fully verified now than then, leaves its tooth-mark in the flesh—the badge of the opprobrious letter which he ought to be wearing no less than Hester. His life withers away, and he falls into the habit of constantly placing his hand over the spot on his breast where chronic pain is fixing its imprint. Roger Chillingworth, who is installed as physician to the suffering minister, has got some clew to his guilt, and sets himself to play upon his fears, and worm his way, if may be, into the dark secret which is undermining his health, till at last Dimmesdale's life is consumed with sighing, and he stands shuddering on the brink of insanity. The physician plies his victim with medicine, half invites his confidence, tells him of omens which appear upon the graves of those who die with their sins unacknowledged. To tyrannise more completely over the soul of this fallen man he falls into a plan—apparently in the interests of the minister's health—of occupying the same apartments with him, so that he may have him under a cruel scrutiny day and night. The walls of their sitting room happen to be adorned with tapestries representing David, Bathsheba, and the prophet Nathan. One day the physician inquisitor unfastens the neck-band of the minister as he is sleeping, and gets a passing glimpse of the mark that remorse is fast writing there in lines red as fire. Like a wild beast he dissects his way into the very heart of this man who has wronged him, and gloats over its daily tremors and quivering pains. The death of his victim would be too poor and disappointing a revenge to satisfy such cold, calculating vindictiveness. It was this one motive which kept Roger Chillingworth, year after year, in the insignificant Puritan township.

In the course of time the minister is driven by his unresting remorse to a midnight penance that stops short, however, of a frank, public avowal of his sin. He takes his stand upon the platform where, seven years ago, Hester was pilloried before the hard, pitiless eyes of her neighbours. As the form of Arthur Dimmesdale, veiled by the darkness, looms from his coign of ignominy, an old minister, who has just been returning from attendance at a death-bed, creeps by, lantern in hand, and the young man thinks he will surely be discovered. The lonely woman and her child happen to be passing by, for she has been to the house of death to measure for a funeral robe the body of a man who was passing away at midnight. He bids them mount and take their stand by his side, he holding one hand of little Pearl whilst the mother holds the other. "Wilt thou stand here with mother and me to-morrow noontide?" asks the child, who seems to be always hovering curiously round the secret, and pining for an acknowledgment which will deliver her from the isolation and contempt in which she is being brought up. The minister could only answer that he would stand together with them at the judgment day, and Pearl mocks him for this make-believe penance, and his delay in avowing the relationship that exists. Then the flash of a brilliant meteor all at once lights up the heavens, and, to Dimmesdale's imagination, it looks like the letter "A," proclaiming his scandalous backsliding before the whole universe. As the night begins to pale into morning twilight, the form of Roger Chillingworth is seen hovering near the pillory, like one of the fiends of the judgment day. The minister loathes the very sight of the man; but, prostrated by all the terror of the night, allows himself to be led back by the physician to his lodgings. The next Sabbath morning, at the close of the service, the sexton returns to the minister a glove which he had dropped on the gibbet, assuming that it was one of the wiles of the devil himself to compromise the reputation of the much revered teacher.

This scene is followed by one in the forest, where Hester has resolved to intercept Arthur Dimmesdale on his return from a visit to an Indian mission settlement, and save him, if possible, from the clutches of the man who is fast hunting him into insanity. She tells him that the physician who haunts his life, and, under the guise of ministering to his physical weakness, has acquired such disastrous mastery over him, is her own husband. He is aghast, and declares that he cannot forgive Hester for suffering this diabolic plot against his peace and well-being to be carried out for years without protest. The poor woman's regret and importunate pity now create a new temptation for them both. After taking counsel together they determine to depart for some foreign shore, where the shame of the past will be unknown and Chillingworth's clutch upon his victim will be relaxed. They will make their home amongst strangers, and find healing for their remorse in a mutual love, that for the moment they scarcely realise is unlawful. Hester flings away the "Scarlet Letter" into the depths of the forest; but when Pearl comes back from her play by the brook, she shuns her mother and repels her call and her caressing affection, till the familiar symbol has been picked up and fastened to her dress again. This scheme of running away from the duty of public confession, and repeating elsewhere the untrue life of the past, seems to let loose a legion of devils in the soul of the faithless minister. As he comes out of the forest he is strangely impelled to pour a torrent of blasphemies into the ear of one of his godliest deacons, and he scarcely knows how he is kept back from the outrage. He meets a pure maiden who has just been received into Church membership, and who is full of reverence for her spiritual guide, and he can scarcely keep himself from interjecting lewd suggestions into her spotless mind. He is prompted to hiss atheism into the ear of an aged saint, who has been accustomed to treasure every syllable of comfort he has addressed to her. When he passes a group of drunken sailors he has a terrible wish to join himself to their company, and bandy obscene jests with them.

Of this interview in the forest Roger Chillingworth soon had suspicion, if not actual knowledge. Like a haunting shadow, he prepares to follow them in their journey across the sea. Before many days are over, to the horror of the intended fugitives, it is clear that he has arranged for himself a passage in the same vessel by which they have planned to go. At this stage in the history a new governor was to be invested, and Arthur Dimmesdale was appointed to preach the election sermon. He feels bound to fulfil this duty before taking his flight. The sermon is delivered with extraordinary pathos to a crowded meeting-house, and makes an amazing impression upon the hearers. In the crowd outside are Hester and Pearl, listening to the distant cadences of the preacher's voice, and feeling that they belong to another world than that in which the preacher is the centre of attraction. As the procession returns from the church to the market-place, Arthur Dimmesdale suddenly leaves his place amongst its dignitaries, calls Hester and Pearl to his side, and in defiance of the deprecation of Roger Chillingworth, who feels that his power as torturer will be destroyed by the confession, with pale face and tottering knees mounts the place where Hester had once stood alone. Tearing away the ministerial band from his breast, he exhibits the burning symbol, the sharper and more terrible counterpart of that worn by Hester, written there. Roger Chillingworth feels that in this act the victim, whose awful wound he has been gleefully fretting for years, has escaped him. The sin proves itself a sin unto death, and in the act of making his confession, his soul attains a long waited for and merciful release.

The persons and the groups of persons in this thrilling romance represent influences providentially appointed to stimulate the laggard conscience to the ever present task from which it shrinks—Brocken shadows, may we not call them, of the common conscience of the race? The moral sense of the community, accustomed to show itself at that primitive period in rude, coarse protests and manifestoes against sexual laxity and all other deadly sins, was essentially right at its core, and put its wall of fire for a defence around the sanctities of the family. Its severities were a just reminder of the divine wrath, which has declared itself against sin; and weak and wavering consciences, like that of the backsliding minister, need to be stung and stimulated by the common conscience, so that unreality may be cast aside, and the salvation of the soul wrought out with fear and trembling. And then Hester stands before him, or flits to and fro with her child, a mute appeal to his sense of honour, and an object lesson of the milder stripes laid upon those to whom concealment is no longer a necessity, and who bear the just reproaches of their transgressions. She carries alone the shame of the past, and at heart suffers less than the man, who is leading a life that is to a great degree false. The very distance he was compelled to observe in his public encounters with her did constant violence to his own sense of truth. And the part played by Pearl is not without its significance in the moral scheme of the story. By her strange reserve and mocking laughter, by the semi-prophetic discernments peculiar to childish innocence, she puts a barrier of ice between herself and the minister, whose instincts of fatherhood are immolated at the base dictates of falsehood and expediency. This strange child seems scarcely human till Arthur Dimmesdale, by his last confession, has made himself of the same circle as Hester and herself. Her kiss on the scaffold is the minister's absolution, and the birth of a new life in her own soul. The voice of this elfish child was a voice appealing to his conscience, and helping his final redemption. In the cold, studious, persistent malice of Roger Chillingworth, the minister recognised a terrible instrument needed in the process of subduing his pride and bringing himself back to spiritual hope, and with his last breath thanks God for the stupendous pressure put upon him by this old man, who, however much wronged at the outset, had for years set himself to do work that seems simply fiendish. But all these forms through which the ever burning wrath against transgression visited him were less than the inward stripes he was compelled to lay upon his own soul. Indeed, his gratitude for the torture with which he has been plied through years shows that remorse is more cruel, envenomed, insatiable than the most ingenious agencies of outward revenge which wait about our pathway.

Obviously the theory worked out in these stories is that the paramount punishment of sin is inward. That is true for this life, and, by parity of reasoning, likewise for the life to come. A strange power is ever pressing the offending soul to the sternest and most awful acts of self-judgment. But man is treated as a compound being, and the flesh is not left out of the judicial reckoning. Conscience, chafing under the recollections of past misdoing, and working from an invisible centre outwards, undermines the strength, wrecks the fair fabric of the physical life, and puts even its burning brand of infamy and reproach upon the outward frame of the transgressor. The lictors who carry out the sentences of eternal right have their home within us, and the woeful stripes they inflict show at last through the vesture of the body.

The emphasis Hawthorne puts upon the obligation to confess sin is significant. In his conception of religion the act of confessing sin becomes, if not a sufficient, at least the best practicable atonement. Perhaps the antinomianism sometimes found in the New England Churches, which makes light of the human conditions of salvation, may have suggested the necessity for a strong testimony on this subject, such as is borne in many of his writings. Hester gained in both personal character and the respect of the community by the open reprobation to which she was subjected. The love of her child threatened to leave her when she wished to cover up the errors of the past, and it was only after she made some vague admission of her sin, under the parable of meeting the black man in the forest, that the heart of Pearl could rest in her. Such comfort and healing had she found in wearing the symbol which openly announced her disgrace, that after Dimmesdale's death, and when Pearl was married and settled in a far off land, she came back to live in the old cottage by the beach, and put the old symbol upon her dress, and to extreme age lived on as the ministering angel of her neighbours. Whilst the offending minister continued in the odour of a spurious sanctity, he sank every day into the deeper mire of the pit, and it was in a confession open as the noonday that he found momentary rest, followed by the absolving release of death. In his last moments the preacher declares that he can scarcely hope to be a companion spirit with Hester in a purer sphere, for their separation from each other in the life to come may be the penalty of their violated reverence for each other's souls here. The law to be satisfied is strict and eternal; no term can be put to the disabilities engendered by sin, and in the farewell words of the minister, as well as in the reassumption by Hester of the discarded badge, there is a touch of inevitable melancholy, and even a suggestion of mild despair. Confession cannot do all we expect, and there are limits to its efficacy. At the same time, we need the lesson of the romance that there can be no healing for the conscience which does not begin in absolute truth of lip and of life.

One great defect makes itself felt—in the undeclared theology which forms a subtle framework behind most of Hawthorne's stories. Without a compensating doctrine of sacrifice and mediation, it is scarcely to be wondered at that the strict and sustained introspection he delineates should end in a remorse scarcely distinguishable from insanity. The balm of atoning love is needed to heal the conscience, or the solitary and continuous contemplation of the past must, sooner or later, have one sure and frightful result. If sin is punished by the conscience, and the conscience itself is a direct instrument of the divine will, sin must be dealt with by some method which gives a due and fitting place to the principle of righteousness. Hawthorne is a stern and solemn schoolmaster, who makes us feel our need of an atonement which satisfies the claim of both justice and love. Said Roger Chillingworth, looking darkly at the clergyman, who is just mounting the scaffold to openly avow the sin of the past, "Hadst thou sought the whole earth over, there was not one place so secret, no high place, no lowly place where thou couldst have escaped me, save on this very scaffold." The demand for confession is inexorable, and there can be no salvation without moral honesty; but surely the place where we bow in sackcloth and ashes, the altar at which we find reconciliation with God and peace with our consciences, needs a higher consecration than that of our penitential tears. Conscience, no less than the divine righteousness which it reflects, asks something more. To come awhile under the guidance of a man of extraordinary insight into the workings of the moral life, to watch that life as his imagination makes invisible spiritual histories visible to us, without keeping at the same time the fact of redemption by divine love in view, makes the very flesh creep with horror.

The wise, solemn, sagacious ethic of Hawthorne, hidden not infrequently under the veil of fantasy and romance, is a much needed corrective to the ribaldry of those fools of an ephemeral fiction who make a mock at sin, and have no sense of its criminality before God. He dramatises with transcendent skill some of those great facts of human nature which are at the very roots of all theology.

W. D. Howells, "Hawthorne's Hester Prynne," in *Heroines of Fiction* (New York: Harpers, 1901), I, 161-174.

There had been among the friendlier prophets overseas a vague expectation that the genuine American fiction, when it came, would be somehow aesthetically responsive to our vast continental spaces and the mighty forces that were taming the forests and prairies, the lakes and rivers, to the use of man. But when it came, the American fiction which owed nothing to English models differed from English fiction in nothing so much as its greater refinement, its subtler beauty, and its delicate perfection of form. While Dickens was writing in England, Hawthorne was writing in America; and for all the ostensible reasons the romances of Hawthorne ought to have been rude, shapeless, provisional, the novels of Dickens ought to have been fastidiously elect in method and material and of the last scrupulosity in literary finish. That is, they ought to have been so, if the obvious inferences from an old civilization ripened in its native air, and the same civilization so newly conditioned under alien skies that it seemed essentially new, were the right inferences. But there were some facts which such hasty conclusions must have ignored: chiefly the fact that the first impulse of a new artistic life is to escape from crude conditions; and subordinately the fact that Hawthorne was writing to and from a sensitiveness of nerve in the English race that it had never known in its English home. We need not deny the greatness of Dickens in order to feel a patriotic content in the reflection that he represented English fiction in his time, and Hawthorne represented American fiction, as with the same implications Carlyle represented English thought and Emerson American thought.

I

Apart from the racial differences of the two writers, there was the widest possible difference of ideal in Dickens and Hawthorne; the difference between the romanticistic and the romantic, which is almost as great as that between the romantic and the realistic. Romance, as in Hawthorne, seeks the effect of reality in visionary conditions; romanticism, as in Dickens, tries for a visionary effect in actual conditions. These different ideals eventuated with Hawthorne in characters being, doing, and suffering as vitally as any we have known in the world; with Dickens in types, outwardly of our every-day acquaintance, but inwardly moved by a single propensity and existing to justify in some fantastic excess the attribution of their controlling quality. In their mystical world, withdrawn afar from us in the past, or apart from us in anomalous conditions, the characters of Hawthorne speak and act for themselves, and from an authentic individuality compact of good and evil; in times, terms, and places analogous to those in which actual men have their being, the types of Dickens are always speaking for him, in fulfilment of a mechanical conception and a rigid limitation of their function in the drama. They are, in every sense, *parts*, and Hawthorne's creations are *persons*, rounded, whole. This fact appears in what has already been shown of Dickens, and it will appear concerning Hawthorne from any critical study of his romances.

II

There is, of course, a choice in Hawthorne's romances, and I myself prefer "The Blithedale Romance" and "The Scarlet Letter" to "The Marble Faun" and "The House of the Seven Gables." * * * From the first there is no affectation of shadowy uncertainty in the setting of the great tragedy of "The Scarlet Letter." As nearly as can be, the scenes of the several events are ascertained, and are identified with places in actual Boston. With a like inward sense of strong reality in his material, and perhaps compelled to its expression by that force in the concept, each detail of the drama, in motive, action, and character, is substantiated, so that from first to last it is visible, audible, tangible. From Hester Prynne in her prison—before she goes out to stand with her unlawful child in her arms and the scarlet letter on her breast before the Puritan magistracy and ministry and people, and be charged by the child's own father, as her pastor, to give him up to like ignominy—to Hester Prynne, kneeling over her dying paramour, on the scaffold, and mutely helping him to own his sin before all that terrible little world, there is the same strong truth beating with equal pulse from the core of the central reality, and clothing all its manifestations in the forms of credible, of indisputable personality.

In its kind the romance remains sole, and it is hard to see how it shall ever be surpassed, or even companioned. It is not without faults, without quaint foibles of manner which strike one oddly in the majestic movement of the story; but with the exception of the love-child or sin-child, Pearl, there is no character, important or unimportant, about which you are asked to make believe: they are all there to speak and act for themselves, and they do not need the help of your fancy. They are all of a verity so robust that if one comes to declare Hester chief among them, it is with instant misgivings for the right of her secret paramour, Arthur Dimmesdale, and her secret husband, Roger Chillingworth, to that sorrowful supremacy. A like doubt besets the choice of any one moment of her history as most specific, most signal. Shall it be that dread moment on the pillory, when she faces the crowd with her child in her arms, and her lover adjures her to name its father, while her old husband on the borders of the throng waits and listens?

"The Rev. Mr. Dimmesdale bent his head, in silent prayer, as it seemed, and then came forward. 'Hester Prynne,' said he, leaning over the balcony and looking down steadfastly into her eyes, . . . 'if thou feelest it to be for thy soul's peace, and that thy earthly punishment will thereby be made more effectual to salvation, I charge thee to speak out the name of thy fellow-sinner and fellow-sufferer! Be not silent from any mistaken pity and tenderness for him; for, believe me, Hester, though he were to step down from a high place, and stand there beside thee, on thy pedestal of shame, yet better were it so, than to hide a guilty heart through life. . . . Heaven hath granted thee an open ignominy, that thereby thou mayest work out an open triumph over the evil within thee, and the sorrow without. Take heed how thou deniest to him—who, perchance, hath not the courage to grasp it for himself—the bitter, but wholesome, cup that is now presented to thy lips!' The young pastor's voice was tremulously sweet, rich, deep, and broken. The feeling that it so evidently manifested, rather than the direct purport of the words, caused it to vibrate within all hearts, and brought the listeners into one accord of sympathy. Even the poor baby, at Hester's bosom, was affected by the same influence; for it directed its hitherto vacant gaze towards Mr. Dimmesdale, and held up its little arms, with a half-pleased, half-plaintive murmur. . . . Hester shook her head. 'Woman, transgress not beyond the limits of Heaven's mercy!' cried the Rev. Mr. Wilson, more harshly than before. . . . 'Speak out the name! That, and thy repentance, may avail to take the scarlet letter off thy breast.' 'Never!' replied Hester Prynne, looking, not at Mr. Wilson, but into the deep and troubled eyes of the younger clergyman. 'It is too deeply branded. Ye cannot take it off. And would that I might endure his agony, as well as mine!' 'Speak, woman!' said another voice, coldly and sternly, proceeding from the crowd about the scaffold. 'Speak; and give your child a father!' 'I will not speak!' answered Hester, turning pale as death, but responding to this voice, which she too surely recognized. 'And my child must seek a heavenly Father; she shall never know an earthy one!' 'She will not speak!' murmured Mr. Dimmesdale, who, leaning over the balcony, with his hand upon his heart, had awaited the result of his appeal. He now drew back, with a long respiration. 'Wondrous strength and generosity of a woman's heart! She will not speak!' "

III

One could hardly read this aloud without some such gasp and catch as must have been in the minister's own breath as he spoke. Yet piercing as the pathos of it is, it wants the ripened richness of anguish, which the passing years of suffering bring to that meeting between Hester Prynne and Arthur Dimmesdale in the forest, when she tells him that his physician and closest companion is her husband, and that Chillingworth's subtlety has divined the minister's relation to herself and her child. The reader must go to the book itself for a full comprehension of the passage, but no one can fail of its dramatic sense who recalls that Hester has by this time accustomed the little Puritan community to the blazon of her scarlet letter, and in her lonely life of usefulness has conciliated her fellow-townsfolk almost to forgiveness and forgetfulness of her sin. She has gone in and out among them, still unaccompanied, but no longer unfriended, earning her bread with her needle and care of the sick, and Dimmesdale has held aloof from her like the rest, except for their one meeting by midnight, when he stands with her and their child upon the scaffold, and in that ghastly travesty forecasts the union before the people which forms the catastrophe of the tremendous story.

In certain things "The Scarlet Letter," which was the first of Hawthorne's romances, is the modernest and maturest. The remoteness of the time and the strangeness of the Puritan conditions authorize that stateliness of the dialogue which he loved. The characters may imaginably say "methinks" and "peradventure," and the other things dear to the characters of the historical romancer; the narrator himself may use an antiquated or unwonted phrase in which he finds color, and may eschew the short-cuts and informalities of our actual speech, without impeaching himself of literary insincerity. In fact, he may heighten by these means the effect he is seeking; and if he will only keep human nature strongly and truly in mind, as Hawthorne does in "The Scarlet Letter," we shall gratefully allow him a privilege which may or may not be law. Through the veil of the quaint parlance, and under the seventeenth-century costuming, we see the human heart beating there the same as in our own time and in all times, and the antagonistic motives working which have governed human conduct from the beginning and shall govern it forever, world without end.

Hester Prynne and Arthur Dimmesdale are no mere types of open shame and secret remorse. It is never concealed from us that he was a man whose high and pure soul had its strongest contrast in the nature

"Mixt with cunning sparks of hell,"

in which it was tabernacled for earth. It is still less hidden that, without one voluntary lure or wicked art, she was of a look and make to win him with the love that was their undoing. "He was a person of a very striking aspect, with a wide, lofty, and impending brow; large, brown, melancholy eyes, and a mouth which, unless he compressed it, was apt to be tremulous. . . . The young woman was tall, with a figure of perfect elegance on a large scale. She had dark and abundant hair, so glossy that it threw off the sunshine with a gleam, and a face which, besides being beautiful from the regularity of feature and richness of complexion, had the impressiveness belonging to a marked brow and deep black eyes. She was ladylike, too, after the manner of the feminine gentility of those days; characterized by a certain state and dignity, rather than by the delicate, evanescent, and indescribable grace which is now recognized as its indication." They were both of their time and place, materially as well as spiritually; their lives were under the law, but their natures had once been outside it, and might be again. The shock of this simple truth can hardly be less for the witness, when, after its slow and subtle evolution, it is unexpectedly flashed upon him, than it must have been for the guilty actors in this drama, when they recognize that, in spite of all their open and secret misery, they are still lovers, and capable of claiming for the very body of their sin a species of justification.

We all know with what rich but noiseless preparation the consummate artist sets the scene of his most consummate effect; and how, when Hester and Pearl have parted with Roger Chillingworth by the shore, and then parted with each other in the forest, the mother to rest in the shadow of the trees, and the child to follow her fancies in play, he invokes the presence of Arthur Dimmesdale, as it were, silently, with a waft of the hand.

"Slowly as the minister walked, he had almost gone by before Hester Prynne could gather voice enough to attract his observation. At length, she succeeded. 'Arthur Dimmesdale!' she said, faintly at first; then louder, but hoarsely, 'Arthur Dimmesdale!' 'Who speaks?' answered the minister. . . . He made a step nigher, and discovered the scarlet letter. 'Hester! Hester Prynne!' said he. 'Is it thou? Art thou in life?' 'Even so!' she answered. 'In such life as has been mine these seven years past! And thou, Arthur Dimmesdale, dost thou yet live?' . . . So strangely did they meet, in the dim wood, that it was like the first encounter, in the world beyond the grave, of two spirits who had been intimately connected in their former life, but now stood coldly shuddering, in mutual dread; as not yet familiar with their state nor wonted to the companionship of disembodied beings. . . . It was with fear, and tremulously, and, as it were, by a slow, reluctant necessity, that Arthur Dimmesdale put forth his hand, chill as death, and touched the chill hand of Hester Prynne. The grasp, cold as it was, took away what was dreariest in the interview. They now felt themselves, at least, inhabitants of the same sphere. Without a word more spoken—neither he nor she assuming the guidance, but with an unexpected consent—they glided back into the shadow of the woods, whence Hester had emerged, and sat down on the heap of moss where she and Pearl had before been sitting. . . . 'Hester,' said he, 'hast thou found peace?' She smiled drearily, looking down upon her bosom. 'Hast thou?' she asked. 'None!—nothing but despair!' he answered. 'What else could I look for, being what I am, and leading such a life as mine?' . . . 'The people reverence thee,' said Hester. 'And surely thou workest good among them. Doth this bring thee no comfort?' 'More misery, Hester!'—only the more misery!' answered the clergyman, with a bitter smile. . . . 'Had I one friend—or were it my worst enemy—to whom, when sickened with the praises of all other men, I could daily betake myself, and be known as the vilest of all sinners, methinks my soul might keep itself alive thereby. Even thus much of truth would save me! But, now, it is all falsehood!—all emptiness! all death!' Hester Prynne looked into his face, but hesitated to speak. Yet, uttering his long-restrained emotions so vehemently as he did, his words here offered her the very point of circumstance in which to interpose what she came to say. She conquered her fears, and spoke. 'Such a friend as thou hast even now wished for,' said she, 'with whom to weep over thy sin, thou hast in me, the partner of it!'—Again she hesitated, but brought out the words with an effort.—'Thou has long had such an enemy, and dwellest with him, under the same roof!' The minister started to his feet, gasping for breath, and clutching at his heart, as if he would have torn it out of his bosom. 'Ha! What sayest thou!' cried he. 'An enemy!' And under my own roof! What mean you?' . . . 'O Arthur,' cried she, 'forgive me! In all things else I have striven to be true! Truth was the one virtue which I might have held fast, and did hold fast, through all extremity; save when thy good—thy life—thy fame—were put in question! Then I consented to a deception. But a lie is never good, even though death threaten on the other side! Dost thou not see what I would say? That old man!—the physician!—he whom they call Roger Chillingworth!—he was my husband!' The minister looked at her for an instant, with all that violence of passion which—intermixed, in more shapes than one, with his higher, purer, softer qualities—was, in fact, the portion of him which the Devil claimed, and through which he sought to win the rest. Never was there a blacker or fiercer frown than Hester now encountered. For the brief space that it lasted, it was a dark transfiguration. But his character had been so much enfeebled by suffering, that even its lower energies were incapable of more than a temporary struggle. He sank down on the ground, and buried his face in his hands. . . . 'O Hester Prynne, thou little, little knowest all the horror of this thing! And the shame!—the indelicacy!—the horrible ugliness of this exposure of a sick and guilty heart to the very eye that would gloat over it! Woman, woman, thou art accountable for this! I cannot forgive thee!' 'Thou shalt forgive me!' cried Hester, flinging herself on the fallen leaves beside him. 'Let God punish. Thou shalt forgive!' With sudden and desperate tenderness, she threw her arms around him, and pressed his head against her bosom; little caring though his cheek rested on the scarlet letter. He would have released himself, but strove in vain to do so. Hester would not set him free, lest he should look her sternly in the face. All the world has frowned upon her—for seven long years had it frowned upon this lonely woman—and still she bore it all, nor even once turned away her firm, sad eyes. Heaven, likewise, had frowned upon her, and she had not died. But the frown of this pale, weak, sinful, and sorrow-stricken man was what Hester could not bear and live! 'Wilt thou yet forgive me?' she repeated, over and over again. 'Wilt thou not frown? Wilt thou forgive?' 'I do forgive you, Hester!' replied the minister, at length, with a deep utterance, out of an abyss of sadness, but no anger. 'I freely forgive you now. May God forgive us both! We are not, Hester, the worst sinners in the world. There is one worse than even the polluted priest! That old man's revenge has been blacker than my sin! He has violated, in cold blood, the sanctity of a human heart. Thou and I, Hester, never did so!' 'Never, never!' whispered she. 'What we did had a consecration of its own. We felt it so! We said so to each other! Hast thou forgotten it?' 'Hush, Hester!' said Arthur Dimmesdale, rising from the ground. 'No; I have not forgotten!' . . . 'Thou must dwell no longer with this man,' said Hester, slowly and firmly. 'Thy heart must be no longer under his evil eye!' 'It were far worse than death!' replied the minister. 'But how to avoid it? What choice remains to me? Shall I lie down again on these withered leaves, where I cast myself when thou didst tell me what he was? Must I sink down there, and die at once?' 'Alas, what a ruin has befallen thee!' said Hester, with the tears gushing into her eyes. 'Wilt thou die for very weakness? There is no other cause.' 'The judgment of God is on me,' answered the conscience-striken priest. 'It is too mighty for me to struggle with!' 'Heaven would show mercy,' rejoined Hester, 'hadst thou but the strength to take advantage of it.' 'Be thou strong for me,' answered he. 'Advise me what to do.' 'Is the world, then, so narrow?' exclaimed Hester Prynne, fixing her deep eyes on the minister's, and instinctively exercising a magnetic power over a spirit so shattered and subdued that it could hardly hold itself erect. 'Whither leads yonder forest track? . . . Deeper it goes, and deeper into the wilderness, less plainly to be seen at every step, until, some few miles hence, the yellow leaves will show no vestige of the white man's tread. . . . Is there not shade enough in all this boundless forest to hide thy heart from the gaze of Roger Chillingworth?' 'Yes, Hester; but only under the fallen leaves,' replied the minister, with a sad smile. 'Then there is the broad pathway of the sea!' continued Hester. 'It brought thee hither. If thou choose, it will bear thee back again.'. . . 'O Hester!' cried Arthur Dimmesdale, in whose eyes a fitful light, kindled by her enthusiasm, flashed up and died away, 'thou tellest of running a race to a man whose knees are tottering beneath him! I must die here! There is not the strength or courage left me to venture into the wide, strange, difficult world, alone!'. . . 'Thou shalt not go alone!' answered she, in a deep whisper. Then, all was spoken."

There is a greatness in this scene which is unmatched, I think, in the book, and, I was almost ready to say, out of it. At any rate, I believe we can find its parallel only in some of the profoundly impassioned pages of the Russian novelists who, casting aside all the common adjuncts of art, reveal us to ourselves in the appeal from their own naked souls.

Hawthorne had another ideal than theirs, and a passing love of style, and the meaning of the music of words. For the most part, he makes us aware of himself, of his melancholy grace and sombre power; we feel his presence in every passage, however deeply, however occultly, dramatic; he overshadows us, so that we touch and see through him. But here he is almost out of it; only a few phrases of comment, so fused in feeling so fused in feeling with the dialogue that they are like the voice of a chorus, remind us of him.

It is the most exalted instant of the tragedy, it is the final evolution of Hester Prynne's personality. In this scene she dominates by virtue of whatever is womanly and typical in her, and no less by what is personal and individual. In what follows, she falls like Dimmesdale and Chillingworth under the law of their common doom, and becomes a figure on the board where for once she seemed to direct the game.

In all fiction one could hardly find a character more boldly, more simply, more quietly imagined. She had done that which in the hands of a feeble or falser talent would have been suffered or made to qualify her out of all proportion and keeping with life. But her transgression does not qualify her, as transgression never does unless it becomes habit. She remains exterior and superior to it, a life of other potentialities, which in her narrow sphere she fulfils. What she did has become a question between her and her Maker, who apparently does not deal with it like a Puritan. The obvious lesson of the contrasted fates of Dimmesdale and herself is that to own sin is to disown it, and that it cannot otherwise be expropriated and annulled. Yet, in Hester's strong and obstinate endurance of her punishment there is publicity but not confession; and perhaps there is a lesson of no slighter meaning in the inference that ceasing to do evil is, after all, the most that can be asked of human nature. Even that seems to be a good deal, and in "The Scarlet Letter" it is a stroke of mastery to show that it is not always ours to cease to do evil, but that in extremity we need the help of the mystery "not ourselves, that makes for righteousness," and that we may call Chance or that we may call God, but that does not change in essence or puissance whatever name we give it.

George Woodberry, ***Nathaniel Hawthorne*** **(Boston: Houghton Mifflin, 1902), pp. 189-203.**

"The Scarlet Letter" is a great and unique romance, standing apart by itself in fiction; there is nothing else quite like it. Of all Hawthorne's works it is most identified with his genius in popular regard, and it has the peculiar power that is apt to invest the first work of an author in which his originality finds complete artistic expression. It is seldom that one can observe so plainly the different elements that are primary in a writer's endowment coalesce in the fully developed work of genius; yet in this romance there is nothing either in method or perception which is not to be found in the earlier tales; what distinguishes it is the union of art and intuition as they had grown up in Hawthorne's practice and had developed a power to penetrate more deeply into life. Obviously at the start there is the physical object in which his imagination habitually found its spring, the fantastically embroidered scarlet letter on a woman's bosom which he had seen in the Puritan group described in "Endicott and the Red Cross." It had been in his mind for years, and his thoughts had centred on it and wandered out from it, tracking its mystery. It has in itself that decorative quality, which he sought in the physical object,—the brilliant and rich effect, startling to the eye and yet more to the imagination as it blazes forth with a secret symbolism and almost intelligence of its own. It multiplies itself, as the tale unfolds, with greater intensity and mysterious significance and dread suggestion, as if in mirrors set round about it,—in the slowly disclosed and fearful stigma on the minister's hidden heart over which he ever holds his hand, where it has become flesh of his flesh; in the growing elf-like figure of the child, who, with her eyes always fastened on the open shame of the letter on her mother's bosom or the hidden secret of the hand on her father's breast, has become herself the symbol, half revealed and half concealed, is dressed in it, as every reader remembers, and fantastically embodies it as if the thing had taken life in her; and, as if this were not enough, the scarlet letter, at a climax of the dark story, lightens forth over the whole heavens as a symbol of what cannot be hid even in the intensest blackness of night. The continual presence of the letter seems to have burnt into Hawthorne's own mind, till at the end of the narrative he says he would gladly erase its deep print from the brain where long meditation had fixed it. In no other work is the physical symbol so absorbing present, so reduplicated, so much alive in itself. It is the brand of sin on life. Its concrete vividness leads the author also by a natural compulsion as well as an artistic instinct to display his story in that succession of high-wrought scenes, tableaux, in fact, which was his characteristic method of narrative, picturesque, pictorial, almost to be described as theatrical in spectacle. The background, also, as in the early tales, is of the slightest, no more than will suffice for the acting of the drama as a stage setting sympathetic with the central scene,—a town, with a prison, a meeting-house, a pillory, a governor's house, other habitations on a street, a lonely cottage by the shore, the forest round about all; and for occasion and accessories, only a woman's sentence, the incidental death of Winthrop unmarked in itself, a buccaneering ship in the harbor, Indians, Spanish sailors, rough matrons, clergy; this will serve, for such was Hawthorne's fine economy, knowing that this story was one in which every materialistic element must be used at its lowest tone. Though the scene lay in this world, it was but transitory scaffolding; the drama was one of the eternal life.

The characteristic markings of Hawthorne's genius are also to be found in other points. He does not present the scene of life, the crowd of the world with its rich and varied fullness of interest, complexity of condition and movement, and its interwoven texture of character, event, and fate, such as the great novelists use; he has only a few individual figures, and these are simplified by being exhibited, not in their complete lives, but only in that single aspect of their experience which was absorbing to themselves and constituted the life they lived in the soul itself. There are three characters, Hester, the minister, and the physician; and a fourth, the child, who fulfills the function of the chorus in the old drama, in part a living comment, in part a spectator and medium of sympathy with the main actors. In all four of these that trait of profound isolation in life, so often used before in the earlier tales, is strongly brought out; about each is struck a circle which separates not only one from another, but from all the world, and in the midst of it, as in a separate orb, each lives an unshared life. It is inherent, too, in such a situation that the mystery that had fascinated Hawthorne in so many forms, the secrecy of men's bosoms, should be a main theme in the treatment. He has also had recourse to that method of violent contrast which has been previously illustrated; on the one hand the publicity of detected wrongdoing, on the other the hidden and unsuspected fact; here the open shame and there the secret sin, whose sameness in a double life is expressed by the identity of the embroidered letter and the flesh-wrought stigma. But it is superfluous to illustrate further the genesis of this romance out of Hawthorne's art and matter in this earlier work, showing how naturally it rose by a concentration of his powers on a single theme that afforded them scope, intensity, and harmony at once. The new thing here is the power of his genius to penetrate, as was said above, deep into life.

The romance begins where common tales end. The crime has been committed; in it, in its motives, circumstances, explanation, its course of passion and human tide of life, Hawthorne takes no interest. All that is past, and, whatever it was, now exists only as sin; it has passed from the region of earthly fact into that of the soul, out of all that was temporal into the world where eternal things only are. Not crime, not passion, not the temptation and the fall, but only sin now staining the soul in consequence is the theme; and the course of the story concerns man's dealing with sin, in his own breast or the breasts of others. It is a study of punishment, of vengeance if one will; this is the secret of its gloom, for the idea of salvation, of healing, is but little present and is not felt; there is no forgiveness in the end, in any sense to dispel the darkness of evil or promise the dawn of new life in any one of these tortured souls. The sin of the lovers is not the centre of the story, but only its initial source; that sin breeds sin is the real principle of its being; the minister is not punished as a lover, but as the hypocrite that he becomes, and the physician is punished as the revenger that he becomes. Hester's punishment is visibly from the law, and illustrates the law's brutality, the coarse hand of man for justice, the mere physical blow meant to hurt and crush; it is man's social way of dealing with sin, and fails because it makes no connection with the soul; the victim rises above it, is emancipated from its ideas, transforms the symbol of disgrace into a message of mercy to all who suffer, and annuls the gross sentence by her own higher soul-power. The minister's punishment, also, is visibly from the physician, who illustrates man's individual way of dealing with sin in another; but it is not the minister's suffering under the hand of revenge working subtly in secret that arrests our attention; it is the physician's own degeneracy into a devil of hate through enjoyment of the sight and presence of this punishment, that stamps him into the reader's mind as a type of the failure of such a revenge. "Vengeance is mine, saith the Lord" is the text here blazed forth. In the sphere of the soul human law and private revenge have no place. It is in that sphere that Hester is seen suffering in the touch of the child, being unable to adjust the broken harmonies of life; her incapacity to do that is the ever- present problem that keeps her wound open, not to be stanched, but rather breaking with a more intimate pain with the unfolding of little Pearl's wide-eyed soul. In that sphere, too, the minister is seen suffering—not for the original sin, for that is overlaid, whelmed, forgotten, by the second and heavier transgression of hypocrisy, cowardice, desertion,—but merely from self-knowledge, the knowledge that he is a living lie. The characters, so treated, become hardly more than types, humanly outlined in figure, costume, and event, symbolic pictures of states of the soul, so simplified, so intense, so elementary as to belong to a phantasmagoric rather than a realistic world, to that mirror of the soul which is not found in nature but in spiritual self-consciousness, where the soul is given back to itself in its nakedness, as in a secret place.

Yet it is in the sense of reality that this romance is most intense. It is a truthful story, above all; and only its truth could make it tolerable to the imagination and heart, if indeed it be tolerable to the heart at all. A part of this reality is due to the fact that there is a story here that lies outside of the moral scheme in which Hawthorne's conscious thought would confine it; the human element in it threatens from time to time to break the mould of thought and escape from bondage, because, simple as the moral scheme is, human life is too complex to be solved by it even in this small world of the three guilty ones and the child. This weakness of the moral scheme, this rude strength of human nature, this sense of a larger solution, are most felt when Hawthorne approaches the love element, and throughout in the character of Hester, in whom alone human nature retains a self-assertive power. The same thing is felt vaguely, but certainly, in the lack of sympathy between Hawthorne and the Puritan environment he depicts. He presents the community itself, its common people, its magistrates and clergy, its customs, temper, and atmosphere, as forbidding, and he has no good word for it; harshness characterizes it, and that trait discredits its ideals, its judgements, and its entire interpretation of life. Hester, outcast from it, is represented as thereby enfranchised from its narrowness, enlightened, escaped into a world of larger truth:—

"The world's law was no law for her mind. It was an age in which the human intellect, newly emancipated, had taken a more active and a wider range than for many centuries before. Men of the sword had overthrown nobles and kings. Men bolder than these had overthrown and rearranged—not actually, but within the sphere of theory, which was their most real abode—the whole system of ancient prejudice, wherewith was linked much of ancient principle. Hester Prynne imbibed this spirit. She assumed a freedom of speculation, then common enough on the other side of the Atlantic, but which our forefathers, had they known it, would have held to be a deadlier crime than that stigmatized by the scarlet letter. In her lonesome cottage, by the sea-shore, thoughts visited her, such as dared to enter no other dwelling in New England; shadowy guests, that would have been as perilous as demons to their entertainer, could they have been seen so much as knocking at her door."

This is the foregleam of the next age, felt in her mind, the coming of a larger day. Hawthorne does not develop this or justify it; he only states it as a fact of life. And in the motive of the story, the love of Hester and Arthur, much is left dim; but what is discerned threatens to be unmanageable within the limits of the scheme. Did Hester love her lover, and he love her, through those seven years in silence? Did either of them ever repent their passion for its own sake? And when Hester's womanhood came back in its bloom and her hair fell shining in the forest sunlight, and she took her lover, hand and head and form, in all his broken suffering to her affectionate care and caress, and planned the bold step that they go out together across the seas and live in each other's lives like lovers in truth and reality,—was this only the resurrection of a moment or the firm vital force of a seven years' silent passion? Had either of them ever repented, though one was a coward and the other a condemned and public criminal before the law, and both had suffered? Was not the true sin, as is suggested, the source of all this error, the act of the physician who had first violated Hester's womanhood in a loveless marriage as he had now in Arthur's breast "violated in cold blood the sanctity of a human heart"? "Thou and I," says Arthur, "never did so." The strange words follow, strange for Hawthorne to have written, but better attesting his truth to human nature than all his morality:—

"Never, never!" whispered she. "What we did had a consecration of its own. We felt it so! We said so to each other! Hast thou forgotten it?"

"Hush, Hester!" said Arthur Dimmesdale, rising from the ground. "No; I have not forgotten!"

That confession is the stroke of genius in the romance that humanizes it with a thrill that is felt throughout every page of the stubborn, dark, harsh narrative of misery. It was not a sin against love that had been committed; it was a sin against the soul; and the sin against the soul lay in the lack of confession, which becomes the cardinal situation of the romance solved in the minister's dying acknowledgment. But the love problem is never solved, just as the hate problem in the physician is never solved; both Hester and Roger Chillingworth, one with her mystery of enduring love, the other with his mystery of insatiable hatred, are left with the issue, the meaning of their lives inexplicable, untold. Yet it is from the presence of these elements in the story that something of its intense reality comes.

It remains true, however, that the essential reality lies in the vivid sense of sin, and its experience in conscience. Hawthorne has not given a historical view of New England life; such a village, with such a tragedy, never existed, in that environing forest of the lone seacoast; but he has symbolized historical New England by an environment that he created round a tragedy that he read in the human heart, and in this tragedy itself he was able also to symbolize New England life in its internal features. One thing stood plainly out in our home Puritanism,—spirituality; the transcendent sense of the reality of the soul's life with God, its conscience, its perils, and its eternal issue. Spirituality remained the inheritance of the New England blood; and Hawthorne, who was no Puritan in doctrine or sympathy even, was Puritan in temperament, and hence to him, too, spirituality in life was its main element. He took that sin of passion which has ever been held typical of sin against the purity of the soul's nature, and transformed it into the symbol of all sin, and in its manifestation revolved the aspects of sin as a presence in the soul after the act,—the broken law disturbing life's external harmonies but working a worse havoc within, mining all with corruption there, while it infects with disease whatever approaches it from without. It is by its moral universality that the romance takes hold of the imagination; the scarlet letter becomes only a pictorial incident, but while conscience, repentance, confession, the modes of punishment, and the modes of absolution remain instant and permanent facts in the life of the soul, many a human heart will read in this book as in a manual of its own intimate hours.

The romance is thus essentially a parable of the soul's life in sin; in its narrower scope it is the work of the moral intellect allegorizing its view of life; and where creative genius enters into it, in the Shakespearean sense of life in its own right, it tends to be a larger and truer story breaking the bonds of its religious scheme. It has its roots in Puritanism, but it is only incidentally a New England tale; its substance is the most universal experience of human nature in religious life, taking its forms only, its local habitation and name, from the Puritan colony in America, and these in a merely allegorical, not historical manner. Certain traits, however, ally it more closely to New England Puritanism. It is a relentless tale; the characters are singularly free from self-pity, and accept their fate as righteous; they never forgave themselves, they show no sign of having forgiven one another; even God's forgiveness is left under a shadow in futurity. They have sinned against the soul, and something implacable in evil remains. The minister's dying words drop a dark curtain over all.

"Hush, Hester, hush!" said he, with tremulous solemnity. "The law we broke!—the sin here so awfully revealed!—let these alone be in thy thoughts! I fear! I fear! It may be that, when we forgot our God,—when we violated our reverence each for the other's soul,—it was thenceforth vain to hope that we could meet hereafter, in an everlasting and pure reunion."

Mercy is but a hope. There is also a singular absence of prayer in the book. Evil is presented as a thing without remedy, that cannot change its nature. The child, even, being the fruit of sin, can bring, Hester and Arthur doubt, no good for others or herself. In the scheme of Puritan thought, however, the atonement of Christ is the perpetual miracle whereby salvation comes, not only hereafter but in the holier life led here by grace. There is no Christ in this book. Absolution, so far as it is hinted at, lies in the direction of public confession, the efficacy of which is directly stated, but lamely nevertheless; it restores truth, but it does not heal the past. Leave the dead past to bury its dead, says Hawthorne, and go on to what may remain; but life once ruined is ruined past recall. So Hester, desirous of serving in her place the larger truth she has come to know, is stayed, says Hawthorne, because she "recognized the impossibility that any mission of divine and mysterious truth should be confided to a woman stained with sin, bowed down with shame, or even burdened with a life-long sorrow." That was never the Christian gospel nor the Puritan faith. Indeed, Hawthorne here and elsewhere anticipates those ethical views which are the burden of George Eliot's moral genius, and contain scientific pessimism. This stoicism, which was in Hawthorne, is a primary element in his moral nature, in him as well as in his work; it is visited with few touches of tenderness and pity; the pity one feels is not in him, it is in the pitiful thing, which he presents objectively, sternly, unrelentingly. It must be confessed that as an artist he appears unsympathetic with his characters; he is a moral dissector of their souls, minute, unflinching, thorough, a vivisector here; and he is cold because he has passed sentence on them, condemned them. There is no sympathy with human nature in the book; it is a fallen and ruined thing suffering just pain in its dying struggle. The romance is steeped in gloom. Is it too much to suggest that in ignoring prayer, the atonement of Christ, and the work of the Spirit in men's hearts, the better part of Puritanism has been left out, and the whole life of the soul distorted? Sin in the soul, the scarlet flower from the dark soil, we see; but, intent on that, has not the eye, and the heart, too, forgotten the large heavens that ensphere all—even this evil flower—and the infinite horizons that reach off to the eternal distance from every soul as from their centre? This romance is the record of a prison-cell, unvisited by any ray of light save that earthly one which gives both prisoners to public ignominy; they are seen, but they do not see. These traits of the book, here only suggested, have kinship with the repelling aspects of Puritanism, both as it was and as Hawthorne inherited it in his blood and breeding; so, in its transcendent spirituality, and in that democracy which is the twin-brother of spirituality in all lands and cultures, by virtue of which Hawthorne here humiliates and strips the minister who is the type of the spiritual aristocrat in the community, there is the essence of New England; but, for all that, the romance is a partial story, an imperfect fragment of the old life, distorting, not so much the Puritan ideal—which were a little matter—but the spiritual life itself. Its truth, intense, fascinating, terrible as it is, is a half-truth, and the darker half; it is the shadow of which the other half is light; it is the wrath of which the other half is love. A book from which light and love are absent may hold us by its truth to what is dark in life; but, in the highest sense, it is a false book. It is a chapter in the literature of moral despair, and is perhaps most tolerated as a condemnation of the creed which, through imperfect comprehension, it travesties.

Theodore T. Munger, "Notes on The Scarlet Letter," *Atlantic Monthly*, 93 (April 1904), 524-535.

* * * What shall be said of the Scarlet Letter; where shall it be located in the realm of Letters? It is not a love story, nor a romance, nor an allegory, nor a parable, nor a historical novel, though it has something of each. It comes near being a dogma set in terms of real life, and made vivid by intense action; but Hawthorne cared nothing for dogma of any sort. What then shall it be called? It must go without classification. It is a study of a certain form of sin made graphic by conditions best calculated to intensify each feature. Mrs. Hawthorne said that during the six months he was writing it, his forehead wore a knot. So will the reader's, if he reads as carefully as Hawthorne wrote.

It was published in 1850, when Hawthorne was forty-six years of age. It has, first of all, this distinction: it is—as Mr. James says—"the finest piece of imaginative writing yet put forth in the country." In the half-century since, a true and full American literature has been produced; authors of high merit have secured a lasting place; and others of less merit have given us works of fiction that sell almost by the million, but none that are worthy to stand by the side of this short story of sin and shame and remorse. What is claimed for it in this country is freely accorded abroad, though, of course, no comparisons are made with the long annals of English literature, where there are names that defy comparison. It is, however, read more widely there than here, and is held in steadier estimate than we accord, who read as gregariously as sheep crop the grass. We simply state the consensus in which it is held in our American world of letters when we say that it is the most consummate work in literature yet produced in this country.

The explanation of the permanent high estimate of the Scarlet Letter—for it would be as safe to wager on it as on the Bank of England—is the absolute perfection of its art and corresponding subtilty and correctness of thought, and, not least, a style that both fascinates and commands. If it is criticised on slight points,—as that it has too much symbolism, that the story is mixed with parable, and the like,—we grant or deny as we see fit; but we brush all this aside, we turn to the book again and close it with a sigh, or something deeper than a sigh,—even thought, and pronounce it perfect.

It is a simple story, told of a simple age, Greek in its severity, having only four characters: a wife forgetful of her vows; a clergyman forgetful of more than his vows; a wronged husband, left in England, but brought forward; a little child,— these and no more, save the people, individually unimportant, but necessary to form a background for the tragedy. Boston is not yet half a century old, Puritan to the core, hot still with a hatred of the tyranny and sin it had crossed the ocean to escape, governed by the letter of Scripture wherein was found the command that an adulteress should die. But some mercy had begun to qualify the Hebrew code, and instead of death or branding with a hot iron, Hester Prynne was condemned to stand upon the pillory-platform, wearing upon her breast the letter A wrought in scarlet, not only then, but ever after. With her babe in her arms she faces the people, and sees her husband among them,—an old and learned man,—who unexpectedly appears and takes his place as an avenger. The real history of the tragedy begins when the young minister, Mr. Dimmesdale, is required by the magistrate to appeal to Hester to reveal the partner of her guilt. Dimmesdale is at no time in the story represented as wholly contemptible. However sinful his characters may be, Hawthorne always clothes them with a certain human dignity. From the first he is the victim of his sin,—suffering the tortures of remorse to a degree impossible to Hester, because to the first sin he added that of concealment and hypocrisy by continuing in his holy office; and, heavier than all, was the sense that he was dragging the cause, in both church and state, for which the colony was founded, down to the level of his own degradation. It was not for this that Hester, when adjured by him, refused to make the declaration for which he called, but for love only. The story, at the outset, is lifted out of all carnality. Shame and remorse have burned up that dross, until in time only the capacity to suffer is left, while in her heart love remains,—pure always, and made purer by acquiescence in her punishment and the discipline of motherhood. The story moves on, most human, but inexorable as fate. The scarlet letter on Hester's breast almost ceases to do its office. A sense of desert and undying love and pity make her shame endurable. But Dimmesdale finds no relief. The scarlet letter burns itself into his flesh, and he dies in late confession for love, if not for his soul.

It would be difficult to find elsewhere so close an analysis of the play of the soul in the supreme moments of life as that of the leading characters,—all brought to the logical conclusion of their history. The blending of spiritual insight and literary art forms one of those triumphs the like of which one may look for in vain until one reaches the great masters in drama. It also suggests a problem in theology that has vexed the souls of men from the beginning, and will continue to vex them so long as sin and conscience stand opposed to each other. The problem is that of forgiveness: it is ever fully won? The plot goes no further than their contrasted destiny. The curtain drops when the chief actor dies. If here and there it is lifted for a moment, or swept aside by some gust of irrepressible grief, it springs from hope, not from the main purpose. It is in Hester that riddance from sin comes nearest a possibility. Her acceptance and patient endurance of her penalty, without suffering it wholly to break her heart or her will, become a natural and real atonement that yields, if not peace, something of more value. The current of her life ran on in its natural channel in the light of day, before the eyes of the people. The contrast at the last between her strength and his weakness was not between a strong woman and a weak man,—each such by nature,—but between them as each came to be under the discipline of the seven years of experience so differently borne. Dimmesdale was not originally a weak man; had he been, the story would have lost point and emphasis, and would have sunk to the level of a vulgar scandal of every-day life. Hawthorne quickly lifts the narrative out of that region, and confines it to the world where only moral and spiritual forces fill the stage. But under the concealment of his sin Dimmesdale gave way at every point; all the sources of his strength were dried up by the hypocrisy in which he had wrapped himself, and he grew steadily weaker, while Hester gained a certain robustness of will without loss of her love. Hawthorne here comes very near preaching. Indeed, he seldom does anything else; it is the function of genius to preach. Give him a text, put on him the Geneva gown, and you have a preacher of universal orthodoxy fulfilling his calling with awful veracity.

But Hawthorne will not allow the tragedy to sink into the hopelessness of reprobation,—not that he cared for the doctrine one way or the other, but, as an interpreter of evil and as a literary artist, he could not leave Dimmesdale absolutely where his sin placed him; for, in one character, he saw that evil, simply because it is evil, is a mystery, and as an artist he could not map out human passion in mathematical lines. It had stripped Dimmesdale of all that was best, obscured his judgment, defeated his love, blinded him to the distinction between good and evil, overthrown his will, involved his body in the sin of his soul, and brought him to the verge of death; but something is left that revives as soon as he clasps the hand of his child, and—leaning on Hester—he mounts the scaffold where she at first had stood alone and taken on herself the punishment he should have shared with her. Under his decision to confess he revives, and begins to move aright. The scene changes. Each character is transformed. Confession begins to do its work. A far step is taken in the next word: " 'Is not this better,' murmured he, 'than what we dreamed of in the forest?' "—meaning flight together, at Hester's suggestion, for his sake. Here he regains something of himself; better to die a true man than to flee a false one. Hester can see the matter in but one light. She had slowly worked out a conscious redemption through "shame, despair, and solitude." She had not sunk to his depth, and she could not rise to the height to which confession was lifting him. She cannot escape the constraint of her love and pity. She had freed herself; she thought she could free him. " 'I know not,' she replied. 'Better? yea: so we may both die, and little Pearl with us!' " In Hester the passion of love dominates; let it be death if we can die together; but in him the passion of a soul achieving deliverance from sin in the only possible way is stronger, and he is ready to die even if it be alone. He exults in the confession he is about to make before the people. It is the fifty-first Psalm over again. Had Hawthorne read St. Augustine? Or was it the insight of genius brooding in long silence on the way of a guilty soul emerging from the hell of measureless sin? Nowhere does Hawthorne rise so high in tragic skill and power as in the confession that follows when Dimmesdale uncovers his breast and shows burnt into his flesh the letter Hester had worn openly upon her bosom. Here are the stigmata of the early saints, brought out by sin instead of by self-absorption in the crucified One. The final and only atonement is made, and he sinks upon the scaffold to die. Forgiving his tormentor whom he had wronged, he turns to his child where the tragedy completes itself.

Pearl is the one consummate flower of Hawthorne's genius,—unsurpassed by himself and absolutely original. There is woven into her the entire history of these two suffering but diverse souls, which she must fulfill and yet preserve her perfect childhood. She sets forth the sin of her parents without a trace of its guilt, yet reflects the moral chaos in which it has involved her. This is done with matchless art:—"an elf child," the people called her, passing from one mood to another as though a double nature, an Undine as yet without soul, but restless because it is withheld; or, as Mr. Dimmesdale himself had described her, having no "discoverable principle of being save the freedom of a broken law;" and there is added a far-reaching word: "whether capable of good, I know not." Hawthorne does not here hint at inheritance of natural disposition, but has in mind a possible transmission of the confusion springing out of a violation of the moral order. It was not a dream of human love that passed into her being, but something stronger than love.

His thought here runs very deep. This child of guilty passion inherited not the passion, but a protesting conscience that always put her at odds with herself. As Chillingworth was the malignant conscience that destroyed Dimmesdale, Pearl was the natural conscience that wholesomely chastened her mother so long as the inevitable penalty lasted. This ministration is strikingly brought out in the profoundest chapter of the book, where Hester's inner life is disclosed. One is tempted, as one follows it, to ask if Hawthorne suffered his own thoughts to wander into the region where the question of woman's place and rights in human society was undergoing heated discussion. The din of it filled his ears unless he closed them, as he usually did when anything like reform met them. But in this tender and sympathetic chapter he tells where Hester's thoughts often led her, and where she surely would have followed them had she been free to fulfill her dreams. It certainly was where his thoughts would not have gone. But as in Tennyson's Princess a child solved the problem, so here Pearl and motherhood dispelled her dreams and kept her within the lines of natural duty. In every case Pearl dominates the situation, whether she be regarded as a symbolized conscience or as a child. The story throughout is a drama of the spirit; the real and the spiritual play back and forth with something more than metaphor, for each is both real and spiritual. She is woven with endless symbolism into every page; from the first wail in the prison where she was born, the child sets the keynote and keeps it to the end. The brook in the forest ran through black shadows and through sunshine, and babbled in two voices. " 'What does this sad little brook say, mother?' inquired she. 'If thou hadst a sorrow of thine own, the brook might tell thee of it, even as it is telling me of mine.' " Here is a sermon in running brooks deeper than the Duke heard,—the response of nature to the inner spirit of man.

But this contradiction that ran through the child passes away as soon as the purpose of confession enters the heart of Dimmesdale, whom before she had shunned so long as he and her mother talked of flight. As the two meet upon the scaffold after treading their bitter but diverse paths, and become spiritually one through this confession, the child mingles her life with theirs through the truth that now invests them, and proves that "she has a heart by breaking it." Here we have the purest idealism, Greek in the delicacy of its allusions, and Hebrew in its ethical sincerity. What Hawthorne has in mind all along is that a sin involving hypocrisy can in no way be undone or gotten over except by confession, and so getting back into the truth. Dramatic art requires that it shall involve all the actors,— Chillingworth as well as Hester. Though a wronged husband, he was fiendish in his revenge, and as false as Dimmesdale. Any other writer of Romance would have hurled him to a doom of fire or flood. But Hawthorne has other uses for him. He is the malignant conscience of Dimmesdale as Pearl is the beneficent conscience of Hester. All the dramatis personae must be subdued into the likeness of the common motive; and so Hawthorne places Chillingworth on the scaffold, where the mingled atmosphere of unconquerable love and repentance enfolds him. He calls it a defeat; "thou hast escaped me," he said to Dimmesdale; but it was more than defeat. Hawthorne leaves room for the thought at least that something of good found its way into his poor soul and stayed there.

We must acquit Hawthorne here, and on every other page of his works, from aiming at mere effect, but we cannot fail to see that in this last scene he comes near losing himself and letting his pity carry him beyond the point where the logic of his story left Dimmesdale; for to have wholly absolved him from his sin would have carried the writer beyond his purpose to unfold the working of broken law,—a thing not to be tampered with by an over-sympathetic pen. Hawthorne was neither a skeptic, nor a pessimist, nor a cold-hearted man; he was widely the reverse of each. It was the intensity of his faith in the moral laws and in the reality of goodness, and the delicacy and strength of his sympathy, that made him capable of writing in an unfailing strain of justice tempered, but not set aside, by pity.

But behind these qualities was the artistic sense, which—in a great man—is one with his power and insight, and he could write only what he saw and knew; for art is authoritative. Tennyson was once asked why he did not give In Memoriam a happier ending,—a Paradiso with its vision of God instead of a great hope only. He replied, "I have written what I have felt and known, and I will never write anything else." Hawthorne could say the same of himself; and we might add that his sense of art, as well as his sense of truth, held him in leash. His reserve, however temperamental, is a sign of his consummate skill as a literary artist. On what page, in what sentence, does he fall short? The reader turns over the last page and feverishly demands the next scene in the tragedy, but finds only hints or nothing at all; the characters sink back into the mystery from which they emerged. They move like spirits in a world unreal except as their truth makes it real. Hence their intangibleness; they haunt one in the guise of the quality they set forth, but beyond that they do not exist. They stand for no person, but only for some law— kept or broken—which they symbolize. There is no Dimmesdale, nor Hester, nor Pearl, nor Chillingworth, but only shadows of broken law working out its consequences in ways of penalty wrought into the Eternal Order. They stay but a moment, and—like a faded pageant—disappear; but while they stay, the deepest meanings of life are set before us in forms of transcendent power, and become permanent in ourselves.

This ready impartation of ideas is everywhere a marked feature of Hawthorne's works, due to the absolute sincerity of their ethical elements, their perfection of literary form, and their pervasive humanity. To doubt the last factor is to rob his genius of its mainspring. The severity of his treatment grows out of the accuracy of his logic. He deals with mystery and, therefore, says little, only enough to show that whatever a man does he does to himself; that obedience is light, and disobedience is darkness in which, because nothing can be seen, there is nothing to be said.

Still, Hawthorne does not hold it to be contrary to his opinions or his art to suffer gleams of hope to illumine even the darkest of his pages. With a masterly touch at the very beginning of the Scarlet Letter, he expressly states this to be a feature of the story he is about to tell. He puts by the door of the prison, where Hester was confined, "a wild rosebush," and says, "it may serve, let us hope, to symbolize some sweet moral blossom, that may be found along the track, or relieve the darkening close of a tale of human frailty and sorrow." Therefore, in the last scene there are almost forecasts of a good outcome. In the child the spell that drove her apart from her father is broken, and with tears she kisses his dying lips. Hester raises the unconquerable question of love: " 'Shall we not spend our immortal life together? Thou lookest far into eternity with those bright dying eyes! Then tell me what thou seest?' " Hester was mistaken. Her cleansed eyes could see, but his could not with any certainty; he had lived in the dark too long for clear vision. And yet Hawthorne will not hide the end behind so dark a pall. The rose at the prison door blossoms into a hope. The moralizing of the great master is not forgotten: "There is some soul of goodness in things evil." Dimmesdale remembers that there is recovery through suffering, and that it is a sign of mercy. Having set his ignominy before the people, his death becomes triumphant, and he departs with words of praise and submission. Still, Hawthorne will neither assert nor deny, but leaves each to read the story in his own way.

It is not well to look for a doctrine in this masterly and carefully balanced picture. Hawthorne did not intend one; he drew from a broader field than that of dogma. One may hope where one cannot well believe. Belief is special; hope is universal. Dimmesdale stated his own case correctly,—a confused and conflicting statement, because having long lived a lie its bewildering confusion impregnated all his thought. In Hester life has done its worst and its best, and, brooded over continually by truth, she emerges clear-eyed, and sees—shall we say heaven or hell?—She cared not, so long as she could be with him. One is here reminded of Dante's Francesca in the Inferno, "swept about the never resting blast" of hell with Paolo,—her only consolation being that they would never be separated. Mr. Dinesmore, who calls attention to this resemblance in his able book, the Teachings of Dante, thinks that Hawthorne—not having then learned Italian—came to it alone. It may well be so, for it is the quality of love to transcend all motives beside its own; and not seldom does it cast itself with loss of all that it has in time or eternity, for so it chooses, rather than give up itself,—not voluptuous love, but that spiritual passion which makes of two souls one. They have no life if they are separated. Such was Hester's love. Penance had not weakened, but rather had refined it, until its spiritual essence only was left with its commanding power. This Hawthorne sees by the light of his own genius. But to unwind the thread of human fault, and hold it up so that it shall shine in a brighter color, is a task that he hints at, but does not attempt.

Still, he touches sin with a firm hand, and traces it without flinching to the point where it culminates,—always the same; it separates man from God and his fellows, and at last from himself; it returns in retribution, and the evil he has done to others he does to himself. A casual reading may set this down as a Puritan dogma. It is Puritan, but it is universal before it is Puritan. Hawthorne in his greater works touched nothing that was only and distinctively Puritan. His characters wear the garb, but underneath is simply the human soul. This distinction is to be made because it helps to a right understanding of the book, and redeems both it and its author from the charge of provincialism,—a derogation not to be made concerning a genius whose province lay among themes as broad and universal as human nature.

Hawthorne put no unmeaning words into the Scarlet Letter, and the question may arise how far he intended to include Chillingworth in the scene of redemption on the scaffold,—for such it may be called. The answer must be found in Chillingworth's exclamation: "Thou hast defeated me!" Why did he say that? Because Dimmesdale had taken himself out of the world of lies, and put himself into the hands of the

God of truth, and thus brought not only himself, but all about him, under the redeeming influences that filled the air, for even the people went home, as it were, smiting their breasts. If the story be a parable, the harassing conscience must be set at rest; it is defeated, and Chillingworth no longer has a vocation. Dimmesdale had done what he had advised him to do: "Wouldst thou have me to believe, O wise and pious friend, that a false show can be better—can be more for God's glory, or man's welfare—than God's own truth?" His advice, given in answer to Dimmesdale's specious paltering with an eternal reality, deepened his victim's agony and so fed his revenge; but when acted on, his patient passed beyond his reach. He had gone deeper than he knew, and had brought to the surface a spiritual power that outmastered his own. Shall we say that Hawthorne did not intend to hint that Chillingworth came under this greater power, and that, finding himself a defeated man through his own suggestion, he felt its divineness? He utters no word of malice, no confident boast, no plan of further revenge. Instead, what else is seen of him is beneficent, and in accord with a nature originally sound and high-minded. Along with others, he has been involved in a furious storm of human passion, but it passes by when truth wins the victory. Hawthorne, like the consummate artist that he is, never asserts or paints in full, but only intimates and leaves the rest to the reader; and so we may believe that the tragedy pauses at the door of Chillingworth. At the close Hawthorne plays uncertainly and with jest over this strange yet natural character. Chillingworth is reduced to nothingness and withers away,—a logical end, but he reappears in a new light as enriching Hester and Pearl,—a strange thing to do unless some goodness is left in him. Then the author jests and sends him literally to the devil where "he would find tasks enough," and receive "his wages duly." If Hawthorne ever falters it is when he plays between the Parable and the Romance. Here he drops the former, and ends his story—in Walter Scott fashion—with a word for each. Evidently he writes with a weary pen, yet not with an unpitying heart. In the next sentence he would fain be merciful to "all these shadowy beings, so long our near acquaintances,—as well Roger Chillingworth as his companions;" and finally, after a bit of psychological byplay, by no means serious,—on the possible identity at bottom of hatred and love,—raises the question whether the old physician and the minister may not find "their earthly stock of hatred and antipathy transmitted into golden love." Thus, though the Scarlet Letter is a sad book, the author would not leave it black with hopeless sorrow. Even as an artist Hawthorne knew better than to paint his canvas in sober colors only; and as a man he had no right to bruise the human heart with needless pain. Sad as the Scarlet Letter is, we need not think him forgetful of Madame Necker's saying that "the novel should paint a possible better world." But if better, it can be such only through truth and never through lies.

What renders the Scarlet Letter one of the greatest of books is the sleuth-hound thoroughness with which sin is traced up and down and into every corner of the heart and life, and even into nature, where it transforms all things. Shakespeare paints with a larger brush, and sets it in great tragic happenings; but its windings, the subtle infusion of itself into every faculty and impressing itself upon outward things, are left for Hawthorne's unapproachable skill. This leads us to speak of the criticism of Mr. Henry James upon the twelfth chapter, where the story reaches its climax. Dimmesdale and Hester and Pearl stand at night upon the scaffold, where Hester had stood alone with her babe seven years before. His remorse had reached its lowest depth; its sting lay in the fact that she wore the scarlet letter while he went clad in robes of unquestioned sanctity. It is the letter that torments him, and carries the guilt and shame of the whole bitter history. He has come into a condition where, because he can think of nothing else, he can see nothing else. A meteor flashes across the black sky and paints upon a cloud the fatal letter. A page of magnificent writing describes the objective picture and the heart within which only it exists. Mr. James regards it as overworked, and, along with a general charge of the same over-doing here and there, intimates that the author "is in danger of crossing the line that separates the sublime from its intimate neighbor." That Hawthorne should be termed ridiculous after being described as "a thin New Englander with a miasmatic conscience" should occasion no surprise. It shows how wide apart are the realist and the idealist; and also how much nearer the idealist comes to the facts of the case in hand.

That Dimmesdale should transfer what he saw and felt within to the external world is a well-known psychological possibility; and we appeal from the realist to his brother the psychologist, who says in his recent book that "it is one of the peculiarities of invasions from the sub-conscious region to take on objective appearances." It is needless to say that literature, from the Bible down, abounds in this transfer of inward feeling to outward form. When Balaam had sold his prophetic gift for a price, it was not the ass that rebuked him, but his own smiting conscience. It was not the witches, but Macbeth, who sang, "Fair is foul, and foul is fair,"—after which all things were inverted: his thoughts became ghosts and daggers and a knocking at the gate like thunders of doom. Lady Macbeth can see nothing but blood on her white hands. Beckford in his Vathek (where possibly Hawthorne found the suggestion of Dimmesdale's habit of placing his hand upon his heart) made the dwellers in the Hall of Eblis happy in all things except that each held his hand over his heart, which had become "a receptacle of eternal fire." Mr. James seems to underestimate the mental condition into which Dimmesdale has fallen; he strikes the key of the tragedy too low, and refers what he regards as excessive to Hawthorne's Puritanism. Now, Puritanism is a capacious thing, but it cannot hold all that is cast into it; and much is set down to its credit that belongs to a false conception of it. Mr. James, in his able biography, insists on two things, to which we have already referred, as explanatory of Hawthorne; that he was provincial, and that he was largely influenced by his Puritan blood. Each is to be taken with due allowance. Of course, every man, however great his genius, strikes his roots down into native soil and draws his life from such air as is about him. Something of root and air will enter into his mental composition, and in some measure he will think with or from his environment, and his heart will throb with ancestral blood. But it is a quality of genius that it is not subject to such limitations. Genius belongs to the domain of nature; it is cosmic, spiritual, universal. It treats these limitations in one of three ways: it lifts them into their ideals; it transcends them; or it extracts their thin essence or spirit. The last may be said of Hawthorne. Little of Puritanism remained in him except its spirituality, by which we mean its profound sense of the reality of moral law. Much that is set down to him as Puritan was a family idiosyncrasy,—an individualism that passed all the bounds of early or later Puritanism. It favored, however, the play of his genius in its chosen field.

To regard him as provincial because Salem was provincial, or because habits were simple in Massachusetts in the first half of the century, is to miss the source of his strongest quality. Hawthorne, by virtue of his brooding solitude and the lofty character of his thought, which was rooted in his own peculiar genius and was fed by an imagination that had no need to go outside of itself for ideas or theories, was shut off from provincialism save perhaps in some matters of personal habit. The nearest sign of it was an intense love of New England and indifference to the mother country where he had lived for years,—an unweaned child of his native land. There is more in him that offsets Puritanism than identifies him with it. In fact, it outdid itself, as has continually happened, and created in Hawthorne an individualism that separated him from itself. A system whose central principle is individualism cannot count upon holding together its own adherents. It is by its own nature centrifugal, though none the worse for that; it makes man a denizen of the heavens rather than of his mundane sphere. But the way is long, and at great cost is it trod.

It is Hawthorne's peculiarity that he cannot be identified with any school of thought. He was a recluse down to the last fibre. He did not hate men, but he would not mingle with them. He was shy, but in a lofty way. Any real alliance in thought or action with others was impossible for him. His individualism was absolute, but it was temperamental. Socially he was closely identified with the transcendental way of thinking, but it found no access to his mind. He and Emerson were neighbors, but not intimates. When they walked together in Concord they discussed the weather and the crops, but not philosophy, nor religion, nor politics. Oftener they were silent, as great men, who know each other as such, can afford to be. Tennyson and Carlyle once sat together of an evening for three hours, smoking, and neither uttering a word, except Carlyle's good-night: "Come again, Alfred; we have had a grand time." This aloofness from men, and at the same time this power of dragging to light the hidden secrets of their souls, is the inexplicable gift of genius; it has an eye of its own; one glance, and it looks the man through and through. He mingled frequently with the North Adams frequenters of the village tavern, but he was off on the mountain-side, among the limekilns, weaving the threads of Ethan Brand. He spent a year at Brook Farm, but spoke lightly of its socialism and of his own part as "chambermaid to the oxen,"—a wasted year, but it gave us the Blithedale Romance, which Mr. James places at the head of his works. He hated Socialism, but Puritanism, its opposite,—being spiritual and social individualism,—won in him no following save as it furnished him standing ground and materials for his work. Had he lived anywhere where conscience and law had full recognition and sin was possible, he would have written in the same strain,—as in the Marble Faun, where Donatello serves his purpose as well as Dimmesdale. The crime and its effect in each belong to the general field of ethics, where sin reveals its nature in soul experiences that are common to all men. Indeed, he has but one deep and permanent interest: the play of conscience under sin. He is a student of the soul. He watches its play as a biologist watches an animal under varying conditions; but in each case it is the study of a soul,—not degraded, but only wounded, as it were, and while it is keen to feel, and while the good and evil in it are full of primal energy.

It is sometimes said, in halfway derogation of Hawthorne's genius, that his tales are parables. Why should they not be so regarded? It is not easy to escape the parable, in literature or in life. What are the world and humanity but parables of the Eternal Mind? The only question in literature is, are the parables well told? If they are, the witness of a vast company of great authors in all ages and tongues is theirs. Hawthorne was full of dreams, fantasies, symbols, and all manner of spiritual necromancy,—turning nature into spirit and spirit back into nature, but—however wild the play of his imagination—the idea underlying it always has three characteristics: it is real, and true, and moral. Hence, the Scarlet Letter,—devoid of history and of probability; illusive; nature transformed to create and to receive meanings; personality sunk in ideas and ideas made personal; so far away that our hearts do not reach it with sympathy, and it is read with unwet eyes, but with thoughts that lie too deep for tears;—still it is one of the truest and most moral of books, because the human soul that lies behind it and plays through it is true to itself whether it does good or evil. Hawthorne knew evil under its laws. Neither sentiment, nor art, nor dogma deflected him from seeing the thing as it is, and setting it down with relentless accuracy. His claim to genius would be impeached if it were not accurate; and the reason why it stands clear and unquestioned is because no taint of morbidness nor Puritan inheritance lessens the absolute veracity of his estimates. Each may have had something to do with the selection of his subjects, but nothing whatever with his own ethical opinions. His literary art and execution, faultless as they are, would not alone secure for him the admiration and reverence of all lovers of good literature. For, at last, it is truth alone for which men care; and truth only is strong enough to win unquestioned and universal verdicts.

And yet he is criticised on the score that the Scarlet Letter, especially, is sad, and sometimes it is added that it is pessimistic. So are Lear and Balzac's Alkahest sad, but neither deserves the latter term. Nothing in literature is pessimistic that accurately describes a violation of the order of the world and of human life, if it be in the interest of truth and justice. Dimmesdale and Hester could not escape the pangs they suffered; they were not going through their parts in a world of pessimism, but in a world of order which they had violated, and for which they were undergoing inevitable yet redemptive penalty. There is no pessimism so long as the just laws of society are working normally,—the very point on which Hawthorne insists,—however hard they are bearing on the individual. Pessimism is an indictment of the moral order of the world, and is essential atheism. Hawthorne stood at the opposite pole. His main function in literature was to illustrate the tragical consequences of broken law when the law was fundamental in character or in society. He was almost slavishly logical,—putting Dimmesdale into the lowest hell of the Inferno, and Hester in Purgatorio, where penalty purifies and makes the sufferer glad.

Absolute as was his insight, and perfect as was his art, he has not escaped criticism. There is general agreement that his pages are overcharged with symbolism. But which flower will you uproot in that garden "of a thousand hues," though "Narcissus that still weeps in vain" blossoms too often there?

Graver criticism is sometimes heard,—as that he has no sympathy with his characters in their suffering. So far as it touches the Scarlet Letter it should be sufficient refutation to read what he himself says in his English Note-Books, in comparing Thackeray's "coolness in respect to his own pathos," with his own emotions when he read the last scene of the Scarlet Letter to his wife, just after writing it,—"tried to read it rather, for my voice swelled and heaved, as if I were tossed up and down on an ocean as it subsides after a storm."

It is not well to search an author too closely as to his feeling over the creatures of his imagination. You may find nothing or everything, according to temperament or literary sense. The great author hides himself behind his canvas. Hawthorne, the most reticent of men and with the keenest sense of literary propriety, is the most impersonal of writers in his greater works. He tells us nothing except what may be inferred from characteristics constantly recurring throughout his pages. Now nothing is more revealing in an author than his style; it is almost a better witness to his character than his assertions. It is like the voice in conversation that speaks from the soul rather than the mind. There are in Hawthorne's style four invariable features,—reverence, sincerity, delicacy, and humanity; each is nearly absolute. Together they stand for heart. No matter how silently it throbs, a writer who puts these qualities into his pages is to be counted as one who pities his fellow men even when most relentless in tracing their sins. It may also be set down as a general principle, that truth is akin to pity, as pity is akin to love. The great virtues do not lie far apart.

The criticism is oftenest urged in connection with Hester, who is both the centre of interest and of the problem. Hawthorne takes utmost pains to make it clear how she lived. Whether she was happy or not he did not undertake to say; he would not raise so useless a question. The tragedy is pitched at too high a key for happiness. Possibly there may be victory after slow-healing wounds, but there can be no amelioration by circumstance or by deadening of sensibility. Study the thirteenth chapter—Another View of Hester—if you would seek an answer to the question whether in her case the book gravitates toward despair or points to recovery and life.

This exquisite rehearsal of Christian service and temper might well win for her canonization. It is the picture of a saint. The very things that Christ made the condition of acceptance at the last judgment she fulfilled; and the graces that St. Paul declared to be the fruit of the Spirit were exemplified in her daily life. Plainly, this is not a picture of despair, nor even of suffering, except that which necessarily haunts a true soul that has done evil. God forbid that it should be different with any of us! Forgiveness is not lethean. To forget our past would defraud the soul of its heritage in life. The Scarlet Letter faded out and even acquired another meaning. Her life came to blessed uses, with rewards of love and gratitude from others that reached even unto death. The logic of this tender picture of a saintly life—a gospel in itself—must not be overlooked. Hawthorne certainly did not mean that the reader should miss the point. How could recovery from sin be better told, or be more complete? When Peter had denied his Lord and wept bitterly over it, all he was told to do was to feed his Master's sheep. Hester's forgiveness did not shape itself in the form of ecstatic visions, but of service in the spirit of Him who bore witness to the truth; and by herself bearing witness to it she won the reward of its freedom.

To the last touch of his pen Hawthorne keeps up the symbolism that both hides and reveals his meaning, and leaves us in such a mood as when, on some autumn day, we watch mountain and river and sky faintly shrouded in haze until we wonder if these and life itself be real,—an experience tenderly rendered by Longfellow in his poem on Hawthorne. He lived in his dreams, but his dreams were as real as the earth and as true as life.

Strangers in Boston still search the burial ground of King's Chapel for the grave of Hester Prynne: so true a story, they think, must be true in fact. If it had been found they might have asked, What does the armorial device mean?

"ON A FIELD, SABLE, THE LETTER A, GULES."

Does the scarlet letter stand for sin or for cleansing? Is the epitaph a word of despair or of hope? In what direction did Hawthorne intend to lead our thought? If asked, he would have said, Read out of your own heart.

William C. Brownell, "Hawthorne," ***Scribner's*****, 43 (January 1908), 83-84.**

"The Scarlet Letter" is not merely a masterpiece, it is a unique book. It is not a story of adultery. The word does not, I think, occur in the book—a circumstance in itself typifying the detachment of the conception and the delicate art of its execution. But in spite of its detachment and delicacy, the inherent energy of the theme takes possession of the author's imagination and warms it into exalted exercise, making it in consequence at once the most real and the most imaginative of his works. It is essentially a story neither of the sin nor of the situation of illicit love—presents neither its psychology nor its social effects; neither excuses nor condemns nor even depicts, from this specific point of view. Incidentally, of course, the sin colors the narrative and the situation is its particular result. But, essentially, the book is a story of concealment. Its psychology is that of the concealment of sin amid circumstances that make a sin of concealment itself. The sin itself might, one may almost say, be almost any other. And this constitutes no small part of the book's formal originality. To fail to perceive this is quite to misconceive it. As a story of illicit love its omissions are too great, its significance is not definite enough, its detail has not enough richness, the successive scenes of which it is composed have not an effective enough cohesion. Above all, Chillingworth is a mistake, or at most a wasted opportunity. For he is specialized into a mere function of malignity, and withdrawn from the reader's sympathies, whereas what completes, if it does not constitute, the tragedy of adultery, is the sharing by the innocent of the punishment of the guilty. This inherent element of the situation, absolutely necessary to a complete presentment of it, the crumbling of the innocent person's inner existence, is absolutely neglected in "The Scarlet Letter," and the element of a malevolent persecution of the culpable substituted for it. The innocent person thereby becomes, as I have already said, an expedient, and though in this way Hawthorne is enabled to vivify the effect of remorse upon the minister by personifying its furies, in this way, too, he sacrifices at once the completeness of his picture and its depth of truth by disregarding one of its most important elements.

He atones for this by concentration on the culpable. It is *their* psychology alone that he exhibits. And though in this way he has necessarily failed to write the *chef-d'oeuvre* of the general subject that in the field of art has been classic since monogamy established itself in society, he has produced a perfect masterpiece in the more detached and withdrawn sphere more in harmony with his genius. In narrowing his range and observing its limits he has perhaps even increased the poignancy of his effect. And his effect *is* poignant and true as reality itself. In confining himself to the concealment of sin rather than depicting its phenomena and its results, he has indeed brought out, as has never been done elsewhere, the importance of this fatal increment of falsity among the factors of the whole chaotic and unstable moral equilibrium. Concealment in "The Scarlet Letter," to be sure, is painted in very dark colors. In similar cases it may be a duty, and is, at all events, the mere working of a natural instinct—at worst a choice of the lesser evil. But surely there is no exaggeration or essential loss of truth in the suggestion of its potentialities for torture conveyed by the agony of the preacher's double-life. The sombre close, the scarcely alleviated gloom of the whole story are in fit keeping with the theme, which is the truth that, in the words of the tale itself, "an evil deed invests itself with the character of doom," and with its development through the torture of concealment to the expiation of confession.

Here, for once, with Hawthorne we have allegory richly justifying itself, the allegory of literature not that of didacticism, of the imagination not of the fancy, allegory neither vitiated by caprice nor sterilized by moralizing, but firmly grounded in reality and nature. Note how, accordingly, even the ways of the wicked fairy that obsessed him are made to serve him, for even the mirage and symbolism so dear to his mind and so inveterate in his practice, blend legitimately with the pattern of his thoroughly naturalistic tapestry. Is the fanciful element excessive, the symbolism overdone? I think not, on the whole. Hawthorne seems to have been "possessed" by his story as to have conducted the development of its formal theme for once subconsciously, so to speak, and with the result of decorating rather than disintegrating reality in its exposition. At all events to this possession (how complete it was as a matter of material fact all his biographers attest) two notable and wholly exceptional results are due. In the first place he *felt* his theme, as he never felt it elsewhere, and consequently presented it with an artistic cogency he never elsewhere attained. The story, in other words, is real and true. If it is thought to show a bias in pushing too far the doom of evil, to ignore the whole New Testament point of view, as it may be called, epitomized in the Master's "Go and sin no more," the answer is that though in this way it may lose in typical value, it gains in imaginative realism, since it is a story of that Puritan New England where it sometimes seems as if the New Testament had been either suspect or unknown. Besides, there is enough deomonstration of its text on the hither side of what it is necessary to invoke the Puritan *milieu* to justify. Every erring soul may not suffer the extremity of Dimmesdale's agony, but it suffers enough, and the inevitability of its suffering was never more convincingly exhibited than in this vivid picture, softened as it is into a subdued intensity by the artist's poetized, however predetermined, treatment.

For, in the second place, it is here alone that Hawthorne seems to have felt his *characters* enough to feel them sympathetically and so to realize them to the full. They are very real and very human. What the imagination of a recluse, even, can do to this end when held to its own inspiration and not seduced into the realm of the fantastic, may be seen in the passage where Hester pleads for the continued custody of her child. Pearl herself is a jewel of romance. Nothing more imaginatively real than this sprite-like and perverse incarnation of the moral as well as physical sequence of her parents' sin exists in romance. Her individuality is an inspiration deduced with the logic of nature and with such happy art that her symbolic quality is as incidental in appearance as it is seen to be inherent on reflection. Mr. James, who objects to the symbolism of "The Scarlet Letter," nevertheless found her substantial enough to echo in the charming but far less vivid Pansy of his "Portrait of a Lady." Chillingworth, the other symbolic character, is in contrast an embodied abstraction—the one *expedient*, as I have said, of the book. But it cannot be denied that he performs a needful function and, artistically, is abundantly justified. As a Puritan parallel of Mephistopheles he is very well handled. "The Scarlet Letter" is, in fact, the Puritan "Faust," and its symbolic and allegorical element, only obtrusive in a detail here and there at most, lifts it out of the ordinary category of realistic romance without—*since nothing of importance is sacrified to it*—enfeebling its imaginative reality. The beautiful and profound story is our one prose masterpiece and it is as difficult to overpraise it as it is to avoid poignantly regretting that Hawthorne failed to recognize its value and learn the lesson it might have taught him.

Harry Thurston Peck, "Hawthorne and 'The Scarlet Letter,' " in *Studies in Several Literatures* **(New York: Dodd, Mead, 1909), pp. 117-130.**

If Nathaniel Hawthorne had never written *The Scarlet Letter*, it is almost certain that to-day he would be remembered only as one of America's minor writers. *The Scarlet Letter* has won readers for his other books and has raised him to the position of a classic. When he began its composition, he was in the forty-fifth year of his life. He had struggled hard to win success in literature and had lamentably failed.

His inventiveness had given him material for scores of tales and sketches. He had edited the manuscripts of other men. He had contributed to many publications. Yet only a very few paid much attention to him as a writer, and those few were largely influenced by their personal regard for him. His pen could not provide for him even a meagre livelihood, and he felt the pinch of actual poverty. There was a time when, with his devoted wife, he lived at Concord on the products of his kitchen-garden. He chopped wood, and cooked the scanty meals, and even washed the dishes in the back-parlour of the Old Manse. He recorded the *menu* of his Christmas dinner in 1843 as "quince, apples, bread-and-cheese, and milk." * * *

The novel in its final form was published in 1850. Two editions of it were almost immediately exhausted. At the age of forty-six, the "obscurest man of letters in America" took rank among the few who have achieved a lasting fame.

When Hawthorne wrote *The Scarlet Letter*, he did, for the one time in his whole life, exactly what he meant to do. He has himself recorded that he penned its pages at a white heat, thrilled by the emotions that were excited in him,—"as if I were tossed up and down upon an ocean." For once, his grasp was firm. Physical energy sustained the effort of intellectual power. And so, in its own way, the story is very nearly perfect—all except the anticlimax of the last few pages.

There were reasons for Hawthorne's doubt, expressed to Fields, as to whether the book was very good or very bad. Had its author been merely a clever writer and not a man of genius, his work would have sunk to the level of melodrama. As Hawthorne actually wrought it out, it is dramatic and something more. It may, indeed, be styled theatric, and I might go still further and call it operatic. No wonder that it has been taken by a living composer for musical interpretation. The libretto fairly leaps out of its pages. The scenes are already indicated with sharp distinctness, for the whole tale is episodic. The grim and weather-beaten prison with its oaken, iron-clamped door—the pillory—a balcony projecting from beneath the church's eaves—beyond, the harbour with a glimpse of high-decked ships—a beautiful but guilty woman wearing the Scarlet Letter on her breast and passing from the prison to the pillory—here is a strangely vivid setting for the *lever de rideau*. How much colour and picturesqueness in the chorus, or the stage mob, if you please! Aged women and young girls, stern Puritan inhabitants of Old Boston with bell-crowned hats and gloomy looks, an Indian or two in paint and feathers, and a group of swaggering buccaneers, garbed strangely,—it is of the essence of the operatic stage.

Then think of those especial episodes which stand out most vividly. The chorus greets Hester Prynne as she walks proudly to the pillory, and it gives the clue to what has gone before. Then comes the trio between Wilson, the old clergyman, Arthur Dimmesdale and Governor Bellingham; followed by the impassioned appeal of Dimmesdale to Hester, urging her to tell the truth, if it be for her soul's peace. His appeal is broken by her short and sharp refusals, and by the deep voice of Roger Chillingworth— obviously a basso. Think also of the operatic possibilities of the prison scene, where Roger plays the physician and is alone with Hester, the wife who dishonoured him by reason of her love for some man whom he threatens to discover and of whom he says: "Let him live! Let him hide himself in outward honour, if he may. None the less, he shall be mine!"

And again, the crafty, stealthy arts of Chillingworth, suspecting Dimmesdale, and playing with malignant skill upon that tortured conscience, until at last, the misshapen seeker after vengeance learns the secret of the minister, and finds upon his breast the great scarlet A. And the forest scene, where Hester meets her former lover, while the uncanny little Pearl sports near them, is full of dramatic and operatic possibilities. The powerful climax is worked up with all the mastery of stage effect that the most skilful playwright could imagine. Here the chorus is diversified by the introduction of soldiers in burnished steel who enter to the strains of military music. The procession of the Governor and magistrates varies the spectacle, while the tense excitement of the moment is raised to a still higher pitch by the seaman's message which shows that the devilish Roger has prevented the escape of Dimmesdale and Hester. And at last, Dimmesdale, in the hour of his seeming triumph, which is also the hour of his death, mounting the scaffold where once Hester stood, reveals his guilt, and with convulsive hand tears open his black vestment and displays the scarlet symbol of his shame and hers.

The genius of Hawthorne is clearly shown in the art with which he has done so much with such slight material. There are only three characters in the story. There is, first of all, Hester Prynne, noble and strong and pure of heart, in spite of the transgression which has marred her life. If she has sinned, it is because of the great law of Nature which gives to every woman the desire for love. There is Arthur Dimmesdale, gifted, sensitive, and with the instincts of a saint; yet still a sinner, guilty of a double sin because of his holy calling, and swayed by moral cowardice which ties his tongue until the end and lets him live a hypocrite. And finally, there is Roger Chillingworth, cold-hearted, implacable, and showing that malignant spirit which so often goes with physical deformity. These three—the confessed and branded sinner, the undetected sinner, and the man who is a self-appointed instrument to scourge the other two—these are the only figures on which the author has concentrated the glaring light of his imagination. Yet out of what would seem to be the meagerest of material, he has created something for which there is no parallel in English literature. How skilfully he manages the physical aspects of his story! In it he was almost the first to cast the glamour of pure romance about the harshness and severity of New England. Old Boston, as he limns it, is as quaint and full of fascinating possibilities as any Rhenish town with a whole millennium of legend. The trackless woods which circle it, seem, under Hawthorne's magic touch, to teem with mystery as though he had transported the Schwarzwald to the Western world. The beauty of its silent glades, where the sunlight sifts through the greenery, makes it enchanted ground; while the lurking Indians who now and then appear so silently, take not so strong a hold upon the fancy as do the dark hints concerning what takes place at night when in the gloom, grim hags steal out to meet the Black Man who has bought their souls. There is a smell of witchcraft in the air, as Hawthorne tells the story; and his reticence and half-spoken intimations are proofs of his consummate art.

Hawthorne was a symbolist, one who spoke in allegory, and let the concrete always serve as a clue to the intangible yet more intense reality of what lay behind it. Thus, the scaffold on which Hester stood to be stared at by a thousand eyes, is a symbol of her public shame. The prison is another symbol. The forest, where she yielded to her lover, reminds us always of the guilt that has been hers as well as Dimmesdale's. But it is the scarlet letter which is the one pervasive and almost terrifying symbol, giving in itself the *motif* of the whole. As Mr. Woodberry has well expressed the thought: "It multiplies itself, as the tale unfolds, with greater intensity and mysterious significance and dread suggestion, as if in mirrors set round about it; . . . and as if this were not enough, the scarlet letter, at a climax of the dark story, lightens forth over the whole heavens as a symbol of what can not be hid even in the intensest blackness of night." This recurrence of a physical object to keep the meaning of the book before the reader's mind forever, is an instinctive bit of art in Hawthorne. It was employed with conscious purpose by Émile Zola three decades later, in the great brazen still of *L'Assommoir*, in the reeking mine-pit of *Germinal* and in the Napoleonic bees of *La Débâcle*.

But it is not the outward aspects of *The Scarlet Letter* that excite the deepest and most lasting interest. This is to be found in its subtler phases, in its moral lesson, if there be one, and in its revelation of the inner mind of him who wrote it. And to understand these things, we must ever so briefly scan the lesson of heredity which helps explain so much. Hawthorne's first ancestor on American soil exhibited a strange *mélange* of tastes and tasks. He was a warrior, a preacher of great eloquence, a reader of fine English prose, and a stern magistrate who ordered the public whipping of women because they were proven to be Quakers. His son condemned to death women who were reputed witches; and he showed such savagery and blood-lust in the courtroom, that one whose wife was sentenced by him, cursed him and the children of his children's children, in a curse that was Oriental in its fury and completeness, and that was not forgotten after many generations.

Hawthorne's father was a sailor, the captain of a Salem vessel, and he bore the reputation of being black and stern to those whom he commanded. When he died, in far-off Surinam, his wife was only twenty-seven years of age. Yet she, too, had the intensity and deep passion of the family which she had entered. She called young Hawthorne, with his sisters, to her room, and told them dryly that their father was now dead. Then she sent her children to her own father's house and for forty years lived in a solitude that was rarely broken. Long after Hawthorne had grown to manhood, he wrote to a friend of having eaten dinner with his mother—"for the first time in my life that I can remember."

Recalling, then, his ancestral traits, we can in part explain Nathaniel Hawthorne as a man, and more especially the Hawthorne of *The Scarlet Letter*. All the sunshine of his nature was lavished on his wife and children, with whom his every hour was an hour of unclouded happiness. But to the world at large he was the true descendant of the men who scourged the Quaker women and doomed the witches and terrified the sailors, as he was also the son of her who let her whole life wither for what she felt to be a "principle." Hawthorne had friends who loved him well, yet he never spared them in his criticism. He was burdened with a secret pessimism which was ever a dark blot on his secret soul. He wearied both of men and places in a little time. When he left his native Salem, he described it as "an earthly cavern." When he left Brook Farm, he wrote: "Even my custom-house experience was not such a thraldom and weariness." When at last, by the kindness of President Pierce, he left America for the lucrative consulship at Liverpool, he was glad, so his biographer informs us, "to get away from his native land, upon which . . . he looked back with the feeling that he never desired to return to it." Yet in England he was wholly discontented and displeased. He refused to meet many of the famous men who would have been glad to offer him their hospitality. One instance of almost incredible tactlessness has been preserved in a brief, surly note which he penned from Liverpool to a Mr. Bright, who had striven to make this difficult genius happy. "Dear Mr. Bright," wrote Hawthorne, "I have come back (only for a day or two) to this black, miserable hole." His contempt for England he has recorded in the pages of *Our Old Home*. The English he described as "beefish, muttonish, portish, and porterish." Yet he was unwilling to meet such Englishmen as Tennyson and Thackeray and Macaulay, who were not beefish and muttonish. He did not care for men of letters. It is hard to say for what, precisely, he did care. At heart, he was a pessimist, a man of gloom, a fatalist, a Yankee Heraclitus. And with it all there was a moral sternness, a relentlessness which his biographers have called Puritanism. Yet in Hawthorne it was not really Puritanism, since the deep religious conviction which was the moving force, the mainspring, of Puritanism, was in his case lacking. For Puritanism, while ascetic and severe in doctrine, was not always unsparing, pitiless, relentless. There were the "uncovenanted mercies of the Lord," and even Jonathan Edwards did not forever preach of dire damnation and the glaring flames of hell. There was a place even in his stern creed, for charity and hope. Therefore, it seems to me that Hawthorne's ultimate belief was rather Paganism—not the joyous, gladsome, irresponsible Paganism of the Greeks, but Paganism of a darker hue,—the Paganism of the Orientals.

In this sense, *The Scarlet Letter* is the fullest revelation of his innermost convictions. Hence, in its last analysis, it is a deeply hopeless book, tinged with morbid thoughts. It means that sin can not be forgiven in this life; that its taint, of which the scarlet letter is a symbol, must remain forever. That which is done can never be undone. Though years of expiation pass, though the sinner repent in tears, and sweat great drops of blood, and eat the bread of bitterness, his sin is unforgiven. If he confess it, he is exposed to public shame. If he conceal it, he is riven by remorse. Love and affection may minister to him, as wild-flowers and green ivies grow about a fire-scarred trunk in the forest—yet the marks of scorching flame are there, and the charred stump can never be again a stately tree. In all this there is no Christ, no hint of gentleness and grace and pity. *The Scarlet Letter* brings to mind a very different work of genius written by a very different type of man, yet one of which the moral is the same,—Rossetti's *Jenny*. There the man of much experience muses over the street-waif as she sleeps, and he thinks of all the problems of existence. He, too, like Hawthorne, feels the mystery of life and death, of sin and sorrow, and he turns away perplexed; for though it is a mystery that stares men always in the face, not one has ever fathomed it.

Carl Van Doren, "The Flower of Puritanism," *Nation*, 8 December 1920, pp. 649-650.

When Hawthorne, seventy years ago, in "The Scarlet Letter" gave the world the finest flower of three hundred years of American Puritanism, he passed quietly by the ordinary surfaces of life, not for lack of talent in portraying them, but for lack of interest in them. In thus being a Puritan to the extent that he rarely lifted his gaze from the human spirit in its sincerest hours, he was also a poet. During his long experimental stage as a writer of brief tales he had brooded over the confused spectacle of mankind, posing for himself one after another of the soul's problems and translating them into lucid forms of beauty; now he posed a larger problem on a larger scale. If his matter was at once that of the Puritan and that of the poet, so was his manner. The Puritan's parsimony in Hawthorne lies very close to the artist's passionate economy.

The impact which the story makes may be traced back of Hawthorne's art and personality to the old Puritan tradition which, much as he might disagree with it on occasion, he had none the less in his blood. Some ancestral strain accounts for this conception of adultery as an affair not of the civil order but of the immortal soul. The same strain in his constitution, moreover, makes of these circumstances more than the familiar triangle. A Frenchman might have painted the joy of Dimmesdale, the lover, with his forbidden mistress; an Italian might have traced the fierce course of Chillingsworth, the husband, to a justified revenge; a German might have exhibited Hester, the offending wife, as actually achieving an outer freedom to match that one within. Hawthorne transfers the action to a different plane. Let the persons in the triple conflict be involved as they may with one another, each of them stands essentially apart from the remaining two, because each is occupied with a still vaster conflict, with good and evil as the rival elements which continually tug at the poor human creature. Small wonder, then, that the flesh, to which the sin was superfically due, should go unsung; that the bliss of the senses should hardly once be attended to. After such fleeting pleasures comes the inexorable judgment, which is of the spirit not of the body. To the Puritan imagination, journeys begin, not end, in lovers meeting. The tragedy of Dimmesdale lies in his defeat by evil through the temptation of cowardice and hypocrisy, which are sins. Chillingsworth tragically, and sinfully, chooses evil when he decides to take a treacherous vengeance into his own hands, though vengeance, he knows, is another's. Hester alone emerges from her guilt through her public expiation and the long practice of virtue afterward.

So far "The Scarlet Letter" agrees with the doctrines of the Puritans. Its broader implications critically transcend them. In what dark slumber during these seven years has that Jehovah wrapped himself whom the elder Puritans invoked day and night about all their business, praying for the remission of sins through the merciful affection of his son? What prayers go up! Who counts upon the treasury of grace from which any sinner might hope to obtain salvation if his repentance were only sore enough? The theology which for seventeenth-century men was almost as real as religion itself had come to be for their profound descendant no more authoritative than some remote mythology except as it shadowed forth a cosmic and moral order which Hawthorne had himself observed. In one respect he seems sterner than the elder Puritans, for he admits into his narrative no hope of any providential intervention which might set these jangled bells again into accord. Dimmesdale will not encourage Hester to hope for a compensating future life even. The consequences of deeds live forever. At the same time, Hawthorne has drawn the action down from heaven's pavement, where Milton would have conducted it, to earth, and has humanized it to the extent that he centers it in human bosoms. The newest schools of psychology cannot object to a reading of sin which shows Dimmesdale and Chillingsworth as the victims of instincts and antipathies which fester because unnaturally repressed while Hester Prynne is cleansed through the discovery of her offense and grows healthier by her confession. All the Christian centuries have known the truth here represented.

But only certain of those centuries—and not the Puritan seventeenth—have been capable of viewing love as Hawthorne views it and unfolds its tragedy. To the actual contemporaries of Hester and Dimmesdale it would have seemed a blasphemy worse than adultery for the lovers to agree, in their meeting at the brookside, that "what we did had a consecration of its own." These are Hester's words, and so it was to Hester that eventually "it seemed a fouler offense committed by Roger Chillingsworth than any which has since been done him, that, in the time when her heart knew no better, he had persuaded her to fancy herself happy by his side." Hester thus becomes the type—subtly individualized but yet a type—of the moving principle of life which different societies in different ways may constrain but which in itself irresistibly endures. Her story is an allegory of the passion through which the race continues. She feels the ignominy which attends her own irregular behavior and accepts her fate as the reward of evil, but she does not understand it so far as to wish uncommitted the act which her society calls a sin. A harder woman might have become an active rebel; a softer woman might have sunk passively down into unavailing penitence. Hester stands erect, and thinks. She asked herself whether women as life was constituted could be happy. "As concerned her own individual existence, she had long ago decided in the negative, and dismissed the point as settled." Yet her mind, though dismissing her particular case as a malady without hope, still ranges the universe for some cure for the injustice her sex inherits. "The world's law was no law for her mind." In this manner those whom the world crushes always take their surest revenge. Hester finds no speculative answer; and so she turns to action, plays her necessary part, and gives herself to the nurture of her child, no less a mother than if approved by every human ordinance. A universal allegory of motherhood, her story is also a criticism of the Puritan attempt to bind life too tightly. In the midst of the drab circumstances of Salem this woman of such radiance of beauty and magnificence of life rises up and cracks the stiff frame of the time. Great as her own suffering is, she has in some measure contributed to let a little light into the general tragedy of her sex. "The Scarlet Letter" is not merely a Puritan story. A spirit larger than Puritanism, as large as the whole world's experience, informs and ripens the book.

Hester, who out of some trait of whimsy embroiders and illuminates the statutory label of her offense until it is a bright token of the "rich, voluptuous, Oriental" luxuriance of her nature, has a sister of somewhat similar stature in Zenobia, heroine of "The Blithedale Romance," in which she represents the fullest flood of life, fire and color, passion and experience. Both of these women, it must be noted, come into Hawthorne's New England from other regions; both to be gorgeous, he appears to think, had to be exotic. This may be taken as his tacit accusation that magnificence of personality did not ripen on that rock-bound coast. His imagination, however, could and did go out to find abundance and ripeness where they lived. A chapter appealing beyond almost anything in the history of American literature might be written upon the dreams of beauty and splendor which visited Hawthorne during the long years which he spent in the gray Salem of his birth and in his restless wanderings over the face of New England in the search for materials of romance. * * *

In a world, he asked himself, where human instincts are continually at war with human laws, and where laws, once broken, pursue the offender even more fiercely than they hedged him before, how are any but the more docile spirits to hold their course without calamity? The Puritan Fathers to the same inquiry, which they asked hardly more frequently than Hawthorne, could point in answer to election and atonement and divine grace. Hawthorne had inherited the old questions but not the old answers. He did not free himself from the Puritan mode of believing that to break a law is to commit a sin, or that to commit a sin is to play havoc with the soul; but he changed the terms and considered the sin as a violation less of some supernatural law than of the natural integrity of the soul. Whereas another romancer by tracking the course of the instincts which lead to what is called sin might have sought to justify them as native to the offender and so inescapable, Hawthorne accepts sin without a question and studies the consequences. He brought to his representation of the theme sanity without cynicism and tenderness without softness; he brought also, what is rarer than depth of moralism, an art finely rounded, a rich, graceful style, a spirit sweet and wholesome. He found a substance apparently as unpromising as the original soil upon which the Puritans established their commonwealth, and no less than they with their stony province he tamed and civilized it— going beyond them, moreover, by lifting it into an enduring loveliness which at least in "The Scarlet Letter" has been enriched rather than diminished by seventy years.

Elizabeth Deering Hanscom, "Introduction" to *The Scarlet Letter* (New York: Macmillan, 1927), pp. vii, xv-xx.

"The Scarlet Letter" marks the center of the life of Nathaniel Hawthorne. It was the climax of his artistic efforts, the turning point of his personal fortune; on it his earlier works focus; by it his later works are measured. * * *

In the years that have passed Hawthorne and all pertaining to him have been studied minutely, critically, constantly; and always the criticism has pivoted upon "The Scarlet Letter." Here for the first time he showed complete mastery; here his art came to full flower; here, unconfined by the self-imposed limitations of the tale, he expended his imagination on a problem that required both time and space for its exposition; and here he evoked characters that grew and changed by the force of external circumstance and by inner compulsion. The work has rare, indeed complete harmony. The language, the style, the descriptive and narrative method, the environment, the action, the characters *belong*. It is almost impossible to separate them. If we try to change any one of the many elements that go to the making of the whole, we find how absolute is this harmony. This may be taken as the first of many characteristics that make this New England romance comparable with Greek tragedy. It is not merely a classic; it is classic. The background is strictly limited and absolutely necessary. Nowhere else could this tragedy have been worked out in this fashion, not even in an English Puritan community of the seventeenth century; for in England Puritanism was always a part of a whole; in New England, at that time, it was the whole. In a manner suggestive of the laboratory method then beginning to revolutionize the study of science, Hawthorne isolated his material, subjecting his characters to careful, impersonal scrutiny. It is this which in part accounts for the coldness, the lack of sympathy that many feel in reading the romance. Certainly to those bred in the sentimental school of fiction this objectivity was marked and frequently not agreeable. The natural background is elemental, the sea before, separating from the old safe ways and the old tried life; the forest behind, stretching back to impenetrable depths, black and fearsome. The social background is hard, yet pervasive, expressed by groups of persons suggestive of Greek choruses, ministers, townspeople, hideously righteous and cruel children.

Against this background three or, if Pearl be counted, four persons are projected after a great sin has been committed. About the sin itself Hawthorne has little direct interest, certainly no curiosity. Doubtless he knew the insidious approaches, the sudden flare of passion; surely he understood the weak excuses, the false justification with which the sinners tried to cheat themselves; but he turns from all that material so alluring to vulgar minds to study the effects of sin. Here again one notices the directness and clarity of the vision, the firmness of the execution. Sin, suffering, conscience, self-mastery, self-abnegation—Hawthorne had no doubts on these points, nor does he assume doubts on the part of his readers. There are some self-evident facts in the moral as well as in the material world; he wasted no effort in proving the axiomatic. Puritan or classic? It is not necessary to label. The theme is clear; not the study of sin; not the effect of sin; but the efficacy of the punishment of sin. One is prone to fall back on the vocabulary of older days and to use words that seldom, if ever, came from Hawthorne's pen, but never could have been far from his thought: repentance, forgiveness, atonement, purification. As one use them, there grows the realization that none of them is truly applicable; and here perhaps is the central fault of the tale. Set in Puritan time and place, dealing with Puritan conventions and formulae, it is untrue to the inner spirit of Puritanism. Puritanism in its essence was Christian. It endeavored, albeit imperfectly, to interpret Christianity; and the central theme of Christianity is salvation by the mediation of Jesus Christ. Not alone, even against a God capable of predestination and foreordination, was man left to struggle; but in "The Scarlet Letter" the characters, in complete spiritual isolation, work out whatever of salvation they achieve, with no suggestion even in the tortured mind of Dimmesdale, a professed minister of the Gospel, that there could be divine aid or mediation. It is this, as much as the scientific and objective treatment of the characters, that makes the book cold. It is true in all but the essential.

The three elements of tragedy are here: struggle, suffering, the inevitable linking together in causal sequence; catharsis also, that mingled satisfaction and elevation, that sense of sharing with human nature in experiences so great, so noble that happiness, personal well being, can no longer raise even a question, so insignificant has it become.

With the letter on her breast, the baby in her arms, Hester faces her world, wins from it respect, even honor; and repents? Let her beaming eyes, her flushed cheeks in the forest answer. We are told much about her; occasionally we see her clearly. By the method of strongly contrasted moments, practised in many of his best tales, Hawthorne reveals her in flashes until at last she stands forth a beautiful, conquering figure, one of the world's sorrowing mothers.

Torn by mental conflict, corroded by remorse, Arthur Dimmesdale adds to his first sin that of hypocrisy, knows and yet persists, and at the end breaks through the hideous coil by a confession he was too weak to make when it could have helped either himself or others. The character is more complicated than Hester's, consequently the treatment is more subtle; the analysis of hypocrisy, the self-deception alternating with mercilessly clear self-recognition, the cowardice and the devotion to that which honestly the man held as the highest good, all these are given with sureness that is never hard and subtlety that is never vague.

These two, Hester and Dimmesdale, are the centers of interest, united by sin, separated by suffering. Between them winds the cruel, gloating Chillingworth, taking upon himself the task of the avenger. The character is not studied as closely as are the others; it had not in it that which was to Hawthorne the very heart of the problem, consciousness of sin.

Pearl is the incarnation of the sin of her parents; could their suffering for a moment cease, there she is to renew it, brilliant, wayward, the expression of a broken law. A creation of imagination but with more than one touch of reality drawn from Hawthorne's idolized and fascinating oldest child, an emanation of the problem, an exposition of the theme, a living symbol, flashing color, light, vibrant motion into the darkened, awful quiet of the tale—all this and far more is Pearl; and the ultimate wonder is that in addition she is a reality.

In material symbolism the book is rich; to some it seems overloaded, but not to those who know the background Hawthorne was reproducing. Widely read in New England history, avid for tradition and legend of his own people, Hawthorne knew the lurid superstition, the allegorizing tendency, the projection of internal experience into external expression, and the translation of phenomena in terms of consciousness, especially in terms of the Divine Will. Using the medium that he had perfected in the lonely years, he filled his romance with symbolism, the rosebush by the jail door, the scarlet letter itself, the minister's gesture, the brook and the forest, and finally the flaring sign in the sky. Nowhere in the romance is he truer to the spirit of early New England than in this final treatment of the symbol.

In his acceptance of moral law Hawthorne is allied at once with the Hebrew and with the Greek poets. Living in the middle of the nineteenth century, he was inevitably affected by the romantic movement; and those who like to trace affinities find a rich field along this line of inquiry. Slightly, more slightly in "The Scarlet Letter" than in some of his writing, he was touched by the New England form of idealistic philosophy known as Transcendentalism. As an artist, he was almost entirely independent, self-directed, unique. But in his attitude toward life, in his inner thought, he was bone of the bone, blood of the blood of Puritan New England.

William Lyon Phelps, "Introduction" to *The Scarlet Letter* (New York: Modern Library, 1927), pp. ix-xvi.

Hawthorne is the most consummate literary artist in American literature, and *The Scarlet Letter* is the greatest book ever written in the Western Hemisphere. It is not relatively, but absolutely great; it holds its place among the fifteen best novels of the world. As so much American literature is both second-rate and second-hand, rising above mediocrity when most imitative, and shaggy with crudity when most original, it is well to remember that in *The Scarlet Letter* we have a work of art profoundly original in conception and design, profound in its revelation and interpretation of human nature, accurate in its historical setting and written in a style almost impeccable.

Hawthorne was, as Hutton called him, "The ghost of New

England"; he came of a long line of Puritan ancestors, he was born at Salem in 1804, he was graduated at Bowdoin College, spent twelve lonely years in one room learning to write, married exactly the right kind of wife, and had that shyness and unconquerable reserve that sometimes accompany the artistic temperament. Politically and socially, he had a genius for the inopportune; he was born on the Fourth of July, he remained a Democrat when nearly all his intimate friends were Abolitionists, and when Emerson declared that John Brown had made the gallows as memorable as the Cross, Hawthorne remarked, "No man was ever more justly hanged."

Upon his New England and Puritan foundation, he superimposed seven years' residence in Europe, and died in 1864.

When he lost his position in the Custom House at Salem, he came home in despondency, and told his wife that his occupation was gone. To his surprise, she greeted this information with delight, and said, "Now you can write your book." "And what shall we live on while I am writing it?" Her reply was to exhibit a little hoard of money which she had saved from the meagre weekly wage he had given her for household expenses. She told him she had always known he was a genius, and that the time would come when it would be necessary for him to have leisure.

In a year he wrote *The Scarlet Letter* (1850). Its greatness was instantly recognised; he found himself famous. In 1851 the German translation appeared, and in 1853 the French. It has been translated into all the leading languages of the world, has been dramatised, made into a grand opera, and lately received the dubious honour of the screen.

Hawthorne is original in his background; it is a background of sombre greys and browns, on which his brilliant figures stand out in sharp relief. There is a shadowy region which he has made entirely his own. It is not the ghoul-haunted region of Weir, for there is little in common between Poe and Hawthorne, however inevitable the comparison. The difference is that between the physical and spiritual; Poe is uncanny, high-pitched, sensational; Hawthorne is subdued and subtle. To read him is to experience a change in the atmosphere rather than a change in the scenery.

His world of shadows is quite terrestrial; we do not really leave the earth. Over his creations hangs a thin veil of fantasy, poetry, romance, and we see his characters through this transparent, gossamer, silver-grey mist, analogous to the light covering the pictures of Andrea del Sarto. This atmosphere is never "worked-up," nor can it possibly be detached from the story, any more than the air can be lifted off the grass.

Hawthorne is an ideal realist. He is not a romance-writer, like Cooper; he is not primarily interested in happenings and adventures. Yet he is by no means a realist like Zola, nor for that matter like George Eliot; perhaps Turgenev more nearly resembles him than any other writer. It is realism seen through a poetic medium.

The Introduction on the Custom House—which building was unfortunately burned in 1921—was written I suppose mainly to relieve his own mind. Here his ironical humour found a subject made to his hand. Little did the bench-warmers who decorated his office suspect that the shy man was shrewdly judging them, and storing them up for literary material. As so often happens, both parties in these casual conversations regarded the other with secret contempt. Hawthorne's advantage was in having an outlet.

Apart from the intense human interest of the narrative, *The Scarlet Letter* expresses the sombre side of Puritan life. That was not the only side, for life even then went on its accustomed course. Young lovers kissed each other in the moonlight, as they have always done; and there must have been some frivolity, else why were such measures taken to repress it? But the most striking, the most picturesque aspect of Puritan life, as we look back on it from laxer times, was its austerity. I suppose those who suffered the most were the children—for there was no place for them in the Puritan regime. Their mature masters would doubtless have heartily approved of the following pedagogic recommendations, given out by a German moralist in the eighteenth century.

> Play must be forbidden in any and all of its forms. The children shall be instructed in this matter in such a way as to show them the wastefulness and folly of all play. They shall be led to see that play will distract their hearts and minds from God and will work nothing but harm to their spiritual life.

The times have changed. Now the entire family revolves around the nursery, where dwells the seat of authority, and the desires of the child are the law of the home. Probably the children are making the most of it, while the good weather lasts.

The sombre background of Puritanism brings out the flame of *The Scarlet Letter*. The colours of the book are a notable part of its scheme. Sunshine and shadow alternate in the great scene by the brook, where for once the accursed letter leaves Hester's bosom, youth and charm return to her face, only to fade when Pearl refastens the symbol. Pearl herself, the child of passion, flutters across the dark pages of the book, like a brilliant, exotic bird across a sullen sky. For, in that cold community, she is as exotic as a tropical visitor, coming as she does, from a country not only unvisited, but unmentionable.

Private sin was followed by public shame. They wore their rue with a difference, but they wore it. In the Colony Records of New Playmouth, dated June, 1671, we find (see Alice Morse Earle, *Curious Punishments of Bygone Days*), that the detected ones were forced

> to wear two Capitall Letters, A.D., cut in cloth and sewed on their uppermost garment on the Arm and Back; and in any time they shall be founde without the letters so worne while in this government they shall be forthwith taken and publickly whipt.

Not only is this novel a study of Puritan life externally— the spiritual foundation of the book is Puritanism. The consciousness of sin is the core of the tragedy. The four characters are linked indissolubly together by one caprice. A sin by many considered lightly; the source of vulgar jest since the dawn of history; the object of religious worship by some ancient Pagans and by some modern novelists, is here painted in the deepest grain; painted with its inevitable consequences. There are many who rebel fiercely against what they regard as the unfairness of the punishment, for there are many who are trying to play the game of life without obeying the rules.

Had the Puritan Jonathan Edwards written the book, instead of the cool artist Hawthorne, he could not have depicted sin in more powerful language. Thus I could wish that Hawthorne had not added the final chapter, but had let the book close with the dying confession of the minister, and its echo from the crowd.

George Woodberry says,

> It is a relentless tale; the characters are singularly free from self-pity, and accept their fate as righteous; they never forgave themselves, they show no sign of having forgiven one another; even God's forgiveness is left under a shadow of futurity. . . . A book from which light and love are absent may hold us by its truth to what is dark in life; but, in the highest sense, it is a false book.

I dislike to differ from such a critic, and from one who adds to his critical perception so sure a sense of moral values. But here he misses the point. To answer his main contention, regard Chillingworth, remembering that it was often Hawthorne's way to show an idea negatively. Chillingworth is transformed from a calm, benign scholar, with the impersonal expression of an investigator, into a fiend; hell has dominion over him, and his eyes glow with the glare of the pit. This degradation is brought about by the subtle poison of revenge; because he cannot forgive, and be free. His face changes by the slow cancer of hate into something inhuman.

Light and love are not absent from the book; over the scaffold there is a celestial glory. And the objection of Mr. Woodberry, that "the characters are singularly free from self-pity," is not this one of Hawthorne's greatest triumphs? Think of the vast number of people to-day, in and out of novels, who insist on their "right to happiness," no matter by what degradation it is attained, nor by what pain caused to others. Arthur and Hester are made of sterner stuff, as became the age in which they lived, as became their sense of responsibility, as became their respect for each other's soul. They were free from the insidious weakness of self-pity.

Another leading idea in the book is the contrast between the loss of public respect and the loss of private respect, self-respect. Hester suffers the worst possible punishment that may befall a woman—public ostracism. There are those who say they do not care what anybody thinks of them; granting that they are speaking truly, a difficult admission, how if such a one were shunned on the streets as if one had some disgusting and contagious disease? How if every public appearance meant the derisive hooting by small boys, the studious crossing to the other side by former acquaintances, enforced isolation worse than a prison cell? That is what Hester has to endure. But the worst has happened; she at all events has nothing to fear. She suffers more on the street than in the solitude of her own room. There she has peace.

Compared with the minister, she is enviable. He is the public idol. What gall, what wormwood, it must be to him to hear his praises sung to his face, to be told by adoring parishioners of the good his sermons have wrought, to be saluted on the street with all the marks of reverence—and to have the scarlet letter burning in his breast! How intolerable his solitude!

Not only is the book a revelation of the powers of the air, but even the *bodies* of the chief actors express their souls. This has already been pointed out in the case of Chillingworth; consider the varied thoughts of Hester in her varied meetings with Arthur, and how her face changes with them; consider the minister, with his hand on his heart, his body wearing thin from the inner fire till it becomes almost transparent; consider the whimsical fancies of Pearl, and how they are reflected in her eyes. Such presentations remind us of the words of Donne, speaking of the young girl:

> Her pure and eloquent blood
> Spoke in her cheeks, and so distinctly wrought,
> That one might almost say, her body thought.

It is instructive by contrast to compare Flaubert's *Madame Bovary* with Hawthorne's *Scarlet Letter*. Both men were equally deliberate artists. In *Madame Bovary* we have a picture of degeneration ending in despair. Life has no solution. In *The Scarlet Letter*, we have sin and its consequences, illumined at last by the light of heaven. Flaubert has nothing but scorn for his characters, whereas Hawthorne treats all of his people with dignity. He did not show the sympathy with his characters that we find in Dickens and Thackeray, but he was deeply moved by their fate.

There is another difference between these two masterpieces. Flaubert was interested in the sin itself, and is not sparing of details. Hawthorne is interested only in the mental consequences. Hence he purposely began his story after the crime, in order to concentrate wholly on the spiritual and mental results. It is falling action.

The evolution of the story is flawless. The plot unfolds as naturally and with as little apparent effort as the petals of a flower. In this respect, Hawthorne is superior to Balzac; for in the works of the French giant we feel the expense of energy. Here we have a natural beginning, a natural development, with an inexpressibly affecting conclusion. *The Scarlet Letter* illustrates Hardy's definition of a novel, that it should be a living organism.

Modern Criticism

Neal Frank Doubleday, "Hawthorne's Hester and Feminism," *PMLA*, 54 (September 1939), 825-828.

When G. P. Lathrop wrote his *A Study of Hawthorne* (1876) he found it necessary, in discussing the interpretation of *The Scarlet Letter*, to protest against the identification of Hawthorne's own beliefs with those given to Hester.[1] Lathrop's protest—which has not much affected subsequent criticism—was directed against a violent review by Arthur Cleveland Coxe, one of three early reviews which mark the beginning of a persistent misapprehension (as it seems to me) in the interpretation of *The Scarlet Letter*.[2] It has almost become a convention to insist that Hawthorne means to advocate a new standard of sex morality in passages like Hester's words: "What we did had a consecration of its own. We felt it so! We said so to each other!"[3] Austin Warren has found sufficient reason to point out again that Hawthorne is careful to characterize the rebellion of Hester as the rebellion of one who "had wandered without rule or guidance, in a moral wilderness," and that Hawthorne is careful to say that "Her intellect and heart had their home . . . in desert places . . . . Shame, Despair, Solitude! These had been her teachers . . . and they had made her strong, but taught her much amiss."[4]

It is the purpose of this note, not to discuss any moral question, but to present one argument against seizing upon the "consecration" of Hester's love as the theme and moral of *The Scarlet Letter*. There are (I believe) other and more important refutations of this interpretation than the one here offered. But this interpretation, whether combined with approval or disapproval, has obscured an interesting aspect of the character of Hester: the way in which she represents feminist thought in Hawthorne's own time. And this aspect of Hester is important to the proper interpretation of the book, for if Hester is in part a type feminist, Hawthorne would hardly have intended an identification of her views and his own. Austin Warren has called Hester "A feminist in advance of the season."[5] Our question will be: how far are Hester's feminist attitudes further evidence for Warren's contention that she cannot be supposed to speak Hawthorne's own view or the book's moral?

Feminist ideas were part of the intellectual climate in which Hawthorne lived, and they converged in a movement which, O. B. Frothingham says, "more definitely than any other . . . can trace its beginning and source of its inspiration to the disciples of the transcendental philosophy."[6] Now what Hawthorne has to say in *The Scarlet Letter* on Hester's position plainly has contemporary reference, and plainly accords with his remarks on feminism elsewhere. Hester, in her distress, falls into errors that are like opinions Hawthorne saw as errors in his own time. Chapter XIII is, almost in its entirety, a discussion of them. Hester had been estranged from the normal existence of woman, in a different way from the feminists among Hawthorne's contemporaries, but still estranged, as they too were estranged. "Some attribute had departed from her, the permanence of which had been essential to keep her a woman." In turning away from the normal life of a woman, "She assumed a freedom of speculation"; and her speculation was, "Was existence worth accepting, even to the happiest" of women? Hawthorne proceeds to outline the task of the feminist as he sees it.

> She discerns, it may be, such a hopeless task before her. As a first step, the whole system of society is to be torn down, and built up anew. Then, the very nature of the opposite sex, or its long hereditary habit, which has become like nature, is to be essentially modified, before woman can be allowed to assume what seems a fair and suitable position.

But not only will these impossible changes have to precede the effective operation of feminist ideals, but woman will have to change her own essential nature, and what then? "Perhaps," Hawthorne answers, "the ethereal essence, wherein she has her truest life, will be found to have evaporated." If a woman have a normal life, these problems do not arise; if she be in normal emotional balance, they solve themselves:

> A woman never overcomes these problems by any exercise of thought. They are not to be solved, or only in one way. If her heart chance to come uppermost, they vanish. Thus, Hester Prynne, whose heart had lost its regular and healthy throb, wandered without a clew in the dark labyrinth of mind: now

> turned aside by an insurmountable precipice; now staring back from a deep chasm. There was wild and ghastly scenery all around her, and a home and comfort nowhere.[7]

This is not the splendid example of self-reliance some of Hester's interpreters would have her be; it is, rather, an infinitely pathetic Hester, in whom, to borrow Newton Arvin's words, passion and feeling have given away to thought "expressive not so much of her whole being as of a specialized and 'unwomanly' function," and to whom is lost the sense of human reality.[8]

It is Hawthorne's treatment, in *The Blithedale Romance*, of Zenobia and her feminism which offers the closest parallels to his remarks on Hester's speculations concerning women's sphere, although other passages may be cited.[9] It is—before Zenobia has learned by experience—her belief and prophecy "that, when my sex shall achieve its rights, there will be ten eloquent women where there is now one eloquent man." Her sphere shall be "the living voice" and by it she shall compel the world's recognition. Coverdale's reflection on all this seems to be Hawthorne's own:

> What amused and puzzled me was the fact, that women, however intellectually superior, so seldom disquiet themselves about the rights or wrongs of their sex, unless their own individual affections chance to lie in idleness, or to be ill at ease. They are not natural reformers, but become such by the pressure of exceptional misfortune. I could measure Zenobia's inward trouble by the animosity with which she now took up general quarrel of woman against man.[10]

Finally, when Zenobia has suffered the loss of Hollingsworth's love, Hawthorne makes her describe her own condition in much the same terms that he used to describe Hester's, although her speech is, of course, in character, and she retains her resentment. The moral is, she says, "That the whole universe, her own sex and yours, and Providence, or Destiny, to boot, make common cause against the woman who swerves one hair's-breadth, out of the beaten track." But her judgment of herself is, it will be noted, exactly parallel to Hawthorne's judgment of Hester: "Yes, and add (for I may as well own it now) that, with that one hair's- breadth, she goes all astray and never sees the world in its true aspects afterwards."[11] Zenobia, her natural affections "ill at ease," though for a different reason from Hester's, like Hester "assumed a freedom of speculation." In both feminism is the product of abnormal adjustment. Both "wandered without a clew."

It need not detract from anyone's appreciation of the emotional richness of *The Scarlet Letter* to recognize that, in his treatment of

Hester, Hawthorne embodies his criticism of a movement contemporary with him, for the portrait of Hester is sympathetic, not satirical. And this aspect of Hester's thinking does show Hawthorne aware of the life and thought about him. Hawthorne's position is plain: there is no abstract solution for a problem so complicated by the nature of humanity itself. He has Hester learn, finally, that a woman estranged from normal experience in whatever way cannot see her own problems in perspective; she recognizes at last "the impossibility that any mission of divine and mysterious truth should be confided to a woman stained with sin, bowed down with shame, or even burdened with a life-long sorrow."[12] No one, certainly, is under an obligation to agree with Hawthorne, but there is no reason why one should not attend to what he says.[13]

[1]G. P. Lathrop, *A Study of Hawthorne* (Boston, 1876), pp. 214-222.

[2]George B. Loring, *Massachusetts Quarterly Review*, III (September, 1850), 484-500; Orestes Brownson, *Brownson's Quarterly Review*, new series IV (October, 1850), 528-532; Arthur Cleveland Coxe, "The Writings of Hawthorne," *Church Review*, III (New Haven, January, 1851), 489-511. Lathrop incorrectly says (*op. cit.*, p. 222) that Loring's review followed and answered Coxe's but it seems likely that Coxe's attack was in reality inspired by Loring's review. See Coxe, *loc. cit.*, p. 503 and M. D. Conway, *Life of Nathaniel Hawthorne* (London, 1895), p. 130. The difference between the two reviews is not a matter of interpretation, but one of attitude.

[3]*The Scarlet Letter*, p. 234. (References are to the Riverside edition of Hawthorne.) For examples of the identification of Hester's words and Hawthorne's own attitude see Conway, *op. cit.*, pp. 130-131; George E. Woodberry, *Nathaniel Hawthorne* (Boston, 1902), pp. 197-198; Lloyd Morris, *The Rebellious Puritan* (New York, 1927), pp. 229-230; Carl Van Doren, *The American Novel* (New York, 1933), pp. 90-92; John Erskine, *C.H.A.L.* II, 26-27. Morris's discussion is an extreme example.

[4]*The Scarlet Letter*, pp. 239-240. See Warren, *Nathaniel Hawthorne* (New York, 1934), p. xxxiv.

[5]Warren, p. xxix.

[6]*Transcendentalism in New England* (New York, 1876), p. 175. The actual movement for women's political and economic rights seems to have grown more immediately out of the antislavery movement. See C. R. Fish, *The Rise of the Common Man 1830-1850* (New York, 1935), pp. 270-271. Of course feminism was not entirely new in the forties.

[7]*The Scarlet Letter*, pp. 198-201.

[8]*Hawthorne* (Boston, 1929) pp. 188-189.

[9]Hawthorne compares Hester to Ann Hutchinson (p. 199). In "Mrs. Hutchinson," one of Hawthorne's early essays, he says: "We will not look for a living resemblance of Mrs. Hutchinson, though the search might not be altogether fruitless. But there are portentous indications, changes gradually taking place in the habits and feelings of the gentle sex, which seem to threaten our posterity with many of those public women, whereof one was burden too grievous for our fathers" (*Sketches*, p. 217). The question recurs in Hawthorne's last period, and in *Septimius Felton* he make Sibyl Dacy speculate upon what she will do for women in the aeons of existence Septimius promises her. But at the end of her questioning she finds no answer: "And then if, after all this investigation, it turns out—as I suspect—that woman is not capable of being helped, that there is something inherent in herself that makes it hopeless to struggle for her redemption, then what shall I do? Nay, I know not. . ." (p. 406). Compare Hawthorne's remarks on women novelists, Caroline Ticknor, *Hawthorne and his Publisher* (Boston, 1913), pp. 141-142.

[10]*The Blithedale Romance*, pp. 456-457.

[11]*The Blithedale Romance*, p. 573.

[12]*The Scarlet Letter*, p. 311.

[13]An amusing sidelight on all this is to be found in a letter from Mrs. Hawthorne to her mother, which comments upon some article of Margaret Fuller's—probably the *Dial* paper which was later expanded into *Woman in the Nineteenth Century*. Mrs. Hawthorne writes in much the terms Hawthorne himself might have put into the mouth of a happily married woman, had he portrayed one. She says: "It seems to me that if she were married truly, she would no longer be puzzled about the rights of woman. This is the revelation of woman's true destiny and place, which never can be *imagined* by those who do not experience the relation. In perfect, high union there is no question of supremacy. . . . Had there never been false and profane marriages, there would . . . be no commotion about woman's rights . . . " (Quoted in Julian Hawthorne, *Hawthorne and his Wife* [Boston, 1885], I, 257. The letter is of 1843). Hawthorne perhaps considered Elizabeth Peabody as among the thwarted women who turned to some activity or agitation as compensation. At least he writes from Liverpool in 1855, evidently in some annoyance: "I sometimes feel as if I ought . . . to endeavor to enlighten you as to the relation between husband and wife . . . . But the conjugal relation is one God never meant you to share, and which therefore He apparently did not give you the instinct to understand; so there my labor would be lost" (Quoted in Randall Stewart, *American Notebooks* [New Haven, 1932], p. 328).

Chester E. Eisinger, "Pearl and the Puritan Heritage," ***College English*****, 12 (March 1951), 323-329.**

I

Pearl, the perverse love-child in *The Scarlet Letter*, "is perhaps the most modern child in literature," D. H. Lawrence remarks somewhat facetiously, because she is, on the one hand, loving and understanding and, on the other, ready to hit you across the mouth. Risking prophecy, Lawrence asserts that "she'll be a devil to men when she grows up."[1] It is true that Pearl is one of the most difficult children in literature. Not only is she endowed with an extraordinary capacity for downright orneriness and, seemingly, a supernally granted intelligence with regard to the several dilemmas of her parents, but she has also been a perennial problem for critics who seek to understand her function in the novel and who are dissatisfied with the obvious explanation that she is the symbol of sin. The difficulties surrounding Pearl are complex, but few if any of them are to be explained on the basis of her modernity. On the contrary, it is the purpose of the present paper to indicate that Pearl is an old-fashioned child—in fact, a child whose wayward course through the novel, culminating in a happy marriage and an apparently stable life (Lawrence's prophecy notwithstanding), is based on orthodox Puritan postulates of the seventeenth century.

Criticism has done so much to mark-out and define the influence of puritanism upon Hawthorne that we need not dwell upon the matter here. Suffice it to say that the evidence of Hawthorne's indebtedness to the Puritans is overwhelming.[2] The proposition that little Pearl may be understood by reference to the Puritan theories of nature and liberty, therefore, is not as far-fetched as it might appear. The claim put forward here is that Pearl is a "natural" child not only in her illegitimacy but in the natural, i.e., unfettered, condition of her life. As wild and as free as nature, she owes allegiance to the domain of nature. She is, as a consequence, virtually beyond the reach of divine salvation and is completely outside human society. Now Hawthorne, believing as the Puritans did that each individual soul is precious, is under obligation to release Pearl from her bondage to nature, find her a place in human society, and make her a consciously human creature. Then she will be susceptible to God's grace should it be offered her. He meets his problem by subjecting Pearl to a kind of psychic shock when Dimmesdale, in his expiation scene, recognizes her as his daughter and awakens through suffering all her human sympathies, thus sweeping her into the community of men. Before this she was unable to obey civil and divine law. Now she may, if she will.

It is necessary at this point to set forth the portions of Puritan thought relevant to this discussion: the view of nature and the conception of polity. No sharp distinction can be made between the two because certain basic assumptions are prevalent in all aspects of Puritan thought.

According to Puritan theory, adherence of the unregenerate man to nature and natural law will lead to a life of riot and confusion. Such a man is a creature of instincts, carrying his appetites and ambitions to excess. No one can doubt, says John Cotton, "the depravation of nature."[3] For the regenerate man, however, nature is good. The Puritan defined nature as the art of God,[4] but, since the Fall has invalidated the efficacy of human reason, only those men who through faith have been granted God's salvation can read aright the lessons of nature. The Puritan held that no one, whether or not in a state of grace, can live by nature alone.

Nature and the unregenerate man are factors necessary to a discussion of Puritan polity, for they are integral to a discrimination between natural and civil liberty and between natural and civil government. The natural man, according to the Puritans, enjoyed natural liberty, which was antithetical to civil liberty and led to excesses in conduct. To live by natural liberty was to deny the authority of God and the doctrine of original sin. The social covenant could be preserved only by adherence to the doctrine of civil liberty. A sound Puritan commonwealth, therefore, could not tolerate the exercise of natural liberties nor abide the presence of those who lived by them. Only those individuals who were conscientiously working toward salvation or those who had already attained it could be admitted into Puritan society. These could be trusted to honor the ends and observe the limitations of civil liberty.

These ideas were given definitive form in John Winthrop's famous speech to the General Court in July, 1645. Here natural and civil liberty were distinguished. The first is common to man and beast and is liberty to do evil as well as good. It will not brook the restraint of just authority, and it makes men "grow more evil." Civil liberty, on the other hand, recognizes the covenant between God and man and bows to the authority of magistrates who govern according to "the rules of God's law." This is the liberty "to that only which is good, just, and honest."[5] In much the same fashion, Samuel Willard concludes that natural liberty and laws might have been valid before the Fall, but now that man is in a state of sin "necessity requires . . . the establishment of Civil Government."[6] Obedience to civil law and repudiation of natural law assure an orderly existence within a stable state.

II

In the opening chapter of *The Scarlet Letter* Hawthorne calls our attention to "a wild rose-bush" growing at the side of the prison door. Its flowers "might be imagined to offer their fragrance and fragile beauty to the prisoner as he went in, and to the condemned criminal as he came forth to his doom, in token that the deep heart of Nature could pity and be kind to him." What was the origin of the rosebush? With characteristic diffidence, Hawthorne suggests alternate possibilities: it has survived out of the wilderness, or perhaps "it had sprung up under the footsteps of the sainted Anne Hutchinson." Why does Hawthorne bring the rosebush into his story at this point? With a quiet cynicism he has been observing, prior to mention of the rosebush, that new colonies, utopian as they might be in intention, always establish at the outset a cemetery and a prison. These are the marks of civilization; the latter, especially, is a symbol of government and law. The rosebush, in obvious contrast, is wild. It is a throwback to the wilderness that existed before civil society in New England. Or its genesis is associated with Anne Hutchinson, who was, in the eyes of the Puritans, a criminal and who was thrust out of their society. Nature, therefore, has especial affinities with the wild or with the criminal, with that which is beyond the pale of civil society. Behind the prison door are Hester and Pearl. It seems clear that Hawthorne is seeking to identify the wildness of nature with sin against society: the first symbolized by the rosebush, the second personified by Hester and Pearl.

As the book progresses, Hawthorne seems to reinforce this identification. When Pearl and Hester visit the Governor's mansion, they walk into the garden, where the child, sighting the Governor's rosebushes, begins to cry for a red rose. Confronted by the dignitaries of church and state, among them the good Mr. Wilson, who seeks to catechize the child, Pearl acts perversely. She refuses to say who made her and finally announces that she "had not been made at all, but had been plucked by her mother off the bush of wild roses that grew by the prison-door." Although she is well aware of the answer expected of her, she prefers in her perversity this fanciful explanation that links her with the natural wildness of the uncultivated plant. Her departure from orthodoxy shocks the Governor, who is convinced of the darkness of her soul and of its depravity.

In still other portions of the novel Hester is granted a kinship with a real and moral wilderness that carries her beyond accepted Puritan attitudes toward society and theology. Hawthorne speaks of the wildness of her nature, which awakens the sympathy of the forest and its dwellers. He points out that Hester had been outlawed from society, and so freed, in a sense, she had developed an intellectual range far greater than Dimmesdale's. Her speculation had led her, however, into a "moral wilderness; as vast . . . as the untamed forest. . . . Her intellect and heart had their home, as it were, in desert places, where she roamed as freely as the wild Indian in his woods. . . . The tendency of her fate and fortunes has been to set her free." Freedom and nature stand on one side; on the other stand the stability, security, and orderliness that are embodied in the divinely directed Puritan community.

Hester, however, is not our principal interest, although it is useful to observe how Hawthorne works out the selfsame idea with respect to her and to Pearl.[7] Furthermore, it is clear that the moral wilderness has engulfed Hester partially as a consequence of a sin, of which Pearl is the living symbol.[8] Pearl is heir, then, not only to a passion that transcended the moral law but to an intellect that was at once free and subject to confusion. In short, Pearl's mother, having conceived the child in sin by giving way to natural passion, brings down upon herself and the child social and religious ostracism and forces herself and the child into a sympathetic relation with nature. As Hawthorne says, "The child's own nature had something wrong in it, which continually betokened she had been born amiss,—the effluence of her mother's lawless passion."

Indeed, if the reader attends to the consistent imagery applied to Pearl, he must come to regard her as an untamed, wild, even nonhuman creature. She is of nature but not of man. She is endowed with "natural dexterity" and "natural grace." On one occasion she is a lovely flower, possessed, a page later, with a "wild-flower prettiness." On at least five occasions she is likened to a bird: "a wild tropical bird, of rich plumage," a "floating sea-bird," and so on. On innumerable occasions she is a sprite, an imp, an elf, a dryad. Hawthorne endows her with "airy charm" and "elfish intelligence"; Pearl is hardly a human child but is an airy sprite, a little elf gathering handfuls of wild flowers. She is capable of an eldritch scream, and Hawthorne, indulging the Puritan appetite for demonology, has Mistress Hibbens suggest that the child is of the "lineage of the Prince of the Air!"

Certainly it is some instinctive, hardly human portion of the child's makeup that gives Pearl her feeling of affinity to Dimmesdale. As a mere babe she stretches her arms toward him. At the Governor's mansion, when he defends Hester's right to keep the child, Pearl, "that wild and flighty little elf," steals up to the minister and caresses him in an "unwonted mood of sentiment" and display of human emotions. She reverts immediately to airy indifference. It is as though the elfish and human portions of her soul were warring for mastery. In this struggle Dimmesdale holds the key. Throughout the novel, until Dimmesdale's confession, Pearl seeks recognition from her father and, being rejected, remains the "natural" child allied to the birds and to the creatures of the nether world. Not until Dimmesdale acknowledges her publicly, as we shall see, does she become a full-fledged human being.

For her kinship with nature is the dominant fact of her existence. Whenever she is outdoors, particularly in the wilderness, there seems to be a conscious desire on her part to merge with natural objects; while on the part of natural objects there is a tendency to absorb Pearl. She plays with her reflected image in a pool of water and seeks "a passage for herself into its sphere of impalpable earth and unattainable sky," as though she would become one with the elements. Again, when Pearl stands on one side of the brook, that "boundary between two worlds," and Hester and Dimmesdale summon her to the other side, Pearl seems to have melted into a natural environment, caressed by the sun, enveloped by and identified with the brook. Hester feels herself estranged from the child who seems to have "strayed out of the sphere in which she and her mother dwelt together" into the realm of Pan or the Druids. She gives up throwing pebbles at a flock of beach-birds after wounding one "because it grieved her to have done harm to a little being that was as wild as the sea-breeze, or as wild as Pearl herself." In the forest, when Hawthorne manipulates light and shade so magnificently, the sun seems deliberately to avoid Hester at first. But Pearl catches the sunshine, and "the light lingered about the lonely child, as if glad of such a playmate." Later, even the "great black forest . . . became the playmate of the lonely infant." Finally, Hawthorne makes explicit what has been evident for some time: "The truth seems to be . . . that the mother-forest, and these wild things which it nourished, all recognized a kindred wildness in the human child." Not always is she a human child, for when she decorates herself with wild violets, anemones, and columbines, she becomes a "nymph-child, or an infant dryad, or whatever else was in closest sympathy with the antique wood."

Hawthorne leaves us in no doubt as to the significance of Pearl's identification with nature. A disciple of neither the eighteenth century's belief in nature's simple plan nor the Romantic notion of living in harmony with nature, this latter-day Puritan looked askance at the uncontrolled and uncontrollable realms of nature. Pearl is wild because she is a child of nature. Nature is wild, untrammeled, because man cannot put his stamp upon it and regulate it. In the great colloquy in the forest, between Hester and Dimmesdale, the former announces firmly that the minister must escape his torture by fleeing to another land. Dimmesdale is tremendously relieved. He feels the "exhilarating effect . . . of breathing the wild, free atmosphere of an unredeemed, unchristianized, lawless region." Now, while Hawthorne does not say that this area is the domain of nature, he does make it quite clear that Dimmesdale is preparing to depart, spiritually as well as bodily, from the Christian community, which is the very antithesis of that region just described. Furthermore, nature seems to approve of this decision, as well as of this region. For no sooner do the lovers begin to savor the effects of their decision than the gloom of the forest vanishes. "Such was the sympathy of Nature—that wild, heathen Nature of the forest, never subjugated by human law, nor illumined by higher truth—with the bliss of these two spirits!" If Pearl is a child of this realm, then her wildness is understandable, as is her position with respect to the organized society of her time.

The Christian community does not admit Pearl or recognize her as one of its members because she belongs to nature and not to man or to human society. Nature finds a kindred wildness in Pearl; society demands that she be submissive. The ideals of the two areas are irreconcilable, and Pearl must become a part of one or of the other.

As a matter of fact, she has no choice in the matter. Society thrusts her out, while nature, as we have seen, takes her in. Her character and her origin determine in part the direction of her allegiance. Hawthorne tells us that, while Pearl's character possessed depth and variety, "it lacked reference and adaptation to the world into which she was born. The child could not be made amenable to rules. In giving her existence, a great law had been broken; and the result was a being whose elements were perhaps beautiful and brilliant, but all in disorder." Pearl is passionate and ungovernable. Her mother is forced to "permit the child to be swayed by her own impulses." Chillingworth remarks that " 'there is no law nor reverence for authority, no regard for human ordinances or opinions, right or wrong, mixed up with that child's composition.' " The only " 'discoverable principle of being' " governing her is " 'the freedom of a broken law,' " as Dimmesdale, so eminently qualified to make the judgment, says. The result is that Pearl is cut off from society and even from mankind. She was born an "outcast of the infantile world" who "had no right among christened infants." Puritan children of the community sensed something "outlandish, unearthly" in both Pearl and Hester, who "stood together in the same circle of seclusion from human society." No wonder, then, that Pearl looks upon the world as adverse. No wonder that she is likened to a "creature that had nothing in common with a bygone and buried generation, nor owned herself akin to it. It was as if she had been made afresh, out of new elements, and must perforce be permitted to live her own life, and be a law unto herself." The continuity of life that links most of us to society and to humanity is denied Pearl.

Yet, all the time, Hawthorne means to reclaim Pearl from nature and to restore her to the jurisdiction of God and man. He clings to the notion that a child of God can return to God. The Puritans held, after all, that God created both man and nature. While Pearl seems to be allied almost completely with nature, Hawthorne never allows us to forget that she has an immortal soul that God will eventually judge: God granted Hester a lovely child who could finally be a "blessed soul in heaven." Illegitimate though she may be, the authorities of the colony are concerned for her spiritual well-being in the interest, again, of her immortal soul. It is this concern that impels the Governor to propose that Pearl be taken from Hester. In the debate over this matter, Dimmesdale, who is defending Hester's interest in the child, argues that Pearl has " 'come from the hand of God' " to act on Hester as a blessing and a retribution and to teach her that if " 'she bring the child to heaven, the child also will bring its parent thither!' " These passages demonstrate conclusively that Hawthorne never abandons the child.

It is through Dimmesdale's expiation that Pearl becomes a human being. Her ultimate salvation rests with God, but her fate as a woman in this life lies in her father's hands. When he confesses his sin, Pearl is reclaimed from the realm of nature, and her wildness and perversity wither away. Or perhaps one could say that they are blown away by the kiss of love and recognition that Dimmesdale exchanges with Pearl when they come together on the scaffold in the revelation scene. "Pearl kissed his lips. A spell was broken. The great scene of grief, in which the wild infant bore a part, had developed all her sympathies; and as her tears fell upon her father's cheek, they were the pledge that she would grow up amid human joy and sorrow, nor forever do battle with the world, but be a woman in it." Into these sentences Hawthorne has packed virtually the complete significance of Pearl. Once the sin of her birth has been acknowledged, a psychic transformation overtakes her. When Dimmesdale reveals himself, the long search for the father is ended. A sense of certainty, even of social status, in a way, is now possible for Pearl. All the latent human emotions rise up in this crisis to overwhelm that wildness that had linked her to nature. Thus the expiation of the sin gives every expectation that Pearl will grow into a woman at one with the world, partaking of its good and of its bad as do all human beings. Mankind and society have claimed their own.

As the book trails off, Hawthorne gives us adequate assurance that Pearl has at last adapted herself to society. She becomes the richest heiress of her day in the New World. Probably "her wild, rich nature had been softened and subdued, and made capable of a woman's gentle happiness." We may safely surmise that, equipped with money and a receptive feminine disposition, Pearl makes a good marriage and bears children. She treats her mother with love and consideration. Pearl stands at the end as an apotheosis of Puritan morality.

III

The naturalistic characteristics of her morality are not the only Puritan attributes ascribed to Pearl, as we have seen. She is the hypostatization, in miniature, of the Puritan conception of nature and notion of the state. She is, until the end, a lost soul because her master is not God but nature. In the end, however, Dimmesdale's regeneration releases Pearl from the thraldom of nature. She is not saved, to be sure, but she is humanized. She is now in a position to follow God, if she will, whereas before this she must needs follow nature.

Shorn of her wild, rebellious spirit, Pearl is ready to live in society and to submit to its institutions and conventions. Before Dimmesdale confesses, Pearl is a symbol of natural liberty, perverse and wilful, consulting her own impulses and following them wherever conflicts arose. She is antisocial. She will not be governed by any human will or law. She is as unruly as nature and is therefore unfit for civil society. Only when these natural qualities are washed away in Dimmesdale's salvation does Pearl become a responsible human being, ready for admission into the community of men and, when Chillingworth's money came to her, even into the Puritan community.

[1] *Studies in Classic American Literature* (New York, 1923), pp. 143 and 145.

[2] Perceptive accounts of the author's relationship to his Puritan heritage may be found in Herbert Schneider, *The Puritan Mind* (New York, 1930), pp. 256-64; Yvor Winters, *Maule's Curse* (Norfolk, 1938), pp. 3-22; F. O. Matthiessen, *American Renaissance* (New York, 1941), pp. 179-368 *passim*; and Barriss Mills, "Hawthorne and Puritanism," *NEQ*, XXI (March, 1948), 78-102. A typical example of Hawthorne's use of Puritan doctrine is illustrated by Matthiessen's comment about Roger Chillingworth: "The physician's own transformation is handled with strictest accord to the Puritans' belief in how an erring mind could

become so divorced from God that it lapsed into a state of diabolic possession" (*op. cit.*, p. 306).

[3]Quoted in *The Puritans*, ed. Perry Miller and Thomas H. Johnson (New York, 1938), p. 50.

[4]Herbert W. Schneider, *A History of American Philosophy* (New York, 1946), p. 7.

[5]John Winthrop, *History of New England*, ed. James K. Hosmer (New York, 1908), II, 238-39.

[6]*The Character of a Good Ruler*, reprinted in *The Puritans*, pp. 250-51.

[7]It must be noted that Hawthorne does not accord the same treatment in all respects to Hester and to Pearl. The mother is a responsible human being throughout the novel and consciously accepts, in accordance with Puritan ways, the fate thrust upon her. Her penance is voluntary and lifelong and, ultimately, rewarding.

[8]There is abundant evidence for this assertion. Pearl is the "scarlet letter endowed with life" and the link in the sin of Hester and Dimmesdale: these two aspects of her symbolism are emphasized.

Darrel Abel, "Hawthorne's Hester," ***College English*****, 13 (March 1952), 303-309.**

Hester Prynne, the heroine of *The Scarlet Letter*, typifies romantic individualism, and in her story Hawthorne endeavored to exhibit the inadequacy of such a philosophy. The romantic individualist repudiates the doctrine of a supernatural ethical absolute. He rejects both the authority of God, which sanctions a pietistic ethic, and the authority of society, which sanctions a utilitarian ethic, to affirm the sole authority of Nature. Hester, violating piety and decorum, lived a life of nature and attempted to rationalize her romantic self-indulgence; but, although she broke the laws of God and man, she failed to secure even the natural satisfactions she sought.

Many modern critics, however, who see her as a heroine a la George Sand, accept her philosophy and regard her as the central figure of the romance—the spokesman of Hawthorne's views favoring "a larger liberty." Hawthorne's women are usually more sympathetic and impressive than his men; because Hester is more appealing than either her husband or her lover, it is easy to disregard their more central roles in the story.[1] Furthermore, the title of the romance is commonly taken to refer mainly to the letter on Hester's dress and thus somehow to designate her as the central figure; but, in fact, the ideal letter, not any particular material manifestation of it, is referred to in the title. Actually its most emphatic particular manifestation is the stigma revealed on Dimmesdale's breast in the climaxing chapter of the book, "The Revelation of the Scarlet Letter."

Hester's apologists unduly emphasize circumstances which seem to make her the engaging central figure of the romance, and they ignore or even decry the larger tendency of the book, which subordinates her and exposes her moral inadequacy. "She is a free spirit liberated in a moral wilderness."[2]

> She has sinned, but the sin leads her straightaway to a larger life. . . . Hawthorne . . . lets the sin elaborate itself, so far as Hester's nature is concerned, into nothing but beauty. . . . Since her love for Dimmesdale was the one sincere passion of her life, she obeyed it utterly, though a conventional judgment would have said that she was stepping out of the moral order. There is nothing in the story to suggest condemnation of her or of the minister in their sin. . . . The passion itself, as the two lovers still agree at the close of their hard experience, was sacred and never caused them repentance.[3]

This opinion sublimely disregards Hawthorne's elaborate exposition of the progressive moral dereliction of Hester, during which "all the light and graceful foliage of her character [was] withered up by this red-hot brand" of sinful passion. It even more remarkably ignores her paramour's seven-year-long travail of conscience for (in his own dying words) "the sin here so awfully revealed."

The most recent and immoderate advocate of Hester as the prepossessing exponent of a wider freedom in sexual relations is Professor Frederic I. Carpenter:

> In the last analysis, the greatness of *The Scarlet Letter* lies in the character of Hester Prynne. Because she dared to trust herself to believe in the possibility of a new morality in the new world, she achieved spiritual greatness in spite of her own human weakness, in spite of the prejudices of her Puritan society, . . . in spite of the prejudices of her creator himself.[4]

It is a tribute to Hawthorne's art that Hester's champion believes in her so strongly that he presumes to rebuke her creator for abusing her and rejoices in his conviction that she triumphs over the author's "denigrations."

In fact, Hawthorne does feel moral compassion for Hester, but her role in the story is to demonstrate that persons who engage our moral compassion may nevertheless merit moral censure. We sympathize with Hester at first because of her personal attraction, and our sympathy deepens throughout the story because we see that she is more sinned against than sinning.

The prime offender against her is Roger Chillingworth, who married her before she was mature enough to know the needs of her nature. There is a tincture of Godwinism—even of Fourierism—in Hawthorne's treatment of Hester's breach of her marriage obligations. Godwin held that marriage was "the most odious of all monopolies" and that it was everyone's duty to love the worthiest. After her lapse, Hester told her husband, "Thou knowest I was frank with thee. I felt no love, nor feigned any." According to Godwinian principles, then, her duty to him was slight, especially if a man came along whom she could love. Chillingworth freely acknowledged that he had wronged her in marrying her before she was aware of the needs of her nature: "Mine was the first wrong, when I betrayed thy budding youth into a false and unnatural relation with my decay." His second, less heinous, offense was his neglectfully absenting himself from her after their marriage. His experience understood what her innocence could not foresee, that the awakening passion in her might take a forbidden way: "If sages were ever wise in their own behoof, I might have foreseen all this." His third and culminating offense was his lack of charity toward her after her disgrace. Although he admitted his initial culpability in betraying her into "a false and unnatural relation," he refused to share the odium brought upon her in consequence of the situation he had created. True, he plotted no revenge against her, but cold forbearance was not enough. He was motivated not by love but by self-love; in his marriage and in his vengeance he cherished and pursued his private objects, to the exclusion of the claims of others, whose lives were involved with his own. He regarded his wife jealously, as a chattel,[5] not as a person with needs and rights of her own. Her error touched his compassion only perfunctorily, but it gave a mortal wound to his *amour-propre*. Hester's adulterous passion was nobler, for she wished that she might bear her paramour's shame and anguish as well as her own. Thus Chillingworth triply offended against her: he drew her into a relationship which made her liable to sin, did not duly defend her from the peril in which he had placed her, and cast her off when she succumbed.

The nature of Dimmesdale's offense against Hester is too obvious to require specification, but both Hester's conduct and his own deserve whatever extenuation may be due to the passionate and impulsive errors of inexperience: "This had been a sin of passion, not of principle, nor even purpose." The minister's conduct toward Hester, then, is less blameworthy than her husband's, who had knowingly and deliberately jeopardized her happiness and moral security; Dimmesdale tells Hester: "We are not, Hester, the worst sinners in the world. There is one worse than even the polluted priest!" A distinction must be made, however, between Dimmesdale's moral responsibility and Hester's; her sin was contingent upon his, and her conduct is therefore more deserving of palliation than his. Besides, he had moral defenses and moral duties which she did not have. He had a pastoral duty toward her and a professional duty to lead an exemplary life. Also, according to Hawthorne's view of the distinctive endowments of the sexes, Hester depended upon her womanly feeling, but he had the guidance of masculine intellect and moral erudition. Above all, he was free to marry to satisfy "the strong animal nature" in him, but Hester met her happiest choice too late, when she was "already linked and wedlock bound to a fell adversary." But the minister's really abominable fault was not his fornication; it was his unwillingness to confess his error, his hypocrisy. Hester wished she might bear his shame as well as her own, but he shrank from assuming his place beside her because his perilous pride in his reputation for sanctity was dearer to him than truth. Like Chillingworth, he wronged Hester and left her to bear the punishment alone.

Society wronged Hester as grievously as, though less invidiously than, particular persons wronged her. Hawthorne distinguished between society under its instinctively human aspect and society under its institutional aspect. Society as collective humanity sympathized and was charitable: "It is to the credit of human nature, that, except where its selfishness is brought into play, it loves more readily than it hates." But society under its institutional aspect pursued an abstraction, conceived as the general good, which disposed it vindictively toward errant individuals. Hawthorne remarked in "The New Adam and Eve": "[The] Judgment Seat [is] the very symbol of man's perverted state." A scheme of social justice supplants the essential law of love which is grounded in human hearts; any system of expedient regulations tends to become sacrosanct eventually, so that instead of serving humanity it becomes a tyrannical instrument for coercing nonconformists.

Harsh legalism has been remarked as a characteristic of the Puritan theocracy by social historians: "The effect of inhumane punishments on officials and the popular mind generally . . . [was apparently] a brutalizing effect . . . , rendering them more callous to human sufferings."[6] "To make the people good became the supreme task of the churches, and legalism followed as a matter of course."[7] "The theory was that Jehovah was the primary law-giver, the Bible a statute-book, the ministers and magistrates stewards of the divine will."[8] Hester, then, Hawthorne tells us, suffered "the whole dismal severity of the Puritanic code of law" in "a period when the forms of authority were felt to possess the sacredness of Divine institutions." Her punishment shows how society had set aside the humane injunction that men should love one another, to make a religion of the office of vengeance, which in the Scriptures is exclusively appropriated to God. The wild-rose bush, with "its delicate gems," which stood by the prison door, and "the burdock, pigweed, apple-peru, and other such unsightly vegetation" which grew with such appropriate luxuriance in the prison yard symbolize the mingled moral elements in "the dim, awful, mysterious, grotesque, intricate nature of man."[9] Puritan society, unfortunately, had cultivated the weeds and neglected the flowers of human nature and attached more significance to "the black flower of civilized life, a prison," than to the rose bush, "which, by a strange chance, has been kept alive in history" "to symbolize some sweet moral blossom." There is powerful irony in Hawthorne's picture of the harsh matrons who crowded around the pillory to demand that Hester be put to death: "Is there not law for it? Truly, there is, both in Scripture and the statute-book." Surely Hawthorne was here mindful of the question which the scribes and Pharisees put to Jesus concerning the woman taken in adultery: "Now Moses in the law commanded us that such should be stoned: but what sayest thou?" The harshness of this tirade reflects the perversion of womanliness which has been wrought among this "people amongst whom religion and law were almost identical." A man in the crowd offered timely reproof to the chider: "Is there no virtue in woman, save what springs from a wholesome fear of the gallows?"—a reminder that virtue must be voluntary, an expression of character, and that there is little worth in a virtue that is compulsory, an imposition of society.

The ostracism called too lenient a punishment by the perhaps envious matrons of the town was almost fatal to Hester's sanity and moral sense, for it almost severed "the many ties, that, so long as we breathe the common air . . . , unite us to our kind." "Man had marked this woman's sin by a scarlet letter, which had such potent and disastrous efficacy that no human sympathy could reach her, save it were sinful like herself." Even children "too young to comprehend wherefore this woman should be shut out from the sphere of human charities" learned to abhor the woman upon whom society had set the stigma of the moral outcast. The universal duty of "acknowledging brotherhood even with the guiltiest" was abrogated in the treatment of Hester:

> In all her intercourse with society, . . . there was nothing which made her feel as if she belonged to it. . . . She was banished, and as much alone as if she inhabited another sphere, or communicated with the common nature by other organs and senses than the rest of human kind. She stood apart from moral interests, yet close beside them, like a ghost that revisits the familiar fireside, and can no longer make itself seen or felt.

The peculiar moral danger to Hester in her isolation was that it gave her too little opportunity for affectionate intercourse with other persons. Hawthorne regarded a woman's essential life as consisting in the right exercise of her emotions. His attitude toward women is that of Victorian liberalism; he looked upon them as equal to men, but differently endowed. To him, the distinctive feminine virtues were those characteristic of ideal wifehood and motherhood: instinctive purity and passionate devotion. His prescription for the happiest regulation of society was "Man's intellect, moderated by Woman's tenderness and moral sense."[10] Dimmesdale's history shows the corruption of the masculine virtues of reason and authority in a sinner who has cut himself off from the divine source of those virtues; Hester's history shows the corruption of the feminine virtues of passion and submission in a sinner who has been thrust out from the human community on which those virtues depend for their reality and function. In this essential feminine attribute, the working of her moral sensibility through her feelings rather than her thought, she bears a strong general resemblance to Milton's Eve (who is, however, more delicately conceived). She is a pure (as Hardy used the term) or very (as Shakespeare would have said) woman: that is, a charmingly real woman whose abundant sexuality, "whatever hypocrites austerely talk," was the characteristic and valuable endowment of her sex.

In consequence of her ostracism, Hester's life turned, "in a great measure, from passion and feeling, to thought"; she "wandered without a clew in the dark labyrinth of mind." Reflecting bitterly upon her own experience, she was convinced equally of the injustice and the hopelessness of a woman's position in society:

> Was existence worth accepting, even to the happiest among them? As concerned her own individual existence, she had long ago decided in the negative. . . . [A woman who considers what reforms are desirable discerns] a hopeless task before her. As a first step, the whole system of society is to be torn down, and built up anew. Then, the very nature of the opposite sex, or its long hereditary habit, which has become like nature, is to be essentially modified, before woman can be allowed to assume what seems a fair and suitable position. Finally, all other difficulties being obviated, woman cannot take advantage of these preliminary reforms, until she herself shall have undergone a still mightier change; in which, perhaps, the ethereal essence, wherein she has her truest life, will be found to have evaporated.

Although Hawthorne to some degree sympathized with Hester's rebellious mood, he did not, as Stuart P. Sherman averred, represent her as "a free spirit liberated in a moral wilderness," but as a human derelict who "wandered, without rule or guidance, in a moral wilderness." "A woman never overcomes these problems by any exercise of thought," and Hester's teachers—"Shame, Despair, Solitude!"—had "taught her much amiss." Thus, unfitted by her intense femininity for intellectual speculations, as well as by her isolation from the common experience of mankind, which rectifies aberrant thought, she unwomaned herself and deluded herself with mistaken notions.

The pathetic moral interdependence of persons is strikingly illustrated in the relations of Hester, Dimmesdale, and little Pearl. Dimmesdale acceded to Hester's plan of elopement because his will was enfeebled and he needed her resolution and affection to support him, but he was well aware that her proposals would be spiritually fatal to them. He evaded this death of the soul by the grace of God, who granted him in his death hour the strength to confess and deliver himself from the untruth which threatened his spiritual extinction. His dramatic escape fortuitously prevented Hester from surrendering her soul to mere nature in flight from her unhappiness. The rescue of her soul is as much a matter of accident as the shipwreck of her happiness had been. It is one of the truest touches of Hawthorne's art that Hester was not reclaimed to piety by the edifying spectacle of Dimmesdale's death in the Lord but that persistent in error, even as he expired in her arms breathing hosannas, she frantically insisted that her sole hope of happiness lay in personal reunion with him—in heaven, if not on earth.

One channel of moral affection in her life, however, had never been clogged—her love for little Pearl. This had sustained her in her long solitude by affording a partial outlet for her emotions, and Hawthorne's rather perfunctory and improbable "Conclusion" informs us that, when she had abated her resentment at being frustrated of worldly happiness, the affection between her and little Pearl drew her into a state of pious resignation and thus served as a means of positive redemption.

In the last analysis, the error for which Hester suffered was her too-obstinate supposition that human beings had a right to happiness. "Hester's tragedy came upon her in consequence of excessive yielding to her own heart."[11] Hawthorne remarked in his notebooks that "happiness in this world, if it comes at all, comes incidentally. Make it the object of pursuit, and it leads us a wild-goose chase, and is never attained." The proper pursuit of man, he thought, was not happiness but a virtuous life; he inherited the Puritan conviction that

> the good which God seeks and accomplishes is the display of infinite being, a good which transcends the good of finite existence. If the misery of the sinner is conducive to such a display, which it must be because sinners are in fact miserable, then it is just and good that sinners should be punished with misery.[12]

Although we are expected to love and pity Hester, we are not invited to condone her fault or to construe it as a virtue. More a victim of circumstances than a wilful wrongdoer, she is nevertheless to be held morally responsible. In her story Hawthorne intimates that, tangled as human relationships are and must be, no sin ever issues solely from the intent and deed of the individual sinner, but that it issues instead from a complicated interplay of motives of which he is the more or less willing instrument. Even so, however strong, insidious, and unforeseeable the influences and compulsions which prompted his sin, in any practicable system of ethics the sinner must be held individually accountable for it. This is harsh doctrine, but there is no escape from it short of unflinching repudiation of the moral ideas which give man his tragic and lonely dignity in a world in which all things except himself seem insensate and all actions except his own seem mechanical. The Purtians were no more illogical in coupling the assumption of moral determinism with the doctrine of individual responsibility to God than is our own age in conjoining theories of biological and economic determinism with the doctrine of individual responsibility to society. The Puritan escaped from his inconsistency by remarking that God moves in a mysterious way; we justify ours by the plea of expediency. Hawthorne, however, was content merely to pose the problem forcibly in the history of Hester Prynne.

[1]"Hester Prynne . . . becomes, really, after the first scene, an accessory figure; it is not upon her the denouement depends" (Henry James, *Hawthorne* [New York, 1879], p. 109). James had a virtue excellent and rare among readers: he attended to his author's *total* intention and exposition. Apparently Hester's modern champions are misled by their prepossessions; they share the general tendency of our time to believe more strongly in the reality and value of natural instincts than in the truth and accessibility of supernatural absolutes.

[2]Stuart P. Sherman, "Hawthorne: A Puritan Critic of Puritans," *Americans* (New York, 1922), p. 148.

[3]John Erskine, *CHAL*, II, 26-27.

[4]"Scarlet A Minus," *College English*, V (January 1944), 179.

[5]"Woman is born for love, and it is impossible to turn her from seeking it. Men should deserve her love as an inheritance, rather than seize and guard it like a prey" (Margaret Fuller, *Woman in the Nineteenth Century* [Boston, 1893], p. 337).

[6]L. T. Merrill, "The Puritan Policeman," *American Sociological Review*, X (December, 1945), 768.

[7]Joseph Haroutunian, *Piety Versus Moralism: The Passing of the New England Theology* (New York, 1932), p. 90.

[8]Merrill, *op. cit.*, p. 766.

[9]Hawthorne remarked, in the *American Notebooks*, that "there is an unmistakeable analogy between the wicked weeds and the bad habits and sinful propensities which have overrun the moral world." There is an excellent explication of the symbolism of *The Scarlet Letter* in H. H. Waggoner's "Nathaniel Hawthorne: The Cemetery, the Prison, and the Rose," *University of Kansas City Review*, XIV (spring, 1948), 175-190.

[10]Tennyson wrote in "The Princess" that "woman is not undeveloped man, but diverse," and looked for a happier state of society

when there should be "everywhere/Two heads in council, two beside the hearth,/Two in the tangled business of the world." Then, man would "gain in sweetness and in moral height," and woman in "mental breadth."

[11]F. O. Matthiessen, *American Renaissance* (New York, 1941), p. 348.

[12]Haroutunian, *op. cit.*, p. 144.

Nina Baym, "Passion and Authority in *The Scarlet Letter*," *New England Quarterly*, 43 (1970), 209-230.

With the composition of *The Scarlet Letter*, Nathaniel Hawthorne, after two decades of hesitation and experimentation, finally accepted his vocation as an author and produced a major work. In this book he defined the focus of all four of his finished novels: the conflict between forces of passion and of repression in the psyche and in society. The book also gave definitive symbolic shape to a number of elements in his continuing exploration of this theme. In Hester, he developed the "dark lady" type of his stories into an embodiment of the soul's creative and passionate impulses; this type is subsequently varied to form Zenobia and Miriam. In Dimmesdale he presented the most memorable version of the guilt-prone, emotionally divided young men who are so often at the center of his work. And, having treated the Puritans in a number of ways in his short stories and sketches, he fixed on a use for them as symbols of authority and repression in both society and the self.

The sexual encounter which forms the *donnee* of *The Scarlet Letter* was an act neither of deliberate moral disobedience nor of conscious social rebellion. The two characters had forgotten society, and were thinking only of themselves, their passion, and momentary joy. Yet, in the world of this novel, where the community dominates all life, to forget the claims of society is to sin against it. But the sin has no reference beyond its social dimension, and society has no reference beyond itself. The community in which Hester and Dimmesdale live is represented as the historical New England Puritan community, but the entire world view within which this historical community conceived of itself is missing.

The Puritans demanded a far-reaching surrender of self-hood to society, it is true, but always in the service of the vital and holy work which had brought them to the New World. This work involved an expansion of the Christian faith into new geographical territories, and, more importantly, a retrenchment of it through the re-creation of the true, biblically ordained, forms of worship and communal life. References to that purpose are continuous in Puritan writings. Winthrop, in his "Model of Christian Charity," gave it the most memorable utterance:

> For the work we have in hand, it is by a mutual consent through a special overruling providence, and a more than ordinary approbation of the churches of Christ to seek out a place of cohabitation and consortship under a due form of government both civil and ecclesiastical. In such cases as this the care of the

> public must oversway all private respects. . . . We are entered into covenant with Him for this work; we have taken out a commission. . . . For this end, we must be knit together in this work as one man . . . always having before our eyes our commission and community in the work, our community as members of the same body.

In everything they did, the Puritans made constant reference out from the act to the divine purpose for which they acted, and the greater will they were bound to serve.

Remove this sense of communal purpose and service, and a self-satisfied secular autocracy remains—precisely what we find in *The Scarlet Letter*. Although the settlement has been in the New World but a little more than a decade when the action of the novel begins, there is nothing of this crucial context provided. Reading through the first scaffold scene carefully, we find a rhetoric remote from that of the Puritans, with God referred to only by the nebulous phrase "Heaven" and even that word used only three times. There are no references to the community's "work," to its "covenant," and none even to the divine commandment that Hester has broken. Though much is said about sin, little of this discourse is directly presented, and what Hawthorne does give us bears little resemblance to Puritan theology. On the one hand, there is no vivid sense of Hell, and on the other, there is a doctrine which appears to suggest that man is bound for heaven unless and until he commits a sinful act. Even if Hawthorne's Puritans believe that man is more likely than not in the course of his life to commit such an act, the implication of their words are that man's sinful nature is, at birth at least, potential rather than actual. But Puritan dogma, which consigned new-born babies to Hell, implies quite another understanding of "natural depravity."

It is clear that Dimmesdale holds this unpuritan view of sin, for he seems to think that until he met Hester in the forest he was a sinless man. Nor do we find him thinking of sin as, ultimately, a hardness of heart signifying alienation from God, which the sinner could not hope of his own accord to overcome; nor of the vital corollary of grace (a term which does not once occur in the novel) as God's free and unearned gift of salvation. We miss God almost entirely in Dimmesdale's mental life—that overwhelming sense of Divine presence which is never absent from the devout Puritan's reflections, expressed as a desire to be swallowed up in Him, to lie low before Him, to be melted with love for Him. Dimmesdale's is no soul to exclaim, with Jonathan Edwards:

> My wickedness, as I am in myself, has long appeared to me

> perfectly ineffable, and swallowing up all thoughts and imagination, like an infinite deluge, or mountains over my head. . . . And it appears to me that were it not for free grace, exalted and raised up to the infinite height of all the fulness and glory of the great Jehovah, and the arm of his power and grace stretched forth in all the majesty of his power, and in all the glory of his sovereignty, I should appear sunk down in my sins below hell itself, far beyond the sight of everything but the eye of sovereign grace, that can pierce even down to such a depth.

Nor can he plead with Edward Taylor:

> Oh! That thy love might overflow my heart
> To fire the same with love; for love I would.
> But oh! My straitened breast! My lifeless spark!
> My fireless flame! What chilly love and cold!
> In measure small, in manner chilly, see!
> Lord, blow the coal! Thy love enflame in me.

There are only two instances of impassioned religious utterance from Dimmesdale, the first in Chapter 8 where he pleads that Hester be allowed to keep Pearl, arguing in most unorthodox fashion that Pearl is "the Creator's sacred pledge, that, if she bring the child to heaven, the child also will bring its parent thither!"[1] Later, in Chapter 10, he resists Chillingworth's prying in these words: "if it be the soul's disease, then do I commit myself to the one Physician of the soul! He, if it stand with his good pleasure, can cure; or he can kill! Let him do with me as, in his justice and wisdom, he shall see good. But who art thou, that meddlest in this matter?—that dares thrust himself between the sufferer and his God?" (p. 137). Dimmesdale's antipathy is justified here, of course, but his argument is poor. What Puritan, who had been admitted to church fellowship precisely because he had been able to stand up before the members and give convincing public witness to his conversion (the novel is set before the installation of the Half-way Covenant) would insist that his relationship to God was a private matter? How, indeed, in the presumed context of public detection and punishment of sins against God, can Dimmesdale even frame such an argument?—only because the presumed and actual contexts of this novel are not the same. The ministerial qualifications listed by Hawthorne in Chapter 10 are such as might fit Dimmesdale for this calling at some later era, but not in the Puritan age: "high aspirations for the welfare of his race, warm love of souls, pure sentiments, natural piety, strengthened by thought and study, and illumined by revelation" (p. 130). Hawthorne's emphasis here, on Dimmesdale's humanitarian and humanistic temper, relegates Christianity to minor importance.[2]

Dimmesdale is a seriously distorted Puritan, and the settlement is distorted in like manner (no true Puritan community, really convinced that Roger Chillingworth was "Satan himself, or Satan's emissary," would have left him unmolested, waiting "with an unshaken hope, to see the minister come forth out of the conflict, transfigured with the glory which he would unquestionably win" [p. 128]) because Puritan religion has been replaced by nineteenth-century sentimental piety. The God of this book is a remote, vague, occasional concept ceremonially invoked at the last minute and in cases of emergency. He is not the immediate, personal, overwhelmingly present, inescapable Alpha and Omega of Puritan life and thought. Discussions of *The Scarlet Letter* generally overlook this crucial distortion. The questions "why does Hawthorne use the Puritans," or "how does Hawthorne use the Puritans," conceal within them the assumption that he uses them accurately. It is generally believed that he shared their "gloomy" view of human nature and found it an important corrective to the optimistic meliorism of his own day. While a story like "The Celestial Railroad" supports this belief, on the whole Hawthorne's view of human nature, though gloomy, is not Puritan, and the Puritans he uses are the Puritans he invents. He must be held accountable as one of the first shapers of that myth of the Puritans which turned them into dour Victorians. His distortions cannot be attributed to ignorance, for he was well- read in Puritan writings; they must be attributed to design. Nor can that design be explained as a pious unwillingness to speculate about ultimates, for ultimates are not in question: the question is the accurate portrayal of a historical community. It might be argued that he is "translating" Puritanism into forms meaningful to his own day, but the point is then that his translation cuts the spirit away from the forms, leaving behind a residue of empty institutions. Hawthorne's Puritan community considers its own laws the ultimate moral framework of the universe to the point where such laws define, rather than reflect or contain, morality as well as good and evil.[3] This community invokes God to sanction its own social system and to enforce the general will on individual members of the group. In sum, in *The Scarlet Letter* Hawthorne has created an authoritarian state with a Victorian moral outlook. He examines the struggles, within this state, of two people who differ from one another not as beings more or less religious, but as beings differently bound to the community, and differently affected by it.

Power in this community is vested in a group of elders, ministerial and magisterial, who blend its legal and moral strands into a single instrument, and, acting as a group, make that power appear diffuse and impersonal. This is the Puritan oligarchy as an outsider or an unbeliever might perceive it. The patriarchal nature of this oligarchy is important for Hawthorne's scheme, which contrasts youth with age, and women with men. The oligarchy is aptly personified in Governor Bellingham,

> a gentleman advanced in years, and with a hard experience written in his wrinkles. He was not ill fitted to be the head and representative of a community, which owed its origin and progress, and its present state of development, not to the impulses of youth, but to the stern and tempered energies of manhood, and the sombre sagacity of age; accomplishing so much, precisely because it imagined and hoped so little. (p. 64)

The impetus of the Puritan movement, as Hawthorne presents it here, runs directly counter to the "American dream," being neither romantic nor libertarian, but distinctly authoritarian and conservative. Pointing out that the people accept forms of authority as divinely sanctioned, and hence worship authority in and for itself, Hawthorne notes the symbols of physical might with which the Puritan rulers surround themselves: the halberd-bearing sergeants in the scaffold scene, the governor's armor in Chapter 7 (reflected in which, Hester's A is monstrously enlarged), and the "weapons and bright armour of the military company" (p. 237) in the final procession. The rulers justify their authority by its forms, and thus the whole system is self- enclosed. They are dedicated to preserving the values and purposes of aging men, "endowments of that grave and weighty order, which gives the idea of permanence, and comes under the general definition of respectability" (p. 238). "Respectability" is a key term in Hawthorne's discourse; in his next novel, the most complete of his villains, Jaffrey Pyncheon, will be characterized as its very embodiment. And of the oligarchy's kindest representative, Hawthorne says that he "had no more right than one of those [darkly engraved] portraits [which we see prefixed to old volumes of sermons] would have, to step forth, as he now did, and meddle with a question of human guilt, passion, and anguish" (p. 65).

Dimmesdale is the only young man among these patriarchs, and he holds this position by a kind of resolute clinging to childhood. He strenuously avoids contact with the world, hoping thereby to stay sinless. He "trode in the shadowy bypaths, and thus kept himself simple and childlike; coming forth, when occasion was, with a freshness, and fragrance, and dewy purity of thought, which, as many people said, affected them like the speech of an angel" (p. 66). By retaining his childish naivete, Dimmesdale tries to avoid the dangerous period of young manhood and achieve old age without the usual "hard experience" that precedes it. This requires continuous self-restraint. His sin consists in an inadvertent relaxation of that self-restraint, with a consequent assertion of youth against the restrictions of the elders—an assertion of the passionate, thoughtless, wilful, and impulsive in his nature. As a result of this act, the minister becomes a man, ceases forever to be the Senior James's "dimpled nursling of the skies." Although both James and Hawthorne share the interesting view that the guardians of the nursery are male, Hawthorne, lacking James's optimism, is convinced that they do not welcome their charge's coming of age. Dimmesdale knows that if his deed is discovered, he will be thrown out of what is, to him, Heaven—the society of elders. It is typical both of Hawthorne and the romantics in general, that the assertion of manhood involves a shift of allegiance away from the values of a male-dominated ethos towards those held rather by a female.

The plot of *The Scarlet Letter* moves from this prior sin of "omission," the undeliberate breakthrough of suppressed passion, to a more important sin of commission. All the years of punishment and pseudo-repentance operate only to bring the lovers back to the scene of their original deed, there to resolve on a far more radical and shocking action. Now, they deliberately reject the judgment society has passed on them—by deciding to leave the community they in effect repudiate its right to punish them. Responsibility for this decision is mainly Hester's, whose seven years of solitude have turned her into what she was at most only implicitly before, a rebel. Responsibility for the subsequent catastrophe is mainly Dimmesdale's, who, momentarily inflamed by Hester's beauty as well as her argument, is led out of the path natural to his feet and then dramatically returns to it. Unlike Hester, he does accept society's right to judge, as well as its specific judgment; but his dying speech does not convince her, for she undertakes alone the journey that had been planned to accompany him. Not until the fruit of her sin is secured from the consequences of a Puritan judgment on it does she return. And then her return is not entirely a penitent's return, for ultimately, though quietly, she forces the community to admit that the scarlet letter is, after all, a badge of honor and not a token of shame.

In the main, then, *The Scarlet Letter* is the story of the different effect on two unlike characters of an act which seriously transgresses the social code. Conventionally, *The Scarlet Letter* is viewed as being about three characters, a triangle or hierarchy of sinners; yet much is unsatisfactory about this approach. For one thing, it leaves Pearl in a kind of limbo, unrelated, unattached, and unsymmetrical; for another, it involves overlooking (or excusing) much about the way in which Chillingworth is handled. One really cannot accept him as a character in the same sense that the other two can be taken. Not only do Hester and Dimmesdale share a single sin, while Chillingworth's is of another genre entirely; he himself is of a different genre. Martin Green's devastating attack on Hawthorne's technique in this instance makes it clear that the view of Chillingworth as a developed, rounded character is untenable.[4] A character is not developed by being asserted to be growing duskier and more crooked. Much is incongruous in his behavior in terms of the cold, calm, disposition he is originally supposed to have had (which the reader never sees, in any event); his psychology as an abused husband is not realistic. Moreover, we have to deal with the surrealistic manner of his appearance and disappearance in the book, as well as the violently exaggerated rhetoric which is used to describe him. All these factors tell us that Chillingworth operates on a different plane of reality from that of either Hester or Dimmesdale. This is the same plane occupied by Pearl, like him a semi-human but mainly symbolic figure. Pearl stands to Hester in exactly the same symbolic relationship as Chillingworth stands to Dimmesdale.

This symbolic relationship has several aspects. Pearl and Chillingworth represent, to begin with, Hester and Dimmesdale's sin; and since that sin did indeed occur, they have, in the fantasy world of the novel, objective reality. But these characters represent the sin as it is felt and understood by each of the two actors, and since these two feel and perceive very differently about what they have done, the deed assumes a different embodiment in each one's emotional life. Pearl is Hester's sin and Chillingworth is Dimmesdale's, and the difference between them is one of the sharpest and clearest statements about hero and heroine. Hester perceives her deed in the shape of the beautiful child, wild, unmanageable, and unpredictable, who has been created from it; Dimmesdale sees his in the form of the vengeful and embittered husband who has been offended by it. Lastly, Pearl and Chillingworth, splintered off from the characters to whom they properly belong, represent disharmony and disunity within Hester and Dimmesdale—another result of their passion. Each character is at odds, however, with a different part of his nature: crudely, Hester is tormented by her passions, Dimmesdale by his conscience. The end of the book, when these two symbolic characters disappear, portrays the reintegration of these shattered personalities. As Dimmesdale dies, Chillingworth dies; as Hester, leaving the society that has tortured her, resumes a full humanity, so Pearl becomes a complete and living child.

Hester is torn between a genuine desire to feel that society has judged her rightly, that there is a purpose and a reason for all the suffering she endures, and a far deeper, irrational conviction that what she has done is not sinful.

> Man had marked this woman's sin by a scarlet letter, which had such potent and disastrous efficacy that no human sympathy could reach her, save it were sinful like herself. God, as a direct consequence of the sin which man thus punished, had given her a lovely child, whose place was on that same dishonored bosom, to connect her parent for ever with the race and descent of mortals, and to be finally a blessed soul in heaven! Yet these thoughts affected Hester Prynne less with hope than apprehension. She knew that her deed had been evil; she could have no faith, therefore, that its results would be for good. Day after day, she looked fearfully into the child's expanding nature; ever dreading to detect some dark and wild peculiarity, that should correspond with the guiltiness to which she owed her being. (pp. 89-90)

Here we see Hester accepting, on a conscious level, the idea that Pearl is guilty; yet the name she gives the child indicates her truer conviction. Similarly, her handling of the letter itself reveals rejection of the social definition of her deed. An artist with her needle ("then, as now," Hawthorne comments, "almost the only [art] within a woman's grasp"), she turns the letter into a work of art by gorgeous embroidery. The art there exhibited is fundamentally amoral; that is, sheerly decorative, delighting in itself for its own sake. Hawthorne calls it a "rich, voluptuous, Oriental characteristic,—a taste for the gorgeously beautiful," which finds no possibility for exercise except in the "exquisite productions of her needle." Thus Hester's needlework is self- expressive both because it realizes her energy and because the form (to the extent that she does not punish herself by making coarse garments for the poor—a masochistic enterprise for which Hawthorne reproves her) corresponds to her nature. In the social context, the amoral, sensuous activity of her art takes on moral significance, because by making the letter beautiful Hester is denying its social meaning. The embroidery is a technique by which Hester subverts the letter's literal meaning; this is well understood by the Puritan women:

> "She hath good skill at her needle, that's certain . . . but did ever a woman, before this brazen hussy, contrive such a way of showing it! Why, gossips, what is it but to laugh in the faces of our godly magistrates, and make a pride out of what they, worthy gentlemen, meant for a punishment?" (p. 54)

The godly magistrates, however, lack this sort of insight; as men "distinguished by a ponderous sobriety, rather than activity of intellect," they seldom see beyond the literal. They perceive the letter on Hester's breast, and do not see what she has done with it. But Hester's letter is just what the goodwives say it is: an assertion of her pride in what she has done, and a masked defiance of the authorities. Although she is a far more complex symbol than the letter, a living thing and not an inanimate object, Pearl's identity with it is made abundantly clear both by Hawthorne and Hester herself. Her aptness for the role is evident: she is the living product, the literal realization, of the act; she is the reason that Hester can never be free of the act; she is its consequence as well as its commission. Hester, aware of all this, stresses the child's resemblance to the letter by decorating her in exactly the same style.

> Her mother, in contriving the child's garb, had allowed the gorgeous tendencies of her imagination their full play; arraying her in a crimson velvet tunic, of a peculiar cut, abundantly embroidered with fantasies and flourishes of gold thread. . . . It was a remarkable attribute of this garb, and, indeed, of the child's whole appearance, that it irresistibly and inevitably reminded the beholder of the token which Hester Prynne was doomed to wear upon her bosom. It was the scarlet letter in another form; the scarlet letter endowed with life! (pp. 101-102)

Pearl, like the letter, is her mother's "work of art" (not, as some critics have argued, Dimmesdale's).[5] Neither symbol is a perfect representation of this idea, but each contributes to it. The letter, though a true artistic production, is created by the play of imagination on a socially received, and basically uncongenial, form which, the magistrates believe, implies guilt in its very shape. This guilt Hester, through the restricted means of surface decoration, attempts to deny. On the other hand, Pearl is an entirely "original" form, springing not only from sources beyond society's control, but from sources largely beyond the artist's control. This "original" Hester tries, somewhat ineffectively, to fit to the letter's meaning. The truth about art, to Hawthorne, lies somewhere in the blend of these concepts of organicism and artifact, and between the social and private imperatives. And the question of artistic creativity is inextricably linked to the question of social guilt. At once accepting guilt as the price of creation, and denying it, Hester is mentally torn. She is torn, too, between a willingness to endure a punishment she cannot truly concur in as the price for remaining near Dimmesdale, and a normal human rejection of misery and suffering.

Pearl embodies more than her mother's deed; she also symbolizes a part of Hester's nature—the wild, amoral creative core of the self. With this part of herself Hester is very much at odds; the splintering of the self is implicit in the very existence of an *alter ego*. The social view of this part of the self is, of course, condemning: this is the sin-producing segment of the soul. Truly to assent to her punishment, Hester must come to feel that the judgment of her nature on which it is based is just. She does make a sincere effort to feel guilty, operating on the time-tested principle that if one behaves as though one feels guilty, patiently and continuously, one will eventually create the condition. She tries to restrain and discipline the child according to society's judgments, but ultimately she cannot be so false to herself. She dresses Pearl like an opulent princess and lets her run wild; here her own wildness has outlet. Perhaps Pearl's most important function as the *doppelganger* is to express all the resentment, outraged pride, anger, and even blasphemy that Hester feels in her punishment, but cannot voice. One recalls the famous catechism scene, where Pearl proclaims that "she had not been made at all, but had been plucked by her mother off the bush of wild roses, that by the prison-door." There is expressed in this speech an angry repudiation of God, of the oligarchs, and of Dimmesdale as well—resentments Hester can barely admit to herself, freely spoken by her uninhibited child.

Hester's ultimately unshakeable belief in the goodness of this part of herself, its wild chaotic nature notwithstanding (although, to be sure, its intensity sometimes appalls and frightens her), saves her from taking the readily available and more common route, the path leading straight from the governor's mansion: witchcraft. The witches are rebellious, of course, but their rebellion is predicated on an acceptance of society's judgment on them. They believe they are evil, and they rejoice in their wickedness. Hester's lonely path, taken less out of conscious decision than out of temperamental necessity, is that of refusing to believe herself evil.

In her solitude, her emotions stifled, she comes to think more and more critically of society. She "assumed a freedom of speculation . . . which our forefathers, had they known of it, would have held to be a deadlier crime than that stigmatized by the scarlet letter." At a later point in the novel, Hawthorne calls her vantage point as estranged from social institutions as that of the "wild Indian," and comments in very significant language that "the tendency of her fate and fortunes had been to set her free" (p. 199). So long as she remains in Boston, she is restrained from showing this newly acquired radicalism by her obligations to Pearl (or, differently put, by her simple instinct for self-preservation), but it is not Pearl who keeps her in Boston.

By the time Hester meets Dimmesdale again in the forest, all social ties but one have disappeared. Only her feeling for Dimmesdale is left. This has bound her to Boston, and so long as she remains there, she must wear the letter. The plot moves Hester towards casting off the letter (just as it moves Dimmesdale towards assuming it), and this action is impossible until Dimmesdale either leaves Boston or otherwise frees her. It is the usual case in Hawthorne's fiction that the "dark" woman is a far more passionate, imaginative, and intellectually daring being than the man,[6] but she is also the less cold, the more loving—and hence her fate is found to be inextricably tied to that more timorous, conventional man. Thus, in the forest, with Dimmesdale, Hester is not permitted to pretend that she is free of the letter; not in the forest, but on the scaffold when Dimmesdale dies, Hester is liberated—insofar, indeed, as woman can hope to be liberated. This is also why Hester, returning later to Boston, looks back on her experience with the hope for the revelation of a new truth which will "establish the whole relation between man and woman on a surer ground of mutual happiness." Having cast off the letter and saved her guilt-conceived child, Hester has been as free as any woman; apparently she has learned that no woman, as society now stands, can be truly free. Probably, too, her very return to Boston is meant to symbolize the limits of a woman's freedom, circumscribed by love.

Hester then, is branded guilty by society, but gradually rejects that brand; Dimmesdale is considered innocent by society, but gradually assumes a stigma of guilt. He is a complete psychological contrast to Hester, except in one crucial respect: both of them *must*, ultimately, at whatever cost, be true to the imperatives of their own natures. Hester *must* reject the judgment of the letter, no matter how she tries to assent to it; and Dimmesdale *must* take that letter on himself, no matter how much a part of him struggles to resist. But where Hester is naturally independent and romantic, Dimmesdale is social and conservative. His choice of profession as well as his astonishing early success in it, make clear that he is a real man of society.

> Mr. Dimmesdale was a true priest, a true religionist, with the reverential sentiment largely developed, and an order of mind that impelled itself powerfully along the track of a creed, and wore its passage continually deeper with the lapse of time. In no state of society would he have been what is called a man of liberal views; it would always be essential to his peace to feel the pressure of a faith about him, supporting, while it confined him within its iron framework. (p. 123)

Never one to give the genesis of his characters' psychic structures,

Hawthorne does not explain why Dimmesdale is inclined to revere authority, but he makes clear that this is a psychological rather than an ethical matter with the minister. Dimmesdale's needs and dependencies mean that he is not hypocritical. It appears, indeed, that he has remained ignorant of his own passionate nature until his encounter with Hester reveals it. Hester plays a role here regularly allotted to women of her type in Hawthorne's fiction: to correspond to and arouse the dormant, repressed, unrealized, or unacknowledged passions of the men. But Hester does not *create* passion in the minister; there is a passionate nature underlying his spirituality all the time, as Hawthorne suggests in a variety of ways. There are signs of a struggle in his constitutional pallor, in the tremor of his mouth denoting both "nervous sensibility and a vast power of self-restraint."

Even more interesting are indications, increasingly emphasized as the novel progresses, that the true source of Dimmesdale's power and influence over his congregation is not the spirituality to which he, in sincere piety, attributes his ministerial gifts, but is that same despised and submerged passion. The chief means by which Dimmesdale sways his listeners is his voice, which is made an instrument of passion.

> This vocal organ was in itself a rich endowment; insomuch that a listener, comprehending nothing of the language in which the preacher spoke, might still have been swayed to and fro by the mere tone and cadence. Like all other music, it breathed passion and pathos, and emotions high or tender, in a tongue native to the human heart, wherever educated. . . . Now [Hester] caught the low undertone, as of the wind sinking down to repose itself; then ascended with it, as it rose through progressive gradations of sweetness and power, until its volume seemed to envelop her with an atmosphere of awe and solemn grandeur. (p. 243)

This sobbing, passionate voice, which "gushed irrepressibly upward" full of plaintiveness and anguish, speaking with "the whisper, or the shriek . . . of suffering humanity" has nothing whatever to do with Dimmesdale's intellectual or spiritual being. By-passing language, reason's instrument, the tones of the voice come straight from the romantic heart. Dimmesdale's power is multiplied manifold after his encounter with Hester, because that encounter has represented the first surfacing of that heart, and because thereafter it can no longer be completely repressed. As ignorant as he about the source of this new art, Dimmesdale's parishioners "knew not the power that moved them thus. They deemed the young clergyman a miracle of holiness." Hawthorne makes the nature of the attraction felt by the people to Dimmesdale even more clear when he comments that "the virgins of his church grew pale around him, victims of a passion so imbued with religious sentiment that they imagined it to be all religion, and brought it openly, in their white bosoms, as their most acceptable sacrifice before the altar" (p. 142).

Passion, which has made him an artist, has made him, as he thinks, a hypocrite as a minister. Dimmesdale is bewildered and horrified by his success. In the social context, art itself is guilty, and a man like Dimmesdale, deeply committed to the furthering of social aims (permanence and respectability) but who is yet an artist, is necessarily the most psychologically ravaged of human beings. In a sense, Dimmesdale's profession (prior to his meeting with Hester) had assuaged his conflict by channeling his energies into accepted social patterns and permitting him to rationalize about the source of these energies. His affair with Hester and the accompanying development of his artistic powers destroy this refuge. His profession becomes a source of torment. Unable to identify his "self" with the passionate core he regards as sinful, he is even less able to admit that this sinful core can produce great, true, sermons. He is obsessed with a feeling of falseness. His act with Hester almost immediately becomes loathsome to him. The part of him which is Puritan magistrate, and which he thinks of as himself, condemns the sinful "other."

The ugliness of his act, as it appears to him, is well expressed in the hideous figure of Chillingworth who materializes, as Hawthorne implies repeatedly, out of thin air, to persecute him. This monster becomes his constant companion and oppressor. If Pearl (to borrow a Freudian metaphor) is a representation of Hester's "id," then Chillingworth represents Dimmesdale's "superego." That he is meant to be part of Dimmesdale's personality is made clear not only by the magical ways in which he appears on and disappears from the scene, and his unrealistic fixation (for a cuckolded husband) on the guilty *man*, but also by the physical and occupational similarities of the two men and their spatial disposition under the same roof.

> The two were lodged in the same house; so that every ebb and flow of the minister's life-tide might pass under the eye of his anxious and attached physician. . . . Here, the pale clergyman piled up his library, rich with parchment-bound folios of the Fathers, and the lore of Rabbis, and monkish erudition. . . . On the other side of the house, old Roger Chillingworth arranged his study and laboratory . . . provided with a distilling apparatus, and the means of compounding drugs and chemicals, which the practiced alchemist knew well how to turn to purpose. With such commodiousness of situation, these two learned persons sat

> themselves down, each in his own domain, yet familiarly passing from one apartment to the other, and bestowing a mutual and not incurious inspection into one another's business. (pp. 125-126)

The identification of Chillingworth with the watchful eye of the personality links him at once with both intellect and conscience.[7] Cut off from punishment in the real world (for reasons we shall shortly consider), Dimmesdale substitutes internal punishment, and this change is symbolized by the replacement of his kindly, benevolent ministerial companion, Wilson, by this malevolent demon. Chillingworth's cruelty represents Hawthorne's idea that the internal judge freed (exactly as Pearl, at the other end of the psyche's spectrum, is freed) from "reference and adaptation to the world into which it was born" is unmitigatedly unforgiving and remorseless. "All that guilty sorrow, hidden from the world, whose great heart would have pitied and forgiven, to be revealed to him, the Pitiless, to him, the Unforgiving!" In all the various speculations about that letter on Dimmesdale's bosom, one likely possibility, that it has been brought out by Chillingworth's "drugs and chemicals," has been peculiarly overlooked. But perhaps this is how Hawthorne allegorized the work of a gnawing conscience.

That Chillingworth is, by virtue of his age, a sort of father figure, suggests a classical Freudian explanation of Dimmesdale's feelings of guilt. On a larger, mythical scale, it symbolizes his sense of having offended the "fathers," the patriarchs, the oligarchs, the male gods. And he has offended them less by having stolen "their" woman, for they are all men without women, and do not appear to covet Hester for themselves, than by having repudiated their values by joining *with* her. In the forest she is clearly presented as an alternative to them. As Chillingworth's wife, she becomes the alternative to *him*: to his sterile paternity she encounters with an image of "Divine Maternity."[8] Dimmesdale, of course, is not "conscious" of the rebellion implicit in his act, for his was a sin of passion, "not of principle, nor even purpose." Sincerely horrified by his deed, he embarks on a long course of self-torture and punishment; but he does not confess. These internal torments, bodied forth most horrifyingly in Chillingworth, are the strategy by which Dimmesdale *keeps from confessing*. His belief that he *is* being punished enables him to keep his guilt secret by pacifying his sense of justice. The question of Dimmesdale's failure to confess, then, is more complicated than it first appears.

Of course, he is terrified by the social consequences of his confession. One who leans so heavily on the social structure would be almost certainly destroyed if he were cast out of it as Hester has been. For a being who defines himself largely by the image he sees reflected back from the watching eyes around him, loss of social place implies a loss of identity. But confession would represent something more: a final and irrevocable capitulation to the sense of guilt. No matter how he persecutes himself, no matter what masochistic free reign he gives to his grotesquely distorted conscience, he does not fully assent to his guilt until he admits it openly, for open admission has irreversible consequences. The failure to confess is the one and only way in which Dimmesdale *resists* the judgment which his conscience attempts to enforce upon him. Chillingworth, thus, as a substitute for the judgment of society, acts also as a strategy for forestalling that judgment, is a buffer or a protection *against* an ultimate condemnation. Once Dimmesdale confesses he has, psychologically, no alternative but to die; Chillingworth the physician does quite literally keep Dimmesdale alive all these years, even if but to torture him. This is, of course, an agonizingly roundabout method—a neurotic method—of resistance, but it is appropriate to Dimmesdale's divided values. Not to confess; to scourge oneself, to fast, endure any kind of private penance, making one's body and soul a veritable playground for internal punitive forces—anything rather than openly to say "I am guilty." This is the technique by which Dimmesdale tries to fend off final acquiescence in the notion of his guilt; if he lacks Hester's will to defy, he has at least something of a will to resist.

But the scene in the forest, where the lovers decide to flee together, has results which break that will. Dimmesdale's own astounding behavior after he leaves the forest convinces him beyond any doubt that he is, indeed, a morally polluted and hideously guilty man. A truly stupifying flood of demons are released from him when he asserts, deliberately, that the social law no longer binds him. He has turned the control of his psyche over to the passionate self that has been clamoring for freedom and recognition all these years. Hawthorne describes it as "a revolution in the sphere of thought and feeling" and a "total change of dynasty and moral code, in that interior kingdom." But rather than finding himself in this revolution, Dimmesdale loses himself. He undergoes a kind of rebirth, but a terrifying one. He recognizes neither his surroundings nor himself. More unsettling than his changed perceptions is his changed behavior—the sequence of blasphemous, lewd, and childishly crude sorts of acts he is tempted to perform. He faces what appears to him incontrovertible evidence of the iniquity of his own passionate nature. This experience of himself, this glimpse into the interior, is decisive. Whatever moral defense he might have been disposed to make for his passionate self, however he might have assented to Hester's "what we did had a consecration of its own" in the forest, when he was led to exclaim,

> "Oh, Hester, thou art my better angel! I seem to have flung myself—sick, sin-stained, and sorrow-blackened—down upon these forest leaves, and to have risen up all made anew, and with new powers to glorify Him that hath been merciful!" (pp. 201-202)

this disposition disappears entirely once he is out of the forest and sees how little his new powers lead him to glorify God—how they lead, in fact, in the opposite direction. He ceases, then, his attempts to evade final punishment. He turns his new burst of life into the writing of his greatest sermon, still bewildered "that Heaven should see fit to transmit the grand and solemn music of its oracles through so foul an organ-pipe as he." Then he delivers it, confesses, and by that confession, executes himself.

On the scaffold, two disintegrated personalities achieve resolutions appropriate to their natures. Hester's change, now that she is freed from the community, is represented by Pearl's disenchantment. By becoming a human being, Pearl effectively disappears as an *alter ego* or an allegorical projection. Instead of two fragments of a single personality we now have two people. Hester then takes her child from the Puritan community into a society where she may better fulfill herself—an ironic reversing of the American dream, for the American is sent backwards in time and space to a more advanced and enlightened Europe. A nature as severely and implacably at war within itself as Dimmesdale's can find peace only in death. This death deprives the parasitic conscience of a host on which to feed, and Chillingworth "positively withered up, shrivelled away, and almost vanished from mortal sight, like an uprooted weed that lies wilting in the sun." Hawthorne's treatment of Dimmesdale, from the encounter in the forest to the expiation on the scaffold, has a convincing psychological inevitability; Hester has certainly meant well, but as Frederick Crews says, she does not really understand Dimmesdale's nature.[9] She imagines him to be a person far more like herself than he really is. "Give up this name of Arthur Dimmesdale, and make thyself another, and a high one, such as thou canst wear without fear or shame," she exhorts. The name, a social label like the scarlet letter, is easily assumed or put aside for Hester, but not for Dimmesdale. He *is* what society calls him. "What hast thou to do with all these iron men, and their opinions?" Hester asks, but released from the iron framework he needs for support, he finds no inner principle to sustain him. His wholly liberated imagination creates not Emersonian images of beauty, but surrounds him with horrors.

This "twist" in the plot is found repeatedly in Hawthorne's fictions. Cut loose from their moorings, the fragile egos of most of his heroes are whirled into frightful, nightmarish fantasies of liberated fears and desires. Young Goodman Brown is perhaps an epitome of this event; but many other examples will come to mind. No one escapes from these nightmares undefeated except the stolid Robin Molineux. The pattern expresses, for one thing, Hawthorne's response, based on his psychological insight, to transcendental optimism about imaginative liberation; and for another, it provides a balance to the romanticism of his own fiction. As much as Hawthorne is drawn to, and moved by, romantic values, he knows too much of the "horrors of the half-known life" to be able to accede to a simple utopian vision. The only values expressed in this novel are romantic; and yet the author despairs of their fulfillment. His conclusions in *The Scarlet Letter*, as he examines these two versions of the struggle between self and society, have a doubly gloomy thrust. On the one hand, he finds (and asserts with increasing vehemence in each succeeding novel) life in society to be the death of art, of love—of the heart. Without denying the wilful, amoral, and chaotic aspects of the unsocial core, he yet asserts its primacy and its basic value. But on the other hand, he does not believe that true self-fulfillment is possible. Men are born into society, and shaped by it. When they strike out towards freedom, the unknown and unimaginable, they are defeated, the stronger by the action of society against them, the weaker by their own internal collapse. Hawthorne's fictions provide an extensive compilation of various kinds of internal collapse: these are different from one case to another, but the vision which informs them is constant: not of a Puritan, but of a Romantic, Hell.

[1]The *Scarlet Letter* (Columbus, Ohio, 1962), 115. All page references to the novel are to this text.

[2]Few of these "precious materials," as Hawthorne calls them, are displayed by the minister during the course of the novel, so self-engrossed has he become.

[3]R. W. B. Lewis, in *The American Adam* (Chicago, 1955) probably speaks for the majority of critics of this novel when he says that "Hester's deed appears as a disturbance of the moral structure of the universe" (112). But this can be the case *only* if the Puritan community is shown to reflect, in its laws and values, that moral structure, for

Hawthorne does not deal (as has so often been pointed out) with absolutes and universals directly. And the care with which he isolates the Puritans in time and space, while refraining from commenting on the truth of such dogmas as he show them to hold, makes it impossible for us to conclude that his Puritans *do* serve as spokesmen for the moral structure of the universe.

[4]*Re-Appraisal: Some Commonsense Readings in American Literature* (New York, 1965), 78-83.

[5]See, e.g., Rudolph Von Abele, *The Death of the Artist* (The Hague, 1957), 45-58.

[6]One must take exception to Roy R. Male's general thesis, in *Hawthorne's Tragic Vision* (Austin, 1957), that the woman is the conservative force holding back the speculative male: Hester and Dimmesdale, Zenobia and Coverdale or Hollingsworth, are only two of many counterexamples.

[7]The identification of Chillingworth with the intellect links him to Hawthorne's gallery, in the stories, of unpardonable sinners. But in this and later novels we see this theme of the intellect-passion or head-heart dichotomy being brought into a much larger context, wherein it is interestingly modified, because intellect is now allied to Puritanical repression, as well as to authoritarian institutions.

[8]One senses here the dim outline of a romantic fiction along lines set down by Northrop Frye, where the "aggressive myths of Judaism, Christianity, and Plato's *Timaeus*, reflect[ing] an urban, tool-using, male-dominated society, where the central figure usually develops out of a father-god associated with the sky" is giving way to a "Romantic redemption myth" where "something of the ancient mother-centered symbolism comes back into poetry." *A Study of English Romanticism* (New York, 1969), 6, 10. Wordsworth, Shelley, Byron, and Blake are all cited as poets centering fictions on a maternal goddess figure who is also, often, sister and bride. In Hawthorne's forest the Apollonian tradition is being rejected for the Dionysian. This is why Chillingworth, who appears superficially at odds with society because of his iconoclastic scientific rationalism, may in fact represent the extreme abstraction of its underlying principles: the repressive and inhibiting male intellect at its most sterile and destructive.

[9]Frederick C. Crews, *The Sins of the Fathers* (New York, 1966), 143.

Robert E. Todd, "The Magna Mater Archetype in *The Scarlet Letter*," *New England Quarterly*, 45 (1972), 421-429.

Duality or ambivalence, as some critics have noted, is an essential attribute of *The Scarlet Letter*. No other book in American fiction, Male believes, is "so dual";[1] and Martin declares that the special quality of Hawthorne's masterpiece inheres in its "essential duality or ambivalence."[2] Much of this duality is expressed through the central figure of Hester Prynne, who has often been interpreted divergently in terms of either saint or sinner.[3] Each of these opposing points of view, held by critics of ability and acumen, is altogether valid in spite of the paradox their polarity presents. For Hester, as Male has said, "is the woman, wedded to guilt yet offering eventual beatitude" to Dimmesdale.[4] Her duality or ambivalence is also typical of that which Jung identified with the "anima" or Magna Mater archetype as it is called in its reflected or projected form:

> Like the "supraordinate personality," the anima is bipolar and can therefore appear positive one moment and negative the next; now young, now old; now mother, now maiden; now a good fairy, now a witch; now a saint, now a whore.[5]

Frye, too, attributes a special archetypal quality to the romance genre that, I believe, is quite evident in Hawthorne's greatest romance and particularly in the character of its heroine, Hester Prynne:

> The essential difference between novel and romance lies in the conception of characterization. The romancer does not attempt to create "real people" so much as stylized figures which expand into psychological archetypes. It is in the romance that we find Jung's libido, anima, and Shadow reflected in the hero, heroine, and villain respectively.[6]

This study is an attempt to demonstrate that Hester Prynne is a figure belonging to the Magna Mater archetype, and that it is in her bipolar role of both "good" and "terrible" mother that she has a decisive influence on the fate of Arthur Dimmesdale. As the "anima" or feminine soul-image of Dimmesdale, she is the bearer of his fate, whose consummation is death.[7]

From the moment when she first appears, a maternal image with the babe at her breast, Hester's kinship with the Great Mother is strikingly evident. The beadle, whose function was to walk before dignitaries with "his staff of office in his hand," first draws her forward from the "darksome apartment" in which she had been confined:

> Stretching forth the official staff on his left hand, he laid his right upon the shoulder of a young woman whom he thus drew forward. . . . She bore in her arms a child, a baby of some three

> months old who winked and turned aside its little face from the too vivid light of day because its existence, heretofore, had brought it acquainted only with the gray twilight of a dungeon, or other darksome apartment of the prison (p. 115).[8]

From the psychological viewpoint of the Magna Mater archetype, the beadle's outstretched staff is quite obviously a phallic image, the dungeon or darksome apartment suggests a symbolic analogue with the archetypal womb, and the emergence of Hester and her baby into the light of day becomes an archetypal birth.[9]

Rising above the crowded marketplace, the wooden scaffold to which Hester is led serves as an altar on which she is the numinous female "spectacle" for a "thousand unrelenting eyes," including those of the governor and the religious leaders of the town. Hawthorne tells us that "her beauty shone out, and made a halo of the misfortune and ignominy in which she was enveloped," while her embroidered letter of scarlet, a "mystic token" not unlike the symbolic cross to which it is later compared, "had the effect of a spell, taking her out of the ordinary relations with humanity, and inclosing her in a sphere by herself" (p. 116). Hawthorne describes the scene with an apparent awareness of Hester's numinous or divine maternity when he compares her to the Virgin Mary, the Roman Catholic surrogate of the Great Mother, who has long shared religious devotion with God the father:

> Had there been a Papist among the crowd of Puritans, he might have seen in this beautiful woman . . . with the infant at her bosom, an object to remind him of the image of Divine Maternity . . . (p. 117).

It is not surprising then to discover that in the first third of the book (Chapters I-VIII) Hester is referred to at least a half- dozen times as pedestaled. As D. H. Lawrence aptly remarked, "Put her [Hester] upon the scaffold and worship her there. Worship her there. The Woman, the Magna Mater."[10]

Not only is the wooden scaffold the "pedestal" for Hester's first, almost ritualistic display of her scarlet letter, it is also the climactic site of Dimmesdale's exalted public confession of his "sin" and of his death in her embrace. In receiving the dying minister, Hester is the same latter-day equivalent of the Magna Mater as the Pieta, who receives the crucified Jesus, embracing him in death as in birth.

Hester's relationship with Dimmesdale, decidedly ambivalent in its effect, is altogether consistent with the essentially ambivalent nature of the Magna Mater archetype in which the "Great Mother, Good Mother, and Terrible Mother form a cohesive archetypal group."[11] Jung said that the most familiar historical example of the ambivalent mother "is the Virgin Mother who is not only the Lord's Mother, but also, according to the Medieval allegories, his cross."[12] Following the same polarized pattern of the archetype, Hester is similarly both a source of destruction and death on the one hand, and a source of love and rebirth on the other.

It is notable that beginning with the first three chapters and ending with the last three, Hawthorne repeatedly reminds the reader of Hester's affinity with the wooden scaffold, which along with the closely related ritual death images of the stake, the gallows, and the cross, is an important symbol of the creative-destructive duality or womb-tomb character of the Magna Mater. Near the end of the book (Chapter XXII) when like the Mother Mary standing at the foot of the cross, Hester stands "statue-like at the foot of the scaffold," Hawthorne summarizes the special cohesive role which that "sacred edifice" played in her life:

> There was a sense within her . . . that her whole orb of life, both before and after, was connected with this spot [the scaffold], as with the one point that gave it unity (pp. 228-229).[13]

As "the figure, the body, the reality of [his] sin," Hester brings spiritual or psychic death to Dimmesdale in the Biblical sense that "the wages of sin is death"; and it is her stigmatic scarlet letter, a scourging and scarring reminder to the minister's mind and flesh of his concealed act of adultery, that is the inspiration for the ascetic, seven-year cross of penitential fasts, closeted flagellations, and introspective vigils that bring about his untimely end. In the visions that often accompanied his masochistic nightly vigils, the ghost of Dimmesdale's mother is presented in an attitude of maternal rejection followed by the spectre of Hester "pointing her forefinger, first, at the scarlet letter on her bosom, and then at the clergyman's own breast" (p. 170). On the other hand, in her role of "Good Mother," Hester is Dimmesdale's "better angel" through whom—during their fateful encounter in the forest—he is "made anew."

It is in his description of the liberating setting of that meeting in the "mother forest" that we also find Hawthorne employing a succession of images that are important symbols of the elemental womb-tomb character of the Magna Mater archetype. The footpath that Hester and Pearl followed to intercept Dimmesdale, the author states, "struggled onward into the mystery of the primeval forest," a mystery traditionally associated with the labyrinthine mystery of the womb;[14] while the "secret dell" in which the two reunited lovers return briefly to their forbidden bliss is described appropriately in language that is pervasively psychosexual in its overtones:

> It was a little dell with a leaf-strewn bank rising gently on either side, and a brook flowing through the midst, over a bed of fallen and drowned leaves (p. 194).[15]

Little imagination is required to grasp the symbolic analogue between the description of the "dell," with its "leaf- strewn bank rising gently on either side," and the female orifice or womb-tomb of the Great Mother. "Gully, ravine, abyss" are, as Neumann has indicated, "the symbols of the feminine earth-womb";[16] and water "is the primordial womb of life, from which in innumerable myths life is born."[17] Freud, too, has noted the symbolic resemblance between "the complicated topography of the female sexual organs" and the "landscapes, with rocks, woods, and water."[18]

When Dimmesdale happens along the footpath and encounters Hester in this forest setting, he is "leaning on a staff," an image which—repeating the earlier mentioned symbolism of the beadle's staff—reaffirms Hester's association as a Magna Mater figure with the male phallus. Another reminder of this symbolic association is Hester's exceptional and widely renowned artistry with the needle, which—with its "fertility and gorgeous luxuriance of fancy"—is a sexually gratifying expression of "a rich voluptuous Oriental characteristic" in her nature. Hawthorne observes that "women derive a pleasure, incomprehensible to the other sex, from the delicate toil of the needle" and that for Hester such activity "might have been a mode of expressing, and therefore soothing, the passion of her life" (p. 133). Hester's skill with the needle relates in a special way as well to the bipolar or womb-tomb nature of her role as Magna Mater, for a significant part of her labors are devoted to decorating the ritual apparel required for the dual events of birth and death. Her needle work, we are informed, "decked the baby's little cap," and "it was shut up, to be mildewed and moulder away, in the coffins of the dead" (p. 133).

The two reunited lovers move hand in hand deeper "into the shadow of the woods" and deeper into its sexual aura and mystery. And, once Pearl is "a good way off, on the otherside of the brook," Hester discards the scarlet letter and then uncovers and lets fall her dark and luxuriant tresses in a dramatic expression of liberated passion. At this point Hawthorne leaves her and Dimmesdale to privacy and the likely renewal of their clandestine relationship,[19] while he—in the manner of the sometimes discreet motion-picture camera—shifts his focus momentarily to record the joyous transformation of a sheltering mother nature that is in empathetic accord with the two lovers:

> And, as if the gloom of the earth and sky had been but the effluence of these two mortal hearts, it vanished with their

> sorrow (p. 204).

The psychic affinity between the situation of the reunited lovers and that of an empathetic nature is continued in the rest of the passage through the use of images that are remarkable for their conjugal figurativeness:

> All at once, as with a sudden smile of heaven, forth burst the sunshine, pouring a very flood into the obscure forest... (p. 204).

These lines, which incidentally appear in a chapter to which Hawthorne gave the heading, "A Burst of Sunshine," not only indicate the sympathetic response of nature but appear as well to be an assimilation, through the immediate and embracing ambience of sun and forest, of the lovers' orgastic climax.[20] The archetypal concept of the solar phallus is fairly common, as is the union of the sun-god with the earth goddess; while the forest into which the sudden burst of procreating sunshine is poured is a traditional symbol of the womb, whose mystery like that of the forest's "heart of mystery" is transformed into a "mystery of joy."

That Hester and Dimmesdale renewed their sexual relationship during this, their "hour's free breath," appears likely. Hawthorne says that the minister "had yielded himself with deliberate choice, as he had never done before, to what he knew was deadly sin" (p. 216). For Bewley "the possible renewal of the adulterous union is seen . . . as a resurrection into life."[21] In any event, it is quite clear that Dimmesdale experiences a transformation or rebirth which he attributes to the regenerative powers of Hester and their "fateful interview":

> O Hester, thou art my better angel! I seem to have flung myself—sick, sin-stained, and sorrow-blackened—down upon these forest leaves, and to have risen up all made anew . . . (p. 204).

Commenting on the change in the minister, Hawthorne declares:

> That the intervening space of a single day had operated on his consciousness like the lapse of years. The minister's own will, and Hester's will, and the fate that grew between them, had wrought his transformation. . . . the same minister returned not from the forest. He might have said to the friends who greeted him,—"I am not the man for whom you take me! I left him yonder in the forest, withdrawn into a secret dell, by a mossy tree-trunk, and near a melancholy brook! . . ." His friends, no doubt, would still have insisted with him,—"Thou art thyself the man!"— but the error would have been their own, not his (pp. 212- 213).

From a psychological point-of-view, Dimmesdale's "rebirth" is a symbol of the psychic process of wholeness and harmony that Jung called *individuation.* Although a detailed analysis of the process of individuation is outside the scope of this essay, a brief explanation may be in order. An important concept in Jungian theory, individuation or self-realization is not individualistic or ego-centered but results, instead, from a synthesis of the conscious and unconscious elements in the personality, which becomes liberated and transformed:

> Consciousness and unconsciousness do not make a whole when either is suppressed or damaged by the other. If they must contend, let it be a fair fight with equal rights on both sides. Both are aspects of life. Let consciousness defend its reason and its self-protective ways, and let the chaotic life of the unconscious be given a fair chance to have its own way, as much of it as we can stand. This means at once open conflict and open collaboration . . . . the suffering iron between them will in the end be shaped into an unbreakable whole, the individual. This experience is what is called—the process of individuation.[22]

By resuming his relationship with Hester and acknowledging his sexual gratification in their original act of adultery, Dimmesdale has finally arrived at a recognition and acceptance of "the dark depths of the unconscious" whose sensual needs and wild irrational intuition, he had painfully denied and repressed for seven years. The result is a psychological wholeness that Jung says "consists partly of the conscious man and partly of the unconscious man"[23] and which is, I believe, reflected in Hawthorne's description of the transformed Dimmesdale:

> Another man had returned out of the forest; a wiser one; with a knowledge of hidden mysteries which the simplicity of the former never could have reached (p. 216).

The character of little Pearl takes on a new and interesting significance when considered within the context of Dimmesdale's individuation, for Jung points out that "the clearest and most significant manifestation" of the child archetype is induced by the process of individuation."[24] Often appearing in dreams as a "son or a daughter," this child has much in common with Pearl, the "Elf-child." According to Jung, this child motif may manifest itself as "the witch's child with daemonic attributes"; or "seen as a special instance of the 'treasure hard to attain' motif," it may assume a variety of shapes, including that of "the pearl."[25] As Male has noted, Dimmesdale's Pearl takes her name from the "one pearl of great price" in *Matthew* 13:45-46.[26]

If, as many critics have contended, mystery is behind *The Scarlet Letter*'s awful course of events, then it is Hester, the Magna Mater figure, who is the heart of that mystery. Although the story of *The*

Scarlet Letter belongs both to her and to Dimmesdale, it is Hester in her ambivalent role of tempting adulteress and redeeming angel who is the generating force for the book's action and denouement. Not only Dimmesdale, but all other forces respond to her influence. The end, as Chillingworth realized, had been "a dark necessity" from the very beginning.

[1]Roy R. Male, *Hawthorne's Tragic Vision* (New York, 1964), 90.

[2]Terrence Martin, *Hawthorne* (New York, 1965), 119.

[3]For example, D. H. Lawrence, *Studies in Classic American Literature* (New York, 1961), 83-89; Theodore T. Munger, "Notes on *The Scarlet Letter*," *Atlantic Monthly*, April, 1904, 521, 535; William Bysshe Stein, *Hawthorne's Faust: A Study of the Devil's Archetype* (Gainesville, 1953), 104-122; and Yvor Winters, *Maule's Curse* (New York, 1938).

[4]Male, 12.

[5]C. G. Jung and C. Kerenyi, *Essays on a Science of Mythology*, translated by R. F. C. Hull (New York, 1963), 173.

[6]Northrop Frye, *Anatomy of Criticism* (Princeton, 1957), 304-305.

[7]For a detailed study of the Magna Mater archetype see Erich Neumann, *The Great Mother*, translated by Ralph Manheim (Princeton, 1955). For an explanation of the "Anima and Animus" see C. G. Jung, *Two Essays on Analytical Psychology*, translated by R. F. C. Hull (New York, 1956), 198-223.

[8]Pagination in this study is based on Nathaniel Hawthorne, *The Complete Novels and Selected Tales of Nathaniel Hawthorne*, Norman Holmes Pearson, editor (New York, 1937).

[9]On the one hand a rod is an instrument of punishment; on the other it is the magic wand, or symbolically speaking the creative phallus. See Neumann, 259. Also my own remarks on the staff of the mysterious Old Man in Chaucer's "The Pardoner's Tale" in "The Magna Mater Archetype in *The Pardoner's Tale*," *Literature and Psychology*, 15 No. 1, 32-40 (1965).

[10]D. H. Lawrence, *Studies in Classic American Literature* (New York, 1969), 88.

[11]Neumann, 21, 30.

[12]C. G. Jung, *The Collected Works*, translated by R. F. C. Hull (New York, 1959), IX, 1, p. 82.

[13]Leland Schubert believes the pattern of *The Scarlet Letter* is built around the wooden scaffold: *Hawthorne the Artist: Fine-Art Devices in Fiction* (Chapel Hill, 1944), 138.

[14]Neumann, 117.

[15]William Frost makes special note of the "pastoral-cum-phallic imagery" in the following speech by Gertrude in *Hamlet* which is, I think, startlingly similar to that cited here: "There is a willow grows aslant a brook/That shows his hoar leaves in the grassy stream." "Shakespeare's Rituals and the Opening of *King Lear*," *Shakespeare: The Tragedies*, Clifford Leech, editor (Chicago, 1965), 193.

[16]Neumann, 170.

[17]Neumann, 47.

[18]Sigmund Freud, *A General Introduction to Psychoanalysis*, trans. Joan Riviere (New York, 1952), 139.

[19]Hester's attempt to seduce Dimmesdale is rather obvious, but whether or not she succeeds is a matter of conjecture. However considering the passionate nature of the attractive Hester and the proven susceptibility of the minister, it appears altogether probable. Rudolphe von Abele declares that during this forest scene Hester's "unregeneracy reasserts itself and infects even Dimmesdale." "*The Scarlet Letter*: A Reading," *Accent*, XI, 222 (Autumn, 1951).

[20]I think it is interesting to note that the motion-picture camera technique that is mentioned here of panning away from the lovers to focus on parallel activity in an empathetic nature was most recently used to advantage in David Lean's film, "Ryan's Daughter." In a review of that film appearing in the *New York Times* for Nov. 22, 1970, Vincent Canby reports that:

> The extraordinary event that one will remember most vividly is Rosy's sexual awakening. As the major makes love to Rosy in a magical forest, dandelions lose their seeds, the sun peers through the leaves to make an effulgent sign of the cross, and the trees themselves go through a little series of ecstatic shudders.

[21]Marius Bewley, *The Eccentric Design* (New York, 1959), 171.

[22]Jung, IX, 1, p. 288.

[23]Jung, IX, 1, p. 175.

[24]C. G. Jung and C. Kerenyi, 78.

[25]C. G. Jung and C. Kerenyi, 79.

[26]Male, 94.

Elizabeth Aycock Hoffman, "Political Power in *The Scarlet Letter*," *ATQ*, NS 4 (March 1990), 13-29.

As a "thorough-going democrat," Hawthorne surely had some admiration for the qualities he gives Hester Prynne in *The Scarlet Letter*. He presents the woman's strength of mind and her self-reliance as a singular contrast to a society that values the conformative citizen. Yet by having her undergo lifelong retribution for her adultery, he indicates an inability to render a completely independent individual. Myra Jehlen recently observed that although granting "rebellion its strongest case by embodying it in his most compelling character," Hawthorne found Hester's defiance "primordial" and thus "an immediate threat to social order." By locating Hawthorne's apparent censure of Hester within the historical context of hegemonic bourgeois values in America, Jehlen's study provides an ideological explanation for his portrayal of his character's punishment (138, 133). Her interpretation differs from past readings of the novel which frequently emphasized the author's personal disapproval of Hester's sexual offense. By privileging Hawthorne's own artistic discretion in the resolution of Hester's fate, the earlier inquiries reinforced the concept of his novel's immunity from political interests. On the other hand, by demonstrating that the author's perception of his character correlates to the middle-class ideology regarding individualism, Jehlen suggests the limitations to the author's creative imagination.

My analysis has an agenda similar to Jehlen's. But while I will show that an ideological conception of individuality enframes Hawthorne's artistic view, I will also argue that he had intended to be more subversive than Jehlen perhaps gives him credit for. I begin with the premise that his "compelling" characterization of the strong-willed Hester in contrast to an extremely regimented society reflects his image of the ideal individual. Drawing from Michel Foucault's observations about disciplining societies, my investigation will demonstrate that Hawthorne's failure to give Hester's individualism complete expression evolves from the restrictive terms of the discourse that he employs. Finally, I will show that although he attempts to differentiate his literary mode of representation from its political counterpart in the culture, the means by which he renders "true" independence in Hester reveal the complicity of his art with those programs that promote domination and subjection in society. To demonstrate this last conclusion, my analysis follows the directives of John Carlos Rowe's deconstructive methodology, especially where they illustrate the importance of examining the meaning-giving process in the literary work.

Hawthorne introduces his interest in an independent conscience in

"The Custom-House" when he dramatizes his lack of imaginative freedom while serving as the Surveyor. In the sketch he satirizes his experience with political patronage, and he obviously targets the Whigs. Much of his bitter irony hinges on the point that while he took a non-partisan attitude in the Custom House and became a "tolerably good surveyor" to the detriment of his artistic powers, his was the "first head" to "roll" when the Whigs took over the national administration (41). In expressing the concern of the American writer who receives little monetary reward for his art, he indicates that dependence on the mercy of politicians and not only offered little security but also enfeebled the imagination. Moreover, the author's lament gestures toward his characterizations of Dimmesdale and Hester, whose creative powers are apprectiated only to the extent that they serve the aims of their society (Baym 142). Indeed, Hawthorne himself imagines his own ancestors' scorn for not taking up a profession that "glorifies God" and is "serviceable to mankind" (10). Given the connection between the author in the sketch and the two characters, we can assume that in the novel proper Hawthorne investigates the methods by which the individual imagination is brought into conformity with the interests of the state.

In this regard, the novel may be seen as a personal "allegory" of the author's experience with conformative pressures when he served in the Custom House (Arac 252). But by placing the disciplining powers within an historical context, he also traces the development of social control in American society since the settlement of the Puritans. Here, another important connection exists: Hawthorne's history of those social mechanisms that individuate members of society and also discipline them resembles Foucault's study of the same topics in *Discipline and Punish*. For example, in the enfeeblement of their will and their simultaneous usefulness to their respective institutions, Hawthorne (in the sketch) and Dimmesdale exhibit a condition which Foucault calls the "docility/utility" produced by disciplining mechanisms in modern societies. According to Foucault, the consciousness of being observed by anonymous or ambiguous observers results in the observed's undergoing an increase in physical output—"in economic terms of utility"—on the one hand, and a diminishment—of these "same forces"—"in political terms of obedience" on the other (138). Obviously, Chillingworth in his disguise as the benevolent, ever-attentive physician attains this power over the minister. If we look to Arlin Turner's biography, we can see that Hawthorne had at least the Whigs in mind in his own case. While they appeared very supportive of his appointment to the Surveyorship (and in Whig- dominated Salem he needed their approval), he was aware that they could punish him for partisan behavior in the Custom House (178). Moreover, by sensing that this projected novel with its critical portrayal of the Puritans could be offensive to the conservative Whigs, he very possibly would have felt constrained in his literary efforts as well. One party leader in particular, the Reverend Charles W. Upham, might have become incensed, for he himself had eulogized the "piety" of the early Puritans in his history of the Salem witchcraft trials (274). He may have played a role in getting Hawthorne appointed to the Custom House, and he definitely headed the movement to obtain his ouster (Turner 181- 183). Hence, the author's relieved response to the Whigs' political "decapitation" of him seems understandable. In finding himself publicly recognized as their enemy, he thought himself no longer constrained from taking the individualistic stance necessary to criticize artistically the mechanisms that create conformative societies.

The publicly punished Hester plays out this aspect of the author's life. Hawthorne suggests that her ostracism by society results, as we are to assume his own ejection from the Custom House did, in her achieving a position which enables her to obtain a critical perspective of the disciplining methods in the community. But Hawthorne undermines her critical view—and by extension the novel's—through the very means by which he attempts to justify it. As this study will demonstrate, essentially the same social techniques of discipline which his novel attacks for their ability to obtain unlimited power over the individual mind produced the discourse that enables him to define her as an individual who responds to the workings of her own conscience. Her character is, in Foucault's words, an " 'ideological' representation" of a disciplining society (194). To understand Hawthorne's ideological limitations, however, we must first examine his observations of the political forces that render the conformative individual. In the opening scene around the scaffold he illustrates the initial gestures towards punitive techniques which culminated not only in the "disciplines" of the nineteenth century but also in the language by which the "ideal" individual could be identified.

In telling us that the scaffold was believed to be "as effectual an agent in the promotion of good citizenship, as ever was the guillotine among the terrorists of France"(55), Hawthorne recalls the theory of French penologists who proposed that public decapitations would convey a clear message to the citizens: the swiftness with which the executions could be performed would signify the prompt and certain power of the legal system (Foucault 13). Foucault writes that because eighteenth-century legalists were discouraged by the ineffectual punishments by the king, they looked for more "efficient" methods of using the criminal's body in public penalities as a deterrent against crime. The king's punitive power, which his executioner made manifest on the prisoner's body, often became so excessive that it drew the spectators' attention away from the lesson they were to learn. The crowds became disruptive, showing great hostility towards the king's authority or the prisoner (59-63). In an initial step to end the arbitrary effects involved in the monarch's public discipline, legalists evolved the concept of "making the punishment fit the crime." To communicate a more unified legal code, they developed a penal semiotic which could be prominently displayed on the criminal's body. Each symbol, or each mutilation, was to show a close correspondence between the crime and the punishment so that it would appear as though the latter grew naturally and necessarily out of the former (106-110). Theoretically, inscribing the prisoner's body with "the abstraction of the law itself" had the advantage of concealing the actual intervention of the legal powers that ordered the punishment (13). Spectators were thus expected to concentrate on the certainty and inexorableness of the law and not have their attention, and possibly their hostility, drawn to the punitive authorities behind the law.

As Hawthorne shows in Hester's penalty, the Puritans in the novel have a contractual government that enables them to devise public punishments which do not manifest the king's power. Rather, the Puritan leaders intend to reflect their belief that the theocracy holds a covenant with God, and therefore the laws that govern them hold a relation with the Divine. But, as Hawthorne reminds us, they had to rely on their own interpretations of Scripture to write the "statute book" (152). Moreover, his telling us that the leaders could not disentangle the "mesh of good and evil" in Hester's heart (64) indicates the kind of ambiguity which can only be resolved by making a political judgment against the act itself (Johnson 105-106). But to provide the appearance of certainty in divine retribution, they encode her body with a sign the makes only "the abstraction of the law itself" manifest. Rendering transparent both her crime (adultery) and her punishment (the wearing of the letter), the symbol is intended to communicate to the spectators that the penalty arose naturally and necessarily from the offense. The Reverend Mr. Wilson reinforces this penal semiotic when he says that "the shame lay in the commission of the crime, and not in the showing of it forth" (65-66). By the time he finishes his hell- fire sermon, with "continual references to the ignominious letter," the author informs us that the symbol has "assumed new terrors" as though its "scarlet hue" came from "the flames of the infernal pit" (68-69).

With the absence of any signs of physical intervention, the real power to punish appears to lie within a higher than human authority, and it seems swift and inexorable. The letter thus seems to produce "a spell," which takes Hester "out of the ordinary relations with humanity" and encloses her in "a sphere by herself" (54).

Hawthorne's description in this scene indicates that a far more subtle force than the letter or Mr. Wilson's terrifying sermon works its disciplining effect on the people around the scaffold. Although they make no outward show of their legal power to punish, the Puritan leaders, on the church platform above and behind Hester, perform an important role in the public spectacle. They assume "solemn" demeanor as they look down on the criminal and thus serve as exemplary witnesses of the law's enforcement. Implying the contrast with rowdy crowds at spectacles in which the king displayed his punitive authority, Hawthorne says, "Even had there been a disposition to turn the matter into ridicule, it must have been repressed and overpowered by the solemn" presences on the balcony (56). Eric Mottram applies a Lacanian principle to the subtle play of power in this scene: "The gaze of the Other [the spectators] . . . controls subjectivity, but the subject [Hester] controls the Other's gaze too" (202). This "exchange of looks" and the behaviorial control that it effects extend to the leaders as well.

While the Puritan authorities solemnly gaze at Hester from the balcony, the spectators are not only aware of their presence but also of the latter's ability to observe their behavior. And conversely, in recognizing the importance of their outward demeanor, the men on the balcony must be conscious of their being subject to the glances of the people down below. "Accordingly," the crowd responds to the dignitaries by becoming "sombre and grave" (56), and the rulers, in turn, feel compelled to remain in a like posture in order to express the sacredness of their office and the law they represent. The overall effect quite probably intensifies the "spell" that encloses Hester in her own "sphere." For in feeling the possible gaze of another upon him or herself, each person around the scaffold could quite naturally become self-consciously absorbed with his/her potential for public humilation. Consequently, while all fix their gaze on the letter, many can not be actually thinking of it in relation to Hester, at least not as much as they fear that some stigma will be attached to them. We know for a fact that Dimmesdale experiences this anxiety.

In Foucauldian terms, the power that circulates around the scaffold, via an "indiscreet," yet also "discreet" (because it works "silently"), "exchange of looks" proves an "efficient" means of controlling the behavior of members of a contractual society. Because all are subject to the gazes of others and no one can tell who might possess a penetrating look, the powers of observation operate "anonymously" and freely back and forth from the bottom to the top of the social hierarchy, punishing the criminal but moreover disciplining the potential or secret offender (176-177). Ideally, in an egalitarian society power should be balanced through an exchange of gazes between subjects and others. In Hawthorne's novel the initial scene around the scaffold illustrates this symmetrical pattern of power. While the Puritan leaders have appropriated Hester's physical person as an object through which they communicate the legal code, their bodies and those of the spectators are also subject to the gazes of others. Only the symbol on her breast, the penal semiotic, differentiates Hester from the remainder of the community. In presenting this historical moment in which two types of punitive power have begun operating in a quasi-democratic society, the author examines the one, a subtle, ambiguous power, for its means of obtaining the conformity of the individual, and the other, a definite, public punishment, for its ability to liberate the individual mind. But by looking first at the punitive relation between Chillingworth and Dimmesdale, we will find that Hawthorne's concept of the self-reliant, self-willed individual is inseparable from the political powers of discipline.

For his portrayal of the Chillingworth/Dimmesdale relationship, Hawthorne used several sources. Leslie Fiedler has shown the the author's reading of Jean-Jacques Rousseau's *Julie, ou la nouvelle Heloise* the year before he began *The Scarlet Letter* provided him with material for the triangular relation between husband, wife, and lover (496). But there are other significant comparisons. Although Clarens differs from Boston in that it is a "class society," mechanisms of surveillance function there as well. Through the continual "exchange of gazes" between the "master and servant," the former make themselves visible examples for the servants to imitate while, conversely, the masters' constant visibility prevents them from concealing any vices (O'Neal 59). And also as in Boston, there is at Clarens a more intimate yet anonymous disciplining force operating. As we find with Chillingworth, Julie's husband Wolmar is a cold-hearted empiric who prides himself on his ability to read the hearts of others and then use that knowledge to manipulate them for his own satisfaction. Having secretly discovered her illicit affair before their marriage, Wolmar succeeds in discreetly directing Julie's passions away from vice and towards virtue so that she becomes the epitome of morality in her society. While Julie's husband expresses the most benevolent intentions, he ultimately causes her as much torment as Chillingworth causes

Dimmesdale, though the physician has contrasting reasons (Rousseau 719-720). Through their empirical observations of another's sexual passions ("heart-knowledge") and their consequent disciplining techniques, the two men become completely engaged in "a schema of power- knowledge," a process in which the autonomous powers of the investigated become transferred to the investigator (Foucault 226-227). Hawthorne's characterization of the old physician as a "leech" offers a graphic description of the transference of the minister's "own proper strength": while behaving like a benevolent friend to Dimmesdale, Chillingworth engorges himself on the power that his torturous examinations of the minister provide and thereby drains the latter of his own life force. Since Julie also loses her will to live, Wolmar's disciplining "love" could be said to follow a like pattern.

Hawthorne's portrayal of Chillingworth's punitive relation to Dimmesdale also shows his familiarity with the penological model of discipline within the prison system in his own day. Two articles in the *North American Review*, which he apparently read, demonstrate that while the reformation of the criminal was the aim, nineteenth-century prison officials had the opportunity to enter into a "schema of power-knowledge" with the convicts under their supervision. The article of 1848 compares the interior of a penitentiary to a "grand theatre" and states that with the surrender "body and soul" of the convict to the "constant and irresistible control of the prison-keeper," penologists can conduct "the trial of all new plans in hygiene and education, physical and moral reform." While the writer reports that a survey conducted in 1847 cites an alarming number of enfeebled prisoners—both in body and mind—in the Philadelphia prison system, he questions the method of incarceration rather than the penitentiary officials' unlimited powers per se (152-153, 158). According to the article of 1839, penologists theorized that if the prison provided the proper solitary environment, the inmate would be forced to confront his/her "vicious mind" and thereby receive the punishment "inflicted by conscience" (20-21). Hawthorne apparently recognized that in observing the spectacle of the convict's self-recriminations, prison supervisors marginalized or repressed the effects of their own investigatorial procedures. As he shows in his portrayal of Chillingworth, the discreet powers of observation can produce physical signs of a guilty conscience in the observed. As with the magistrates' orchestration of Hester's penalty, intervention is concealed in order to establish a necessary correlation between crime and punishment.

In the novel Hawthorne extends the penological model of discipline to other sectors of society to demonstrate that social institutions, such as the medical sciences, are given the opportunity to conduct empirical observations of individuals and thereby gain enormous power over them. Enlisted by the Puritans to become Dimmesdale's physician, a role which, according to the author, implies the "license" to investigate a patient's most deeply hidden secrets (124), Chillingworth represents "the political counter-part" to the legal system. While, as Foucault has shown, the law itself limits the "exercise of power" by one individual over another, it also sets no definite restraints on the mechanisms of surveillance that operate within social institutions and enable the "asymmetrical" power relations to develop (222-223). Hawthorne suggests the connection between the "discipline" of medicine and the law when he tells us that Chillingworth began his "investigation" of Dimmesdale with the cool objectivity of a "judge" (129). While Chillingworth's sense of his own personal betrayal increasingly draws him into his vengeful relation to the minister, the "knowledge/power" that the physician gains from his close observations of his patient becomes as fascinating as it gratifying to torture the other. Chillingworth enacts the role of the modern "inquisitor" whose goal, rather than being the extraction of the offender's confession, is to continue indefinitely an examination of the prisoner's body for evidence of his soul or conscience (Foucault 226-227). After secretly discovering some sort of stigma on Dimmesdale's breast, he does not wish to confront the other openly. Instead, he prefers the role of "chief actor" in the clergyman's "interior world" which, between the latter's acutely sensitive imagination and his own machinations, is much like the "grand theatre" in a prison. Disguised as a benevolent doctor, Chillingworth manages to keep Dimmesdale "for ever on the rack" through an interrogation designed to effect excruciating pains of remorse upon the interrogated (139-140).

But as Hawthorne's term "leech" indicates, Chillingworth has no more independent strength than Dimmesdale has. Both are used by the community for its own disciplining purposes. Because he shows the promise of performing "great deeds for the now feeble New England Church," Dimmesdale's deteriorating health concerns the Puritan community, and its leaders appropriate the physician's skills to diagnose the illness and recommend a cure (120-122). As the punitive relation develops between the two men, their society finds another use for them. Living examples of good and evil serve as a disciplining technique in Boston. Consequently, when many of the people observe that since the beginning of their relationship the minister's physical appearance has become increasingly enfeebled and the deformed Chillingworth has developed a sinister aspect, they decide that they are witnessing the drama of a saint's inevitable struggle with the torments of Satan or his agent. No one doubts that the demon will lose the conflict. But Hawthorne reveals the bitter irony of a society that enables an obviously asymmetrical power relation to continue. In response to the people's treating the destructive relation as a spectacle for its own instructive purposes (Dimmesdale's "certain victory" will exemplify the way to salvation), Hawthorne says that "it was sad to think of the perchance mortal agony through which he [Dimmesdale] must struggle towards his triumph" (128). The people's worshipful respect for the minister does not preclude their accepting his life as expendable in the process of advancing communal interests.

Through Dimmesdale's character the author further undermines disciplining mechanisms which keep persons in conformity with the utilitarian principles of the community. Although the minister hides his crime because he fears the people's disapproval, he attempts to convince himself that his better service to society lies in not exposing his "black" and "filthy" self to the public eye because he could then do no more good. But in telling himself that he suffers more by keeping his painful secret, he cannot ignore the other side of the argument which Chillingworth proposes; the greater way to serve one's fellow humans is to make "manifest the power and reality of conscience" (132-133). Since the Puritan community employs living examples of good and evil, Dimmesdale confronts an irresolvable question about which would be the more useful—the revelation of his crime or its concealment. And to demonstrate that the minister remains obedient to the last to the utilitarian values of his community, Hawthorne portrays Dimmesdale playing out the dual roles of saint and sinner in his dying hours.

While moral readings of Dimmesdale's ascent to the scaffold argue that he at last finds the strength of will to reveal his crime, his "revelation" does not equate to a confession. He essentially replicates before the public eye his obsession with the disciplining process which has created "the power and reality of [his] conscience." Having constantly felt the gaze of others watching his every move, he has developed an extreme egocentricity which is characterized by his becoming the subject and object of his own observations. Earlier, in the privacy of his room, he exhibits this pattern when he plays out the roles of the accuser and the accused, the punisher and the punished, during his grueling self-examinations and self-flagellations. And his "revelation" on the scaffold constitutes another enactment of these dual roles. He begins with the first-person voice—"behold *me* here ... the one sinner of the world," and after pointing to the letter that has been Hester's punishment, he shifts to the third person to draw attention to this stigma— "It was on *him*" (254-255, emphasis added). Referring to himself as an object indicates that, in a literal sense, he has gone out of his mind. He in fact shows the "highly disordered mental state" that Hawthorne observes in him when he interprets the comet in the midnight sky as a sign (the letter "A") meant just for him.

The author explains that the minister's delusion about the comet results from his extending his "egotism over the whole expanse of nature." Moreover, the author says, Dimmesdale's denial of reality includes his simultaneous awareness that Chillingworth is observing him on the scaffold with an expression of "malevolence" on his face (155-157). Hawthorne indicates that, as he has often done in the past, the minister finds himself hating the inquisitive physician at the very moment when he feels most tortured by his guilt. But rather than allowing himself to make the connection between his pain and Chillingworth's presence, he sublimates the latter's participation in his punishment, thus enabling the old man's punitive procedures to create an extreme effect. By intensifying the minister's awareness of his hidden offence, Chillingworth's constant examinations create the circumstances in which Dimmesdale magnifies his own criminality and inflicts on himself a correlative punishment.

And this pattern typifies his behavior after he yields to Hester's scheme to flee the colony. In his meeting with the old man afterwards, he knowingly comes face to face with his "enemy." But he also senses that Chillingworth has discerned his most recent liaison with Hester (224). Responding in his habitual manner, Dimmesdale exaggerates his own guilt while simultaneously sublimating his awareness of the physician's ever-observant eye, as his "revelation" demonstrates. On the scaffold he declares himself "the one sinner of the world" and refers to the stigma on his breast as the evidence of "God's judgment" (254-255). But his repetition of a behavioral pattern that Hawthorne had earlier described as symptommatic of a mental disturbance undermines his claim. Aware that an external force perceives his guilt, the egocentric man represses his knowledge that Chillingworth played the punitive role in his "interior world" and attributes the penetrating gaze to supernatural powers.

Dimmesdale's "revelation" also recalls Hester's initial appearance on the scaffold when the magistrates concealed their intervention in her punishment. Paralleling their use of the letter, the minister presents the stigma on his breast as "witness" of a divine law that mandates a necessary relation between his crime and its retribution (255). The mark on his body, like Hester's brand, thus appears to have the effect of individuating him by suggesting that he occupies an "isolated sphere" where punishment comes of necessity from a supernatural source. But as Hawthorne shows, the intervention of subtle political powers of discipline produces Dimmesdale's egocentric conception of uniqueness. Accordingly, the author intends a contrast between the meaning he ascribes to the minister's stigma and that which he attaches to the sign on Hester's bosom.

While the letter is first shown as a political-legal discourse (its purpose lies in deterrence as well as punishment), Hawthorne demonstrates that over the years Hester finds a personal significance in it. Its ability to isolate her in a "sphere of her own" does not prevent her sense of painful humiliation when the gaze of others focuses upon the sign of her adultery. But because her offense has been made public, she is not susceptible to the ambiguous forces of discipline in society that operate on secret offenders like the minister. Through her needlework and charitable deeds, she becomes a useful member of society, and since she holds a hostile view of popular opinion, her actions appear volitional. Hawthorne indicates that if she intends her generosity to the poor and sick to be a penance, she does not seek to win the Puritans' approval in the process. When Chillingworth tells her that her good works have possibly earned her a pardon, she responds that "it lies not in the pleasure of the magistrates to take off this badge . . . . Were I worthy of it, it would fall away of its own nature, or be transformed into something that should speak a different purport" (169). She has obviously transformed the Puritan leaders' illusion of non- intervention, when they forced her to stand on the scaffold, into a reality: she will not allow their interference in the punishment of her crime. Moreover, in her determination that a higher than human law governs the term of her penalty, Hawthorne does not suggest the extreme egocentricity which he exhibits in Dimmesdale.

Yet she is the subject and object of a disciplining technique similar to that which enfeebles the minister's will. In their solitary "sphere" Pearl acts as the disciplinarian. Through the child's character, Hawthorne attempts to differentiate his own model of discipline from the political one by suggesting a spiritual paradigm of necessary retribution. "God," he tells us, "as a direct consequence" of Hester's "sin" gave her a "lovely child" (89). But Pearl's mechanisms of surveillance diverge very little from Chillingworth's. Although described as a "messenger" from the "spiritual world" (256, 165), Pearl provides her mother with the kind of "trials" that take place behind the prison walls where the crime itself is no longer the reason for the punishment.

Pearl does not need to know the exact meaning of the letter to torture her mother. Perceiving Hester's sensitivity to the sign whenever she draws attention to it, the child converts the knowledge she obtains from the woman's physical responses into the power to torment her. Although Pearl does not engage in the "schema of power/knowledge" with the same vengeance which Chillingworth exhibits with Dimmesdale, her method of surveillance operates with essentially the same ambiguity and produces similar effects. Her "peculiar" and "uncanny" "tendency to hover about the engima of the scarlet letter" seems to Hester the Providential "design of justice and retribution" (180), and she submits to her daughter's punishment. The woman's belief that her "retribution" arises from a supranatural force differs little from Dimmesdale's perception of the origins of his punishment. Yet Hawthorne validates her notion of a divine "justice" by referring to her daughter as "God"-sent and by showing that Pearl's discipline results in her mother's strengthened mind, in contrast to the minister's enfeeblement. Within their solitary "sphere," however, the woman's ineffectiveness in controlling Pearl's wild behavior and her docile response to the child's tormenting attention to her "badge of shame" illustrate their asymmetrical power relation. Again like Dimmesdale, Hester perceives her individuality through a punitive process that particularizes her at the same time that it operates ambiguously.

Rather than being the transcendent power of the "spiritual world," the discipline that produces Hester's individuality can be placed in the historical context of modern penology. Individualized punishment, such as that which Pearl administers to her mother, grew out of the legalists' efforts to correlate the penalty with the offense in the public spectacle. In the prison cell, according to penal theorists, the "real" punishment would necessarily come from the inmate's conscience as he/she reflected on his/her deviant past. While to the community the letter singles the woman out as a "type of shame," it describes only the adultery, making the crime itself the object of the punitive gaze of others. Moreover, the woman's stoic bearing in public represses any outward show of her personal feelings. With the symbol on her bosom as the focal point, her physical person becomes practically invisible—a "bare and harsh outline"—which manifests no signs of her former, passionate self (163). Under Pearl's observant eye, however, the woman's "whole" existence becomes the visible object of the child's power. By reminding Hester of her past, Pearl's aberrant behavior shows the "knowledge/power" that Foucault has related to the extensive documentation of prisoners' lives (189). Seeing a "shadowy reflection of the evil that had existed in herself," Hester finds in her daughter's "wild flow of spirits" the "lawless passion" that led to her adultery (91-94; 165).

The woman reasons that the child could have absorbed her own distraught emotions while being carried in her womb. And although Hester arrives at a natural explanation for her daughter's hyperactivity, the "perverse" yet "intelligent" look in Pearl's eyes as she launches into one of her wild sprees renders the mother powerless to bring the tormenting behavior to an end. Hawthorne himself describes the child's knowing look as "inexplicable," indicating that a mysterious force is behind it (92). Yet modern psychology would demonstrate that having learned to read her mother's facial expression in infancy, Pearl began to detect those emotions which paralyzed Hester's will to control her daughter's aberrant actions. On the other hand, the dynamic of power involved here—the complete transference of Hester's strength to her daughter—recalls the parasitic relation Chillingworth holds with Dimmesdale. Moreover, it suggests the political program that individuates as it disciplines.

Foucault finds that prior to the modern age relatively few persons below the highest levels of society were singled out for attention. But at the historical moment when the examinations of the disciplines became engaged with measuring thoughts and behaviors against established "norms," a new mode of individualization appeared that operated throughout the social hierarchy. According to Foucault, one achieves the status of "individual" not through those aspects that characterize a "normal, healthy, law-abiding adult," but through traits that depart from fixed standards (191-194). The political nature of this process of particularization and normalization becomes apparent when we recall the opening scene of the novel where the discreet yet ambiguous exchange of gazes produces a pose of "solemn demeanor" in everyone around the scaffold. Sombreness serves as the "norm," and no one dares depart from it for fear of being singled out for observation. Here, since all are subject to the gaze of others, the powers of discipline function in an egalitarian manner. In the relation between Chillingworth and Dimmesdale, however, the imbalance of power is obvious. And the same asymmetrical power relation exists between Pearl and Hester. Although she is a child, Pearl's oddly expressive gazes (97) and the knowing look with which she acts out the "lawless passion" (165) of the woman's former life make Hester intensely aware of the difference between her own motherhood and that which accords with the "norm."

Because Pearl's ignorance of the actual offense enables her "intelligent" glances to operate with both discreetness and subtle ambiguity, they strike Hester with the sense that her own life has acquired some kind of visibility. When Hester witnesses Pearl's wild behavior, she is not tormented by the child's actions per se, but by their comment on her own life—"the evil that had existed in herself" (94). Moreover, by providing Hester with torturous reminders of her former deviancies, they make the correlation between the crime and the punishment appear to be a natural process to produce a self-disciplined woman. Hawthorne describes the child at these instances as appearing "shadowy" or like an "airy sprite" (92, 94). While he uses these artistic expressions to point up Pearl's "peculiar" agency in a heaven-sent retribution, the child's invisibility in relation to her mother's visibility also resembles the dynamics of power within the disciplines. The aim—to bring the individual within the bounds of "normative behavior"—seems Hawthorne's intention as well. Since Hester's strength contrasts significantly to Dimmesdale's enfeebled mind, the disciplining technique he portrays through the child seems most effective towards that end. Accordingly, the woman's independent conscience in relation to the conformative pressures of popular opinion points to the author's "norm" or ideal—the self-discipline and courage of his own convictions which he hoped to find in himself after leaving the Custom House.

Like that of many artists, Hawthorne's purpose in the novel lies in overturning a false perception with a true one. In providing parallel models of discipline, he valorizes his own by replacing the intervention of overtly political powers of discipline with that of a child whose "uncanny" behavior reminds the parent of the "wild" past. Each model has the ability to make the miscreant aware of the need for discipline, but his would seem to illustrate a more natural method. In Dimmesdale's case, the popular gaze and Chillingworth's techniques of surveillance keep his attention focused on his public image, thus producing the predominant self-perception of the hypocrite rather than of the adulterer. Hawthorne suggests that while the two images are interrelated, the former prohibits direct confrontation with the "primal" self, the self of uncontrollable passions that Pearl's character is intended to point up. According to Hawthorne, by lacking this self-perception, Dimmesdale cannot obtain the higher truth regarding justice that Hester gains. Interestingly, like Hester's, the minister's outward submission to the discipline of his public image conceals an inner rebellion. But Hawthorne indicates that his hostility arises solely from the guilt produced by the popular view of his sanctity. His barely repressed impulses to shock and horrify the people during his "midnight vigil" on the scaffold and upon returning from his forest meeting with Hester are reflexive reactions to the tormenting mockery of his popular image (Moers 67-68).

On the other hand, by showing that Hester submits to the guilt reflected in a private image of herself—through Pearl's agency, Hawthorne provides a "reality" to her perception. He suggests that by making her mother constantly aware of the lawless, passionate self, Pearl enables Hester to recognize a higher than human law that authenticates the necessity of discipline. Hester's consciousness of a transcendent "design of justice" would then seem to validate her—and the novel's—critical observations on the disciplining mechanisms within "human institutions" (199). His subversion of the obviously political model of punishment suggests that he found in the ambiguous powers of popular opinion and of the scientific empiricists an unnecessary disruption of a process by which the individual confronts the "real," primal self and thus perceives the "real" need for discipline. And except for the brief hour in the forest with Dimmesdale, the woman is depicted as remaining true to this principle, which the sign on her breast represents. Hawthorne implies that by acting on the enfeebled minister's "heart- knowledge" (260). Hester displaces her awareness of her own guilty passions, her removal of the letter symbolizing the lapse in self-perception. When Pearl succeeds in forcing her mother to resume wearing her "badge of shame," he justifies the child's intervention by saying, "So it ever is, whether thus typified or no, that an evil deed invests itself with the character of doom" (211).

Yet by needing Pearl's character to render the "truth" about the necessity of punishment, he undermines his artistic model of discipline. Referred to as her mother's "guilt and torture" (102), the child is needed to transform the original political- legal meaning of the letter's semiotic into the personal, transcendent "truth" for Hester. Since the first necessity (Pearl's intervention) overturns the primacy of the second (the necessary relation between the offense and its retribution), his literary model subverts his critical observations about the expediencies of political mechanisms of social control. Christian dogma, upon which his own discourse is based, may teach the inevitability of retribution, "typified or no" in this world. But a political program of discipline created the need for intervention. Contrary to Jonathan Arac's claim, "authorial meaning" alone cannot differentiate a literary model of discourse from its political counterpart in the culture (261-262). As John Carlos Rowe has shown, the way in which the author realizes his meaning must also be considered. Rowe's methodology demonstrates that while a writer's "truth" can repress or marginalize the relation of his discursive mode of representation with the political, the intervening space between the signifier of a discourse and its signified provides the crucial key to the process which enables the expression of artistic meaning (11, 25- 26). In his representation of literary "truth," Hawthorne's description of Pearl as a "God"-sent consequence suppresses the political nature of her mediating position between her mother's adultery and its punishment. Yet just as the examinations of the disciplines produced the "reality" of the individual, Pearl's replication of her mother's "lawless" past provides the "truth" of her mother's selfhood.

Hawthorne apparently recognized that the disciplines created the need for their own interventions. He seems to have seen that their measurements of behaviors against established "norms" made their own mechanisms of discipline and normalization appear necessary. But, as he indicates in his portrayal of Chillingworth, he perceived their interventions arising from an obsession with "power/knowledge." On the other hand, his portrayal of Pearl shows his concurrence with the ideology of an aboriginal self, the "noble savage" as it were. The conception of a dualistic, pre-social self apparantly suggested to him that a corresponding transcendent law originates the need to discipline the passions. Unlike Rousseau, however, Hawthorne found that contractual forms of government, though seeming to offer the ideal setting, could actually displace the higher instinct by emphasizing the social or public self. Consequently, he points to the family unit, the "private sphere," as the proper environment to bring out this innate quality. But in using Pearl's character, his literary model repeats the gestures of the political program whose representation of the "noble savage" enabled it to justify the necessity of intervention and domination.

The political rhetoric that employs binary oppositions— "deviancy" versus "normality," "savage" versus "noble," and like contrarities—is central to his own method of rendering "truth." As both Derrida and Foucault have shown, the power to create meaning originates in the intermediate position between antithetical signs. In terms of the disciplines, Hawthorne situates Pearl in the space from which aberrant behaviors receive their "reality" through references to acceptable standards. In using her character to transform the political-legal semiotic of the letter into a personal, artistic discourse, he describes her as a living counterpart to the sign. Yet she is more like the function of political writings than like a real child. By enabling the "necessary" correlation between an illicit past and a punitive conscience, Pearl inscribes Hester's character with a "truth" that was created by the written histories of the reformed criminal. And the woman's lifelong retribution demonstrates the successful internalization of this "truth." At the novel's conclusion, by returning Hester to New England without Pearl, Hawthorne shows that the woman remains faithful to the semiotic of the letter: her leaving a grown daughter who, according to the author, could give her love and warmth (262) evidences her refusal to accept reward from an illicit love. But moreover, his presenting the self-denying woman as exemplary points up his own complicity in the political program that effects the subjection of the individual through the ideological representation of substandard or abnormal behaviors.

Works Cited

Arac, Jonathan. "The Politics of *The Scarlet Letter*." *Ideology and Classic American Literature*. Ed. Sacvan Bercovitch and Myra Jehlen. Cambridge: Cambridge University Press, 1986. 247-266.

Baym, Nina. *The Shape of Hawthorne's Career*. Ithaca, New York: Cornell University Press, 1976.

Fiedler, Leslie. *Love and Death in the American Novel*. Cleveland and New York: The World Publishing Company, 1962.

Foucault, Michel. *Discipline and Punish*. Trans. Alan Sheridan. New York: Vintage Books, 1979.

Hawthorne, Nathaniel. *The Scarlet Letter*. Vol. I. of *The Centenary Edition of the Works of Nathaniel Hawthorne*. Ed. William Charvat et al. 18 Vols. to date. Columbus: Ohio State University Press, 1962-.

Jehlen, Myra. "The Novel and the Middle Class in America." *Ideology and Classic American Literature*. Ed. Sacvan Bercovitch and Myra Jehlen. Cambridge: Cambridge University Press, 1986. 125-144.

Johnson, Barbara. *The Critical Difference*. Baltimore: The Johns Hopkins University Press, 1980.

Moers, Ellen. "*The Scarlet Letter*: A Political Reading." *Prospects* 9 (1984): 49-70.

Mottram, Eric. "Power and Law in Hawthorne's Fictions." *Nathaniel Hawthorne: New Critical Essays*. Ed. A. Robert Lee. London: Vision Press Ltd., 1982. 187-228.

O'Neal, John C. "Morality in Rousseau's Public and Private Society at Clarens." *Revue de Metaphysique et de Morale* 89 (1984): 58-67.

"Prison Discipline." *North American Review* 49 (1839): 1-43.

Review of *Prison Discipline in America* by Francis C. Gray. *North American Review* 66 (Jan. 1848): 145-190.

Rousseau, Jean-Jacques. *Julie, ou la Nouvelle Heloise*, Vol. 2 of *Oeuvres Completes*. Ed. Bernard Gagnebin. 4 Vols. Paris: Gallimard Editions, 1961.

Rowe, John Carlos. *Through the Custom-House*. Baltimore: The Johns Hopkins University Press, 1982.

Turner, Arlin. *Nathaniel Hawthorne: A Biography*. New York: Oxford University Press, 1980.

Upham, Charles W. *Lectures on Witchcraft, Comprising a History of the Delusion in Salem*. Boston: Carter, Hendee and Babcock, 1831.

Marilyn Mueller Wilton, "Paradigm and Paramour: Role Reversal in The Scarlet Letter"*

Although many early critics of *The Scarlet Letter* regarded Hester as "an accessory figure" (James 109) whose "appeal made it easy to disregard the more central roles of her husband or of her lover" (Abel 303), most modern scholars recognize her primacy in the romance. In fact, Hester's prominence is so strongly delineated that she could be considered the "hero" of the work. This is not, as it might first appear, simply an exercise in semantics but rather the basis for a new perspective on the romance. Recognizing Hester Prynne as the "hero" and Arthur Dimmesdale as the "heroine" acknowledges Hester's dominance in the plot and accords Dimmesdale an important but less essential role. Because she embodies the quintessential attributes of the traditional hero and is central to the plot, Hester can be legitimately referred to as the hero of *The Scarlet Letter*, while Dimmesdale's anti-heroic qualities and secondary function subordinate his status to hers. This striking reversal of traditional male and female literary roles in the plot is the basis for asserting that Hester is its paradigmatic hero while Dimmesdale is its paramour and heroine.

These designations for Hester and Dimmesdale are not entirely new, for Nina Baym refers to Hester as a "hero" in *The Scarlet Letter: A Reading*, and Margaret Thickstun terms Arthur Dimmesdale the work's "heroine" in *Fictions of the Feminine*. However, neither of these writers develops the role reversal in depth or in parallel comparison. Though Baym sees Hester as heroic, she makes no mention of Dimmesdale as a heroine. Instead, she sees Hester as both a heroine and a hero. Stating that Hester can be considered a heroine because "she is deeply implicated in, and responsive to, the gender structure of her society, and because her story, turning on 'love,' is 'appropriate' for a woman," Baym also considers Hester a hero "because she has qualities and actions that transcend this gender reference and lead to heroism as it can be understood for anyone" (62). On the other hand, Thickstun views Dimmesdale as "the bride of Christ whose spiritual chastity is threatened," "the heroine of *The Scarlet Letter*" (134). In her opinion, "Dimmesdale surpasses Hester as the fallen woman because his turning away from God is more serious than her transgression against an earthly husband" (134). But, although Thickstun refers to Dimmesdale as a heroine, she does not regard Hester as particularly heroic. In contrast to the views of Baym and Thickstun, I maintain that a dual role reversal occurs in the story, with Hester assuming the dominant heroic role and Dimmesdale playing the secondary part of the heroine.

Several critics have addressed the issue of Hester's prominence in the plot and Dimmesdale's subordinate function. In "The Significance of Plot in Hawthorne's Romances" (50), Baym notes that Hawthorne establishes Hester's centrality in *The Scarlet Letter* by selecting her as the only character he mentions in the prefatory "The Custom House," by making Hester the focal point of the first two chapters, and by centering a majority of the work's chapters on her. Additionally, both Baym and John C. Gerber consider Hester's return to Boston as critical to the denouement. David Morse and Robert Todd underscore Dimmesdale's weakness of character, thereby bolstering Hester's importance by diminishing Dimmesdale's role. Morse questions Dimmesdale's failure to confess his crime, which "nullifies all his moral earnestness, dedication and spiritual fervor" and shows him to be "a bare vestige of a human being" (200). Both Morse and Todd recognize as well that Dimmesdale's final confession is the direct result of Hester's "regenerative powers" and subsequent influence on him (Todd 427).

Hester embodies the characteristics of a traditional literary hero whereas Arthur Dimmesdale falls short of that title in many respects; Dimmesdale does, however, represent the idealized love figure in the romance, a role normally enacted by the heroine in a work in which the plot is dominated by a strong heroic figure. The heroine is supplementary, though in some ways vital, often assuming a passive role and serving as a foil to highlight the active performance of the hero. Dimmesdale's weakness underscores Hester's strength in precisely this way. In fact, for some readers it is quite difficult to justify Hester's attraction to such a timid person; however, if Dimmesdale is considered the embodiment of "pure, unattainable love"—the heroine—the affinity becomes more plausible.

Throughout the novel Arthur Dimmesdale assumes the role of the "love object," a subordinate stance traditionally taken by a heroine of significantly lesser importance than the hero. Often the hero's love search is a vital underlying component of the plot. In fact, the romantic heroic quest "involves the hero's often desperate attempt to secure a meaningful love relationship" (Wilson 96). Early in *The Scarlet Letter*, Hawthorne alerts the reader to the fact that Hester, though free to leave Boston, feels magnetized to that place for two reasons. Although one of those reasons is Hester's sense of poetic justice in working out her fate ("Perchance, the torture of her daily shame would at length purge her soul, and work out another purity than that which she had lost; more saint-like, because the result of martyrdom"), the second reason that she remains is her deep, continuing love for Arthur Dimmesdale, "although she hid the secret from herself" (80). Even though their love affair was illicit, Hester considers it a sacred and binding union, for, as she admits to Dimmesdale in the woods, "what we did had a consecration of its own" (195). Accordingly, Hester strives to remain true to that relationship, for "there dwelt, there trode the feet of one with whom she deemed herself connected in a union, that unrecognized on earth, would bring them together before the bar of final judgment, and make that their marriage- altar, for a joint futurity of endless retribution" (80). Hester's longed-for love union with Arthur in the afterlife possesses an ethereal, spiritual quality that distances and elevates it from the seedy connotation assigned by the Puritan townspeople who consider it her "sin." For Hester, at least, her love for Arthur is more sacred and binding than her marriage vow with Chillingworth.

The impossibility of the Hester-Dimmesdale relationship mirrors the predicament often apparent in romantic literature. In *The Romantic Heroic Ideal*, James D. Wilson explains that "Typically in romance literature the woman to whom the hero commits himself appears as the 'earthly analogue' of a transcendental ideal . . . . This ideal projection of self usually becomes unattainable" (96). Hester, the scarlet, disdained woman of Boston, is an unlikely mate for Arthur Dimmesdale, who has achieved a position of power in the vehicle of highest honor in Puritan time, the Church. In a very real sense Arthur Dimmesdale is the idealized man who cannot be possessed in love. Hester's search for the Holy Grail of purification and unrequited love in knightly style exalts the distant, pure frozen maiden in the guise of Arthur Dimmesdale.

Literary convention demands that a hero has a touch of defiance in his character. According to Victor Brombert, "The Romantic hero . . . is above all a rebel, searching for a spiritual aristocracy to which he might belong" (19).[1] Undeniably, Hester is the rebel of *The Scarlet Letter* as she asserts her individualism in bold insubordination against the repressive social mores of her time. This denunciation of Puritan values is manifested in several facets of her lifestyle. For instance, Hester gives birth to an illegitimate child and later withholds the name of the father in spite of the admonitions of the powerful magistrates and clergymen. In fact, when the Reverend Mr. Wilson instructs Hester that she must name the baby's father and repent in order to remove the scarlet letter, she defiantly replies, "I will not speak!" (68).[2] Later, Hester's refusal to relinquish Pearl when Governor Bellingham suggests that she is morally inept to guide a young soul is further proof of her contumacy.

A perpetual trademark of Hester's intransigence is her ostentatious display of the scarlet letter. She subverts its intention as an instrument of shame and dishonor by transforming it instead into a flourish of her personality and beauty. In addition, Hester defies Puritan social stratification by sumptuously embroidering her letter A. Only the social elite were normally allowed to wear ornate clothing, for it was considered a badge of status. External splendor distinguished this class of citizens because it was "deemed necessary to the official state of men assuming reins of power." Such raiment was an integral part of the pageantry that symbolized the Puritan theocracy and was "readily allowed to individuals dignified by rank or wealth" (82). By disregarding this protocol with her decorative A, Hester mocks the intentions of her punishers. In one instance Hester's shiny symbol leads to a servant's confusion about Hester's place in society. For when Hester first arrives at Governor Bellingham's mansion, a bond-servant "perhaps judging from the decision of her air, and the glittering symbol in her bosom, [believed] that she was a great lady in the land" (104), indeed an ironic mistake.

Similarly, Hester dresses Pearl, the embodiment of her sin, in conspicuous, colorful clothing. Hester's A and Pearl's unconventional attire are outward signs of Hester's inner rebellion, for they stand in marked contrast to the drab gray conservative dress of the typical Puritan citizenry. As the living "emblem and product of [her mother's] sin" (93), Pearl is the constant reminder of Hester's adulterous liaison—the incarnate exhibit A of her mother's crime. Even the scarlet letter itself can be interpreted as a sign of rebellion. For all the while that Hester seemingly accepts the role of social pariah assigned to her by the community, the ornate scarlet letter is secretly effecting changes in her. However, the changes wrought are not those contemplated by Hester's punishers. In one sense the letter A *is* the stigma or mark of Cain that isolates her from society, but at the same time it serves as testimony of her growing spiritual recalcitrance. As Hester reflects on the fate of woman, wondering whether "existence [is] worth accepting, even to the happiest among them" (165), Hawthorne adds that "The scarlet letter had not done its office" (166), meaning that it has not made her repentant. (This crucial change in Hester's attitude does not occur until the final chapter and is a pivotal event in the novel.) Such an uncompliant attitude toward orthodoxy is often characteristic of the literary hero, who tends to be a rugged individualist and therefore inherently a misfit in the eyes of others.

Hester's ambivalence between conforming to her inner standards of morality while simultaneously trying to etch out a niche for herself and her daughter in a hostile society demonstrates the tension between the individual's and the community's values and is the crux of the denouement. Puritan society's full acceptance of Hester and her return to Boston and resubmission to her role there comprise the "unraveling," the resolution of the plot. Although this complete reconciliation isn't apparent until the final chapter, the tracing of its slow and steady progress consumes much of the narrative.

In the heroic tradition, Hester demonstrates a personal moral strength that transcends her suffering and transforms her punishment into self-designed grace. Even as she is initially placed on public display on the scaffold, Hester discloses a haughty demeanor, as if refusing to allow the punishment to chasten her. Also, Hester's eventual redemption is not achieved within the traditional framework of punishment designed by the hierarchy of Puritanism but rather through her own personalized atonement. This individualized system of expiation illustrates the heroic confrontation of personal values that clash with those of the society in which he or she lives. As Frederick Garber explains of the Romantic hero's value system: "The mind, then, becomes its own source for standards of reward and punishment, and thus one feels guilt according to the scheme of values one's own mind has established" (224). By being true to her internal code of ethics, Hester exemplifies the heroic stance of determining and living by her private moral standards.

Much as her artistry in the design of her scarlet letter inverts the dishonor that the mark was meant to symbolize, so does Hester's plan for redemption follow only the dictates of her own conscience. Her creativity as an artist is woven into the flair with which she works out her penitence; this confirms Hester's "Self-awareness, a recognition of the demands and complexities of [one's] own private being" that is "basic to the position assumed by the romantic hero" (Garber 213). Outwardly, Hester appears to accept the punishment and taunts of the community, suffering in silence with Christ-like equanimity. Her frugal life is punctuated by charitable works, such as sewing clothing for the poor, who often reject her kindness and berate her. By nursing the sick, Hester becomes "self-ordained a Sister of Mercy" (161). In time, her good acts begin to transmute her emblem of "adulteress" into that of "able," and even "angel," representative of her kind works. It is she, not the Puritan lawmakers, who imparts this effect to the A through her self- imposed penance, and some of the Puritans begin to accept her on the basis of her new-found role. Through voluntary acts Hester contrives her own salvation—not through the punishment officially meted out—a heretical yet creative and daring antinomian concept that parallels the example of Anne Hutchinson.[3]

Hawthorne, in fact, employs a direct analogy between Hutchinson and Hester early in the novel. He lends heroic stature to Hester immediately by linking her path with that of "the sainted Anne Hutchinson" (48), and he reinforces this comparison later in the tale by stating that if it had not been for Pearl, Hester "might have come down to us in history hand in hand with Anne Hutchinson, as the foundress of a religious sect" (165). In fact, Hester bears a striking resemblance to that historical character and, by this association, Hawthorne implies a deep respect for the shared courageous traits of the two women.

Although Hawthorne develops all three members of the love triangle in depth in this tale of densely rich characterization, the plot begins and ends with Hester. She is the focus of a majority of the narrative as well. Even before she enters the scene, she is the main topic of conversation, and by the time she makes her dramatic appearance in Chapter II, the author has created a tension that focuses the reader toward her.

Hester's initial appearance is also preceded by the imagery of the "wild rose-bush" amidst the stern, somber hues of Puritanism. Whatever else it may represent, the rosebush may be construed as a symbol of Hester's rugged individualism. By ending the first chapter with the foreshadowing note that the wild rosebush "may serve...to symbolize some sweet moral blossom" (48), the author implies that this is primarily Hester's tale, for she is the stamen of the "sweet moral blossom." In contrast, Dimmedale's importance lies chiefly in the example of moral cowardice he provides. He exemplifies the inverse of Hawthorne's central principle: "Be true! Be true! Be true! Show freely to the world, if not your worst, yet some trait, whereby the worst may be inferred" (260). Hester, on her part, is the story's definitive affirmation of this principle.

Rather than accept defeat at the hands of those who have scorned and rejected her, Hester, in heroic style, determines to forge an independent life for herself and her daughter through her role as a solitary artist on the fringes of society. Although Hester and Pearl are social and physical outcasts living in an isolated hut near the seaside, Hester's fine needlework is in high demand. Her artistic talent is admired and even coveted by the Puritan citizenry, for it seems that the handiwork of a tainted lady lends it a more sensational and lurid air. By becoming a craftswoman who survives through her own talent, Hester demonstrates the heroic qualities of self-sufficiency and regeneration. Slowly she earns cautious acceptance from the townspeople as well.

Several critics have commented on the similarity of artistry between Hester and her creator. David Morse, for instance, asserts that "since Hester's skills are recognized on an aesthetic level, she also figures as the pioneer artist, endeavouring to carve out within American culture a space within which writers such as Hawthorne himself will eventually try (not very successfully) to function" (199). Others suggest that Hester is a symbolic Hawthorne attempting to justify his return to the role of artist after working as a Surveyor in the Salem custom house. This Hawthorne-Hester identification speaks positively for the case of Hester as hero-protagonist of the tale because of the author's strong affinity with her and her creative craft. Baym reinforces this impression with her reading of *The Scarlet Letter* "symbolically as a representation of the situation of the artist in America," noting that in a commercial society the person who "dreams instead of calculating, feels stigmatized for that preference." Furthermore, according to Baym, "Hawthorne suggests that the democratic and commercial American nation has found no place for the artist, has indeed excluded the artist from its roll call of legitimate citizens" (*A Reading* 106). Again, the parallel between Hawthorne and Hester seems telling. Similarly excluded from mainstream society, Hester epitomizes a type of alienated artist severed from the group, admired for her skill yet suspected for her nonconformity.

Much like a traditional hero, moreover, Hester repeatedly rescues the heroine, Dimmesdale. In the first scaffold scene when Reverend Wilson urges Hester to name the father of her child, he unwittingly discloses Dimmesdale's timorous nature by characterizing Arthur's words as bearing "a young man's over- softness" (65). Wilson's statement echoes with dramatic irony and reveals a basic cravenness in Dimmesdale's character that is readily apparent once the reader learns of the minister's complicity in Hester's sin. Reverend Wilson's reiteration of Dimmesdale's counsel to Hester discloses the full impact of Arthur's dastardly nature; for Dimmesdale had previously said "that it were wronging the very nature of woman to force her to lay open her heart's secrets in such broad daylight" (65), a statement that serves both to shield Arthur's identity and to protect his "woman's nature."

Upon Governor Bellingham's direct instruction, Dimmesdale publicly requests that Hester identify the father of her child. However, Dimmesdale prefaces his words to Hester with a hidden reminder to her that "thou . . . seest the accountability under which I labor" (67). He protests, in effect, that "I'm being forced to say this." Then Dimmesdale cleverly attaches a proviso which only Hester can interpret: "*If* [italics mine] thou feelest it be for thy soul's peace, and that thy earthly punishment will thereby be made more effectual to salvation, I charge thee to speak out the name of thy fellow-sufferer" (67). Knowing Hester's irrepressible nature as he does, Arthur realizes that he is on fairly safe ground with his "request." This is evidenced by his "long respiration" of relief at Hester's refusal and in his comment, "Wondrous strength and generosity of a woman's heart! She will not speak!" (68). Hester, sensing the reluctance of her would-be co-confessor, infers his hidden message and responds correctly on cue. This scene reveals Arthur's intentions as self-seeking but Hester's as unselfishly considerate. For though this is a perfect opportunity to share her ignominy with her lover, Hester protects his honor in chivalrous fashion by refusing to name him. This action illustrates the principle that "Love can be for the hero a potentially redemptive force, but not if it is narcissistic; indeed, love serves the heroic quest only if . . . it enables the hero to transcend self-consciousness," a tenet of heroism outlined by Wilson (194).

Hester rescues Arthur on other occasions as well. For example, she saves him when she notices his severe debility and deterioration at the hands of Chillingworth. Although she incurs Arthur's wrath by doing so, Hester tells him that the villainous leech is her husband. She also protects Dimmesdale from his own self-destructiveness by providing him with the sustenance he needs to reclaim his life and make decisions. Until their meeting in the forest, Dimmesdale had been a broken, impotent man.

True to heroic form, when confronted with obstacles, Hester acts. For instance, after reflecting on the seemingly hopeless fate of woman in a society where "the very nature of the opposite sex . . . is to be essentially modified before woman can be allowed to assume what seems a fair and suitable position" (165), Hester accepts the challenge instead of submitting helplessly to it. Rather than lament her destiny, Hester devotes her energies to Dimmesdale's cause, to saving him. "Her interview with the Reverend Mr. Dimmesdale, on the night of his vigil, had given her a new theme of reflection, and held up to her an object that appeared worthy of any exertion and sacrifice for its attainment" (166). Through Hester's self-immolation for her loved one, she becomes the knightly figure waging battle against an evil force to rescue the damsel in distress, Arthur.

In marked contrast to Hester's strong, heroic role, Dimmesdale is essentially passive. He lacks the courage to confess, then repeatedly excuses his hypocrisy by telling himself (and later Chillingworth indirectly) that if he were to admit to his crime all the good that he could have accomplished through his ministry would be lost. Nevertheless, the turmoil of his inner conscience suggests that even he is not entirely convinced by such a rationalization.

Modeling the traditional role of the heroine, Dimmesdale awaits a savior to show him the solution to his problem, for his secret method of atonement is little better than a self-deceptive charade. Accordingly, he charts his final course only after garnering strength from Hester in the forest; however, even then he follows her lead by patterning his disclosure after Hester's own public confession on the scaffold rather than in the church. For although Dimmesdale has numerous chances to redeem himself by confessing his sin publicly from the pulpit, he cannot find the courage or spiritual stamina to do so on his own or in his natural theater. Though he weakly attempts to tell his congregation of his sin—"I, your pastor, . . . am utterly a pollution and a lie!" (143)—his parishioners assume that their pastor's sins are purely imaginary, the ravings of obsessive humility.

Dimmesdale's other attempt to confess is also secretive and safe, performed in the dark on the scaffold in chapter XII. In that scene he appears to be a spurious penitent, imitating Hester in a shallow, insignificant way. That night even little Pearl is observant enough to realize that Dimmesdale's midnight vigil is a poor substitute for Hester's seven-year public penance. In fact, Pearl chides him for his cowardice by saying, "Thou wast not bold!—thou wast not true!" (157)—in other words, you are no hero, Arthur Dimmesdale.

Hester's meeting with Dimmesdale in the forest rejuvenates him and delivers him from his own self-defeating frame of mind.[4] In the throes of utter inertia Dimmesdale tells her to "Be thou strong for me! . . . Advise me what to do" (196). Accordingly, Hester counsels him in great detail, suggesting a number of alternatives. But Dimmesdale replies with torpid languor: "There is not the strength or courage left me to venture into the wide, strange, difficult world, alone!" (198). Not until Hester assures him that she will leave with him does Dimmesdale take courage.

Revived in the flesh if not in spirit, the minister returns from the woods and his interview with Hester filled with "unaccustomed physical energy." As Hawthorne writes, he "leaped . . . thrust himself . . . plunged . . . overcame . . . all the difficulties of the track" (216). This strength affords him the stamina he needs, ironically enough, to undermine the plans he and Hester have laid to leave Boston together. After his Election Sermon, Dimmesdale ascends the scaffold and reveals his scarlet stigma in a performance reminiscent of Hester's scaffold scene. However, Dimmesdale's confession is barely audible, causing onlookers to disagree whether the minister actually confessed.

Unlike Hester, who suffered her disgrace alone, Dimmesdale must rely on her support once again—both figuratively and literally. "Come, Hester, come! Support me up yonder scaffold!" (253). After this quiet confession, Dimmesdale conveniently dies, sparing him more than just a moment's disgrace among the few bystanders who heard and believed his confession.[5] Often in a romance the heroine coldly refuses to accept the love of the hero and sometimes dies before the love promise can be fulfilled. In this scene Dimmesdale, in the style of a true heroine, manages to do both.

Despite his importance to the denouement, Dimmesdale's role is decidedly subordinate, like that of most heroines in narratives strongly dominated by the bold figure of a hero. Compared to Hester's reconciliation with Puritan society in the last pages of the romance, Arthur's scaffold revelation (while certainly the *climax* of the work) seems only a salient event in the subplot. The problem is that Hawthorne has depicted Dimmesdale's death scene so dramatically and forcefully that it upstages all subsequent scenes, thus diverting the reader's attention away from Hester near the end. As a result, the true resolution of the plot—Hester's reintegration into Puritan society and the electric chain of humanity—is lost, or at least de-emphasized. Hawthorne apparently downplayed Hester's role at this point to make his work more palatable to a public unprepared to embrace a scarlet woman as hero.

Following Dimmesdale's dramatic, climactic exit, there is a tendency to gloss over the "Conclusion" to *The Scarlet Letter*, yet it contains several important ideas that affirm Hester's primacy in the romance. For one, we learn that "the story of the scarlet letter grew into a legend," and that "its spell . . . was still potent, and kept the scaffold awful where the poor minister had died, and likewise the cottage by the sea-shore, where Hester Prynne had dwelt" (261). In other words, Hester's stigma remained even in her absence and long after Dimmesdale's death. In essence, his death has changed nothing for her. However, when she returns to Boston and voluntarily resumes "her long-forsaken shame," Puritan society finally accepts her and makes a place for her on her own terms. "The decaying wood and iron [symbols of the Puritans' rigid moral code exemplified by the prison door] yielded to her hand" for "not the sternest magistrate of that iron period would have imposed it" (261, 263). Now, at last, Hester's transformation among the people of Boston is complete because "the scarlet letter ceased to be a stigma . . . and became a type of something to be sorrowed over, and looked upon with awe, yet with reverence too" (263). Hester's return to Boston is vital to the denouement and her heroic status.[6] According to John Gerber, "Years pass in a foreign country before Hester comes to that full sense of responsibility which swells into repentance and the desire to do voluntary penance. When that happens, of her own free will she returns to Boston and resumes the scarlet letter." Gerber explains that "her heart and her intellect have come to rest in a position of equilibrium, and she wins back a useful and even honorable place in the great order of things" (xxx-xxxi).[7]

In the closing pages of the romance, Hester is sought after as a counselor, a sage advisor especially to the young women of the community. She is also something of a visionary; she and her followers look with hope to a brighter future for the world when "a new truth would be revealed, in order to establish the whole relation between man and woman on a surer ground of mutual happiness" (263). Finally, in death, Hester is honored by being buried in a spot where "all around there were monuments carved with armorial bearings," suggesting that people of elevation and rank are now her neighbors; she is on/under equal ground with the eminent dead of the community. In fact, Hester is paid tribute on her grave, for on her "simple slab of slate" there appeared "the semblance of an engraved escutcheon . . . [bearing] a herald's wording: 'On a field, sable, the letter A, gules' " (264). Hester has been formally "knighted" by this heraldry; thus, Hawthorne affirms her centrality and establishes her as the work's hero in these final words of the romance, long after the death of the "heroine" Arthur Dimmesdale.

Notes

[*]This essay has been written for this volume and is published here for the first time.

[1]Brombert discusses this conflict between the hero and society at length, noting that the hero's "uniqueness helps define or condemn social conventions . . . his arbitrariness and self- sufficiency redeem man's submissiveness to despotism" (12-13). Additionally, "The tensions between private will and collective order allow for a sharp focusing on the problems of freedom and morality" (12).

[2]All references to the primary text are taken from Hawthorne's *The Scarlet Letter* (Columbus: Ohio State University Press, 1962).

[3]For interesting background information on Anne Hutchinson, see Ann Stanford, "Images of Women in Early American Literature," in *What Manner of Woman: Essays on English and American Life and Literature*, ed. Marlene Springer (New York: New York Univ. Press, 1977), 187-189. After studying historical notes of the time, Stanford notes that Hutchinson was portrayed as "serving her neighbors, but

stubborn and determined to have her own way, a woman who gloried in her power and her sense of personal revelation, and who ever took hope from the afflictions of excommunication and exile" (189). See also Michael J. Colarcurcio, "The Footsteps of Anne Hutchinson," *ELH* 39 (September 1972): 459- 494, for a detailed discussion of the Hester/Hutchinson parallel.

[4]In *American Romanticism: From Cooper to Hawthorne*, David Morse states that "it is only through Hester's influence that Dimmesdale can summon up, in one final desperate effort, the courage and strength to speak the truth publicly" (200).

[5]Even this act of contrition can be interpreted as egotistical and unheroic, though. As Baym notes, Dimmesdale's "last thoughts on the scaffold are for himself, for dying with a clean conscience, for the institutions rather than the human beings he has failed" ("The Significance of Plot" 56).

[6]Hester's return is critical to the denouement, as Baym comments: "Her return, still wearing her letter, to a community that accepts her and comes to love her, represents a compromise between self and society, a resolution of the problems of the story less glamorous than the lovers' elopement would have been, but more durable" ("The Significance of Plot" 58).

[7]However, Gerber credits this transformation and resolution in plot to Dimmesdale's influence on Hester: "That she should be able to find some peace in so doing comes as the ultimate result of Dimmesdale's confession" (xxxi). On this point I must differ. I see no logical basis for finding in Dimmesdale's confession the source of Hester's serenity, especially inasmuch as there was no consensus among the Bostonians present at his death that the minister actually did confess.

Works Cited

Abel, Darrel. "Hawthorne's Hester," *College English*, 13 (March 1952): 303.

Baym, Nina. *The Scarlet Letter: A Reading*. Boston: Twayne, 1986.

———. "The Significance of Plot in Hawthorne's Romances," in *Ruined Eden of the Present: Hawthorne, Melville, and Poe*. West Lafayette: Purdue University Press, 1981, 56, 59.

Brombert, Victor. *The Hero in Literature*. Greenwich: Fawcett, 1969, 19.

Colacurcio, Michael J., ed. *New Essays on The Scarlet Letter*. London: Cambridge University Press, 1986.

Garber, Frederick. "Self, Society, Value, and the Romantic Hero," in *The Hero in Literature*. Ed. Victor Brombert. Greenwich: Fawcett, 1969, 213.

Gerber, John C. "Introduction" to *The Scarlet Letter*. New York: Random House, 1950.

Hawthorne, Nathaniel. *The Scarlet Letter*. Columbus: Ohio State University Press, 1962.

James, Henry. *Hawthorne*. London: Macmillan, 1879.

Morse, David. *American Romanticism: From Cooper to Hawthorne*. Houndmills, England: Macmillan, 1987.

Stanford, Ann. "Images of Women in Early American Literature," in *What Manner of Woman: Essays on English and American Life and Literature*. Ed. Marlene Springer. New York: New York University Press, 1977, 189.

Thickstun, Margaret Olofson. *Fictions of the Feminine: Puritan Doctrine and the Representation of Women*. Ithaca: Cornell University Press, 1988.

Todd, Robert E. "The Magna Mater Archetype in *The Scarlet Letter*," *New England Quarterly*, 45 (1972): 429.

Wilson, James D. *The Romantic Heroic Ideal*. Baton Rouge: Louisiana State University Press, 1982.

The Scarlet Letter on Stage and Screen

"Amusements," ***Boston Transcript*****, 2 January 1877, 4:3.**

"*The Scarlet Letter,*" in the dramatization made by Count de Nargae and Mrs. Lander, was produced at the Boston Theatre last evening, before a small but intelligent audience; indeed the notabilities in letters and art of Boston and Cambridge were a very large proportion of it. We suppose no reasonable person expected to find the whole incomparable riches of Hawthorne's masterpiece put upon the stage. Its artistic motives and beauty and power lie too deep, are too purely spiritual or intellectual, to be adequately expressed in any spoken language or fitly portrayed by any actors save the sympathetic creations of each reader's own fancy. Most of the rarest beauty and delight of Shakspeare escapes the acting versions, and it is only one actor in a thousand that does not grossly coarsen the ideals of the characters conceived by the reader in his closet. Bearing in mind these universal limitations, one would surely agree that the dramatists of the "Scarlet Letter," as presented last evening, have done their work well. Certain it is that a drama most powerful and affecting has resulted, taking rank in its classification—by virtue of its original's lofty plane in "high art," its masterly poetic treatment, its universal human types working out their representative passions, sins, and sorrows,—with Goethe's "Faust" and Shakspeare's "Hamlet." To accomplish this was mostly a work of selection from the splendid materials of our greatest American romance, and it must be gratefully conceded that, on the whole, the most characteristic and comprehensive scenes have been chosen for the five acts of the play; that the dialogue is much of the time Hawthorne's own words; that the plot is developed clearly and connectedly; and that the progress and relations of the scenes have been so artistically treated and accented as to build up effective dramatic climaxes to each act. This is not to say that every lover of Hawthorne does not miss many incidents and touches that for him perhaps contain the very flavor of the whole. But the limits of the possible are soon reached, even in a five-act drama, with such "embarrassment of riches" as the "Scarlet Letter" provides.

Every good Bostonian must feel a comfortable gratification—higher than the common local vainglory—at seeing Hawthorne's classic story of our most distant and romantic epoch, the one vista in American history deep enough to be softened and beautified by legendary lore thus honored and popularized in so respectable a drama. It is not exactly gracious, therefore, to look narrowly for errors of historic detail. The "local color" given in the scenery, the dresses, and the accessories of the stage, is very artistic at all events, and near enough to the pictures and relics of the fathers to be strongly suggestive and vividly illustrative. When the time comes for the production of the "Scarlet Letter" in the dramatic form of which it is best worthy—as a grand opera, by, say, some Cambridge doctor of music, performed by the regular company of our future municipal Academy of Music—then it will be worth while looking sharply to learn whether Rev. Arthur Dimmesdale was such a spoiled favorite in the Puritan settlement as to be permitted to wear so vain an adornment as a moustache, or whether such evidences of a sunny south of France or Italian climate existed in the scenery round about Boston, or the first New Englanders so much resembled in dress and merrymaking the traditional "lords," "peasants," and "villagers" of the stage. * * *

But while it is unjust to be hypercritical with a play so reverently following Hawthorne and so richly illustrative of the splendor of his poetic and artistic genius, it is but a pious duty to object to the acting of one of the two principal parts. Mrs. Lander would no doubt have received unstinted praise, unalloyed gratification and increased pecuniary reward had she been content with the exhibition of her ripe artistic taste and talents in the authorship of a grand drama like this. Assuming the part of Hester Prynne, she stands in the way of its success. She does not "look the part" and her voice and acting constantly betray the old-school artificiality and exaggeration that are as far removed from nature as Mr. Turveydrop's "deportment" from good breeding. Her conceptions of the role is of course intelligent, but with her constant consciousness of effort in "elocution," the figure in the drama around which the interest and sympathy of the whole should centre becomes a barren unreality. Mr. Theodore Hamilton as Arthur Dimmesdale has a fine face, dark, handsome and expressive, and he draws his portraiture in strong lines—so strong and heavy, sometimes, as to approach perilously the melodramatic. The next character in importance—we doubt if it should not rank as the first in importance as the parts are acted—is Pearl, the child of Hester, which is played by a child under six years of age in a manner simply wonderful. With a little round face and piquant profile, as perfect and fascinating a childlike beauty as Frere or Rouse ever drew— little Mabel Struthers unites what appears to be a really intelligent appreciation of the character and knowledge of the means of artistic expression. Into this wayward, imp-like little creature, the apt embodiment as well as sign of her mother's errors and character, Hawthorne threw much of his favorite supernatural element, and in Pearl's infantile caprices, so shocking and so deeply significant, almost all the supernaturalism brought into the drama is comprehended. Like Goethe's Mignon in "William Meister," Pearl runs through the "Scarlet Letter" like a *scarlet* thread. Upon the stage her quaint, long-skirted scarlet frock, fantastically embroidered, flashes hither and thither in contrast to the black velvet doublets of the Puritan men and the prim gowns of the Puritan women, just as her defiant and surprising turns of wilfulness startle the habitual submissive and deferential habit of those around, while the unconscious meaning of her likes and dislikes adds heightened charm or poignancy to the dramatic situation. In this truly phenomenal little actor's performance there is a remarkable degree of absence of consciousness of sign of drill or prompting, and the effect of her talent applied to Hawthorne's masterly poetic fancy and inventive ingenuity is extraordinary. Mr. Shewell's personation of Roger Chillingworth was carefully restrained, yet not wanting great dignity, fire and force. Mr. Maguinnis did his trifling part with all the fine wit and intelligence that he brings to a Shakspearian clown—as was worthy and fitting.

"Hawthorne/His 'Scarlet Letter' Dramatized/How Gabriel Harrison Has Done the Work/The Romance and the Play Compared/A Worthy Work Fairly Performed," ***Brooklyn Eagle*****, 7 January 1877, 3:8-9.**

* * * With the pure English and perfect sentiment of Washington Irving and Nathaniel Hawthorne, not to mention the other greater writers of fiction whose names are linked with the history of our country, there lies before the appreciative student of literature a mine of dramatic treasure. It is singular that no effort has been made properly to popularize the works of such men by the most distinguished of our dramatists, and it is with pleasure that we refer to the work of one of our own residents and a theatrical manager of some standing,

Mr. Gabriel Harrison. The task he has attempted is the dramatization of Hawthorne's "Scarlet Letter."

Mr. Harrison has caused but one hundred copies of his work to be printed, and this fact coupled with copious stage directions with which it is enriched, suggests the belief that is intended for stage representation. If this is the case he will be in competition with the Count Nargae, who has written a piece for Mrs. Lander, similarly entitled and derived without question from the same source. It is one of the difficulties of the adapter's task that he must leave the author's descriptive work to the judgment and skill of the actors who personate the characters of his piece, and still further condense the story to bring it within the limits of stage representation. But in doing this he must preserve the sequence of events and individuality of character, selecting such incidents as shall at once aid in the development of plot and character, and at the same time possess the dramatic qualities which appeal at once to the eye and ear. To adhere closely to the original and still to fit the selections coherently presents oftentimes a dilemma out of which the adapter can emerge only with the nicest skill. We select from the novel a passage which is of strong dramatic interest—the meeting of Dimmesdale and Hester Prynne in the forest. The story told in the novel takes several pages and opens thus:

THE PASTOR AND HIS PARISHIONER.

Slowly as the minister walked, he had almost gone by before Hester Prynne could gather voice enough to attract his observation. At length she succeeded.

"Arthur Dimmesdale!" she said, faintly at first, then louder, but hoarsely. "Arthur Dimmesdale!"

"Who speaks?" answered the minister.

Gathering himself quickly up, he stood more erect like a man taken by surprise in a mood to which he was reluctant to have witnesses. Throwing his eyes anxiously in the direction of the voice, he indistinctly beheld a form under the trees, clad in garments so sombre, and so little relieved from the gray twilight into which the clouded sky and the heavy foliage had darkened the noontide, that he knew not whether it were a woman or a shadow. It may be that his pathway through life was haunted thus by a spectre that had stolen out from among his thoughts.

He made a step nigher, and discovered the scarlet letter.

"Hester, Hester Prynne!" said he. "Is it thou? Art thou in life?"

"Even so," she answered. "In such life as has been mine these seven years past. And thou, Arthur Dimmesdale, dost thou yet live?"

It was no wonder that they thus questioned one another's actual and bodily existence, and even doubted of their own. So strangely did they meet in the dim wood, that it was like the first encounter in the world beyond the grave, of two spirits who had been intimately connected in their former life, but now stood coldly shuddering in mutual dread, as not yet familiar with their state, nor wonted to the companionship of disembodied beings, each a ghost and awe stricken at the other ghost! They were awe stricken likewise at themselves; because the crisis flung back to them their consciousness and revealed to each heart its history and experience as life never does except at such breathless epochs. The soul beheld its features in the mirror of the passing moment. It was with fear and tremulously, and as it were by a slow, reluctant necessity, that Arthur Dimmesdale put forth his hand, chill as death, and touched the chill hand of Hester Prynne. The grasp, cold as it was, took away what was dreariest in the interview. They now felt themselves, at least, inhabitants of the same sphere.

This is a beautiful scene, and much of its charm lies in the picture of the two guilty souls meeting, as the author describes them, like disembodied spirits. How it can be rendered on the stage in order to convey the same ideas we cannot judge. We can only present the dialogue as Mr. Harrison gives it, and leave the realization to the witness of the scene, the audience, aided by such skill as the actor possesses. Here is the passage from the drama, given rather more extensively:

HESTER (to Pearl)—There, go yonder where the sun is shining on that bit of beautiful meadow; gather the wild flowers, and when I shall call you, come. (*Exit Pearl.*) Arthur Dimmesdale! Arthur Dimmesdale!

DIMMESDALE—Who speaks? Hester Prynne, is it thou?

HESTER—Even so, if I am in life, and if it be life as I have lived these seven years.

DIMMESDALE—Hast thou then found no peace?

HESTER—None; hast thou?

DIMMESDALE—Nothing but misery.

HESTER—Thou wrongest thyself in this. Thou hast deeply repented. The people reverence thee, and surely thou workest good among them! Doth this bring no comfort?

DIMMESDALE—More misery, Hester! Only the more misery! As concerns the good I may appear to do, I have no faith in it. It must need be a delusion. What can a ruined soul like mine effect toward the redemption of other souls? And as for the people's reverence, would that it were turned to scorn and hatred! Can'st thou deem it a consolation that I must stand up in my pulpit and meet so many eyes turned upward to my face, as if the light of heaven were beaming from it, and see my flock listening to me as if a tongue of Pentecost were speaking? I have laughed in bitterness and agony of heart at the contrast of what I am. And Satan laughs at it.

HESTER—Thou wrong'st thyself. Is there no reality in the penitence thus sealed and witnessed by good works?

DIMMESDALE—There is no substance in it. It is cold and dead and can do nothing for me. Of penance I have had enough. Of penitence there has been none; else should I long since have thrown off these garments of mock holiness, and have shown myself to mankind as they will see me at the judgment seat. Happy are you, Hester Prynne, that wear the Scarlet Letter openly on your bosom! Mine burns in secret. Thou little knowest what a relief it is after the torments of a seven years' cheat to look into an eye that recognizes me for what I am. Oh! had I but one friend, or even an enemy, to whom I could betake myself, and be known as the vilest of sinners. Even this much truth would save me, for now all is falsehood and emptiness.

HESTER—Such a friend as thou hast even now wished for, with whom to weep over thy sin thou hast in me, the partner of it. Thou hast long had such an enemy, and dwellest with him—under the same roof.

DIMMESDALE—Ha! What sayest thou, an enemy? and under mine roof. What sayest thou?

This is about half the scene, which takes many pages of the story. It will be seen that Mr. Harrison has shown no little skill in thus abridging the text without sacrifice of the sentiment or other points which so exquisitely serve to illustrate the fate of the two offenders. The dialogue throughout has been preserved, with little alteration, but sentences have been merged together in order to give as much as possible of the author's meaning with the least possible sacrifice of his language. The scene we have selected happens to be the most dramatic in the volume, as well as in the play, and its treatment is a fair example of the manner in which Mr. Harrison has done his work. The character of Hester Prynne is firmly outlined, that of Roger Chillingworth is not less well portrayed. The three leading characters are, indeed, as faithfully represented as it is possible for the dramatist to picture them. There is margin enough given the illustrative artist to amplify them for the stage, and as an acting piece the "Scarlet Letter" should be successful. It must be remembered, however, that the novel depends entirely upon the bright and luminous style of the author for contrast with the sombre hue of the story. In its stage dress the *chiaroscuro* is impaired. There is little relief in the pictures, which, no matter what their strength and boldness of outline, are gloomy and tragic throughout.

Mr. Harrison has not strengthened the piece by the introduction of a number of Indian characters to give an incantation scene over which Mistress Hibbins is made to preside. The fourth scene of the second act is thus described:

A glen—full depth of the stage. Trees and wild-vines overhanging embankments. The full moon is seen rising through the trees. In centre of the stage a large caldron hanging from a tripod, with a blazing fire underneath. Groups of Indians and wild looking white men and women sitting around the stage, beating on Indian drums, etc., while others are dancing round the caldron, etc. Spearhead drops a fox's haunches into the caldron.

SPEARHEAD—And this I bring that's full of meat!
HIBBINS—A fox, indeed, is rare and sweet!
FLEETWING—And I these birds all fresh and clean.
HIBBINS—The finest batch I have ever seen!
SWAMP LILY—And I these fish, the black and blue!
HIBBINS—Indeed a prize; well done for you!
BLIGHTED TRUNK—And here are legs of toads and frogs, I caught but now in clumpy bogs.
CHORUS—Around, around the caldron fly,
While yet the moon fills yonder sky, etc.

This scene is, of course, suggested from "Macbeth," and very feebly imitated. The mixture of mysticism and colloquialism makes it ridiculous, simply without being impressive. The fact is that Hibbins has little to do with Mr. Harrison's story, and the whole scene is injudiciously interpolated. But beyond this there is little to find fault with, and much to commend in the work done by the adapter.

"The Scarlet Letter/A Dramatic Version of Hawthorne's Novel Produced in London," ***New York Times*****, 5 June 1888, 4:7.**

LONDON, June 4.—Shorn of its poetry and dealing simply with the guilt of Hester Prynne, Hawthorne's "Scarlet Letter," dramatized by the Hon. Stephen Coleridge, was presented tonight at the Royalty Theatre by Eleanor Calhoun and her company. In 1876 Joseph Hatton first presented a dramatic version of this novel to provincial audiences under the title of "Hester Prynne; or, The Scarlet Letter," and the author of that version was an interested spectator of Coleridge's version. The play, although crude and sketchy, proved interesting, and not until almost the fall of the curtain did anything occur to disturb the approbation of the house. The ending of the novel is changed, and now Roger Chillingworth is charged with being the father of the child. He strenuously denies the charge and denounces Dimmesdale. The crowd rushes upon him. He flies from them and is pursued, and as the minister is about to confess his guilt news is brought to the Governor that Chillingworth has been killed by the mob. Hester exclaims: "It is the hand of God!" and the curtain falls.

Miss Calhoun, though lacking in sympathy, played the part of Hester with rare intelligence and naturalness, and made a considerable success. Forbes Robertson was too robust in his acting of Dimmesdale, but was satisfactory to the audience. The blot in the performance was the weak and contemptible conception which Norman Forbes gave of the part of Chillingworth. The play was well put on the stage, but cannot prove financially successful.

"The Scarlet Letter," ***Theatre*****, 2 July 1888, pp. 41-42.**

New play by ALEC NELSON, with an Original Prologue by CHARLES CHARRINGTON. (Founded on Nathaniel Hawthorne's Story.) First produced at the Olympic on Tuesday afternoon, June 5, 1888.

In the version given here Mr. Charrington bore in mind that the present generation were not so well up in Hawthorne's powerful story, and therefore wrote for it a prologue, which shows the early love that grew up between Hester Prynne and Arthur Dimmesdale. The scene is in England, and we find the mere girl married to a man considerably her senior, who, without being actually unkind, is cold, undemonstrative, and wrapped up in his studies and scientific pursuits. Dimmesdale, the young clergyman, is supposed to be handsome, kindly, and attentive; he feels he cannot struggle against his passion, and therefore accepts a call to go forth as a pastor to Salem in Massachusetts, and soon after old Roger Prynne, returning from a long journey, announces that he and his young wife are also going to America. Once there we are led to suppose that Prynne has almost deserted his wife, spending years among the aborigines, and, when he reappears to learn the shame that has fallen on his wife, it is as an Indian Sachem. Then follows her condemnation to wear the brand of shame, the hold that Roger Prynne obtains over Dimmesdale, haunting him as his shadow, never for a moment letting him forget his sin, and at length, when the young clergyman is insensible, discovering that on his breast he also has the "scarlet letter." The ending is in accordance with Hawthorne's book. After preaching the election sermon, Dimmesdale is at the very pinnacle of esteem in all good men's eyes, revered and loved by all around him. Hester Prynne has also lived down her shame by continuous deeds of charity and goodness, and it has been considered whether she may not now be allowed to remove the scorching badge she has worn. Then in the Market-place does Dimmesdale call her and their child to him, and mounting with them on the scaffold confesses his past iniquity. The divulgence of his long-pent-up secret, the sufferings he has borne, tortured as he has been by remorse, prove too much for an already weakened heart, and he dies tearing open his dress and revealing the "scarlet letter" burnt in upon his breast. Save for the introduction of Mistress Hibbins, whose maunderings in the forest and elsewhere become wearisome, I prefer the Olympic version; there is more to study in the character of Roger Prynne, and the relentless hate of the man was splendidly delineated by Mr. Fernandez. Miss Janet Achurch's performance as Hester Prynne was unequal; she was excellent in the prologue, but in the play itself frequently lost command over her voice and was too restless; still, taken altogether, her rendering was powerful. The Arthur Dimmesdale of Mr. Charles Charrington exhibited some fine points, but was a little too melancholy. Miss Gertrude Kingston acted well as Mary Barton, and Mr. William Lugg, Mr. John Tresahar, Mr. Hamilton Knight, and Miss Roma deserve favourable mention. Miss Grace Murielle was wonderfully clever as the elfish dancing child Pearl.

"Hawthorne's Romance 'The Scarlet Letter' in Dramatic Shape/ Mr. Joseph Hatton's Version is Not an Ideal Play, but It Serves Theatrical Purposes and Deeply Interests an Audience/Mr. Richard Mansfield's Dimmesdale/Some Curious Blunders of Costuming and Stage Management Which Go Far to Mar the Puritan Picture/A Stageworn Trick That Ought to Go," ***New York Herald*****, 18 September 1892, 14:1-3.**

The appearance amid the mass of raw, inconsequential, uninteresting and, for the most part, wearisome stuff which has been foisted upon this long suffering public under the name of farce-comedy, farce, melodrama, or what you will of such a performance as that of Mr. Mansfield in "The Scarlet Letter," which was seen during this last week at Daly's Theatre, is like an oasis of green to the tired wanderer among wastes of sand.

It is not that "The Scarlet Letter" is a play above criticism or that its performance has not its weak spots, and plenty of them. The task set Mr. Hatton, who has made the present dramatic version, was of no ordinary difficulty. He had to make vivid upon the stage a psychological study of remorse clothed by Hawthorne in language so delicate and subtle that it seems almost like sacrilege to utter it amid the glare and tinsel of the footlights.

The easiest and simplest way of treating the problem proved to be the most effective. Mr. Hatton, so far as possible, lets Hawthorne tell the story in his own language. There are whole pages literally transcribed from the romance, and these make the most effective passages of the play.

———

For instance, Hawthorne's description of the Rev. Mr. Dimmesdale's appeal to Hester, made in compliance with the wish of the Governor, exhorting her to confess the truth, is as follows in the book. The scene, it will be remembered, is in the market place. Hester stands on the scaffold of the pillory, with below her the jeering, noisy mob. She holds her child in her arms and is apparently unconscious of her surroundings as she waits for the verdict of the judges who are to pronounce penalty for her grievous sin of having disgraced that Puritan community and brought into the world a child whose father she will not name.

The Rev. Mr. Dimmesdale bent his head, in silent prayer, as it seemed, and then came forward. "Hester Prynne," said he, leaning over the balcony, and looking down steadfastly into her eyes, "thou hearest what this good man says, and seest the accountability under which I labor. If thou feelest it to be for thy soul's peace, and that thy earthly punishment will thereby be made more effectual to salvation, I charge thee to speak out the name of thy fellow-sinner and fellow sufferer. Be not silent from any mistaken pity and tenderness fo him; for, believe me, Hester, though he were to step down from a high place and stand there beside thee, on thy pedestal of shame, yet better were it so, than to hide a guilty heart through life. What can thy silence do for him, except it tempt him—yea, compel him, as it were—to add hypocrisy to sin? Heaven hath granted thee an open ignominy, that thereby thou mayest work out an open triumph over the evil within thee, and the sorrow without. Take heed how thou deniest to him—who, perchance, hath not the courage to grasp it for himself—the bitter but wholesome cup that is now presented to thy lips!"

This is transcribed verbatim into the play. Again, in the final scene, although Mr. Hatton brings about Dimmesdale's determination to make confession by letting him know that Roger Chillingworth has taken passage in the ship in which Hester and he are to sail, while Hawthorne makes no note of this and brings about the confession simply as the final bursting of the bonds under which Dimmesdale has writhed during seven years, he uses the exact words of the text:—

"People of New England!" cried he, with a voice that rose over them high, solemn, and majestic,—yet had always a tremor through it, and sometimes a shriek, struggling up out of a fathomless depth of remorse and woe,—"ye, that have loved me!— ye, that have deemed me holy!—behold me here, the one sinner of the world! At last!—at last!—I stand upon the spot where, seven years since, I should have stood; here, with this woman, whose arm, more than the little strength wherewith I have crept hitherward, sustains me, at this dreadful moment, from grovelling down upon my face! Lo, the scarlet letter which Hester wears! Ye have all shuddered at it! Wherever her walk hath been,—wherever, so miserably burdened, she may have hoped to find repose,—it hath cast a lurid gleam of awe and horrible repugnance round about her. But there stood one in the midst of you, at whose brand of sin and infamy ye have not shuddered!"

It seemed, at this point, as it the minister must leave the remainder of his secret undisclosed. But he fought back the bodily weakness,—and, still more, the faintness of heart,—that was striving for the mastery with him. He threw off all assistance, and stepped passionately forward a pace before the woman and the child.

"It was on him!" he continued, with a kind of fierceness; so determined was he to speak out the whole. "God's eye beheld it! The angels were for ever pointing at it! the Devil knew it well, and fretted it continually with the touch of his burning finger! But he hid it cunningly from men, and walked among you with the mien of a spirit, mournful, because so pure in a sinful world!— and sad, because he missed his heavenly kindred! Now, at the death-hour, he stands up before you! He bids you look again at Hester's scarlet letter! He tells you that, with all its mysterious horror, it is but the shadow of what he bears on his own breast, and that even this, his own red stigma, is no more than the type of what has seared his inmost heart! Stand any here that question God's judgment on a sinner? Behold! Behold a dreadful witness of it!"

With a convulsive motion he tore away the ministerial band from before his breast. It was revealed!

It is entirely probable that hundreds of persons who know "The Scarlet Letter" by heart and who have a high opinion of Mr. Mansfield's capacity as an actor, went to see his performance in the expectation of witnessing at the very most a brilliant failure. Attempts have been made so often to make a good play out of the romance and have failed so uniformly that nothing much was expected of Mr. Hatton's version. Action is essential to a good play, and there is no action to speak of in "The Scarlet Letter." But even those who expected least were fairly certain that the actor would make an interesting fiasco of his attempt. The many who went to see this failure of a more or less brilliant sort remained to enjoy an exceedingly interesting play so far as one could be made with this unpromising material, and to applaud a bit of acting which for sincerity of purpose and felicitous light and shade stands near the top of what Mr. Mansfield has done.

If the test of a play's merit be the effect left upon an audience of intelligent persons may be accepted, "The Scarlet Letter," as given now at Daly's Theatre is a good play—that is to say, it rouses the interest at once and holds it to the end of the performance; it leaves the audience deeply impressed at the close of each act. Whether the most that can be made of this subtle study of Hawthorne's has been made by Mr. Hatton and Mr. Mansfield need not be here discussed. The fact remains that nothing heretofore so full of color, of impressiveness, of deep feeling has been done with "The Scarlet Letter," and for this much let us be thankful. Here is a play which gives us lines of much beauty by one of the few inspired writers this country has produced, which places them in a setting that robs them as little as possible of their moral and poetic significance. If there are writers who can make a better play out of "The Scarlet Letter" and actors who can more deeply impress an audience with its lines, I should be glad to welcome their work. Because the present achievement falls short of the ideal seems to be taken in some quarters as sufficient reason for denouncing the attempt instead of encouraging one of the rare efforts of that serious work upon which we have to congratulate ourselves.

———

Where Mr. Hatton departs from the actual text, in so far as concerns Dimmesdale, his words show care and sympathy. At the close of the second act Dimmesdale, during his midnight vigil, alone upon the scaffold, is made to utter the soliloquy that Hawthorne merely quotes as the confession that for years had hung upon the minister's lips. The scene represents the sleeping city, the moonlight coming and going through rifts in the clouds:—

DIMMESDALE (alone)—What right had infirmity like this to burden itself with crime? Crime is for the iron nerved, who have their choice either to endure, or—if it press too hard—to exert their fierce and savage strength to fling it off at once. This feeble and most sensitive of spirits can do neither and thus there is entwined within me the unravelled knot! The agony of Heaven defying guilt and vain repentance. The lights are out—the city sleeps and I—there is never rest for me. You poor, misguided creatures. You deem me a miracle of holiness. You fancy me the mouthpiece of Heaven's messages of wisdom and rebuke and saintly love. In your eyes the very place on which I stand is sanctified. The place on which I stand! Yonder is the place where I should stand—not in the pulpit—but here (he ascends the scaffold)—I, whom you behold in these black garments of the priesthood. I, who ascend the sacred desk and turn my pale face heavenward. I, in whose daily life you discern such sanctity. I, whose footsteps, as you suppose, leave a gleam along my earthly track. I, who have laid the hand of baptism upon your children. I, who have breathed the parting prayer. I, your pastor, whom you so reverence and trust—am utterly a pollution and a lie.

The effect of this impassioned monologue, rising by degrees from mournful dejection to frenzied intensity is, perhaps, the most effective bit of the play from a theatric point of view.

Having said so much as to the merits of this production I feel at liberty to express some surprise concerning the blemishes—very glaring—which Mr. Mansfield allows to mar the play. In a dramatic version of the "Scarlet Letter" which was seen in Boston about twenty years ago, if I remember rightly, the scene in the forest was made something of a comedy and Dimmesdale actually rejoices over the possibility of running away with Hester and Pearl. It was a sort of happy family reunion, and this was supposed to lend lightness to an otherwise tragic story; it was its one gleam of sunlight. Mr. Hatton has had better taste than this and has followed Hawthorne's spirit in making Dimmesdale barely acquiesce in any suggestion of an escape from the misery he bears. It is absurd to imagine that a man of Dimmesdale's training and character should throw off the cloud at any time.

But in his desire to lighten up the present play there are other things in this production quite as absurd as this. The scenes between the gossips of the town, the recrimination between the sensible and light-hearted village girl, Mary Willis, who believes in Hester's goodness and virtue, and the vituperative old gossips; finally, the love scenes between Mary Willis and her several admirers, among them the fatuous jailor, Master Brackett, and Captain Hiram Weeks—all these are accomplished in a very inoffensive manner fairly in keeping with the spirit of the play. They were a necessary evil and have been minimized.

But why, in the name of all that is wonderful, should Captain Hiram Weeks, a Massachusetts smuggler by profession and an honest tar in the opinion of his fellow townspeople, be dressed and comport himself like the buccaneer at a fancy ball? Thus berigged with ribbons of all colors of the rainbow he would make the central picture of a comic opera performance, and he disports himself in a manner that fits his gorgeous clothes.

While speaking of costume it may also be worth while to note that both Hester and little Pearl are absurdly overdressed. Hawthorne notes that Hester was a good needlewoman and that the scarlet letter she embroidered was well done. Her garb is also spoken of as picturesque, but this is scarcely an excuse for dressing her in brilliant figured silks. As to little Pearl, she was a delightful picture out of Kate Greenaway's most exaggerated sketches. Her gowns were so exquisite in design and texture that they must have cost the year's income of a good Puritan burgher of that day. There was a sad lack of Puritan simplicity in the matter of costuming.

As to stage management, it was fair upon the whole, although the scene of Hester's appeal upon behalf of her child might better have been placed, as Hawthorne has it, in Governor Bellingham's house instead of in the market place. The behavior of the mob was also entirely too vociferous. Moderation here would have meant strength.

"The Scarlet Letter Dramatized," ***Illustrated American*****, 8 October 1892, pp. 287-288.**

Mr. Richard Mansfield opened his fall season with a dramatic version of Hawthorne's imperishable story, "The Scarlet Letter," at Daly's Theatre, New York city. This scholar and actor is entitled to the applause of the public for his efforts to make the stage a place of intellectual profit as well as entertainment. Every season we find him delving into the classic precincts of literature for dramatic material, and every season closes with achievements which add to his fame as an actor and a man of letters.

No writer of fiction holds a higher place than our own countryman, Nathaniel Hawthorne. His tales will live until language is no more, and the impression they have made is potential, universal, and never-fading.

To all of us who have our ideas of his celebrated characters, Mr.

Mansfield's production of "The Scarlet Letter" is of uncommon interest. We do not consider it a play in which Mr. Mansfield's talents as an actor can be discussed.

We believe he will enjoy great success in it, but gain no great honors. Considered as a dramatization of the book, we are of opinion that it has not caught the strange movement of Hawthorne's genius; indeed, the subtleties of Hawthorne's writings can not be seized by the dramatist any more than life in an uncorked bottle of champagne can be recaptured by the vintner.

A WOMAN'S CRITICISM OF "THE SCARLET LETTER."

The stage as a vehicle for great moral effects is as depressing to an audience as the cholera page of a contemporaneous journal is to stocks. No such forcible sermon as "The Scarlet Letter," interpreted by Mr. Mansfield and his wife, was ever preached by Sam Jones from a text. It is a religious melodrama from start to finish. At the end of the play, one comes forth into the glare of Broadway with the sensations of Sunday and worship clinging to one; the Reformation measures of Luther's grand old choral, "Ein Feste Burg," haunt one's memory. Sin and its long retribution, the world's scorn and contumely for the woman's one false step, involving contingencies, never found more apt and terrible exemplification than in such pictured scenes. But the play leaves a bad taste in the mouth. It hints at the futility of reparation, expiation, and repentance, all good and advisable things in their way, and makes death the only loophole for entangled souls. This, although tolerated in a novel where much clever writing softens the edges of things, is inadmissable in a play. It is quite too brutal. Nevertheless, the dramatic story touches our common humanity with the electric spark of truth. Despite Mr. Mansfield's inadequacy to portray the Reverend Arthur Dimmesdale according to Hawthorne's lines, and despite Miss Cameron's praiseworthy struggles to cope with the passion of her position, there is still the man-and-woman parable back of it all, that appeals to the heart of an audience. When Hester stands upon that platform, hiding with her infant that burning letter, which proclaims her shame, from the hooting, jeering mob, demanding its paternity, white-souled women weep over the cruelty of sex; and when her spiritual advisor adds his urgency to the general clamor, and when she cries out "Never!"—the universal kinship of sympathy has been proven. One hears not alone the story of Hester Prynne and Arthur Dimmesdale, but an epitome of the fall of woman from the beginning.

"In weakness to yield, but in strength ever shield,"—and this is accumulated pathos.

A dull resentment against the piety that suggests a desire to repeat in this sinning woman's case the afflictions of the Biblical Stephen, besets one; that fanatical spirit which made witch-burning the popular pastime of the old Salem days, impels one to utter a secret thanksgiving that such days are long past,—but, to any woman whatever, this story, read or played, is passionately human and true.

If taken merely as a psychological study of remorse, Arthur Dimmesdale's attitude in the play bespeaks a misconception of the way remorse acts upon a man. It never quite reaches the pitch of suicide, but is always just getting there, for seven long weary years. This is impossible. The woman, in the meantime, has been salving her soul by doing much good missionary work, and otherwise expiating her sin as best she could. Along with this, she industriously manufactured stylish red garments for her child, and chaperoned Mary Willis in a certain queer Puritan fashion. The Hamlet-like figure of Mansfield, however, has no such fires of zeal. Now, remorse, unless suicidal, begets activity.

This type is not infrequent in fiction, and in "The Silence of Dean Maitland," a powerful and dramatic story, we have, perhaps, a far better showing of the workings of remorse. Here we have the minister throwing himself with passionate fury into the role he has assumed before the world, and achieving prodigies of soul-saving, unselfishness, fleshly mortification. There is no such priestly enthusiasm in the stage presentation of Arthur Dimmesdale. His wandering manner, trembling voice and hands, aimless and uncertain speech, lead one to infer that Hester was bewitched by nothing less than an imbecile, so disappointing, unsympathetic, and false is Mr. Mansfield's conception of the character. Hawthorne never intended him to be a weak-kneed coward, except secretly and morally; he was the leader and idol of the people, to whom even the Governor deferred. Why, then, are we treated to this puling and pallid specimen? Granted that he was weak—he was, undoubtedly—did it not require a certain positive strength to remain on there as the pastor of the people, when he might so easily have fled? In Mr. Mansfield's Arthur there is too much of the "secret gnawings" business—altogether too much of the quiet, self-contained Puritan and priest. He lacks the quality which made his crime possible, and his remorse probable. We see only a sad, poetical figure wandering amongst trees, napping on the pillory in the market-place, and uttering mournful speeches in heart-broken baritone. Why this absence of high lights? Were there no periods of religious abasement and wrestling—no wails for mercy at the feet of a stricken Christ— no penitential and passionate scourgings? A little of the lashing of conscience would enliven those scenes immeasurably. That dull, spiritless yielding to unpleasant circumstances has a morbid influence. Of course, it is difficult to appreciate at the present day the calamities entailed by a fall of grace, in one occupying the Reverend Arthur's position when the colony of Massachusetts was young; but distress of mind, wan appearance, and choleric behavior generally, do not atone for a lack of the unities in a good play. The hypocritical shepherd, who is neither picturesque nor long-haired—as he should be—makes one very tired. He seems very weary of his lot himself, and plaintively underfed. His soliloquies lack fire and brimstone. In that pillory scene, where he does a certain amount of self-accusation, he loses a magnificent chance to wrestle with his soul—and the audience is sensible of it. Judging him without reference to his cloth, merely as a man, how unsatisfactory is his final confession! As it frightened at the prospect of eternity opening before him, he clears his decks, so to speak, by a bid for atonement of that mutual sin, which the woman, whose strength he invokes for support, has so openly and flagrantly borne for many years, and here is another lost opportunity. The stress of the circumstances impresses the mind of an auditor with trembling expectations of an adequate climax, but the climax is disappointing; and when church is over, and the congregation disperses, there is a painful sensation of something lacking in the service.

To my mind, the most impressive passage in the play was the meeting in the forest, when Arthur inquires of Hester, "Hast thou peace?" This question she, woman-like, parries by the counter- question, "Hast thou?" This is a point the audience is bound to feel, because with such temperaments as theirs, hedged about by the consciousness of sin, and the restrictions of sect, there is no peace this side of the grave, and the force of the situation is powerful in the extreme.

Stephen Fiske, "The Scarlet Letter," ***Spirit of the Times*****, 12 January 1895, p. 889.**

THE SCARLET LETTER, opera in three Acts, by Walter Damrosch, the libretto arranged in rhyme by G. P. Lathrop, excerpts from which were given, at Carnegie Hall, last Saturday, is one of the few serious attempts at setting American classics to music. We remember the opera of Fry, the musical critic of the *Tribune*, based upon Cooper's "Spy" and produced at the old Academy, about a quarter of a century ago, and should like to have its score taken out of some dusty box and heard again, now that it has a worthy successor. The first Act of The Scarlet Letter and the forest scene of the second Act were sung, last

Saturday, by Nordica, as Hester; William Rieger, as Arthur; Campanari, as Chillingworth, Conrad Behrens, as the Governor, and the Oratorio Society chorus as the 400 Puritans, and Damrosch led the Symphony Society orchestra. Of course, the music, and especially the heavy orchestration, is Wagnerian in style; for Damrosch is a Wagnermaniac from foot to baton; but it was enthusiastically received; the introduction of the grand hymn, "Old Hundred," delighted the general audience, and the ladies and gentlemen of the chorus showered the young composer with flowers and handed him a gigantic wreath of laurel. In response to repeated calls, he modestly said that the only way open to him to produce his opera was at such a concert; that the scenery, costumes and dramatic action were necessary to show just what he meant by his music, and that he hoped, before long, to be able to present his American opera properly and in English. We heartily echo this hope; but, practically, the opera would have a better chance of production if translated into German.

The full libretto is published and may be considered apart from the music. Why G. P. Lathrop, who has never done any thing more dramatic than a weak dramatization of "Elaine," should have been selected to write it, Heaven and Damrosch only know. He begins by omitting the part of Little Pearl, because, he says, "the character was obviously impossible in opera." On the contrary, represented by a child singer, the character of Little Pearl would make the opera unique and assure its success. Then he arrogantly claims that he has written, not a dramatization of Hawthorne's story, but an original "dramatic poem," "a new work," partly in rhyme and partly in which he calls "overrhythms." This is all nonsense. The libretto is either a dramatization of Hawthorne or it is rubbish, and Mr. Lathrop adds: "I do not suppose that I have adapted from Hawthorne's pages more than two dozen sentences, if so many." Then Damrosch's Scarlet Letter music requires a new and more faithful libretto.

If Mr. Damrosch will listen to our advice, he will take his opera to some old operatic hand—such as Max Maretzek, who will criticize it all the more justly because he is not Wagner mad— and ask him what it needs for popular and artistic success. Such a reviser would say, at once, that the music of "Old Hundred" must not be flattened to form a background for the solo voices, but must be given in its integrity and must end the Act as a triumphal chorus. He would say that Hester's prayer, in the forest scene, is too reminiscent of "Angels Ever Bright and Fair." He would say that to make the arriving Pilgrims sing a madrigal is absurd. The Pilgrims did not sing madrigals. They had left home and country to get rid of madrigals. For them a solemn, stately march must be composed, or, if Mr. Damrosch will not venture to compete with Wagner, then one of the magnificent old hymn-tunes must be adapted to the situation. The madrigal music is for Pearl, pretty Pearl, dancing about like the sunbeams and singing merrily in defiance of the Pilgrims. He would not allow Hester to tear off the scarlet letter forever in Act second, and sew it on again for Act third. He would suggest an invisible chorus of passing Pilgrims as a background for the duet of Hester and Arthur at the end of the second Act. He would object to the Pilgrims singing such trash as "And a hey for the Pilgrim, hey!" to begin the last Act, and would condemn the glee, as he had the madrigal, for Pilgrim music. Many other suggestions he would doubtless make; but these are the clues to his criticisms, and the result would be the transformation of Mr. Damrosch's ambitious attempt into a genuine and permanent success.

" 'Scarlet Letter' Badly Done/Direction, Writing, Ruin Classic Novel," ***Hollywood Reporter*****, 6 July 1934, p. 3.**

Pity Nathaniel Hawthorne! The production that Majestic Pictures have given his "The Scarlet Letter" almost succeeds in making the old classic ridiculous.

Burdened with the highest of high-flown dialogue, like "Open thy bright, dying eyes and tell me what thou seest in eternity for us," it suddenly is overcome with self-consciousness and tries something like this, with a "What Price Glory?" flavor, "Sayest thou!"; "Sayest!!!" Also, "Oh, yea?" in the accent of "Oh, yeah?"

The fault lies primarily with the direction, by Robert G. Vignola, which is somnolently slow, and with the screen play by Leonard Fields and David Silverstein, which treats the old tale with no respect at all and won't even hand it some crutches when it falls down.

If it were not for the theme, which is insisted upon through the many, many reels (except for the "comedy" sequences), the picture would have some value for children as being a fairly adequate portrayal of life in Massachusetts in the 1600's. However, it is a bitter and bewildering education pill. * * *

It simply is not for any house, anywhere.

"Scarlet Letter," ***Variety*****, 25 September 1934, 14:1-2.**

Darmour production and Majestic release. Stars Colleen Moore, features Hardie Albright. Directed by Robert G. Vignola. Leonard

Fields, David Silverstein, screen play and dialog; Jos. S. Brown, Jr., camera. At Strand, Brooklyn, week Sept. 14, on double bill. Running time, 70 mins.

Hester Prynne	Colleen Moore
Arthur Dimmesdale	Hardie Albright
Roger Chillingworth	Henry B. Walthall
Governor Billingham	William Farnum
Bartholomew Hockins	Alan Hale
Abigail Crakstone	Virginia Howell
Pearl	Cora Sue Collins
Samson Goodfellow	William Kent

———

Another venerated classic is wrecked on the rocks of comedy relief. Otherwise, it is a generally creditable effort. Hawthorne's tense plot is lightened with a John Alden-Miles Standish development that recurs with mathematical precision about every so often to spoil whatever tension the players have been able to create. By no means the first classic to have been bogged down with clumsy comedy, but producers never seem to realize that some plays cannot stand comedy injection.

In this instance the comedy at least matches the nature of the main story. It blends in well and save for one pantalette incident, has been intelligently handled, but it acts as a drag to the suspense and detracts from the main plot. Granting that the story is dismally dark; that it derives most of its power from its tone of hopelessness, it is at least one of the outstanding examples of early American writing and should not be tampered with to make it conform to the Hollywood tradition. It should be offered for what it is since the comedy injections will not make for more business.

Apart from this the script work has been well done. The added dialog conforms to the tone of that extracted from the book. The dialog job is thoroughly well done. But the scenarist has been unfortunate in the selection of his incident. He fails to stress properly the cruelties of Chillingworth against Dimmesdale and Hester, which really is the backbone of the suspense. He fails to develop the real soul-tragedy of the man and woman, working chiefly on the surface story of the community's cruelty to the transgressor. As far as he went he did well enough, but he did not dig below the surface.

The production and direction of Robert Vignola is outstanding in spite of poor photography in spots. The picture owes much to his skill.

It would be difficult to imagine a more happy choice for Hester than Colleen Moore. Her work is informed by gentle humility which gives the part dignity and appeal. She plays with repression, but always with power. Hardie Albright is an excellent Dimmesdale, playing with restraint which makes for effect, while Henry B. Walthall, slightly theatric at times, is good as the husband. Alan Hale and William Kent take care of the comedy and suggest that there is a team in the making. Each foils the other admirably. Other roles are all in competent hands.

Selected Bibliography

I list below the most frequently cited and accessible modern scholarship on *The Scarlet Letter.*

Abel, Darrel. "Hawthorne's Dimmesdale: Fugitive from Wrath," *Nineteenth-Century Fiction*, 11 (September 1956), 81-105.

———. "Hawthorne's Pearl: Symbol and Character," *ELH*, 18 (March 1951), 50-66.

Arac, Jonathan. "Reading the Letter," *Diacritics*, 9 (Summer 1979), 42-52.

Baker, Larry. "The PBS *Scarlet Letter*: Showing Versus Telling," *Nathaniel Hawthorne Journal*, 8 (1978), 219-229.

Baskett, Sam S. "The (Complete) Scarlet Letter," *College English*, 22 (February 1961), 321-328.

Baughman, Ernest W. "Public Confession and *The Scarlet Letter*," *New England Quarterly*, 40 (September 1967), 532-550.

Bayer, John G. "Narrative Techniques and the Oral Tradition in *The Scarlet Letter*," *American Literature*, 52 (May 1980), 250-263.

Baym, Nina. "The Romantic Malgre Lui: Hawthorne in 'The Custom House," *ESQ*, 19, i (1973), 14-25.

Bell, Michael David. "Arts of Deception: Hawthorne, 'Romance,' and *The Scarlet Letter*," in *New Essays on The Scarlet Letter*, ed. Michael J. Colacurcio. New York: Cambridge University Press, 1985, pp.

Bell, Millicent. "The Obliquity of Signs: *The Scarlet Letter*," *Massachusetts Review*, 23 (Spring 1982), 9-26.

Benoit, Raymond. "Theology and Literature: *The Scarlet Letter*," *Bucknell Review*, 20 (Spring 1972), 83-92.

Bensick, Carol. "His Folly, Her Weakness: Demystified Adultery in *The Scarlet Letter*," in *New Essays on The Scarlet Letter*, ed. Michael J. Colacurcio. New York: Cambridge University Press, 1985, pp. 137-159.

Bercovitch, Sacvan. "Hawthorne's A-Morality of Compromise," *Representations*, 24 (Fall 1988), 1-27.

———. "The A-Politics of Ambiguity in *The Scarlet Letter*," *New Literary History*, 19 (Spring 1988), 629-654.

———. The Office of *The Scarlet Letter*. Baltimore: Johns Hopkins University Press, 1990.

Berner, Robert L. "A Key to 'The Custom House,'" *ATQ*, 41 (Winter 1979), 33-43.

Boewe, Charles, and Murray G. Murphy. "Hester Prynne in History," *American Literature*, 32 (May 1960), 202-204.

Branch, Watson. "From Allegory to Romance: Hawthorne's Transformation of *The Scarlet Letter*," *Modern Philology*, 80 (November 1982), 145-160.

Bronstein, Zelda. "The Parabolic Ploys of *The Scarlet Letter*," *American Quarterly*, 39 (Summer 1987), 193-210.

Browning, Preston M. "Hester Prynne as Secular Saint," *Midwest Quarterly*, 13 (Summer 1972), 351-362.

Brumm, Ursula. "Hawthorne's 'The Custom-House' and the Problem of Point of View in Historical Fiction," *Anglia*, 93 (1975), 391-412.

Carpenter, F. I. "Hester, the Heretic," *College English*, 13 (May 1952), 457-458.

———. "Scarlet A Minus," *College English*, 5 (January 1944), 173-180.

Clark, C. E. Frazer, Jr. " 'Posthumous Papers of a Decapitated Surveyor': *The Scarlet Letter* in the Salem Press," *Studies in the Novel*, 2 (Winter 1970), 395-419.

Colacurcio, Michael J. "Footsteps of Ann Hutchinson: The Context of *The Scarlet Letter*," *ELH*, 39 (September 1972), 459-494.

Cottom, Daniel. "Hawthorne versus Hester: The Ghostly Dialectic of Romance in *The Scarlet Letter*," *Texas Studies in Literature and Language*, 24 (Spring 1982), 47-67.

Cox, James M. "*The Scarlet Letter*: Through the Old Manse and the Custom House," *Virginia Quarterly Review*, 51 (Summer 1975), 432-447.

Crews, Frederick J. *The Sins of the Fathers: Hawthorne's Psychological Themes*. New York: Oxford University Press, 1966, 136-153.

Davidson, Edward H. "Dimmesdale's Fall," *New England Quarterly*, 26 (September 1963), 358-370.

Davis, Sarah I. "Another View of Hester and the Antinomians," *Studies in American Fiction*, 12 (Autumn 1984), 189-198.

Diehl, Joanne Feit. "Re-Reading The Letter: Hawthorne, the Fetish, and the (Family) Romance," *New Literary History*, 19 (Spring 1988), 655-673.

Dillingham, William B. "Arthur Dimmesdale's Confession," *Studies in the Literary Imagination*, 2 (April 1969), 21-26.

Downing, David B. "The Swelling Waves: Visuality, Metaphor, and Bodily Reality in *The Scarlet Letter*," *Studies in American Fiction*, 12 (Spring 1984), 13-28.

Dunne, Michael F. "Hawthorne, the Reader, and Hester Prynne," *Interpretations*, 10 (1978), 34-40.

Eakin, Paul John. "Hawthorne's Imagination and the Structure of 'The Custom House,' " *American Literature*, 43 (November 1971), 346-358.

Estrin, Mark W. " 'Triumphant Ignominy': *The Scarlet Letter* on Screen," *Literature/Film Quarterly*, 2 (Spring 1974), 110-122.

Feidelson, Charles. "*The Scarlet Letter*," in *Hawthorne Centenary Essays*, ed. Roy Harvey Pearce. Columbus: Ohio State University Press, 1964, pp. 31-77.

Fogle, Richard H. *Hawthorne's Fiction: The Light and the Dark*. Norman: University of Oklahoma Press, 1952, pp. 106-118

Foster, Dennis. "The Embroidered Sin: Confessional Evasion in *The Scarlet Letter*," *Criticism*, 25 (Spring 1983), 141-163.

Garlitz, Barbara. "Pearl: 1850-1955," *PMLA*, 72 (September 1957), 689-699.

Gerber, John C. "Form and Content in *The Scarlet Letter*," *New England Quarterly*, 17 (March 1944), 25-55.

Gollin, Rita K. " 'Again a Literary Man': Vocation and *The Scarlet Letter*," in *Critical Essays on The Scarlet Letter*, ed. David Kesterson. Boston: G. K. Hall, 1988, pp. 171-183.

Granger, Bruce Ingham. "Arthur Dimmesdale as Tragic Hero," *Nineteenth-Century Fiction*, 19 (September 1964), 197-203.

Gross, Seymour. " 'Solitude, and Love, and Anguish': The Tragic Design of *The Scarlet Letter*," *CLA Journal*, 3 (March 1968), 154- 165.

Hansen, Elaine Tuttle. "Ambiguity and the Narrator in *The Scarlet Letter*," *Journal of Narrative Technique*," 5 (September 1975), 147-163.

Hart, James D. "*The Scarlet Letter*: One Hundred Years After," *New England Quarterly*, 23 (September 1950), 381-395.

Herbert, T. Walter, Jr. "Nathaniel Hawthorne, Una Hawthorne, and *The Scarlet Letter*: Interactive Selfhoods and the Cultural Construction of Gender," *PMLA*, 103 (May 1988), 285-297.

Hoeltje, Hubert H. "The Writing of *The Scarlet Letter*," *New England Quarterly*, 27 (September 1954), 326-346.

Hunt, Lester H. "*The Scarlet Letter*: Hawthorne's Theory of Moral Sentiments," *Philosophy and Literature*, 8 (April 1984), 75-88.

Katz, Seymour. " 'Character,' 'Nature,' and Allegory in *The Scarlet Letter*," *Nineteenth-Century Fiction*, 23 (June 1968), 3- 17.

Kaul, A. N. "Character and Motive in *The Scarlet Letter*," *Critical Quarterly*, 10 (Winter 1968), 373-384.

Kearns, Francis E. "Margaret Fuller as a Model for Hester Prynne," *Jahrbuch fur Amerikastudien*, 10 (1965), 191-197.

Lawrence, D. H. *Studies in Classic American Literature*. New York: Viking, 1964, pp. 83-99.

Leverenz, David. "Mrs. Hawthorne's Headache: Reading *The Scarlet Letter*," *Nineteenth-Century Fiction*, 37 (March 1983), 552-575.

Levi, Joseph. "Hawthorne's *The Scarlet Letter*: A Psychological Interpretation," *American Imago*, 10 (Winter 1953), 291-305.

Levy, Leo B. "The Landscape Modes of *The Scarlet Letter*," *Nineteenth-Century Fiction*, 23 (March 1969), 377-392.

Maclean, Hugh Norman. "Hawthorne's *Scarlet Letter*: The Dark Problem of This Life," *American Literature*, 27 (March 1955), 12- 24.

McNamara, Anne Marie. "The Character of Flame: The Function of Pearl in *The Scarlet Letter*," *American Literature*, 27 (January 1956), 537-553.

Male, Roy R. *Hawthorne's Tragic Vision*. Austin: University of Texas Press, 1957, pp. 90-118.

Manierre, William R. "The Role of Sympathy in *The Scarlet Letter*," *Texas Studies in Literature and Language*, 13 (Fall 1971), 497-507.

Martin, Terence. *Nathaniel Hawthorne*. New Haven: Twayne, 1965, pp. 108-127.

Matthiessen, F. O. *American Renaissance: Art and Expression in the Age of Emerson and Whitman*. New York: Oxford University Press, 1941, pp. 275-282 and passim.

Mellard, James M. "Pearl and Hester: A Lacanian Reading," in *Critical Essays on The Scarlet Letter*, ed. David Kesterson. Boston: G. K. Hall, 1988, pp. 193-211.

Newberry, Frederick. "Tradition and Disinheritance in *The Scarlet Letter*," *ESQ*, 23, i (1977), 1-26.

Nolte, William H. "Hawthorne's Dimmesdale: A Small Man Gone Wrong," *New England Quarterly*, 38 (June 1965), 168-186.

O'Donnell, Charles R. "Hawthorne and Dimmesdale: The Search for the Realm of Quiet," *Nineteenth-Century Fiction*, 14 (March 1960), 317-332.

Pinsker, Sanford. "The Scaffold as Hinge: A Note on the Structure of *The Scarlet Letter*," *College Literature*, 5 (1978), 144-145.

Porte, Joel. *The Romance in America*. Middletown: Wesleyan University Press, 1969, pp. 98-114.

Rahv, Philip. "The Dark Lady of Salem," *Partisan Review*, 8 (September-October 1941), 362-381.

Reynolds, David S. *Beneath the American Renaissance: The Subversive Imagination in the Age of Emerson and Melville*. New York: Knopf, 1988, pp. 118-132 and passim.

Reynolds, Larry J. "*The Scarlet Letter* and Revolutions Abroad," *American Literature*, 57 (March 1985), 44-67.

Rowe, John Carlos. "The Internal Conflict of Romantic Narrative: Hegel's Phenomenology and Hawthorne's *The Scarlet Letter*," *MLN*, 95 (December 1980), 1203-1231.

Rowe, Joyce A. *Equivocal Endings in Classic American Novels*. Cambridge: Cambridge University Press, 1988, pp. 27-45.

Ryskamp, Charles. "The New England Sources of *The Scarlet Letter*," *American Literature*, 31 (November 1959), 257-272.

Sampson, Edward C. "Motivation in *The Scarlet Letter*," *American Literature*, 28 (January 1957), 511-513.

Sandeen, Ernest. "*The Scarlet Letter* as a Love Story," *PMLA*, 77 (September 1962), 425-435.

Scheiber, Andrew J. "Public Force, Private Sentiment: Hawthorne and the Gender of Politics," *ATQ*, NS 2 (December 1988), 285-299.

Smith, Julian. "Hester, Sweet Hester Prynne—*The Scarlet Letter* in the Movie Market Place," *Literature/Film Quarterly*, 2 (Spring 1974), 100-109.

Smolinski, Reiner. "Covenant Theology and Arthur Dimmesdale's Pelagianism," *ATQ*, NS 1 (September 1987), 211-231.

Stanton, Robert. "*The Scarlet Letter* as Dialectic of Temperament and Idea," *Studies in the Novel*, 2 (Winter 1970), 474-486.

Stouck, David. "The Surveyor of 'The Custom-House': A Narrator for *The Scarlet Letter*," *Centennial Review*, 15 (Summer 1971), 309-329.

Stubbs, John Caldwell. "Hawthorne's *The Scarlet Letter*: The Theory of the Romance and the Use of the New England Situation," *PMLA*, 83 (September 1968), 1439-1447.

Swann, Charles. "Hester and the Second Coming: A Note on the Conclusion to *The Scarlet Letter*," *Journal of American Studies*, 21 (August 1987), 264-268.

Tanselle, G. Thomas. "A Note on the Structure of *The Scarlet Letter*," *Nineteenth-Century Fiction*, 17 (December 1962), 283-285.

Tuerk, Richard. " 'An Exceedingly Pleasant Mention': *The Scarlet Letter* and Holden's *Dollar Magazine*," *Nathaniel Hawthorne Journal*, 4 (1974), 209-230.

Van Deusen, Marshall. "Narrative Tone in 'The Custom-House' and *The Scarlet Letter*," *Nineteenth-Century Fiction*, 21 (June 1966), 61-71.

Vogel, Dan. "Roger Chillingworth: The Satanic Paradox in *The Scarlet Letter*," *Criticism*, 5 (Summer 1963), 272-280.

Waggoner, Hyatt H. *Hawthorne: A Critical Study*. Cambridge: Belknap, 1955, pp. 18-50.

Wagner, Linda W. "Embryonic Characterization in 'The Custom House,' " *English Record*, 16 (February 1966), 32-35.

Walcutt, Charles C. "*The Scarlet Letter* and Its Modern Critics," *Nineteenth-Century Fiction*, 7 (March 1953), 251-264.

Warren, Austin. "*The Scarlet Letter*: A Literary Exercise in Moral Theology," *Southern Review*, 1 (Winter 1965), 22-45.

Whelan, Robert Emmet, Jr. "Hester Prynne's Little Pearl: Sacred and Profane Love," *American Literature*, 39 (January 1968), 488- 505.

Woodson, Thomas. "Hawthorne, Upham, and *The Scarlet Letter*," in *Critical Essays on The Scarlet Letter*, ed. David Kesterson. Boston: G. K. Hall, 1988, pp. 183-193.

Young, Philip. *Hawthorne's Secret: An Un-Told Tale*. Boston: Godine, 1985.

Ziff, Larzer. "The Ethical Dimension of 'The Custom House,' " *Modern Language Notes*, 73 (May 1958), 338-344.

Index

About the Editor

GARY SCHARNHORST is Professor of English at the University of New Mexico and coeditor of *American Literary Realism.* His book publications include *The Lost Life of Horatio Alger, Jr.* and *Nathaniel Hawthorne: An Annotated Bibliography of Criticism Before 1900.* His articles have appeared in a wide assortment of academic journals appropriate to American literature as well as essay collections in book form.